THE
HISTORY
OF THE
Roman or *Civil LAW*.

SHEWING

Its ORIGIN and PROGRESS; how, and
when the feveral Parts of it were firft compil'd; with fome Account of the Principal
WRITERS and COMMENTATORS
thereupon: And of the METHOD to be
obferv'd in Studying the fame.

Written originally in *French*,

By *M.* CLAUDE JOSEPH de FERRIERE.

To which is Added,

Dr. *DUCK's* Treatife of the Ufe and Authority
of the CIVIL LAW in *England*.

Tranflated into *Englifh*,

By *J. B.* Efq;

With a new introduction by Michael H. Hoeflich
John H. & John M. Kane Professor of Law, University of Kansas School of Law

THE LAWBOOK EXCHANGE, LTD.
Clark, New Jersey

ISBN-13: 978-1-58477-663-5 (hardcover)
ISBN-13: 978-1-61619-059-0 (paperback)

Lawbook Exchange edition 2005, 2010

The quality of this reprint is equivalent to the quality of the original work.

THE LAWBOOK EXCHANGE, LTD.
33 Terminal Avenue
Clark, New Jersey 07066-1321

*Please see our website for a selection of our other publications
and fine facsimile reprints of classic works of legal history:*
www.lawbookexchange.com

Library of Congress Cataloging-in-Publication Data

Ferrière, Claude Joseph de, d. ca. 1748.
  [Histoire du droit romain. English]
  The history of the Roman or civil law : shewing its origin and
progress : how and when the several parts of it were first compil'd :
with some account of the principal writers and commentators
thereupon : and the method to be observ'd in studying the same /
written originally in French by M. Claude Joseph de Ferriere ; to
which is added Dr. Duck's treatise Of the use and authority of
the civil law in England ; translated into English by J. B. ; with new
introduction by Michael Hoeflich.
    p. cm.
  Originally published: London : Printed for D. Browne, [etc.], 1724.
  Includes bibliographical references and index.
  ISBN 1-58477-663-3 (alk. paper)
  1. Roman law--History. 2. Civil law--History. I. Duck, Arthur,
Sir, 1580-1648. II. Beaver, John, 18th cent. III. Title.
KJA147.F47313 2005
340.5'4'09--dc22   2005006549

Printed in the United States of America on acid-free paper

INTRODUCTION

Claude-Joseph de Ferriére, the son of a noted Parisian lawyer and legal author, was born sometime around 1680 in Paris and died at Paris about 1750. His father, a successful lawyer and jurist who died about 1715 at Rheims, was the author of a number of prominent works on law and legal history as well as a popular French translation of Justinian's *Institutes*, which was first published in 1680. Claude-Joseph, brought up in a scholarly household, followed in his father's footsteps, became a law professor at Paris and published a number of important works on law and legal history as well. He edited new editions of several of his father's works, including, in 1719, the translation of the *Institutes*.

On his own, Claude-Joseph published a number of legal treatises on Roman law and on Canon law. He was best known during his life and after for his *Dictionaire de Droit et de Pratique Contenant l'Explication des Termes de Droit, d'Ordonnances, de Coutumes, & de Pratique*. First published in 1734, this work was reprinted countless times and cited widely as an authority. Of his legal historical works, the volume reprinted here was among the best known. It was first published at Paris in 1718 under the title, *Histoire du Droit Romain, Contenant son Origine, ses Progrès, Comment en Quel Tems les Diverses Parties dont est Composé le Corps du Droit Civil ont été Faites, l'Usage que l'on fait en France du Droit Romain*. It was reprinted a number of times in French during the eighteenth century and an English translation of the work by John Beaver was published at London in 1724.

Ferriére's *History of Roman Law* is not a work of profound scholarship. In fact, much of the work is closely modeled on the earlier history of Roman law by the Italian jurist, Vincenzo Gravina. But Ferriére's work does have a number of points to commend it to the non-expert. First, it is brief and clearly written. The English translation is also quite readable. Second, Ferriére did not attempt to give a detailed history of the development of doctrine. On the contrary, his work is a work of what is often called "external history." It provides the historical background necessary to understand substantive legal developments anduseful biographical information both on ancient Roman jurists and their early modern counterparts. From the perspective of the modern reader it is these latter biographical sketches, along with the chapters on the use of Roman law in pre-revolutionary France that are of the greatest interest and utility.

Also of interest to modern readers are two of the final chapters in the work which provide a brief history of Ferriére's notions on how best to study Roman law and a discussion on the use of quotations and abbreviations in works about Roman law. Ferriére also included discussions of two non-Roman legal sources in the work which are quite valuable. He discusses both the Papal Decretal *Super Specula* as well as the royal *Ordonnance* of Blois. Both of these laws were designed to impede the study of Roman law in France and, in the decretal's case, the rest of Europe. Ferriére's comments on these are quite instructive.

Many English editions of Ferriére's treatise are bound with two other short works. The first of these is an English version of *On the Use and Authority of the Civil Law in the Kingdom of England* by Arthur Duck [1600-1648], a Fellow of All Souls and an advocate of Doctors' Commons. Generally considered his major work, it is a history of the reception of Roman law in Great Britain. The second is John Beaver's translation of a French work generally attributed to either Gabriel Argou or Claude Fleury entitled (in English) *The History of the Origine of the French Laws*, which includes a preface and notes by Beaver "Shewing the Analogy of the Laws of the Antient Gauls and Britons." Gabriel Argou [d.1724] was a French lawyer best known for his *Institution du Droit Français*, a history of French customary law. Claude Fleury [1640-1723] began his career as a lawyer but achieved fame as an ecclesiastical historian. According to the entry in the Harvard Library Catalogue, *The History of the Origine of the French Laws* is a translation of Fleury's 1674 *Histoire Du Droit Français*. The false attribution derives from the frequent habit of binding Fleury's *Histoire* with copies of Argou's *Institution.*

Most modern historians of Roman law concentrate either on the Middle Ages or the nineteenth century in their studies of modern Roman law. The seventeenth and eighteenth centuries are very much terra incognita to today's scholars of Roman law and its afterlife. Similarly, Germany and German scholarship, especially the works of Savigny and Mommsen, is the normal focus of most English-speaking modern scholars of Roman law. French Romanists of the early modern period are rarely studied. This is a shame for they have much to offer us. This reprint of Ferriére's greatest work on Roman law, as well as the works of Fleury and Duck on Roman law and French Law, will help to correct this imbalance.

Michael H. Hoeflich
May 2005

THE
HISTORY
OF THE
Roman or *Civil LAW*.

SHEWING

Its ORIGIN and PROGRESS; how, and
when the feveral Parts of it were firft compil'd; with fome Account of the Principal
WRITERS and COMMENTATORS
thereupon: And of the METHOD to be
obferv'd in Studying the fame.

Written originally in *French*,
By *M.* CLAUDE JOSEPH de FERRIERE.

To which is Added,
Dr. *DUCK's* Treatife of the Ufe and Authority
of the CIVIL LAW in *England*.

Tranflated into *English*,
By *J. B.* Efq;

LONDON,
Printed for D. BROWNE, at the *Black-Swan*, and
F. CLAY, at the *Bible*, without *Temple-Bar*. 1724.

To the Honourable

Charles Colyear, Efquire.

S I R,

IVE me leave to introduce to the Honour of your Acquaintance a *French* Author, in Plain *Englifh* Cloaths; which, tho' not quite fo Genteel, render him more Familiar and Ufeful in this

A 3   Coun-

DEDICATION.

Countrey, than he can be in his Foreign Dreſs.

He and I, Sir, join in inviting you to the Study of the *Civil Law*; for which you are qualified by all the Advantages of a liberal Education, bright Natural Parts, and a Maturity of Judgment rarely to be met with at your Age.

'Tis in this Treaſure, and no where elſe, you may find the moſt perfect Collection of Natural Reaſon and Equity, applied to all the various Tranſactions and Intercourſes between Man and Man: And therefore, all Gentlemen, tho'
                                        they

DEDICATION.

they do not defign to make it
their Profeffion, ought to underftand fo much of the *Civil
Law*, as may ferve for a Rule
to govern their Actions.

You are, Sir, already Confiderable by your Birth and Fortune, and 'tis in your own
Power to make your felf much
more fo, by applying fome
part of your Time to the Study of a Science, the Ufefulnefs
and Excellency whereof is univerfally allow'd.

Forgive me, Sir, the Freedom I have taken in furnifhing
you with a Guide to fhew the
Way, and make your Entrance
eafie

DEDICATION.

easie ; since I assure you, it proceeds from my Natural Inclinations to serve, and earnest Desire to see you both Great and Happy. I am

SIR,

Your most Obedient, and

Most Humble Servant,

John Beaver.

THE

THE
CONTENTS.

CHAP.

The CONTENTS.

CHAP.

The CONTENTS.

---

*O*F *the Use and Authority of the* Civil Law *in the Kingdom of* England. i

THE

THE
HISTORY
OF THE
ROMAN LAW.

INTRODUCTION.

I T is an eſtabliſh'd Maxim, that no Man can arrive at a perfect Knowledge of any SCIENCE, without having firſt examin'd its *Riſe* and *Progreſs:* But tho' this generally holds true, it is in no Caſe ſo naturally applicable, as in the Study of the *CIVIL LAW:* Whether it be owing to the great Variety of *Laws* made upon the ſame Subject, or the different Qualifications of the *Legiſlators* who have govern'd *Rome* at ſeveral times.

FOR,

For, notwithstanding Justice be in it self Immutable, the Administration of it is subject to great Changes ; the *Laws* themselves, which ought to encourage this Vertue in Mankind, are the very Cause thereof : The Disputes which generally give birth to *Laws*, never happen all at the same time ; nor is it in the Power of Man, to foresee all the Consequences of those General Rules they prescribe, or to adapt them to every Case that may arise; from whence it follows, that so profound a Science as the *Law*, could not possibly be brought to that Perfection in which we now see it, but by Degrees, and Length of time. Besides, as our Understanding of the *Roman Law*, depends very much upon knowing what kind of Government the *Romans* were under at the Time of their making ; 'tis plain, nothing can more facilitate that Sudy, than to be acquainted with the Rise and Progress of the *Law*.

This Book therefore, in which I have carefully collected from the Ancients, all that is remarkable or material on this Subject, and which lies dispers'd, or rather buried in a vast Number of Places, will serve those that apply themselves to the *Civil Law*, as an Introduction; and at once make them Masters of several Things, which are apt to discourage Beginners for a time.

THIS *History of the Roman Law*, is so closely link'd to that of the different Forms of their Government, that I flatter my self, it will be no less curious than useful to such as have already any Knowledge of either; it will be highly pleasing to them to have a Prospect of both as it were at one View, and to recollect the *Laws* themselves by comparing them with their Origine. In a Word, it will enable them to form a just Idea of what they had before but a confus'd Notion; and to dive into the Bottom of those Causes, of which they were before contented to admire the Effects only.

THE Force of the *Roman* Arms, and Extent of their Empire, made them formidable throughout the whole World; but how much more were they so by the Wisdom of their *Laws?* Their very name, methinks, commands Respect, and every Work that treats of them, for the sake of its Subject, has a kind of Right to a favourable Reception from the Publick.

BUT I have not confin'd my self to treat only of the manner in which the *Roman Laws* were first establish'd; I propose to shew what success the Body of *Law* compos'd by *Justinian*, had after his Death in the Eastern and Western Empires.

IN the next Place, the Love of Truth engages me to shew the Excellency of the *Civil Law*, and how far 'tis receiv'd in this Kingdom: Nor would it have been just, to write the History of the *Law*, without giving it the Praises it deserves;

and

and fhewing that moſt of the Maxims upon which our *Common Law* is grounded, are borrow'd from it.

As haughty a People as the *Romans* were, they made no ſcruple to own their Obligation to the *Grecians*, for the *Laws* they had from them. How then can we admire and follow the *Romans*, and not imitate their Gratitude?

To make this Work the more compleat, I have added, the true Explanation of the famous Decretal Epiſtle *Super-ſpecula, titulo Decretalium Privilegiis*; and that of the Sixty ninth Article of the *Ordonnance* of *Blois*, concerning the Prohibition to teach the *Civil Law* in the Univerſity of *Paris*; which was a Point, I thought, had not been hitherto ſufficiently cleared up, tho' it ſeem'd to deſerve the Curioſity and Notice of the Learned.

Lastly, The Concluſion of this Hiſtory, will direct young Students how to apply themſelves uſefully to the Study of the *Civil Law*, ſo neceſſary for thoſe who are deſign'd to defend Cauſes or determine Diſputes; and alſo ſhew, what Diſpoſitions they ought to have, who make this Study their Choice.

Having thus given the Reader a View of the Plan of this Work, and inform'd him what it is to contain, I ſhall enter upon the *Hiſtory of the Roman Law*, and purſue that People through all their different Forms of Government.

THE

The CONTENTS.

CHAP. I.

Of the different Forms of Government in ROME.

THE *Roman Law*, having an inseparable Relation to the different Constitutions of the Nation to whose Wisdom it is owing; one cannot arrive at a full and exact Knowledge of it, without being first well acquainted with the several Kinds of Government to which the *Roman* People were subject. This is what I shall endeavour to unfold, after having briefly touch'd upon the Origine of that Empire, which from a very slender Beginning, came in time to be the Greatest and most Powerful that ever was known.

Rome, was so called from ROMULUS; who, in the Eighteenth Year of his Age, laid the Foundations of the City, round about *Mount Palatine*. This was Seven Hundred and Fifty Years before the Nativity of Christ; reckoning Three Thousand Two Hundred and Fifty three Years from the Creation of the World; upon the Twenty first of *April*: A Day celebrated by the Shepherds in Honour of the Rural Goddess *Palilia*.

The *Roman* People, who at first were under the Dominion of ROMULUS, became afterwards subject to Three different Forms of Government.

The First was the *Regal* Government; which lasted Two Hundred and Forty Years, under Seven Kings, *viz.* ROMULUS, NUMA-POMPILIUS, TULLIUS-HOSTILIUS, ANCUS MARTIUS, TARQUIN

B   the

the Firft of that Name, SERVIUS TULLIUS, and TARQUIN the PROUD.

After the Expulfion of the laft King, *Rome* erected it felf into a Republick, and pafs'd into a quite different kind of Government, that of *Confuls*, who were annually chofen. This Confular State lafted about Five Hundred Years, from the firft Confulate of C. *Junius Brutus*, to the time of *Auguftus Cæfar*.

The Third Form of Government was *the Imperial*, under the Emperors; which continued Five Hundred and Fifty eight Years, from the Beginning of the Reign of AUGUSTUS, to that of the Emperor JUSTINIAN; to whofe fuccefsful Endeavours, we are beholden for the Compilation of the Body of the Civil Law, in the Order it has been tranfmitted to Us.

C H A P. II.

Of the Roman Law *under the* Regal Government.

NO fooner had ROMULUS fix'd his Authority, by an Alliance which the *Sabines* were forc'd to contract with him, but he divided the People into Three Parts, which were called *Tribes*, and each *Tribe* into Ten *Curiæ*; and appointed Priefts to offer Sacrifices to the Gods. But the moft remarkable Act of his Reign, was the Eftablifhment of that auguft Affembly, which afterwards became the moft awful of all Tribunals; I mean the *Senate*, which he chofe out of the moft Ancient and Venerable Citizens, to affift him in his Adminiftration.

This *Senate* at firft confifted of a Hundred only; but their Number was afterwards much increafed.

To thefe, he committed the Care of the moft important Affairs of State, but with certain Reftrictions. There were three Things, which he thought not proper to fubmit to their fole Determination; The *Creation* of *Magiftrates*, the making *Peace* and *War*, and *Enacting* of *Laws*. Thefe he referr'd to be debated and decided in a full Affembly of the People.

Nor

Nor did ROMULUS ever after the Establishment of this Great Council, attempt to make any Law, before he had first concerted it with them, and afterwards revis'd it in a General Assembly.

NUMA POMPILIUS, who succeded *Romulus*, turn'd his Thoughts chiefly to settling Religion; his creating of Priests and Augurs, &c. were the Effects of his Zeal for the Establishment of exterior Worship. He made many good Laws, appointed Punishments for Homicides, and regulated the Ceremonies of Funerals. Whatever he propos'd, was eagerly embrac'd by the People; whose Credulity and Superstition he knew so well how to turn to his own Advantage, that he made them believe, he had frequent Interviews with the Nymph *Egeria*, and did nothing but by her Inspiration.

Military Discipline was the chief Study of TULLIUS HOSTILIUS.

ANCUS MARTIUS applied himself particularly to adorn and embellish the City.

TARQUINIUS, afterwards Sirnam'd PRISCUS, did likewise little or nothing towards strengthning or settling the Authority of the Laws. He only invented the Ornament of Distinction, which the Senators ever after preserv'd as a Mark of Superiority, the *Laticlave*; which was a Gown or *Tunique*, sew'd about the Edges with pieces of Purple like great Nails.

SERVIUS TULLIUS did not only cause the Laws of ROMULUS and NUMA, which time had almost abolish'd, to be reviv'd, but enacted himself several new ones, which were transcrib'd into the Law of the *Twelve Tables*.

He was at abundance of Pains to dive into the Knowledge of every Man's Estate and Circumstance, in order to make him contribute proportionably to the Necessities of the Government: And this was the Reason of his instituting the *Census*, or general Review of the People every fifth Year; when all were oblig'd to give in a faithful Particular of

their

their Eftates : Which Review was at firft made by the *Kings* themfelves, afterwards by the *Confuls,* and laftly by the *Cenfors.*

The Laws, according to the Rules prefcribed by R O-MU LU S, were propofed by the Kings to the Senate, whofe Approbation was requifite ; and then carried down to be confirm'd by the Votes of the People, divided into Thirty *Curiæ :* From whence thofe Laws fo pafs'd, were called *Leges Regales & Curiales.*

But after the People came to be divided by S E R V I U S T U L I. I U S into Six Claffes, and a Hundred Ninety four Centuries, the Laws got the Name of *Centuriales.*

The firft Clafs or Divifion, which was compos'd of the Richeft and Principal Citizens, confifted of Fourfcore and Eight Centuries ; and as it was far the moft Numerous, their Confent only was fufficient, unlefs they happen'd to be divided in Opinion.

After the Death of *Servius Tullius,* T A R Q U IN the P R O U D afcended the Throne, whofe predominant Qualities were Pride, Inhumanity and Avarice. He fubdued *Rome* intirely to his Tyranny : He govern'd with a Rod of Iron ; and his Will, howfoever unjuft, was the only Law.

He utterly extinguifh'd the Laws of *Servius Tullius,* and negledted to enforce the Execution of thofe enadted by his Predeceffors, even of *Romulus.* He held the ancient Cuftom of advifing with the Senate and People in fuch Contempt, that he hearkned only to the Advice of Confidents and his own Caprice. His immeafurable Defire of Ruling abfolutely, blinded him to all other Views, and never fuffer'd him to examine whether his Commands were agreeable to the Rules of Juftice : So that having neither Goodnefs enough to govern reafonably, nor Spirit enough to make his Tyranny obey'd, the People waited only for a proper Conjundture to fhake off the Yoke of their Slavery, with which, the Death of the unhappy *L U C R E T I A* foon fupply'd them.

It is well known how *Sextus Tarquinius* this Tyrant's Eldeft Son furpriz'd her alone, what Threats and Violence he offer'd, to force her in fome meafure to condefcend to his Criminal Defires : But fhe had not Courage enough to furvive the Affront. She called for her Relations ; and having
recited

recited to them her Agonies and Misfortune, and recommended the Revenge of the Injury done her, she stabb'd her self with a Dagger.

So remarkable a Death, the Body of this unfortunate Lady which was expos'd to Publick View, and the Harangue *Brutus* made to the People, excited in them so much Pity and Indignation, that they abandon'd themselves wholly to Rage, and meditated nothing else but Arms and Revenge: And *Brutus* improv'd the Occasion so well, that *Rome* set it self at Liberty, and chang'd the Monarchical into Republican Government; and a Law was made, for perpetual Banishment of the Kings of *Rome.* This Law was called *Tribunitia*, because it was made at the Instigation of the same *Brutus*, who was then Tribune of the Cavalry.

But before I end this Chapter, I must take notice, *First*, that under this King's Reign, *Sextus Papyrius* had collected the Laws of the preceding Kings, and digested them into a Volume, which was called, *Jus Civile Papyrianum.*

Secondly, That notwithstanding the Aversion of the *Romans* to Kingly Government, at the time of T A R Q U I N's Expulsion, they did not repeal the *Regal* Laws, but the greatest part of them grew Obsolete; and such as retain'd any shadow of Authority, were made use of only as Usages: So that it is a Mistake to assert, that the *Tribunitian* Law repealed the *Regal* Laws; for the Word *Exsolescere*, which we meet with in the Law, 2. §. 3. *ff. de Origine Juris*, does not signifie to Abolish or Repeal, but to grow Obsolete or into Disuse.

But in order to let us into the true meaning of the Law in this Paragraph, we must read it thus, *Exactis deinde Regibus Lege Tribunitia, omnes Leges hæ exoleverunt*; with the Comma after the Word *Tribunitia*, and not after *Regibus*, as some will have it. In short, *Brutus* was so far from abolishing the *Regal Laws* by the Law *Tribunitia*, that many Authors affirm, the Law *Tribunitia* restor'd the Laws of *Servius Tullius*, which *Tarquin* the *Proud* had abrogated.

However this be, the *Regal* Laws, some time after the Establishment of the Republican Government, ceased to be in use; nor are there the least Footsteps of any of them to be found in the Books of the *Roman Law.*

CHAP.

CHAP. III.

Of the Free State of ROME *in its Infancy ; and the Creation of* Confuls.

TARQUIN the PROUD being thus Banifh'd from *Rome*, which happen'd in the Year Two Hundred Forty four after the Building of the City, the State of Affairs and Government were quite changed. In the Place of Kings, whofe Authority had degenerated into Tyranny, they chofe Two Magiftrates, for the Adminiftration of Publick Affairs ; whofe Power, tho' very great, was not unlimited, nor in-confiftent with their new-purchas'd Liberty.

Thefe Two Magiftrates were called *Confuls, à Confulendo* ; becaufe it was incumbent upon them to take care of the Re-publick ; or becaufe they were oblig'd to give Advice for its good Government, and not to Rule according to their own Fancy.

The firft Confuls were *Junius Brutus* and *Tarquinius Collatinus,* Husband to *Lucretia* ; but the latter was forced not long after, to refign his Place, and go into voluntary Exile, only for the fake of bearing the Name of *Tarquinius,* which became odious to the People ; and becaufe they had made a Law, not to fuffer any of that Name to live in *Rome.*

Thus the Sovereign Power was divided between Two, to prevent the ill ufe a fingle Perfon might make of it. Be-fides, the Limitation of their Office to the Term of a Year, did not give them room to imagine they might act without Controul ; tho' they were in full Poffeffion of all the exterior Ornaments ufed by the Kings, as the *Purple Robe,* the *Twelve Lictors,* the *Fafces,* and other Marks of Diftinction. But to avoid giving Jealoufie to the People, who might think their Condition rendred Worfe rather than Better, by having Two Mafters inftead of One, they agreed to govern alternately by Months ; and that he only who was in Power, fhould be attended by the *Lictors* and *Fafces,* with the *Axes* ; the other, by *One* Gentleman-Ufher only, and Twelve *Lictors,* without either *Axes* or *Fafces.*

But

But altho' thefe *Magiftrates* had all the outer fhew of the ancient *Regal* Majefty, their Power was not the fame. Thofe had no other Law than their own unbounded Wills, and acknowledg'd no Superior : On the contrary, the Confuls were only Depofitaries and Guardians of the Laws, whofe Duty it was to fee them duely put in Execution. It belong'd to them to call together the Affemblies of the People and Senate, but not to conclude any Thing, without the Deliberations of the one, or Decrees of the other. And they were oblig'd to render an Account of their Adminiftration as foon as it ended.

But notwithftanding all the wife Precautions the People of *Rome* could take, to eftablifh their new-gotten Liberty ; the good Effects of it were foon interrupted, by fome enterprizing Citizens, fupported by the Magiftrates ; which gave occafion for the making feveral New Laws, to retrench the Confular Power. Thus the Law *Valeria* was enacted, and took place from the Year 244. by which Liberty was given of appealing from the Magiftrate to the People *. After that, in the Year 261, the Law *Sacrata* was made, concerning the Election of *Tribunes* of the People, to protect them from the Oppreffion of the *Nobility* †. And in the Year 291, the Law *Terentia* was propos'd, to keep the *Confuls* Authority, which was grown exorbitant, within Bounds ; but it was oppos'd by the *Senators*, becaufe the Right of Law-making did not belong to the People ‡.

As for the *Regal* Laws, during the firft Seventeen Years of the *Free State*, they were no otherwife regarded than as Ancient Ufages ; nor had all of them even that Force, but fuch only as were reputed the moft Juft and Equitable.

All this time, there was no fix'd Law at *Rome* ; which occafions that Obfcurity we obferve in the Hiftory of the Civil Law, from the Beginning of the *Confular State*, to the Time of forming the Law of the *Twelve Tables*.

---

* Livy, Book 2. Chap. 8. † Book 2. Chap. 32. ‡ Book 3 Chap. 8.

CHAP.

C H A P. IV.

Of the Creation of Tribunes *of the* People.

THE *Confuls* themfelves aiming 'at Arbitrary Govern‑ ment, encourag'd the *Patricians* to ufurp a Tyrannical Power over the *Plebeians*, and invade their Liberty daily by new Attempts. The People, on the other hand, being no longer able to fupport the extravagant Pride and In‑ folence of the Nobles, nor fuffer the infatiable Avarice of the Rich, who opprefs'd them to death with exceffive Ufury, thought of nothing elfe, but how they might fhelter them‑ felves from all Violences, and throw off the Yoke of their Slavery and heavy Calamities.

Wherefore, about the Year 261, under pretence of march‑ ing againft the *Æqui* and *Sabines*, getting Arms, they re‑ tir'd to *Mons Cruftumerinus*, afterwards called *Sacer*, from the Law *Sacrata* there made. Upon this, the Senate having held feveral Meetings and Confultations about the Retreat of the Commons, refolv'd to Commiffion fome of the moft Reverend and Popular Senators to treat with the People ; of which number was *Appius Menenius*, who addrefs'd himfelf to them in this manner. *Once upon a time the Members and Parts of Man's Body fell out with the Belly, alledging, That they were all forced to toil and moil to provide Neceffaries for the Belly, whilft that lived Idle, and did nothing but enjoy its Plea‑ fures : Whereupon, they refolv'd the Hands fhould not lift the Meat to the Mouth, nor the Mouth receive, nor yet the Teeth chew it ; by which means, whilft they endeavour'd to famifh the Belly, they themfelves, and the whole Body were all ftarv'd, for want of the Nourifhment they received from it.* In the fame manner, faid he, the Senate and People, making but one Body, muft perifh by this Difagreement ; as they will live and flourifh, whilft they maintain a mutual Friendfhip and good Underftanding.

The People feem'd highly fatisfy'd with his Story and home Application, but being defirous of fecuring themfelves againft the future Attempts of the Senators, and to put a ftop to the career of their Violences, would not agree to de‑ part

part and return to the City, till the Senate had confented to the creating of five new Officers yearly, out of their own Body, with the Title of *Tribunes*, whofe fole Power fhould be to give Relief to fuch *Plebeians* as were injur'd, and fuffer none to be oppreſs'd by the *Senate* or *Confuls*.

The *Law Sacrata*, by which thefe new Magiftrates were created, was made on *Mons Cruftumerinus*, in the Year 261: By it, the Perſons of the Tribunes were made Sacred, and none was to offend them upon Pain of Death.

Their Authority was very confiderable; they might afſemble the People whenever they pleas'd, and ſummon any Magiftrate of what Degree or Quality foever, to appear at their Tribunal. No *Senatus-Confultum* was of force, till it had their Confirmation. They were not allow'd to fit in the Senate-Houfe, but ftood without; where they examin'd all Decrees paſs'd within, and either gave their Approbation, by figning them with the Letter T, or rejected them with this Word, *Veto*; without being oblig'd to give any Reafon for their Refufal.

At firft they were elected only out of the Body of the *People*; but afterwards the *Senators* and *Patricians* were admitted to that Office, and accounted it a great Honour to be of their Number; which, in the beginning was *Five*; but that being found too fmall for the Bufinefs, was afterwards increas'd to *Ten*. [*L. 2. §. 2. ff. de Origine Juris.*]

The Senate quickly perceiving the Tribunes Defign was to divide the Government, neglected nothing to elude their Authority, and render it ufelefs: And the People, purfuing their Drift of fharing in the Management of Affairs, enacted feveral Laws, which they called *Plebifcita*, without acquainting or confulting the Senate: Which Mifunderftandings were often the caufe of dangerous Seditions and Tumults in *Rome*.

The particular Meetings in which thefe *Plebifcita* paſs'd, were affembled at the Command of the *Tribunes*, and called *Curiata Comitia*, to diftinguifh them from the General Affemblies of all the Citizens, when the Senate and whole Body of the People were fummon'd to meet, by Order of the Conful, which were call'd *Centuriata Comitia*.

The

The *Senate* could by no means be induced to fubmit to the *Plebifcita :* They urg'd, that the *Tribunes* were created only to protect the People, and not to make Laws. On the other fide, the People refus'd to acknowledge the Laws made by the Senate : Which Difputes, occafion'd many Conferences for fettling a certain *Law,* that might be obligatory to all, and put Matters upon fuch a footing, that the meaner fort might be in no Danger, from the abfolute Power which the Senators pretended to.

At the fame time there arofe a Difpute between the *Patricians* and *Plebeians,* whether the Republick fhould be govern'd by fix'd Laws, or the Authority of the Magiftrate.

The Senators maintain'd, that the Power of the Magiftrates join'd with the Law, was moft advantageous to the Publick ; that the Laws themfelves were in many Cafes unjuft, and being inexorable, fhut the door to all Mercy and Favour.

The People on their parts, pleaded, that the Laws were preferable to any Dependance upon the arbitrary Pleafure of a Magiftrate ; becaufe as they are free from all Paffion, whatever they prefcribe muft be Juft, and ought to be regarded as the Dictates of Heaven : That notwithftanding they might feem to contain fome unjuft Decifions in particular Cafes, that Inconvenience might be eafily remedy'd, by giving them an equitable Conftruction.

The Peoples Argument prevail'd ; fo they fell to work to make a General Law, for a Rule to Great and Small.

CHAP.

CHAP. V.

Of the Decemviri, *and Law of the* Twelve Tables.

NOtwithſtanding the ſtrong Oppoſition made by the Ma-giſtrates and Senators, whom nothing would ſatisfie but an Arbitrary Government, it was reſolved about the Year of *Rome* 299, to ſend Embaſſadors into *Greece*, to bring ſuch Laws from thence, as the Wiſdom of that flouriſhing Nation had eſtabliſh'd.

Upon their Return, in the Year 302, of the ſame Date, the People being aſſembled in *Centuries*, created Ten Ma-giſtrates, to whom they gave the Name of *Decemviri*. The Method they agreed upon, was, that they ſhould govern the Republick by Turns for a Year, and have the ſame Power with that of *Kings* and *Conſuls*.

He only who was in Power, had the *Faſces* and *Axes*, with other Conſular Enſigns carried before him; the other Nine attended him as Aſſiſtants, having only an *Accenſus* or ſort of Beadle going before them.

At length, having with great Exactneſs made a Model, partly from ſuch Laws as were brought from *Greece*, and partly from the Regal Laws and Cuſtoms of their own Ci-ty, they were approv'd of, and by a *Senatus-Conſultum* or Decree of the Senate, ratify'd by a *Plebiſcitum*, order'd to be every where obey'd. This done, they were reduc'd in-to order, and engraven on *Ten* Tables of Braſs, which were expos'd to publick View, in the moſt conſpicuous part of the *Forum*, in the Year of *Rome*, 303.

All Parties ſeem'd extreamly pleas'd with the Conduct of the *Decemviri* for the firſt Year; but ſomething was ſtill wanting to make the Laws compleat, and therefore the ne-ceſſary Supplements were agreed to be made. In order to bring this Work to Perfection, they proceeded to a new Election of *Decemviri*; of whom, Seven were choſen out of the *Patricians*, and Three out of the *Plebeians*; whereas the whole Number of the former Ten were all *Patricians*, to the great Diſſatisfaction of the People.

Theſe

These added *Two* Tables of Law to the Ten that were made the Year before, which together went by the Name of the *Law of the Twelve Tables*, and were look'd upon as the Fountain of all Law both Publick and Private. *Cicero*, in his Book *de Oratore*, commends them highly, and says, *They are a Summary of all that is excellent in the Libraries of the Philosophers.*

CHAP. VI.

Of the Consequences that attended the Law of the Twelve Tables.

THE Laws contain'd in the Two last Tables, were in no Degree so favourable to the People as those before publish'd; which was owing to the Contrivance of *Appius Claudius*, one of the *Decemviri*. Besides, every one of them laid hold of all Occasions to shew their Tyranny and Violence, having previously agreed and promis'd each other by Oath to be of one Mind, never to assemble the Senate or People, to retain the Power in their own Hands, and to be of equal Authority among themselves.

In a word, *Appius Claudius*, one of the *Decemviri*, fell desperately in love with *Virginia*, Daughter of *Virginius*, a *Plebeian*, at that time *Lieutenant* or *Legate* in the Army, on Mount *Algidum*. This Great Man, having no hopes of gaining her Affections, suborn'd one of his Clients to challenge her for his Slave, assuring him of success in his Cause, since the Trial was to be before him. As soon as *Virginius* heard the news, he hasted to *Rome*, where he found his Daughter condemn'd for a Slave; and despairing of any Relief, desir'd he might speak a Word with her, before he parted from her; which being granted, he led her aside, and stabb'd her to the Heart with this Expression, *This, Child, is the only way I have to set thee at Liberty.*

The

The Difguft with which the People were prepoffefs'd by the violent and fanguinary Proceedings of the *Decemvirate*, made them look upon this unjuft Sentence pafs'd by *Claudius*, as an Invitation to extinguifh and deftroy their Power.

Accordingly, *Appius Claudius* was arraigned, as well as his Colleague *Spurius Oppius*, for correcting a Soldier immoderately. The reft of the *Decemvirate* banifh'd themfelves, and fuffered their Eftates to be confifcated.

In a Word, the Confular Government was reftored; and from the Year 304, the People by the Law *Horatia* decreed, that fuch Laws as the Commons enacted, call'd *Plebifcita*, fhould to all intents and purpofes have the Force of Law. By this Law it was provided, that whatever the People ordain'd feparately from the Senate, fhould be of the fame Force and Authority, as if it had been done in the *Comitia Centuriata*, or general Affembly.

But as there afterwards happen'd two other Difputes between the Senate and People, which occafion'd the latter to retire to Mount *Aventine*, and afterwards to the *Janiculum*; the Senate, to entice them to return, were again oblig'd to promife and confent that the *Plebifcita* fhould be received as Laws; which was fettled by the Law *Publia*, in the Year 415, and by the Law *Hortenfia*, in the Year 478.

Thus it appears, that after the Law of the *Twelve Tables* was eftablifh'd, feveral Laws were made, not only by the whole Body of the People in their *Centuriata Comitia*, but many *Plebifcita* in their *Curiata Comitia*.

Moreover, the Interpretation and Determination of the Learned, bred another kind of Law, called *Jus Civile*, Civil Law, the Practice of the Bar, or the *Cuftumary* Law.

About the fame time, certain Forms were compos'd by the Lawyers call'd *Actiones Juris*, or Cafes at Law, which were in a fet and folemn Style, and to be follow'd in all Proceedings, as well as Acts of Court. Of thefe Forms or Cafes at Law, *Appius Claudius* made a Collection, about the Year 473, which his Secretary *Gneus Flavius* publifh'd, under the Title of the *Flavian Civil Law*: But as this Collection was imperfect, *Sextus Ælius* put out foon after a more compleat one, which went by the Name of the *Ælian Law*; [*L.* 2. §. 6. & 7. *ff. de Origine Juris.*] But the Emperors took away the neceffity of keeping to the Words of thofe

Forms,

Forms, ſtill preſerving that of bringing the Action proper
to the Suit commenced. [*L.* 1. *& * 2. *Cod. & Formul. & im-
petrat. Action. ſublat.*]

Several Regulations were alſo made in the time of the
Republican Government, by the Magiſtrates, particularly
the *Prætors*; of which, after having firſt ſpoken ſomething
of the *Laws*, the *Plebiſcita* and *Interpretation of the Laws,*
the Reader ſhall have an Account.

C H A P. VII.

Of the L A W S.

THE Emperor JUSTINIAN, in the Fourth Para-
graph of the Second Title of the firſt Book of his
Inſtitutes, defines a *Law* to be that which is enacted by the
Roman People, upon the Requiſition of a Magiſtrate of the
Senatorian Order ; as for inſtance, of a *Conſul* :

During the time of the Republican Government, when
the People were their own Law-givers, the Laws were
propos'd by the Conſuls, or ſome other Magiſtrate of the
Senatorian Degree, in a General Aſſembly of the People,
who either paſs'd or rejected them, as they ſaw convenient.

The Method obſerv'd was this ; When a Conſul or other
Magiſtrate of the Senatorian Order, moved to have a Law
enacted, he firſt repreſented the Advantage it would bring
to the Publick, and then read it openly on Three different
Days to the People, that being Maſters of the Heads of it,
they might the more eaſily give their Opinions, when it
came to be debated in the General Aſſembly, or if they
foreſaw any Inconvenience, inform the Magiſtrate who had
the Management of it.

On thoſe Three Days publick Notice was given, of the
time the Law was to be put to the Votes of the People ;
which being come, the Magiſtrate demanded in theſe
Words, *Velitis, Jubeatis Quirites ?* That is, *Is it your Pleaſure,
O Romans, this Law ſhall paſs or no ?* If it went in the
Affirmative, their Anſwer was *Uti Rogas, Be it as thou haſt
ask'd.*

aſk'd. But if in the Negative, *Antiquo* was the Word, i. e.
I forbid it.

Here we muſt obſerve, it was at firſt cuſtomary among
the *Romans*, to give their Votes *vivâ voce* ; but afterwards,
to avoid Tumults, they proceeded in another manner, by
giving every Voter two Tables, in one of which were theſe
Two great Letters *U. R.* in the other a great *A.* one of
which they deliver'd into a little Box for that purpoſe, according as they voted for or againſt the Law propounded.

If the Law paſs'd, it was immediately engraven on Braſs
Tables, which were hung up at the Doors of their Temples
and Corners of their Croſs Streets. And it was a Rule
conſtantly obſerv'd, that all Laws ſhould be firſt expos'd to
Publick View, and examin'd, that no Offender might eſcape
unpuniſh'd, under pretence of Ignorance.

This was the Cuſtom obſerv'd in making Laws, during
the Republican Government, which alſo continu'd for ſome
time under the Emperors, as I ſhall ſhew anon, when I
come to treat of the *Roman Law* in their Reigns.

C H A P. VIII.

Of the Plebiſcita.

A *Plebiſcitum*, according to J U S T I N I A N's Definition,
in the Fourth Paragraph of the Second Book of his
Inſtitutes, is what is enacted by the People, without the
Concurrence of the Senators, upon the Requeſt of one of
their own Magiſtrates, that is, of a *Tribune*.

How the *Plebiſcita* were firſt introduc'd, and afterwards
obtain'd the Force of *Laws*, is particularly ſet down in the
Sixth Chapter.

As for the Difference between a *Plebiſcitum* and a *Law,*
it conſiſts in Four Things. The Firſt is, That a *Law* was
made by the whole Body of the People ; but a *Plebiſcitum*
was the Act of the People only, without the Knowledge of
the *Patricians* and Senators.

The

The Second is, That a *Law* had in it felf a coercive Power, whereas a *Plebifcitum* had no fuch Power, but by the Authority of thofe Three Laws before mention'd.

The Third is, That a *Law* was made at the Requeft of fome Magiftrate of the Senatorian Order ; for inftance, of a *Conful, Dictator, Decemvir,* or *Military Tribune ;* whereas a *Plebifcitum,* was made only at the Requeft of the Tribunes of the People, whofe fole Bufinefs it was, to protect them from being opprefs'd by the *Patricians* and *Senators,* as is faid before.

The Fourth is, That a *Law* was made in the General Affembly of the People, call'd *Centuriata Comitia ;* but a *Plebifcita* pafs'd in a Particular Affembly of the People, feparate from the *Patricians* and *Senators,* which they call'd the Tribunes Affembly, or *Curiata Comitia.*

C H A P. IX.

Of the Interpretation of the Lawyers.

THE Obfcurity of the Law of the *Twelve Tables,* occafion'd by its too great Concifenefs foon appear'd, and made the Interpretation of the Lawyers neceffary ; by which, being accommodated to the Practice of the Bar, and receiving a convenient Extent and proper Reftrictions, 'twas thought it might be brought to anfwer Expectation.

For how Judicious and Sagacious foever a *Law-giver* may be, 'tis impoffible but fomething will efcape his Forefight. The Inconveniencies of Laws are rarely difcover'd till they come to be put in Execution. Every one muft agree, the Foundation of all Laws is Equity ; but the great Variety of Circumftances, are frequently the Caufe that the Decifions of the Law have little of Equity in them, when they are to be applyed to Private Cafes. For as the Law, in regulating Matters goes commonly upon general Principles, and according to the ufual Courfe of Things ; it eafily happens, that a Law which in General is very Juft, proves quite otherwife in Private Cafes that may naturally arife.

There-

Therefore it is neceffary the Law fhould be mitigated by Equity; which depends upon the Diverfity of Circumftances: And this is the Reafon the Laws are feldom in that Perfection the Authors of them intend, till they have receiv'd an Equitable Conftruction.

The *Lawyers*, whofe Right it naturally was to interpret the Laws, by common Confent, undertook to explain thofe Paffages of the Law of the *Twelve Tables*, which were either Obfcure, or liable to a Double Acceptation. They agreed upon Rules for limiting the Difpofition of the Law, where it was *Vague*, or too General, and giving it an Extent to Cafes omitted; and how the Severity and Rigour of its Decifions, was to be temper'd with Equity: Which Method they have ever fince follow'd, in explaining other Laws.

This Interpretation of the Lawyers, created a new kind of Law, fo much approv'd of in Practice, that it was call'd *The Civil Law*, or *Ufage of the Bar*.

It acquir'd the Force of Law, by the tacit Confent of all the *Roman* People; who were highly pleas'd to find their Lawyers fo expert in reconciling the ftrict Literal Sence of the Laws, to the Practice of the Bar, and Rules of Equity.

The Credit of thefe Interpreters was fo much the greater, as they were Men of Rank and Fortune; whofe Wealth, join'd to their profound Learning in the Laws, very much contributed to advance the Dignity of their Profeffion, as well as their Perfonal Merit. So true it is, that the Gifts of Fortune will command and increafe Refpect; which bare Merit can but faintly attract.

In making their Interpretations, they follow'd thefe Two Rules. The firft was, to adhere to the Defign of the Law, rather than the Words in which it was conceiv'd. Thus, when the Law was conceiv'd in General Terms, the Interpreters fometimes confin'd it to Certain Cafes, excluding all others. At other times, when the Law mention'd only Certain Cafes, they extended it to others by parity of Reafon; of which the Titles in the *Inftitutes* (*De Pupillari Subftitutione & de Acquifitione per adrogationem,*) furnifh us with Examples; the Conftruction whereof, being drawn directly from the Spirit and Defign of the Law, is with Juftice regarded as the Law it felf. [*Argumento Legis* i. *ff. de Legibus & L.* 68. *ff. de Verborum Significatione.*]

C

The

The other Rule obferv'd in Interpreting, was by the Rule of Equity, without regard to the Letter or Difpofition of the *Law* : But this could not be done openly by the Interpreters, who had no Power to make or directly abrogate *Laws* ; fo that they could not go againft the *Law*, but under fome Colour, indirectly, and by Inferences drawn from the *Law it felf* ; by which they made it evident, that their Interpretation agreed with the Spirit and True Sence of the *Law* ; altho' it feem'd in fome meafure, contrary to the Terms thereof.

Of this manner of Interpreting the *Law*, there are fome Inftances in the Titles of the *Inftitutes : De Exheredatiune Liberorum, & De Inofficiofo Teftamento.*

One thing worth obferving, in this laft Way of Interpreting, is, That as it feem'd to be contrary to the moft obvious Sence of the *Law*, it was not fo readily receiv'd as the other, which was taken from the true Meaning of it : The Truth was, the *Lawyers* could not go againft the Difpofition of the *Law*, but under fome Colour, that their Interpretation was agreeable to the Spirit of it.

Nor were the Interpretations of the *Lawyers* admitted, how Equitable foever, when they were fo directly oppofite and contrary to the formal Determination of the *Law*, as not to be reconcil'd by any Colour whatever : And therefore, when the *Law* it felf was clear, and its Determination evident, the Authority of the *Lawyers* could not alter it ; becaufe that would not be to Interpret, but in Effect to Abrogate the *Law* ; which is not to be done, but by the Supream Power. Befides, 'tis certain, Interpretations were not intended to deftroy or elude the Force of the *Law*, but to preferve its Vigour, and quicken its Execution ; confining it, however, within the Bounds of Equity, according to the Diverfity of Circumftances.

From what is faid, it muft be concluded, that when the *Law* is abfolutely Unjuft in its Principle, or becomes fo by fubfequent Circumftances, fo that it can receive no Interpretation, without rendring it utterly ufelefs; there is no other Remedy, but to have recourfe to the Sovereign Authority, which alone has the Power of giving Relief, by making another to Repeal it. And 'tis to this Cafe we muft apply the Maxim, *That the Power of Interpreting the Laws, is referv'd for him who has the Right of making them.* [L.1. Cod. de Legibus.]   CHAP.

CHAP. X.

Of the PRÆTOR'*s Edicts.*

THE Interpretation of the *Laws,* did not only belong to the *Lawyers,* but the *Magistrates*; particularly to the PRÆTORS. Let us examine what was the first Occasion of their Creation.

The Two *Consuls,* who were chosen principally to fill the Magistracy, were afterwards often interrupted in the Exercise of their Civil Duty, by the Wars, where their Presence became indispensably necessary.

This was the Reason, that in the Year 387, the Republick created a Magistrate to supply the Place of the Consul, in the Administration of Justice. He was call'd *Prætor,* from *Præessendo* or *Præeundo:* And because he partook of the most considerable Branch of the Consuls Office, had the Honour of being styl'd their *Collegue*; and was allow'd the same Ensigns of Distinction as the Consuls themselves.

At first, we must note, all Magistrates were call'd *Prætors*; afterwards, the *Generals* of *Armies*; and at length, the Name became peculiar to the *Magistrate,* whose Office it was to see Justice administred in the City of *Rome.*

After some time, there was another *Prætor* created, to decide Controversies between Foreigners, who resorted in great Multitudes to *Rome:* And to distinguish these *Magistrates,* one was call'd *Prætor Urbanus,* the other *Prætor Peregrinus.*

In short, as Business multiply'd, in proportion to the Increase of the Empire, the Number of *Prætors* was augmented at several times; and at last, they came to *Twelve*; who had each of them different Employments: One was call'd *Tutelaris,* another *Fidei-Commissarius,* and so the rest, according to the principal Object of their respective Duties.

The *Prætor* himself did not judge ordinary Matters, but only certain Causes, such as *the Restitution of Minors:* Things that were to be decided in the Common Form, he committed to Persons of his chusing, and prescrib'd Forms of Writs or Actions to the Complainants.

C 2   Tho'

Tho' the Inftitution of a *Prætor,* was defign'd rather to fee former *Laws* put in Execution, than to make *new Ones;* yet, as he had the Power of amending the *Laws,* when they prov'd Defective, the People fubmitted to his Decifions; and his *Edicts,* had in fome meafure the Authority of *Laws.*

In reality, as the different Kinds of *Laws,* of which we have here unravel'd the Original, did not take in all Cafes, nor were always Equitable in their Determinations ; the People tacitly allow'd the *Prætors* to propofe their *Edicts,* for mitigating the Rigour of the *Law,* and adding their Decifions, where the *Law* was not explicit. Hence it is, that the Emperor JUSTINIAN fays, *The* Prætor *aids the* Civil Law, *fupplies the Defects in its Difpofition, corrects it, and even fometimes oppofes its Decifions.* [Tit. 9. Inftit. in principio.]

It is alfo in this Sence CATO is to be taken, when he fays in his *Difticks, We muft have Recourfe to the Magiftrate, when the* Law *is Unjuft* ; and that *the Laws themfelves defire to be govern'd by* Law ; that is, by the *Judge* who is the Voice and Interpreter of the *Law.*

Befides the *Prætors,* there were other Officers who had the Power of making *Edicts* and *Regulations,* in Explanation of the *Laws:* Thefe were the *Ædiles Curules,* who had the Direction of all Publick Sales, the Care of the Watch, and cleanfing of the Streets.

Of thefe, I fhall only obferve, they had their Names from *Ædibus;* being at firft chiefly appointed to look after the Publick Buildings ; but in procefs of Time, their Office was much enlarg'd, and the Regulation of the Market, Gaming-Houfes, Publick Shews, and generally the whole Civil Government of the City, was put under their Care. They had the Addition of *Curules* from *Curru* ; becaufe they rode in Chariots, wherein there was a Chair adorn'd with *Ivory,* which denoted their being in the Rank of *Chief Magiftrates.*

To return to the *Edicts* of the *Prætors :* Many of them yielding to Favour, or following their own Caprice, made feveral *Regulations* contrary to Equity, and the moft receiv'd Maxims : Wherefore, in the Year 686, the *Plebifcitum Cornelianum,* oblig'd them to fpecifie at their entring into the Office, the Method they intended to obferve in adminiftring

Juftice,

Juftice, through the whole Courfe of their Magiftracy; from which they could not deviate. And 'tis from thefe *Edicts,* the *Law* call'd, *Jus honorarium & viva vox Juris Civilis,* is deriv'd. [*L.* 7. §. 1. *& L.* 8. *ff. de Juſtitia & Jure.*]

The Force of thefe *Edicts* expir'd with the *Prætor's* Office, which was Annual, unleſs they were renew'd by their Succeſſors. This Limitation to a Year, got them the Name of *Leges Annales* ; and as the *Prætors* caus'd them to be wrote on a *White Table,* that was call'd *Album Prætoris.*

Among thefe, there are fome *Edicts* fo very Juft, that they have been perpetuated as *Laws* ; from which there is no departing, without an Offence to Equity and Right Reafon.

It muſt, however, be allow'd, that the vaſt Number of them, diffus'd a great Uncertainty through the whole Law. To remedy which, the Emperor ADRIAN order'd *Julian,* a celebrated Lawyer, out of all thefe *Edicts,* to form a Perpetual one, which might ferve the *Prætors* for a conſtant Rule, to guide them in their Judgments and Adminiſtration of Juftice ; and at the fame time, took from them the Power of making *Edicts* for the future. [*L.* 3. §. 18. *& 21. Cod. de Veteri Jure enucleando.*]

This *Perpetual Edict* was divided into Fifty Books, containing the moſt juft and ufeful Matters of all the *Prætors Edicts* ; and feveral *Roman Lawyers* have made fine Commentaries thereon.

CHAP. XI.

Of the Roman Law under the Emperors.

THE Independant State and Liberty of the *Romans*, receiv'd its firſt ſhock from JULIUS CÆSAR, who laid the Foundation of a *new Monarchy*, in the Ruins of the *Republick*. He diſpos'd of all as if he had been *ſole Maſter*, got himſelf to be created *Perpetual Dictator*, againſt all Rule; and order'd the chief Marks of Sovereign Power to be given him.

But the Republick was utterly extinguiſh'd under AUGUSTUS, in the Year 731, from the Building of *Rome*; at which time, the Sovereignty was tranſlated from the People to his Perſon. It was done by a Decree of the *Senate*; which, with the Conſent of the *People*, reviv'd the *Law Regia*; firſt paſs'd, as 'tis pretended, in favour of ROMULUS, and now renew'd in favour of AUGUSTUS. The Thing happen'd thus;

AUGUSTUS's Ambition made him paſſionately deſirous of the Empire, but his Diſcretion directed him to purſue his Aims after ſuch a manner, as not to forfeit the Good Will of the People. His Deſign was not only not to appear deſirous of the Government, but to bring them to petition him to accept of it. In this View, he pretended to be unable alone to ſupport the Weight of ſo great an Empire; but the more he ſtrove to Diſqualifie himſelf, the more eagerly the People begg'd he would take it upon him. At laſt he conſented to the paſſing of the *Law Regia*, by which the Sovereignty was transferr'd to him; that is, the Right of Law-making, of commanding Generally, and forcing Obedience. This *Law* was always renew'd upon the Acceſſion of the Emperors, to the Reign of VESPASIAN.

Thus the Power of *Law-making*, being transferr'd from the People to the Prince, by the *Law Regia*, we may obſerve, that in the Emperors Reigns, their Determinations had the ſame Authority as thoſe of the People under the

Free

Free State; which produc'd a new Kind of *Law*, call'd, *The Edicts or Constitutions of the Emperors.*

But this was not brought about all at once; for notwithstanding the Sovereign Power had shifted from the People to the Emperor, He was too politick not to leave them some Marks of their late Freedom, in order, the better to establish and strengthen his Government. Wherefore, he kept up the Use of General Assemblies, in which he order'd all his *Edicts* to be publish'd, and that they should still retain the Name of *Laws.*

This faint Mark of the Ancient Liberty, displeas'd TIBERIUS, who succeeded *Augustus* : He suppress'd those Assemblies, under Pretence, that they could not be conveniently held, in Respect of the prodigious Increase of the People, which made it impossible for them to meet any longer in one Place.

This Contrivance he made use of to gain their Consent, that instead of advising with the *People* upon making *new Laws,* the *Senate* only should be consulted : But his Designs were easily seen through. Jealous of his own Power, he resolv'd not to leave the least Shadow of the Ancient Liberty ; nor did he weaken, or rather abolish the Rights the People, and increase those of the Senate, with other View, than that all the Advantages and Prerog[atives] of absolute Sovereignty, should by degrees, at last in Himself.

To this End, whenever he had a mind to pu[blis]h a *new Edict,* he drew it up in his Privy Council, an[d t]hen sent it to the Senate, who never fail'd to make a [D]ecree according to his Pleasure : And by this imagina[ry] Deference to the Judgment of the Senate, his *Edicts* [go]t the Force of *Law,* without the Peoples Approbation.

His Successors practis'd the same Artifice and got their *Edicts,* by an affected Moderation, pass'd [fo]r the real *Senatus-Consulta* ; tho' in truth, they were no[thing] [el]fs the *meer Will* and *Pleasure* of the Emperor, in which [th]e People had no Part.

But in after Ages, the Emperors [p]ublish'd several *Edicts,* without the Formality of the Sen[ate']s Approbation ; most of which, they commanded, shoul[d] go under the Title of *Imperial Constitutions,* in order [to] give the greater Lustre to their Sovereignty.

In

In this manner, the Emperors *Edicts* establish'd a new kind of *Law*.

There are also many *Senatus-Consulta* and *Responsa Jurisconsultorum*, to be met with under the Monarchical Government of the Emperors, which are to be spoken of in this Place; but I think it proper, first to trace, as one may say, the Succession of the *Roman* Emperors, in order to give the Reader some *Idea* of the *Laws* made by them: In doing which, 'tis not my Design to write a History of them, but only to take notice of the Time they Reign'd; and, by the way, of the *Laws* they publish'd: Being convinc'd, that many Difficulties arise in the Study of the *Civil Law*, which cannot be resolv'd, without knowing when the *Laws* were made.

C H A P. XII.

The Succession of the Emperors to JUSTINIAN.

*A*UGUSTUS came to the Empire in the Year of Rome 711, in the manner describ'd in the foregoing Chapter. He made several *Laws*; of which the Chief are, the *Julia de Adulteriis*, for punishing *Adulterers*; prohibits in another Chapter the Alienation of *Land* given in *Dowry*. The Law *Julia Peculatus*, to prevent the Misapplication of *Publick Money*. The Law *Julia de Residuis*, to oblige *Receivers* and *Managers of Publick Treasure* to Account. The Law *Julia de Ambitu*, against Bribing for Employments in the Government. Many other *Laws* were made in this Emperor's Reign, which are too long to give an Account of here.

TIBERIUS succeeded him, in the Year of Christ 23, and Died in 38 of the same Date. He did nothing without first consulting the Senate; and by that means, gave the *Senatus-Consulta* the Force of *Law*.

CALI.

CALIGULA came to the Empire in the Year of Chriſt 39, and was Killed in 42.

The Emperor CLAUDIUS began his Reign in the Year 43, after Chriſt, and continued to the Year 55. He was the Author of many *Laws*, and Repeal'd the *Clauſe* in the Law *Papia Poppea*, relating to the Marriage of Men of *Sixty*, and Women of *Fifty* Years old. Being diſpos'd to marry his Neice *Agrippina*, Daughter of his Brother *Germanicus*; he caus'd a *Senatus-Conſultum* to be made for that Purpoſe, that his Marriage might not be Unlawful.

NERO ſucceeded him in the Empire, in the Year of Chriſt 56, and Kill'd himſelf in 69. The *Senatus-Conſultum Trebellianum* was made in his Time, with ſeveral other *Laws*; among which, One provides, *Ne quis alienum ſcribens Teſtamentum Legatum ſibi adſcriberet*, that *The Writer or Maker of another Man's Will, ſhall not make himſelf a* Legatee *therein.*

GALBA, OTHO and VITELLIUS, were received Emperors ſucceſſively: The Firſt held the Government but Seven Months and Twenty five Days; the Second, Three Months; and the laſt, Eight. So that by the ſhortneſs of their Reigns, they had no Opportunities to make many *Laws*.

VESPASIAN was choſen Emperor in the Year 71, and Reigned Nine Years. The *Law Falcidia*, and the *Senatus-Conſultum Pegaſianum*, were both made in his Time.

TITUS his Son, and Succeſſor in the Empire, govern'd Two Years and Two Months, and Died in the Year 80.

DOMITIAN his Brother, who ſucceeded him, Reigned Fifteen Years, and was Kill'd in 97.

Upon his Death, NERVA was rais'd to the Empire, and Died Sixteen Months after, in the Year 99. He enacted many *Laws*; one of which, fully empower'd the Sol-

diers

diers to make *Military Teſtaments* without any Formality
of *Law.* [*L.* 1. *ff. de Teſtament. Milit.*]

The Emperor TRAJAN, his adopted Son, was his
Succeſſor. He Reign'd Eighteen Years, to the Year 118.
This Emperor made ſome *Laws,* which are Inſtances of his
Mildneß and *Juſtice* : Among the reſt, one obliges the *Father*
who has been too ſevere to his *Son,* to *emancipate him.*

Before I proceed, it will not be amiſs to inform the Reader, that none of the Emperors *Edicts,* from *Auguſtus* to
Trajan, are to be found in *Juſtinian's Code* ; which Collection, conſiſts only of *Edicts* paſs'd by thoſe Emperors that
came afterwards to the Empire ; that is, from *Adrian* to
Juſtinian.

ADRIAN, who was *Trajan's* Couſin-German, was declared Emperor in the Year of Chriſt 118. He Reign'd
Twenty Years and Ten Months, and Died in 139. He
made ſeveral *Laws* upon different Subjects : One was con-
cerning the Property of *Treaſure Trove,* (§. 39. *Inſtit. de rer.
Diviſione.*) He declar'd Children *Legitimate* that were born
in the *Eleventh Month.* He forbad *Maſters* to *kill* their *Slaves.*
He granted the *Twelfth of the Eſtate,* to the Children whoſe
Parents were condemn'd to Die. The *Perpetual Edict* was
compos'd in his Reign by *Salvianus Julianus,* in the Year of
Chriſt 132. As alſo, the *Senatus Conſultum Tertullianum* or
Tertyllianum ; which provides, That the *Childrens Eſtates* ſhall
revert to *their Mothers,* in Default of *Heirs Deſcendants.*

TITUS AURELIUS ANTONINUS, Sirnam'd
PIUS, ſucceeded *Adrian.* He Reign'd Twenty two Years
and Seven Months, and Dy'd in the Year of Chriſt 161.
Among the many *Edicts* which he made, there is One prohibiting *Legacies, Pœnæ nomine* : Upon which, ſee my *Commentaries* on the laſt Paragraph of the Title of *Legacies,*
in the *Inſtitutes.*

The two Brothers, MARCUS AURELIUS, Sir-
nam'd the PHILOSOPHER, and LUCIUS VE-
RUS ſucceeded, and Reign'd jointly about Eighteen Years,
Lucius Verus dying in the Year 170. After which, *Marcus
Aurelius* Reign'd alone till 177 ; and from that Time, took
his

his Son COMMODUS for a Partner in the Empire; with whom he Reigned till the Year 181, in which he Died.

These two Brethren, *Marcus Aurelius* and *Lucius Verus,* are call'd in many *Laws, DIVI FRATRES.* [*Vid. L.* 3. *ff. de Jure Fisci.*] And there are many *Laws* of their making, reported in the *Code.*

The Emperor *Marcus Aurelius* also enacted several, whilst he sat alone in the Throne; many of which are to be seen in the *Code,* under the Title *Ne de Statu defunctorum.* He created a *Prætor* to determine Matters relating to *Tutorship.* In his Time, the *Senatus-Consultum Orphitianum* was made, which admits *Children* to succeed as *Heirs at Law* to their *Mothers:* Upon which, see my *Commentaries* on the Fourth Title of the Third *Book* of the *Institutes.*

After the Death of *Marcus Aurelius,* the Emperor COMMODUS Reign'd alone till the Year 193, in which he was Kill'd.

ÆLIUS PERTINAX was chosen Emperor in his Place, altho' he refus'd to accept of the Government. And tho' he was Kill'd Three Months after, there are several of his *Laws* reported in the *Code.*

JULIAN, Grandson of the Famous *Lawyer,* who was Author of the *Perpetual Edict,* succeeded *Pertinax.* He held the Empire but Two Months, yet some of his *Laws* are in the *Code.*

After him, SEPTIMIUS SEVERUS was elected Emperor, in the Year of Christ 195. He Reign'd Eighteen Years, and Died in 212. He was the Author of the *Senatus-Consultum,* which provides, *Ne prædia rustica aut suburbana minorum alienarentur sine decreto Magistratus t. t. ff. de rebus eorum qui sub Tutela,* &c. Tho' this Emperor was Cruel and Irreligious, he had many Good Qualities: He took Pleasure in doing *Justice,* and had a particular Esteem for the celebrated *Papinian.*

ANTO-

ANTONINUS CARACALLA and GETA, both Sons of *Severus*, were by their Father made *Associates* in the Empire : Which is the Reason we find some *Laws* in the *Code*, bearing the Names of *Severus* and *Caracalla*.

About a Year after *Severus* dy'd, *Caracalla* Kill'd his Brother *Geta*, in the Presence of his Mother *Julia*. He Reign'd alone Six Years, and was then Kill'd. We meet with several *Laws* of his making, dispers'd in the *Code*.

MACRINUS was proclaim'd Emperor, after the Death of *Caracalla*. His Reign lasted only a Year and Two Months, being put to Death in 219. None of his *Laws* appear in the *Code*.

VARIUS ANTONINUS HELIOGABALUS, was in *Macrinus*'s Life-time proclaim'd Emperor by the *Army*. He was reported to be the Natural Son of *Caracalla*. The Name of *Heliogabalus*, was given him, because he was a *Priest of the Sun*, which is denoted by that Word. His Reign lasted only Four Years, being Kill'd in the Year of Christ 223 : Yet there are some of his *Laws* in the *Code*.

AURELIUS SEVERUS ALEXANDER, was his Successor. He Reign'd Thirteen Years, and was Kill'd in 236. He was one of the Greatest and Best Princes in the World ; equally to be admir'd in War and Peace. His chief Care was to see Justice impartially administer'd. He was the *Author* of abundance of *Laws* ; the *Wisdom* and *Equity* of which, give us an *Idea* of his *sound Judgment*, and the *Uprightness of his Heart*. There are no less than Four Hundred and Sixty one in *Justinian's Code* ; upon which, Monsieur *de Chassanée* has made very Learned Commentaries.

After this Emperor, MAXIMINUS, some of whose *Laws* are to be seen in the *Code*, Reign'd Two Years, and was Kill'd in 238.

Then

Then follow'd GORDIANUS, who Reign'd One Month and Six Days. And after him, ABBINUS and PAPIENUS, elected Emperors by the *Senate*, Reign'd about a Year ; and were then both put to Death by the *Soldiers*.

GORDIANUS, the Younger Son of the Emperor juſt mention'd, ſucceeded them. He govern'd Six Years, and Died in 245. There are ſome of his *Laws* in the *Code*.

MARCUS PHILIPPUS, who came after him, Reign'd about as long as his Predeceſſor. He Died in 250. Some of his *Laws* alſo, are to be found in the *Code*.

DECIUS, who ſucceeded him, Reign'd only Two Years, or thereabouts, and Died in the Year 252. The *Code* has ſome of his *Laws*.

GALLUS and VOLUSIANUS ſucceeded him : Their Reign, which laſted only Two Years, ended by their Death, in the Year 254. Some of their *Laws* are to be ſeen in the *Code*.

After theſe, VALERIANUS, and his Son GALIE-NUS Reign'd together Seven Years. In the *Code* we ſee ſeveral *Laws* under both their Names.

Valerianus being dead, GALIENUS Reign'd with VALERIANUS *the Younger* ; but they were both Kill'd in the Year of Chriſt 269. There are ſome *Laws* in the *Code* of their making.

CLAUDIUS *the Second*, who ſucceeded them, Reign'd but Two Years, or thereabouts ; yet we have ſome of his *Laws*.

After this, AURELIANUS Reign'd Six Years, and was Kill'd in 276. We find many *Laws* of his making, in the *Code*.

After

After him TACITUS Reign'd Six Months ; FLO-RIANUS, about a Year : And then PROBUS was rais'd to the Empire, who was Kill'd Six Years after, in 282.

Then follow'd CARUS, with his Sons CARINUS and NUNNERIANUS, whom he made Partners with him in the Empire. After about a Year, the Father being Slain, *Carinus* and *Nunnerianus* Reign'd together for a Year ; and then were both Kill'd, in 285. There are fome *Laws* in the *Code*, which have the Names of *all Three* ; and others, thofe only of *Carinus* and *Nunnerianus*.

DIOCLETIANUS and MAXIMIANUS HER-CULIUS, Reign'd together for the Space of Eighteen or Twenty Years : When *Diocletianus* Refign'd the Empire in favour of CONSTANTIUS CHLORUS, in the Year 304. *Maximianus Herculius* did the fame Two Years after in favour of MAXIMIANUS GALERIUS.

Conftantius was fatisfy'd with *England* and the *Gauls* ; and *Maximianus* had all the reft of the Empire for his Share. There are fome *Laws* in the *Code*, made by *Diocletianus* alone ; others by Him and *Maximianus* ; and fome by *Con-ftantius, Maximianus* and *Galerius*.

CONSTANTINUS, Sirnam'd the GREAT, fuc-ceeded his Father *Conftantius*, the Year 308 ; and Reign'd feveral Years with the Emperors *Galerius*, and *Maxentius* Son of *Maximianus*, the Firft of that Name : After which, he govern'd the Empire alone for Thirteen Years, and Died in 339.

Conftantine the Great, was the firft *Chriftian* Emperor. After conquering *Maxentius* : He enter'd *Rome* in Triumph with a *Crofs* ; and labour'd to perfwade the *Senate* and *People* to embrace the *Chriftian Faith*. There are abundance of his *Laws* in *Juftinian's Code* ; moft of them relating to *Religion* and the *Catholick Faith*, *Bifhops* and other *Minifters of the Church*, and *Places* dedicated to the Service of *God*. All which are uncontef̈table Proofs of this Emperor's great Piety and Zeal.

CON-

CONSTANTINUS *the Younger*, CONSTAN-TIUS and CONSTANS, all three Sons of *Conftantinus* the *Great*, after their Father's Death, divided the Empire between them.

Conftantinus the *Younger*, was Kill'd Three Years after; *Conftans* in the Year 352 : After which, *Conftantius* enjoy'd the Throne alone, till the Year 365. There are in the *Code* fome *Laws*, by the Names of all Three; fome alfo have the Names of *Conftantius* and *Conftans*, and others that only of *Conftantius*.

JULIANUS, call'd *the Apoftate*, becaufe he fell from the Faith of Chrift, was Nephew to *Conftantinus* the *Great*. He came to the Empire in the Year 365, and was Kill'd two Years after. There are fome of his *Laws* extant in the *Code*.

As there are alfo of JOVIANUS who fucceeded him, and Reign'd but Eight Months.

VALENTINIANUS and VALENS, Brothers, were made Emperors in the Year 367; and GRATIA-NUS, Son of *Valentinianus*, the Year following. Thus we find in the *Code*, *Laws* made by *Valentinianus* and *Valens*; and others by *Valentinianus*, *Valens* and *Gratianus*.

Afterwards, *Valens*, *Gratianus*, and VALENTINIA-NUS the *Second*, Reign'd together in 378. And there are feveral *Laws* by thefe Three Emperors Names in the *Code*. But *Valens* was Kill'd Five Months after. So the Two Brothers, *Gratianus* and *Valentinianus*, Emperors of the *Eaft*, with THEODOSIUS, whom *Gratianus* affociated in the Empire, Reign'd together, from the Year 382 to 386. We have feveral *Laws* made in their Reigns.

After the Death of *Gratianus*, *Valentinianus* the *Second*, *Theodofius*, and ARCADIUS his Son, Reign'd till 394. The *Code* has many *Laws* under their Names.

Then *Theodofius* with his Two Sons, *Arcadius* and HO-NORIUS; fome of whofe *Laws* we meet with in the *Code*, Reign'd till the Year 398, in which *Theodofius* Died.

After

After his Death, *Arcadius* and *Honorius*, Reign'd together till 404; and made several *Laws*, whereof some are in the *Code*.

Theodosius the *Great* being Dead, *Arcadius*, *Honorius*, and THEODOSIUS the Younger Son of *Arcadius*, Reign'd jointly till 410. Then *Honorius* and *Theodosius*, to the Year 425. From which time, the latter Reign'd till 427 : And then, taking VALENTINIANUS the *Third*, for a Co-partner in the Government, Reign'd till 452, in which he Died.

Here the Reader must be inform'd, that *Theodosius* the *Younger*, in the Year 438, made a *Code* call'd after his Name ; in which he inserted all his own *Edicts*, with those of *Constantinus* and his Successors ; the greatest part of which, were transcrib'd into *Justinian*'s *Code*. The excellent *Notes* publish'd by *Gothofredus* upon the *Theodosian Code*, may be of very great Use towards the right understanding of all the *Constitutions*, from the Reign of *Constantinus*, to the End of that of *Theodosius* the *Younger*.

Valentinianus the *Third*, having held the Empire alone, for some time after the Death of his Collegue, Reign'd in Conjunction with MARTIANUS to the Year 457 : From which, *Martianus* Rul'd alone till 460. In the *Code* we find several *Laws*, by *Valentinianus* the *Third* alone ; others by him and *Martianus*, and some by *Martianus* only.

LEO succeeded *Martianus :* He govern'd the Empire with MAJORANUS till 463 : After that with SEVERUS, till the Year 468. And then with ANTHEMIUS, who being Dead, he Reign'd alone till 475. There are *Laws* in the *Code* which bare the Names of them both, and some that of *Leo* alone.

LEO the *Younger* and ZENO Reign'd together till 476 ; and *Zeno* alone, till 494. We have *Laws* that go under both their Names, and others of *Zeno* only.

ANASTASIUS succeeded *Zeno*, and Reign'd Twenty seven Years, till 521. There are many of his *Laws* in the *Code*.

His

His Succeſſor was JUSTIN, a *Thracian* by Birth, of low Extraction; having in his Youth been a *Herdſman*: When he grew older, he betook himſelf to the Wars; where, after paſſing thro' ſeveral Military Offices, he came to the Empire, upon the Death of *Anaſtatius*, in the Year 521. He Reign'd alone for above Six Years, and we find many *Laws* in the *Code* which go under his Name only.

In his Seventh Year, he adopted his Nephew JUSTI-NIAN, and made him his Co-partner in the Empire; which is the Reaſon, that in the *Code* we meet with ſeveral *Laws* under both their Names; but there are a vaſt Number of *Juſtinian's* alone; and even ſome made by him, after his *Code* was firſt Compos'd, which were added when he Corrected and Enlarg'd it: Particularly, his *Fifty Deciſions*; upon which, Monſieur *Ragueau* has made an excellent Commentary in *Quarto*.

As Part of this Work was always deſign'd to give an Account of the ſeveral Materials, out of which *Juſtinian* compos'd the Body of the *Civil Law*; I thought it incumbent upon me, to enlarge a little upon his Life; and therefore have allow'd it a ſeparate Chapter.

And indeed, I ſhould be to blame to ſpeak of ſo excellent a Work, without furniſhing the Reader with ſome Notion of the Prince, by whoſe Care it has been tranſmitted to Us, in its preſent State.

D CHAP.

CHAP. XIII.

Of the Emperor JUSTINIAN.

JUSTINIAN, born in the Year of Chrift 483, was the Son of *Sabatius* and *Nigilantia*, both of Obfcure Families; but *Juftinian* receiv'd much Honour from his Parentage: For his Mother was Sifter to the Emperor *Juftin* I. who notwithftanding his bafe Extraction, happily came to the Empire. By this means alfo *Juftinian* was in his Uncle's Reign advanc'd to the Degree of a Patrician, and fucceffively made Conful and General of the Army. At length, being folemnly adopted by *Juftin*, he was made Copartner in the Empire, on the Firft of *April* 527, which happen'd to be *Eafter-Day*, and four Months after, became fole Mafter of the Empire, by the Death of his Uncle and Adoptive Father.

The conftant Succefs which attended this Prince in all his Undertakings, his Piety and Courage, were alone fufficient to attract the Love and Admiration of his Subjects, and even of Foreign Nations; but Providence was pleafed to fecond all thefe in giving him great Generals, and moft Skilful Lawyers, by whofe Affiftance he perform'd fo many Wonders both in Peace and War.

Belifarius conquer'd the *Parthians*, drove the *Goths* out of *Italy*, and the *Vandals*, with all the *Barbarians*, out of *Africa*. *Tribonianus*, *Dorotheus* and *Theophilus* affifted the Emperor in framing his Law, and compiling his *Inftitutes*, *Code* and *Digeft*, which have not a little contributed towards the Glory of his Memory.

And tho' *Suidas* malicioufly reports, with an Intent to blaft this Prince's Reputation, that he was of a dull phlegmatick Conftitution, and utterly unacquainted with Polite Learning, it would be highly unjuft to give an implicit Credit to what he fays, in oppofition to all Hiftorical Evidence to the contrary.

'Tis not to be queftion'd, but this Emperor was endow'd with moft of thofe great Qualities which raife a Man above

bove the Vulgar, efpecially an undaunted Courage, with exemplary Piety. Befides, 'tis plain, he was ever fuccefful in his Wars, and very knowing in Affairs of all kinds.

Procopius tells us, (*Lib.* 1. *de Bell. Goth.*) that *Juftinian* fhew'd always great Refolution and Magnanimity in all his Enterprizes. This he reports fairly: And 'tis highly probable, that many things he fays of him in his Secret Hiftory, proceeded from the Difguft the Emperor had given him.

Paulus Diaconus fpeaks of him in thefe Terms: "This "Prince was fortunate in War, and skilful in managing "Civil Affairs: He profefs'd the Catholick Faith, was "upright in all his Actions, juft in all his Judgments, "and all his Undertakings fucceeded to his Wifh." *Jornandes, Lib. de Rebus Gothicis, in fine,* adds, that by the Valour of *Belifarius*, he triumphed over many Nations, and that no time can obliterate the Glory he has acquir'd.

If we may believe what *Caffiodorus* reports in his *Epiftles* 19, and 22. *Book* 10. *Theobaldus*, King of the *Goths*, addreffes himfelf to this Emperor in this manner: "All Nations "honour you: 'Tis no new thing to hear an Emperor prai- "fed by his own Subjects; but very particular, to fee "Strangers join with them in their Wifhes, which, we may "well conclude, are hearty and fincere, fince they are not "the Effect of Fear.

No Emperor fince *Conftantinus*, has fhewn more Zeal for the Chriftian Religion: All his Sentiments were Orthodox. His Confeffion of Faith is at the Beginning of his *Code*, and truly worthy of him. The Magnificent Temple which he caufed to be built at *Conftantinople*, is another Mark of his Piety.

Thefe, and many other evident Teftimonials of the Vertues and good Qualities of this Great Man, are of too much Weight to be over-balanc'd by the fingle Authority of one *Greek* Hiftorian, who, perhaps, was guilty of the fame Fault, with which *Cicero* in his Oration for *Flaccus*, reproaches the Authors of that Nation. 'Tis believed, *Juftin* II. Son of *Dulciffimus* and *Vigilantia*, *Juftinian*'s Sifter, accufed him of fome things for which he had no grounds. However, 'tis not to be denied, but this Great

Man

Man was too much devoted to the Fair Sex ; and we ſee he always inclin'd to countenance them, and made ſeveral Laws in their Favour.

To conclude, 'tis agreed he was. Two and Forty Years old, when he began to Reign, and that he Died the Thirteenth of *November,* 565. He left *Juſtinus* the Second for his Succeſſor ; who, as we ſaid before, being Jealous of his Predeceſſor's Glory, endeavour'd to tarniſh his Memory, by ſpreading many Falſe and Scandalous Reports of him.

Having before obſerved, that under the Monarchical Government of the Emperors, beſides their *Conſtitutions,* ſeveral *Senatus-Conſulta,* and *Anſwers* of the Learned in the *Law* appear'd ; I am now to explain theſe Two *new* kinds of *Law,* according to the Method I propos'd to follow in this Hiſtory.

But, as the *Senatus-Conſulta,* which are to be our Subject, were made in the *Senate,* and that Auguſt Aſſembly had always the greateſt Share in the Adminiſtration of Publick Affairs, I thought my ſelf oblig'd to give ſome Account of it in this Place, in order to render this Work compleat. Beſides, it muſt be allow'd, it will very much contribute towards informing us, what a *Senatus-Conſultum* was ; and underſtanding of ſome Paſſages in our Books, wherein the *Senate* and *Senators* are mention'd.

CHAP.

CHAP. XIV.

Of the Roman Senate.

THE Inftitution of the *Senate*, follow'd foon after the Eftablifhment of the City of *Rome*; whofe Founder, rightly confidering, that nothing is fo unftable as *Force* without *Wifdom*, refolv'd to govern his State, in Concert with fome of the Members which compos'd it.

His Prudence equally appear'd in the Defign and Execution. He commanded his Subjects to draw *Three Counfellors* or *Senators* out of each *Tribe*; and that the Thirty *Curiæ*, into which the People were divided, fhould alfo choofe Three more; making choice himfelf of *One* only, whom he plac'd at the Head of all the reft: Thus his Council confifted of an Hundred Perfons. But he took particular Care none fhould be advanced to this Eminent Dignity, but fuch as were well recommended by their great Age and Merit.

Hence the *Senators* had their Name, *Quafi fenes*; and were afterwards called *Patres*, to mark out the Refpect which was due to them, or becaufe their Application to Bufinefs, and Care of the Republick, made them regarded as *Fathers*. *Their Bodies*, fays *Saluft*, *were enfeebled by great Age, but their Underftandings were fortified with Wifdom and Experience.*

ROMULUS call'd only a Hundred, as is before obferv'd, to this Dignity; but their Number was afterwards confiderably augmented: Upon which Increafe, the Appellation of *Patres* became peculiar to the old Original *Senators*. The new Ones were called *Confcripti*; and in procefs of Time, both were join'd, and made ufe of to fignifie the whole *Senate*.

At firft, none were admitted into the *Senatorian* Order, but *Patricians*; that is, fuch as were defcended from the Antient *Senators* created by *Romulus*: Afterwards, the *Roman* Knights were receiv'd into it: Which is the Reafon that *Perfeus*, King of *Macedonia*, in *Livy*, calls the *Roman* Knights, *The Chofen of the Youth, and Seminary of the Senate.*

D 3   At

At length, in order to raife an Emulation, which might be advantageous to the Republick, fuch of the People as had born any Chief Offices, were admitted to be *Senators*; but not till they were firft Ennobled.

The ordinary, as well as moft important Part of the *Senators* Bufinefs, was to confult upon Emergencies, and the Scituation of *Publick Affairs.* So the *Senate*, properly fpeaking, was at firft the Prince's Council ; and in time, became that of the Republick : Which makes *Cicero* call it, The *Guardian*, the *Defender*, and *Organ* of the *Commonwealth* ; leaving the *Magiftrates* the Honour of putting their Refolutions in Execution. In fhort, as the *Magiftrate* had the Command over the *People*, fo the *Senate* commanded the *Magiftrate.*

" The *Senate*, fays *Polybius*, had the Difpofal and Diftri" bution of the *Publick Treafure* ; the whole Revenue of " the Government was in their Power, and they order'd all " Expences as they thought proper." He adds, " That " the *Quæftors*, which are thought to have been at *Rome*, " and had the Office of our modern *Comptrollers* of the " Treafury, had no Power to difpofe of a Penny of the " Money in their Hands without a Warrant from the *Se-* " *nate*, unlefs by order of the *Confuls.*

The Appropriation of the Publick Treafure, was fo abfolutely in the *Senate*, that the People never pretended to interfere in it ; and it belong'd to them only to regulate all the Publick Expences, and comptroll the Accounts of fuch as farm'd the Publick Revenue.

When it was neceffary to difpatch *Embaffadors* to Foreign Princes or Nations, or appoint *Lieutenants* for *Generals* of *Armies*, or *Governors* of *Provinces*, the Senate made choice of whom they thought fit to fill thofe Employments.

It was alfo their Right to *receive* and *give Audience* to Foreign Minifters.

The Honours of Triumph could not be had, but by their Permiffion.

No new Religion or Worfhip could be introduc'd, till it had their Approbation.

In a Word, the *Senate* was to the *Republick*, what the *Soul* is to the *Body* : It directed all its Motions, warded off all Dangers, and kept it in Tranquillity, by prudently preferving an exact Harmony in all its Parts.

There

There were frequent Occasions of affembling the *Senate.* In the *Regal* Government, the Kings only had Power to call them together; but under the *Free State,* that Power devolv'd to the *Chief Magiftrate* of the City: So that the *Prætor* had it only in the Abfence of the *Conful*; and that too, upon very preffing Occafions:

There were Two Ways of calling the *Senate* together; one by Proclamation iffued by the *Confuls,* or in their abfence, by the *Chief Magiftrate*: The other, by a Publick Crier, who proclaim'd in the Streets of the greateft Concourfe, the Order of the *Conful* for the *Senate's* meeting: But this was us'd only upon fudden Emergencies, when fpeedy Refolutions were neceffary.

The *Confuls* had a Right to move their Queftion, before any other Magiftrate, and to put it to the Vote; and in their Abfence, that Right belong'd to the *Prætors* or *Cenfors.* But every Member of the *Senate,* upon giving his Opinion, had a Right of making other Propofals.

The Meetings of the *Senate,* were ufually on the *Calends,* *Nones,* or *Ides* of every Month: But in *September* and *October,* the Publick Affairs were manag'd by a *Committee* of the *Senate,* chofen by Lot.

They were not debarr'd from meeting on *Holydays,* but they feldom did; nor upon the fame Days as the *People* affembled, unlefs the Occafion was very preffing; in which Cafe, the *People* adjourn'd their Affembly, to make room for that of the *Senate.*

Their Places of affembling, were always in fome of their *Temples,* or other *Publick Buildings,* which had been Confecrated by the *Augurs.*

The *Magiftrates,* whofe Right it was to call them together, never met, till they had firft offer'd *Propitiatory Sacrifices* to the *Gods.*

Such *Members* as made any Motion or Report in a full *Senate,* were to fpeak Standing; and when any one Voted, he was to be in the fame Pofture; after which, he was allow'd to fit down.

As their chief Bufinefs was to deliberate upon the *Neceffities of the State,* and other *Publick Affairs*; fo there were great Privileges annex'd to the *Senatorian* Office.

They had a Particular Drefs, which diftinguifh'd them from other Citizens, as is before obferv'd.

D 4 All

All Embaffies and Honourable Commiffions, were generally beftow'd upon the *Senators*, and not on the *Roman* Knights.

The Right of fitting in the Chief Places, at *Publick Shews* and *Ceremonies*, contributed very much towards gaining them Refpect.

Whoever offended a *Senator*, was fure to be punifh'd with greater Severity, than if he had done the fame to a common *Citizen*.

Cicero, in one of his Letters to *Sulpicius*, gives us to know, That if a *Senator* had a Suit commenc'd againft him in any of the *Provinces*, he could remove it to *Rome* ; which feems to be very like our Privilege in *France*, granted by *Letters of Committimus*.

A *Plebeian*, had the Liberty of excepting only againft *Three* Judges ; but a *Senator*, by the *Law Cornelia*, of which *Sylla* was the Author, might reject a greater Number.

In the *Provinces*, *Senators* had the Right of being attended by *Lictors* ; which belong'd to them from *Cuftom* ; for no *Law* allow'd them that Prerogative.

All thefe Marks of Honour were common to every *Senator* ; but many of them had peculiar Privileges. They were diftinguifh'd according to the Offices they had born.

For Example ; Such as had been *Confuls*, were preferr'd to thofe that had been only *Prætors* ; and he who was at their Head, took Place of all the reft : He was the Man, whofe Nomination, as I have before obferv'd, *Romulus* referv'd to himfelf ; and generally the moft Ancient of all the *Senate*.

In after Ages, the Honour of *Chief Senator*, belong'd to that Perfon whom the *Cenfor* nam'd firft, in reading over the *Lift* of the *Senators* : But he commonly gave it to an Old *Senator*, who had born fome of the chief Offices, as that of *Conful* or *Cenfor*.

All thefe *Privileges* and *Honours*, were attended with *Penalties*, *Labour*, and *Dangers*.

No *Senator* was permitted to go out of the Confines of *Italy*, without leave, upon fome Lawful Occafion.

They were every one oblig'd to give ftrict Attendance in the *Senate-Houfe*, upon Pain of being feverely reprimanded.

No

No one could attain to the Degree of a *Senator*, unlefs he was poffefs'd of an Eftate to a certain Value, to main-tain the Dignity of his Office : And fuch as by fquand'ring away their Money, were reduc'd to Poverty, were oblig'd to renounce and quit their Places in the *Senate* ; and there-fore, to prevent their Extravagance, they were forbidden to run in Debt above Two Thoufand *Denarii*, which makes about Two Thoufand *French Livres.* In which, the Wifdom of the *Roman* Commonwealth is highly to be admir'd, for obliging the *Senators* to be Rich and Thrifty at the fame Time.

But to entitle Men to be receiv'd into this Chief Order of the State, other Qualifications were requifite.

That of being a *Citizen* was abfolutely neceffary : And if in the Declenfion of the Commonwealth, *Strangers*, and perhaps *Slaves* were admitted to be *Senators*, it was contra-ry to all Rule : And therefore, Hiftory informs us, that *Auguftus* corrected that Abufe, as foon as he came to the Empire.

It was but fit, to ufe the utmoft Precaution in advancing Men to a Place of fo Extenfive a Power, and Exalted Dig-nity ; and therefore, a Good Behaviour and Honourable Actions, were the firft ftep that led to it.

Birth was likewife confider'd, in the Choice of a *Senator.* At firft, we fee, the *Senate* was compos'd of *Patricians* only ; but afterwards, *Plebeians* were admitted ; becaufe the En-trance into the Supream Council, and moft Honourable Or-der of the State, ought to ftand open to the Vertue and Me-rit of every Citizen.

The having well difcharg'd any great Office in the *Ma-giftracy*, was a fair Pretenfion to be made a *Senator* : A Man's good Conduct and Behaviour in his firft Employ-ments, being, as it were, an Earneft of his future Fidelity.

They were alfo limited to a certain Age, before which, no one could be made a *Senator* : 'Tis not exactly known what that Age was, but generally believed to be *Thirty Years.*

As to the Right of chufing *Senators, Romulus*'s Succeffors referv'd it to themfelves ; and the *Roman* Emperors like-wife, kept it in their own Hands. In the Beginning of the *Free State*, the *Confuls* and *People* divided that Right between them ;

them ; the *Confuls* nominating fo many, out of which, the
the *People* chofe fuch as they thought beft qualify'd to fill
fo important an Office.

But after the Creation of *Cenfors,* who were the Reformers of all Orders in the State, they took upon them to
elect *Senators.* As every Fifth Year they review'd the
whole Body of the People, they then fill'd up fuch Vacan-
cies in the *Senate,* as had happen'd by Death, or by Removal
of thofe, whofe ill Conduct render'd them unworthy of fo
eminent a Degree.

C H A P. XV.

Of the Senatus-Confulta.

THE *Senatus-Confultum,* according to the Definition of
it by *Juftinian,* (§. 5. *Tit. Inft. de Jure Natur. Gent. &
Civ.*) is a *Decree* of the *Senate,* by which any Thing is ordain'd and eftablifh'd.

This Ordinance of the *Senate,* is fometimes called plainly a *Decree,* or a *Senatus-Confultum* indifferently ; altho'
fome Authors have obferv'd, that we ought to diftinguifh
thefe Words : For *Senatus Confultum,* in its proper Signification, is meant of thofe *Ordonnances* of the *Senate,* which
concern'd the Affairs of the Government ; whereas a *Decree*
of the *Senate,* is only 'an *Act* that regards the Intereft of
Private Perfons, and not the Publick.

Befides, a *Senatus Confultum* could not be made, but by
the *Senate,* whereas a *Decree* might be pafs'd by the Authority of any other Society ; and fometimes, by that of a
Magiftrate only ; as we fee, there are *Decrees* of *Augurs,
High-Priefts,* &c. Nay the Word *Decree,* is often us'd in the
Law, to fignifie the Judgment given by a Prince, with Cognizance of the Caufe, and which had the Force of *Law.*

The Defign of the Inftitution of a *Senate,* being for the
Management of Publick Bufinefs, no doubt they made at all
times *Senatus-Confulta* upon Affairs of Moment, in which the
Good of the State was concern'd.

Diony-

Dionyfius Halicarnaffeus mentions One made in the Time of *Romulus*, in order to end the War for reftoring the *Sabine Women*, that had been Ravifh'd by the *Romans*.

After *Romulus* died, there was a *Senatus-Confultum* made, to put the Government of the State into the Hands of *Commiffioners*, during the *Interregnum*.

By another *Senatus Confultum*, *Numa Pompilius* was chofen to fucceed *Romulus*; the *People* having on that weighty Occafion, referr'd the Choice to the *Senate*.

In a Word, there have been abundance of *Senatus-Confulta* made, under all the different Governments of the *Romans*; how and when they obtain'd the Force of *Laws*, I fhall hereafter fet forth. Let us now fee in what manner they were made.

It is eafily imagin'd, that the Matters taken into Confideration by the *Senate*, being of the higheft Importance, there was a fix'd Number requir'd to pafs a Lawful *Senatus-Confultum*; but what that Number was, Hiftorians do not exactly inform us.

That which feems moft likely in this Cafe, is, that the Number of *Senators* having been greater or lefs at different Times, that Proportion of them requifite for paffing a Lawful *Senatus-Confultum*, was likewife encreas'd or diminifh'd, according to the whole Number, at the time of paffing it.

The Method was thus; The *Prefident* of the Affembly, collected the Votes of all the *Senators*, and recapitulated their Opinions, in order to Refolve according to the Plurality of Votes.

When they divided, for the more eafie counting the Votes, he order'd them to feparate into Two Parties, oppofite to each other, which he did in thefe Words, *Qui hoc cenfetis huc tranfite; qui alia omnia, in illam partem.*

After they had voted, any one might retract his Opinion, by paffing over and ranging himfelf with the contrary Party.

The Majority carried the Queftion, and the Refolution pafs'd accordingly, but fometimes Variety of Opinions, occafion'd the Determination to be put off till another Day.

When every particular *Senator's* Opinion was afk'd, it was call'd *Senatus-Confultum per relationem factum.*

But in regulating ordinary Matters, the *Senate* gave their Confent all at once, without going into Debates, or asking every Man's Opinion: And then it was a *Senatus-Confultum*

per

per difceffionem factum & tum fententiam pedibus tuliffe Senatores dicebantur.

But a Majority of the Members prefent, called *difceffio in fententiam*, was equally neceffary to the paffing both thefe kinds of *Decrees.* The Difference confifted only *in debating,* or *not* ; becaufe the *Senatus-Confultum quod dicebatur fieri per difceffionem,* was pafs'd in a Moment, as foon as ever it was propos'd, without going into the Merits of the Queftion, or debating it, as they did when the *Senatus-Confultum per relationem fieri dicebatur.*

As foon as a *Senatus-Confultum* was agreed to by a Majority, one of the *Clerks* of the *Senate*, by order of the *Prefident*, read the Refolution aloud ; which being done, the *Prefident* difmifs'd the *Senate* in thefe Words, *Patres Confcripti, nemo vos tenet,* or *Nihil vos moror, Patres Confcripti.* But notwithftanding this leave to depart, a *Chief Magiftrate* might detain them, if he had any other Bufinefs to communicate.

Concerning the Form in which the *Senatus-Confulta* were written, it muft be obferv'd, they firft fet down the Time and Place where every one was made; then the Names of all that were prefent; after that, a fhort State of the Matter regulated and enacted by the *Senate*, with the *Magiftrate's* Name who mov'd the Queftion ; and laftly, the Refolution of the *Senate* thereupon, exprefs'd by thefe Letters, *d. e. r. i. c.* that is, *de ea re ita cenfuerunt.*

When the *Senate* recommended the Execution of any Thing contain'd in the *Senatus Confultum*, to the *Confuls*, they inferted thefe Words, *Si eis videatur.*

In a Word, moft of the *Senatus-Confulta*, efpecially thofe made under the *Free State*, ended with thefe Words, *Si quis huic Senatui-Confulto interceffcrit, Senatui placere, autoritatem perfcribi, & de ea re ad Senatum populumque referri :* Which Claufe was us'd, becaufe of the Oppofition frequently made to the *Senatus Confulta*, by fome of the Principal *Magiftrates*, efpecially the *Tribunes of the People* ; who having been created to counter ballance the Authority of the *Senate*, and preferve the Rights of the *People*, often oppos'd the Refolutions of the *Senate* ; and fometimes, without any other View than to leffen their Power, and increafe their own, by making themfelves more Confiderable.

Before

Before thefe *Magiftrates* were allow'd to enter into the *Senate-Houfe*, they fat upon *Benches* over againft the Door; and as foon as the *Senatus-Confultum* had pafs'd the Forms within, it was brought out to them to examine: Such as were approv'd of, they mark'd with the Letter *T.* and when they rejected any, they wrote the Word *Veto* under it; nor were they oblig'd to give any Reafon for their Refufal, as I have taken notice before in the Seventh Chapter.

On the contrary, all other *Magiftrates* were oblig'd to fhew Caufe, and give Reafons for their Oppofition to a *Senatus-Confultum:* As for Inftance, That the *Senate* was not call'd together by *Lawful Authority*, or held in a Place not *confecrated* by the *Augurs*, or upon a Day prohibited by the *Laws.* And thefe Objections were to be firft remov'd and fettled, before they could proceed upon the *Senatus-Confultum.*

To preferve the Remembrance of their Refolutions, and tranfmit a faithful Account of their Conduct to Pofterity, they had a *Publick Regifter*; in which, all their Debates and *Laws* were written, not omitting thofe that mifcarried by the *Tribunes* Oppofition.

This was commonly the Bufinefs of one of the *Secretaries* to the *Senate*: But when it was neceffary to come to a Refolution which was to be Secret, and not divulg'd till put in Execution, the Office of *Regifter* or *Secretary*, was difcharg'd by a *Senator*: And the *Senatus-Confulta* made in this manner, without the Knowledge of the *Officers* or other *Senators*, were called *Tacita Senatus-Confulta.*

All the *Senatus-Confulta* or *Decrees* of the *Senate*, were for a long Time left in the Hands of the *Confuls*; but as they took upon them to fupprefs fome, and alter others, it was thought proper to remove, and place them in the Temple of *Ceres*, under the Care of the *Ædiles*: At length they were carried to the Temple of *Saturn*, where the Governments Money was lodg'd, as making part of the Publick Treafure.

They went under the Name of the *Magiftrate* who prefided in the *Senate* at the Time of their making: Thus we have *Senatus-Confultum Trebellianum, Pegafianum*, and others of the fame kind.

Having

Having thus fhewn the Method in making the *Senatus-Confulta*, I fhall now fpeak of their Authority, and when they firft acquir'd the Force of *Law*.

They were ever in ufe, both under the *Regal* and *Republican* Government; but far from having the Authority of *Law*.

During the *Free State*, as well as the *Regal* Government, the *Senate* was advifed with, but it was only for their Opinion; and a *Senatus-Confultum* of it felf, was of no Force, till confirm'd by a *Law* made with the Peoples Confent; which occafion'd that Form fo much in ufe among the *Romans*, POPULUS JUBET SENATUS AUTOR EST.

But unforefeen Accidents, often plung'd the Government into fo great Danger, that immediate Help was neceffary; in adminiftring which, the Solemnity of calling a *General Affembly* of the People, and paffing the *Laws* in Form, could not be obferv'd: In which Cafes, the *Decrees* of the *Senate* had the force of *Law*, provided the People tacitly confented.

The *Senatus-Confulta* began abfolutely to obtain the Force of *Law* under the Emperor TIBERIUS; being made at his Requeft, and under his Authority: Therefore, it was called *Senatus-Confultum factum ad Orationem Principis*, and carried a full and perfect Authority. Upon which, it is to be obferv'd, that notwithftanding the *People* loft the Power of making *Laws*, under *Tiberius* and the reft of the Emperors, the *Senate* preferv'd their Right of making *Ordonnances* a long Time. 'Tis in this Sence, and with Reference to thefe *Senatus Confulta quæ fiebant ad Orationem principis*, we are to underftand the Decifion of the Ninth *Law* in the *Digeft. de Legibus*, which has thefe Words, *Non ambigitur Senatum Jus facere poffe*. The Author of this *Law* was *Ulpian*, who lived in the Reign of *Alexander Severus*. Befides the Definition which *Juftinian* gives of a *Senatus-Confultum*, (5 *Tit. de Jure Natural. Gent. & Civil*;) fhews plainly, the *Senatus-Confultum* had the Force of *Law* under the *Roman* Emperors: *Senatus-Confultum*, (fays he) *eft quod Senatus jubet atque conftituit*; not *conftituebat*, as he defines a *Law* and a *Plebifcitum*.

Thefe

Thefe *Senatus-Confulta*, were a Contrivance of *Tiberius*; who inftead of advifing with the *People*, referr'd all Matters to the *Senate*; under pretence, that the Body of the People were grown too numerous to affemble all in one Place. So the Emperor, being invefted with the Authority of the People, by the *Law Regia*, fummon'd the *Senate* to meet, and propos'd to to them fuch *Laws* as he had a mind to Enact : Which *Laws* fo pafs'd, had the fame Force as thofe made in the Time of the *Republick*, not in reality by the Power of the *Senate*, but in Confequence of the *Prince*'s Authority.

Under the latter Emperors, the *Senate* had the Power of making *Regulations* at their own Pleafure ; but it was only in Cafes of fmall Moment, fuch *fumptuary Laws*, to fupprefs Luxury in Apparel. [*L. Unica Cod. de SenatusConfultis.*]

But L E O the *Philofopher*, by his Seventy eighth *Novel*, abrogated the *Law* 1. *ff. de Legibus*, and entirely divefted the *Senate* of the Power of making any *Edicts* or *Laws* whatever.

Yet, 'tis pretended, that the *Senate* in thofe Times, when they were not permitted to make *Laws* themfelves, ftill preferved the Right of examining and approving thofe propos'd by their Princes. (See *L. 8. Cod. de Legibus*.) To which, the Cuftom of Inregiftring our *King's Edicts* and *Declarations* in the *Parliaments*, feems properly enough to refer.

C H A P.

CHAP. XVI.

Of the Lawyers Anſwers.

THE *Lawyers Anſwers*, are the Sentiments and Opinions of thoſe, who were authoriz'd to give *Anſwer* upon *Law-Queſtions* ; for which Purpoſe, there were Perſons
appointed under all the different Governments of *Rome*.

The firſt Interpreters of the *Law*, were the *Senators* and
Nobles, whom *Romulus* enjoin'd to give Advice to their *Clients* ; that is, ſuch as were put under their Protection *.
The *Plebeians*, therefore, ſhelter'd themſelves under ſome
Powerful *Senator*, who was oblig'd, to aſſiſt them with his
good Advice and Credit, in the Management of their Affairs,
explain the *Law*, and do them all manner of good Offices.

Theſe *Plebeians*, on their Parts, gave their *Patron*, under
whoſe Protection they had put themſelves, their *Votes*, in
Elections of *Magiſtrates* ; attended him in all Publick *Pro-
ceſſions*, and engag'd in his Service, whenever there was
Occaſion.

This Relation between *Patrons* and *Clients*, was of *Romulus*'s Invention ; to eſtabliſh a perfect Union among
the Citizens, by a Correſpondence between the Rich and
Poor.

The Right of interpreting the *Laws*, was afterwards ve-
ſted in the *College* of *Pontiffs* and *Prieſts*, when the *Romans*
found it proper to mix *Law* with *Religion* and *holy Ceremonies* : For this Reaſon, *Dion. Caſſius* obſerves, *Auguſtus* aſ-
ſum'd the Title of *Pontifex Maximus*. Nay, the very
Chriſtian Emperors, who abhorr'd the *Pagan* Ceremonies,
and Name of *High-Prieſt*, ſuffer'd themſelves to be ſtyl'd ſo
in their *Addreſſes* and *Medals*.

All whoſe particular Application and Ability had render'd
them knowing in the *Laws*, undertook to reſolve ſuch Queſtions as were brought to them ; but their *Anſwers* were of
no great Weight in the Time of the *Republick*, nor even
under *Auguſtus* ; altho' he allow'd them to give their Opinions publickly. [*L. 2. §. 47. ff. de Origine Juris.*]

* *Dion. Halicarnaſ. Lib. 2.*

In reality, this Emperor, inftead of authorizing every *Lawyer* by a particular Commiffion, to give his Opinion upon Queftions in *Law*, empower'd all by a General One, but, as 'tis thought, limited their Number. However, this gave their Decifions no great Authority ; but they grew into confiderable Credit in the Reign of *Tiberius* ; who order'd, no one fhould prefume to give an Opinion in Law-Matters, but fuch as were licenfed by his Special Favour fo to do.

Yet for all this, the *Anfwers* of the *Lawyers* had not the fame Force as *Law :* For *Tiberius* in his Licences to an-fwer fuch Queftions as fhould be propofed to them, laid no Injunction upon the Judges to regard them as *Laws* in their Determinations : Nor was it practicable, under his Reign, to have given them that Authority, upon account of the Two prevailing Sects of *Sabinians* and *Proculeians,* who generally gave contrary Opinions upon the fame Que-ftion, as fhall be fhewn hereafter.

'Tis likely the *Lawyers Anfwers* were firft confidered as *Law,* under *Valentinian* III. becaufe he confirm'd the Writings of *Gaius Ulpian, Paul Papinian,* and others ; and forbad the Judges to fwerve, in Points of *Law,* from their Opinions.

And becaufe many Inconveniencies arofe from the Diffe-rence of Opinions upon the fame Queftion, He order'd, the Judges fhould be govern'd by the Majority, and in cafe of an Equality, to follow that Side to which *Papinian* adher'd. [*L. Unica Cod. Theod. de refponf. prudent.*]

The Written Opinions of the *Lawyers*, were grown fo Vo-luminous, that in *Juftinian's* Time, they made no lefs than *Two Thoufand Books* ; which render'd a perfect Knowledge of them Impracticable : Befides, they were fo confus'd, that it was very difficult for the moft diligent Reader to reap any great Advantage from them.

Thefe Difficulties *Juftinian* remov'd, by fetting fome to work, to pick out and chufe the *Beft* of this indigefted Heap of *Lawyers Writings* ; which he reduc'd into a certain Order, and took away *Papinian's* Prerogative ; allowing all the *Lawyers* equal Privilege, without Diftinction. [*L.* 1. §. 5. & 6. *Cod. de veteri jure enucleand.*] For, fays the Emperor, *Omnia no-ftra facimus, & ex nobis eis impertitur authoritas.* (Vide *Jacob. Gothofredum ad Leg. unic. Cod. Theod. de Refponf. prudent.*)

E

But

But we muſt take care not to confound theſe *Anſwers*, or *Opinions* of the *Lawyers*, with That which in the *Laws* is call'd, *The Authority of the Interpreters.*

For the *Anſwers* of the *Lawyers* were nothing elſe, but the Opinions of particular Men, as *Papinian, Paul Ulpian*, &c. Whereas the *Interpretations* of the *Lawyers*, ſpoken of in the Ninth Chapter, were the Unanimous Opinion of the whole Society ; or what is call'd the *Uſage* of the *Bar*, and the *Law* introduc'd by *Practice*. Wherefore, every *Anſwer* of the *Lawyers*, having a certain *Author*, they are plac'd among the *Caſes* of the *written Civil Law* ; whereas the *Interpretation* of the *Lawyers*, having no particular *Author*, makes only a Part of the *unwritten*, or what we call the *Law* introduc'd by *Practice.*

But altho' it has been ſaid, that the *Anſwers* of the *Lawyers* were not always Authentick, it muſt be allow'd they were ever in great eſteem ; and thoſe that are reported in the *Pandects*, ſufficiently ſet forth the *Learning, Wiſdom*, and *Eloquence* of thoſe Great Men, moſt of whom were rais'd to the higheſt Dignities of the *Roman* Empire ; and many of them taken into the Emperor's Councils, to aſſiſt them with their *Knowledge* and *Experience*, in the Management of the moſt *weighty Affairs.*

They were juſtly ſtiled *Fathers of the Law*, ſince by their Induſtry it was brought to Perfection : And for that Reaſon, I look upon my ſelf oblig'd to take notice of them in this Hiſtory. Beſides, there are a vaſt Number of *Laws*, which are not to be underſtood, without knowing the Time when they were made : So that I am perſwaded, 'twill be no leſs Uſeful than Curious, to be appriz'd in reading a *Law* in the *Digeſt*, when the Author liv'd, and what Rank he held in the *Roman* Empire.

But as this Detail would lead me into too large a Field, it ſeem'd more adviſable to make a ſeparate Chapter of it, in which I ſhall give a brief Account of all the *Lawyers* that flouriſhed in the *Republick*, or under the Emperors before *Juſtinian.*

And tho' there are no Books remaining that were written by the *Lawyers* who lived under the *Republick*, and but very few *Laws* in the *Digeſt* taken from their Writings ; yet I ſhall not omit mentioning what is moſt remarkable of them.

CHAP.

CHAP. XVII.

Of the most celebrated Roman Lawyers.

PUBLIUS PAPYRIUS, was the first *Roman,* that apply'd himself seriously to the Study of the *Law.* He made a Collection of the *Regal Laws,* in the Reign of *Tarquin* the Proud, as is already observ'd.

APPIUS CLAUDIUS was employ'd in digesting the *Law* of the *Twelve Tables*; which was not finish'd till 304, after the Foundation of *Rome.* As he was an expert *Lawyer,* he had the greatest Share in that excellent Work : But his *Violence* and *Injustice,* drew upon him the Indignation of the People, which threw him into so deep a Melancholy, that 'tis generally believ'd he Kill'd himself in Despair.

APPIUS CLAUDIUS, Sirnam'd CENTIMA-NUS, said to be Grandson of the former, was likewise a great *Lawyer,* and qualify'd for the highest Employments : He was *Consul* in 449.

SEMPRONIUS, a celebrated *Lawyer,* was descended from the Ancient *Patricians.* The People gave him the Sirname of *Wise ;* and conferr'd upon him the chief Employments in the Government : He was *Consul* in the Year 450, and afterwards *General* of the *Army.*

TIBERIUS CARUNCANIUS was the Author of several memorable *Answers,* but none of his Writings are extant. He was *Consul* in the Year 473 : After which, he was *High Priest,* and the first of the *Plebeian* Order that was rais'd to that Dignity. He was also *Censor* and *Dictator :* And so famous for his great Prudence, that his Opinion was follow'd in the most important Cases, both of *Humane* and *Divine Law.*

QUINTUS MUTIUS, was not only an able *Lawyer,* but a great *Politician,* and well vers'd in Business. It was he that was sent Embassador to *Carthage,* to offer them their Choice of *Peace* or *War.*

E 2   After

After him came SEXTUS ÆLIUS, who was firſt *Ædile* and then *Conſul.* He made a Book of the *Elements* of the *Law,* intitled *Tripartita,* bacauſe it confiſted of the *Law* of the *Twelve Tables,* the *Interpretations* of the *Lawyers,* and *Caſes* of *Law.*

PUBLIUS ÆLIUS lived about the ſame Time, that is, in 545. He was alſo *Conſul.*

Scipio Naſica, Publius Attilius, Marcus Porcius Cato and *Marcus Manilius,* flouriſh'd about the Year of *Rome,* 600. SCIPIO NASICA acquir'd great Reputation, as well by his Skill in the *Laws,* of which he was a perfeƈt Maſter, as his upright Conduƈt in the Offices of *Prætor* and *Conſul* ; and the Signal Viƈtories he got over the Enemy, obtain'd him a Decree for a Triumph. He was Sirnam'd OPTIMUS by the *Senate* ; who allow'd him a Houſe in the *Holy Street* at the Expence of the *Publick,* that they might adviſe with him more conveniently.

PUBLIUS ATTILIUS, was of the Family of *Attilius Regulus,* who choſe rather to undergo the Cruel Torments with which the Enemy threatned him, than break his Word. This *Attilius* the *Lawyer,* was the firſt that had the Title of *Prudent* given him by the People.

MARCUS PORCIUS CATO compos'd ſeveral *Law Books* ; 'tis of him probably that *Paulus* ſpeaks in the *Law* 4. §. *Cato. ff. de verb. oblig.* He is ſuppoſ'd to be the Author of the *Regula Catoniana,* treated of in the Seventh Title of the Thirty fourth Book of the *Digeſt.*

MARCUS MANILIUS, according to *Cicero's* Account, was a very great *Lawyer,* (*Lib. de Clar. Oratorib.*) " If any one ſhould ask me, ſays he) who deſerv'd the " Name of a *Lawyer* ; I would anſwer, 'twas that Man who " had a perfeƈt Knowledge of the *Laws* and *Cuſtoms* of the " Place where he profeſſes it ; and knew how to put it in " Praƈtice : And if I muſt produce Examples, I would " name *Sextus Ælius, Marcus Manilius* and *Publius Mucius.*"

Publius Mucius and *Brutus,* flouriſh'd about the Year of *Rome* 630 ; and *Publius Rutilius* about 640.   This

This PUBLIUS MUCIUS, of whom *Cicero* speaks in the Paſſage before cited, compos'd Ten Books' upon *Law-Subjects.* He was deſcended from the famous *Mucius Scævola,* ſo renown'd in Hiſtory.

BRUTUS, equally celebrated for his Actions and Birth, made Seven Books upon the *Law.*

PUBLIUS RUTILIUS RUFUS, who came after him, was firſt *Tribune of the People,* then *Conſul,* in the Year 648; and afterwards *Proconſul* of *Aſia.* His Anceſtors had been both *Cenſors* and *Conſuls.* All that is related of Him, is, that he was in high Eſteem with *Auguſtus,* who ſupported all his own Notions, with the Reaſonings of this great *Lawyer.*

Towards the Year 650, *Paulus Virginius, Quintus Tubero, Sextus Pompeius, Cælius Antipater, Lucius Craſſus* and *Quintus Mucius Scævola* appear'd.

PAULUS VIRGINIUS, who was of a very ancient *Patrician* Family, made ſeveral *Law-Books,* which are loſt.

QUINTUS TUBERO was a *Stoick,* and a good *Lawyer.*

SEXTUS POMPEIUS, was Uncle by the Father's Side to the Great *Pompey.* He is mightily commended by *Cicero* *.

COELIUS ANTIPATER applied himſelf more to the Art of *Speaking* than the *Knowledge* of the *Law;* therefore, all that *Pomponius* ſays of him, (*L.* 2. §. 40. *ff. de Orig. Jur.*) is, that he was an Hiſtorian. However, He was an able *Lawyer;* and *Cicero* gives him that Character, in the Place before quoted. *Quintilian* † ſays, He was a Man of great Parts; that his Diſcourſe was ſolid, pure, correct, entertaining and very lively; and that he was one of the beſt Writers of his Time.

---

* *In Bruto.*

† *Lib.* 10. Inſtit. *cap.* 1. & 2.

PUB.

PUBLIUS CRASSUS, Brother to *Publius Mucius,* was *Quæftor, Ædile,* and afterwards *Conful,* and *High-Prieft* at the fame time. He was reckon'd an Able and Eloquent *Lawyer.*

QUINTUS MUCIUS SCÆVOLA, Son of *Publius,* was *Tribune of the People, Conful,* and *High-Prieft.* He had the Art of expreffing a great deal in a few Words, and was always a clofe Reafoner. He was Mafter of a pure, and very florid Style; and his Thoughts, tho' Sublime, were no lefs Subftantial. There is reafon to believe, that 'tis of him *Cicero* fpeaks, when he fays, " That *Quintus* " *Mucius* was the moft Eloquent among all the *Lawyers,* and " the beft *Lawyer* among the Men of *Eloquence.*" He com- priz'd the whole *Law* in Eighteen Books; and was the Au- thor of the *Cautio Muciana,* which provides, *That if a Man has a Legacy left him, upon Condition of abftaining from a cer- tain Act as long as he lives, he might require the Delivery of the faid Legacy, if he would engage to furrender it in cafe of not performing the Will of the Teftator.* But his Merit, great as it was, could not protect him from the Fury of the Wicked: He was Murther'd in the Temple of *Vefta,* in the Year 672, by one *Simbria,* employ'd by the *Prætor Da- mafippus;* and 'tis reported that the Affaffin fhould fay, *He was Criminal, becaufe he was too Honeft.*

About the Year 680, *Aquilius Gallus, Balbus Lucilius, Sex- tus Papyrius,* and *Gaius Juventius* appear'd upon the Stage. AQUILIUS GALLUS was a very Popular Man: Whilft he was *Tribune,* he got the *Law Aquilia* enacted; which is fpoken of in the Third Title of the Fourth Book of the *Inftitutes.* He was *Prætor* with *Cicero,* who contracted a clofe Friendfhip with him. He was a *Knight,* and of a *Noble Family;* for feveral of his Anceftors had been *Tri- bunes, Confuls* and *Ambaffadors.* He was look'd upon to be fo Learned and Honeft a Man, that the *Prætors* would often Depute him to give final Judgments in Private Caufes; and his Vote was of great Authority in eftablifhing *Laws.* He was Author of the *Novation per ftipulationem Aquilianam;* and fettled the *Cuftom* of inftituting or appointing pofthu- mous

mous Grandchildren to be *Heirs*, upon which we have the famous *Law* Gallus, 28 ff. de Liber. & Posthum.

BALBUS LUCILIUS was a confiderable *Lawyer,* and admir'd both for his Eloquence and Learning.

SEXTUS PAPYRIUS, the Offspring of an Ancient and Illuftrious Family, taught *Servius* the *Elements* of the *Law*; of which he makes grateful Acknowledgment in his Works, and thereby has preferved his Memory.

GAIUS JUVENTIUS, was a great and well-read *Lawyer.*

SERVIUS SULPICIUS, Son of a *Roman* Knight, was the Defcendant of one of the moft Ancient Families of *Rome*. He was the firft *Orator* of his Time except *Cicero*. After *Quintus Mucius* had reproach'd and advis'd him, he applied himfelf fo diligently to his Studies, that he became a moft admirable *Lawyer*. He compos'd feveral Books, wherein he reduc'd the *Science* of *Law* to an *Art*; which before was confufedly taught by others, without Order or Method. After he had difcharg'd the *Prætor*'s Office, the *Republick*, being without *Confuls*, and fallen into great Diforder; by Authority of the *Senate*, the Government was put into his Hands. After that, he was made *Conful*, then Governor of *Greece*; in all which Employments he acquitted himfelf fo well, that dying upon an Embaffy, the People erected a Statue in honour of him, in the Place of Publick Harangues.

Pomponius (Leg. 2. §. 44. *ff. de origine juris)* fays, that *Servius Sulpicius* had ALFENUS VARUS GAIUS, AULUS OFILIUS, TITUS CÆSIUS, AUFIDIUS TUCCA, AUFIDIUS NAMUSA, FLAVIUS PRISCUS, GAIUS ATEIUS, PACUVIUS, LABEO ANTISTIUS, CINNA, *Labeo*'s Father, and PUBLIUS GELLIUS for his Scholars: But *Cujacius* fays, that the putting *Gaius* into this Lift, is a Miftake of *Pomponius*, and that he ought to be ftruck out.

All thefe lived under the Emperors *Julius* and *Auguftus Cæfar*: Eight of them left fome of their Works behind them; out of which *Aufidius Namufa* made a Body of *Law*, divided

E 4   ded

ded into Fifty Books. The moſt celebrated amongſt them were *Alfenus Varus,* who was *Conſul,* and wrote *Forty Volumes* upon the *Law* ; and *Aulus Oſilius* a *Roman* Knight, and *Ju- lius Cæſar*'s boſom-Friend.

Beſides ſeveral Books which he wrote upon the niceſt Points of *Law,* he reduc'd all the *Prætor*'s Edicts, of which *Servius* had publiſh'd too ſhort an Extract, into one Volume.

There were many other *Lawyers,* who lived and were eminent about the ſame Time, as *Trebatius, Aulus Caſcellius, Quintus Ælius Tubero, Ateius Capito,* and *Antiſtius Labeo.*

TREBATIUS was Diſciple to *Cornelius Maximus* ; he labour'd hard at the *Law,* and 'twas at his Inſtigation that *Auguſtus,* who eſteem'd him very much, introduc'd the Uſe of *Codicils.* He had been Baniſh'd for ſiding with *Pom- pey* ; but *Cicero,* who lov'd him, got him leave from *Cæſar* to return home, whom he afterwards ſerved in Qualiry of a *Counſellor* ; and was offer'd by him to be made a *Military Tribune,* and to have a Diſpenſation from attending the *Army* ; which could not be an agreeable Life, to a Man that by choice had preferr'd the *Gown* to the *Sword.*

AULUS CASCELLIUS, who was a Knight, di- ſtinguiſh'd himſelf by his Knowledge, both in the *Law,* and all kinds of polite Learning. *Trebatius* was deeper than *Caſ- cellius,* but in Eloquence he out-did *Trebatius,* and *Oſilius* excell'd them both, as *Pomponius* relates, (*L.* 2. §. 45. *ff. de orig. juris.*) *Antonius Anguſtinus* and *Cujacius* remark, that there is a Fault in the Beginning of this Paragraph, which ought not to be read as it is, but thus, *fuit Aulus Caſcellius Quinti Mucii Voluſii auditor.*

This *Caſcellius* was contented with the *Quæſtorſhip,* and refus'd to accept of any higher Office, altho' *Auguſtus* made him an Offer of the *Conſulſhip.* There is only One of his Books remaining, entitled *Benedictorum.*

Altho' in the *Law, Pomponius* ſpeaks of *Voluſius* only by the Bye, as having been *Caſcellius*'s Maſter, yet it appears, he wrote upon the *Law* ; and *Cujacius,* in his *Notes* upon *L.* 21. §. 2. *ff. de annuis Legatis,* ſpeaks very advantage- ouſly of a Treatiſe written by him upon the *AS* ; and adviſes all Beginners to read it, before they enter upon the *Inſtitutes.*

Q.

Q. ÆLIUS TUBERO, who follow'd *Offilius*, was of an Ancient Family. After having run thro' the Study of *Rhetorick*, and pass'd to that of the *Law*, he wrote several Books of *Law*; but the antiquated Style they are in, makes them very disagreeable to the Reader.

ATTEIUS CAPITO, *Offilius*'s Scholar, understood the *Publick* and *Private Law* perfectly well. He was *Consul* in the Year of *Rome*, 746. He wrote *Commentaries* upon the *Law* of the *Twelve Tables*; Seven Books of the *Sacerdotal Rights*, One of the *Senatorian Office*, and a *Commentary* upon *Publick Judgments*.

ANTISTIUS LABEO, was of a Noble Family, and Son of that *Labeo*, who was *Servius Sulpisius*'s Disciple. This *Labeo* the Son, was educated in the *Law* by *Trebatius*; He had also many Law-Lessons from others. That he might apply himself wholly and solely to the Study of the *Law*, he refus'd to be made *Consul*, being offer'd it by *Augustus*. He spent Six Months of the Year, in conversing with Learned Men, and the other Six in writing of Books. He made a *Commentary* upon the *Law* of the *Twelve Tables*; Thirty Books *ad Edictum Prætoris peregrini*; some upon the *Edict Prætoris Urbani*, and Eight Books *Pithanon*, that is, *credibilium* or *verisimilium* *.

As to these Two last *Lawyers*, 'tis to be observ'd, they were Authors of Two different Sects: For *Ateius Capito*, sticking closely to the common Method, went on still as he was taught, without altering a Tittle; whereas *Labeo*, relying much on his own Judgment and Knowledge, innovated and chang'd many Things, which Division was much widened by Two *Lawyers* that succeeded them, as will be seen hereafter.

Under *Tiberius*, *Claudius*, *Nero*, and *Vespasian*, there appear'd *Cocceius Nerva*, *Masurius Sabinus*, *C. Cassius Longinus*, *Proculus*, and *Nerva* the Son.

---

* See *Aul. Gell.* Book 13. Cap. 10.

COC-

COCCEIUS NERVA, who was a very Eminent *Lawyer*, embrac'd *Labeo's* Party, and was in great Favour with *Tiberius*.

MASURIUS SABINUS, was a *Roman* Knight, and at length made a *Senator*. Among the reft of his Works, he compos'd Twelve Books call'd *Memorabilia*, Three *Commentaries de Indigenis*, and One Book *de Furtis*. Many Places of the *Digeft* are taken from his Works. He was in great Credit with *Tiberius*. He lifted himfelf in *Ateius Capito's* Party, which from thence was call'd the *Sabinian* Sect.

CAIUS CASSIUS LONGINUS fucceeded *Sabinus*. He was *Conful* with *Quirinus* under *Tiberius*, in the Year of *Rome*, 764; and *Governor* of *Syria*, under *Claudius*, in 782, according to *Tacitus, Annal.* 12. The high efteem he was in, as an excellent *Lawyer*, was the Reafon that the Party he efpous'd was call'd the *Caffian* Sect, as the other had the Name of the *Sabinian*.

PROCULUS fucceeded *Nerva*. His profound Learning and Skill in the *Laws*, got him great Reputation under *Vefpafian*. He adher'd to *Labeo's* Party, which afterwards went by the Name of the *Proculeian* Sect.

NERVA the *Son*, was in play at the fame Time; He follow'd his Father in embracing *Labeo's* Party. He has left feveral Books *de ufu capionibus*. If we may believe *Ulpian*, he was fo great and early a Proficient in the *Law*, that he anfwer'd Queftions publickly at the Age of Seventeen.

There was at the fame Time another CASSIUS LONGINUS, of the Order of Knighthood, who was *Prætor:* We find many *Laws* in the *Digeft* taken from his Writings.

CÆLEUS SABINUS, who was *Conful*, was a great Favourite of *Vefpafian's*. He fucceeded *Caffius Longinus*, and was of the fame Sect. He wrote a Book upon the *Edict* of the *Ædiles Curules*.

P E

PEGASUS, who lived alſo in *Veſpaſian*'s Time, was *Conſul*, and *Governor* of *Rome*. *Juvenal* calls him the Beſt and moſt Sacred *Interpreter* of the *Laws*. He was Author of the *Senatus-Conſultum* which goes by his Name, and is ſpoken of in the *Inſtitutes*, under the Title *de Fidei Commiſſar. hæreditatib*. He ſucceeded *Proculus*; and the *Proculeian* Sect, which he follow'd, was afterwards call'd by his Name, the *Pegaſian*.

Under *Trajan*, *Adrian*, and *Antoninus Pius*, there appear'd *Javolenus Priſcus*, *Celſus*, the Father and Son, *Neratius Priſcus*, *Alburnus Valens*, *Tuſcianus*, *Salvius Julianus*.
  JAVOLENUS PRISCUS, ſucceeded *Cæleus Sabinus*; He was *Salvius Julianus*'s Maſter, as appears by the *Law* 5. *ff. de manumiſſ. vindict.*

 CELSUS the Father, was very much eſteem'd by the Emperor *Trajan*, and a Member of *Adrian*'s Council: He ſucceeded *Pegaſius*, whoſe Sect he follow'd.

CELSUS the Son ſucceeded his Father, and adher'd to the ſame Sect: He was twice *Conſul*, and left many Books of *Law* behind him.

NERATIUS PRISCUS follow'd the ſame Sect; that is, the *Proculeian*: He was *Conſul*. He made many Books; among which, the moſt valuable are, the Fifteen concerning the *Rules* of *Law*.

ALBURNUS VALENS, TUSCIANUS, and SALVIUS JULIANUS, ſucceeded *Javolenus*, and embrac'd the oppoſite, that is, the *Sabinian* Sect.
  Valens wrote Seven Books upon *Fiduciary Truſts*. We read nothing of *Tuſcianus*, in any of our Books; which has induc'd ſome to think, that in the *Law* 2. §. *ult. in fine ff. de orig. juris*, inſtead of *Tuſcianus*, it ought to be *Fuſcianus*; becauſe there is a *Conſtitution* of *Antoninus Pius*, directed to *Fuſcianus*, in the *Law* 7. *ff. de Legat. præſtand.*
  Salvius Julianus, Diſciple to *Javolenus*, was *Governor* of *Rome*, and twice *Conſul*. Whilſt he commanded in *Aquitain*, the Emperor *Adrian* wrote to him. *Juſtinian* calls him an
excel-

excellent *Lawyer.* He was the Compofer of the *Perpetual Edict,* whofe Decifions were of fo much weight; to which he added a *Claufe* in favour of the Children of an *Emanci-pated Son,* to entitle them to a Part of their *Grandfather's* Eftate, in Conjunction with their *Father.* The Pleafure he profefs'd to take in Studying, and his great Defire to Learn, can never enough be commended: For he us'd to fay, *Efti alterum pedem in Sepulchro haberem adhuc tamen addifcere vellem.*

Having thus finifh'd the Account of all the *Lawyers* mention'd by *Pomponius;* let us now take a View of thofe he has faid nothing of, and whofe Writings have contributed to the Compofition of the *Digeft.* Firft, let us obferve, that the greateft Number of them never made themfelves Parties to either of the *Two Sects* before-mention'd; but form'd their *Decifions* according to the Rules of *Juftice* and *Equity.*

Of thefe *Lawyers* not mention'd by *Pomponius,* there were Two who flourifh'd in the Reign of the Emperor *Adrian, Tertullianus* and *Affricanus.*

TERTULLIANUS, who was *Conful* under the Emperor *Adrian,* made Four Books of *Queftions,* and One *de Caftrenfi peculio.* He was Author of the *Senatus-Confultum* which bears his Name, and is fpoken of in the Third Title of the Third Book of the *Inftitutes. Cujacius* pretends He wrote upon *Religion;* for which Opinion he quotes *Eufebius,* who fays, that *Tertullian* the *Divine* was alfo a *Lawyer:* But others think they were different Perfons of the fame Name.

AFFRICANUS lived alfo in *Adrian's* Time, and was Scholar to *Salvius Julianus.* 'Tis he that *Aulius Gellius* fpeaks of, under the Name of *Sextus Cæcilius. Cujacius,* in the Beginning of his *Commentaries* upon the Treatifes written by this Author, confirms it, and blames thofe who have afferted that he lived in *Papinian's* Time, and was his Difciple: However that be, 'tis certain *Affricanus* was the moft intricate and unintelligible Author of all the *Roman Lawyers;* and no Commentator of lefs Learning and Penetration than *Cujacius,* could ever have explain'd his meaning,

MARCELLUS, who was one of the Council to *Antoninus Pius,* left feveral Books of *Law,* which are fo many Proofs of his great Learning.

CEREI-

CEREIDIUS or SERVIDIUS SCÆVOLA, who liv'd under *Antoninus,* Sirnam'd the *Philosopher,* reduc'd that Emperor's *Edicts* into Writing. He was *Septimius Severus's* Master. 'Tis remark'd of him, that he took more Pains to resolve the Difficulties of any Question put to him, than any of the *Lawyers.*

GAIUS, one of the most celebrated *Lawyers* that *Rome* ever bred, made abundance of Books which help'd to compose the *Digest.* He flourish'd under the Emperors *Antoninus Pius* and *Marcus Aurelius,* as *Oifelius* proves in his Preface to that *Lawyer's Institutes.* So that supposing there had been a *Lawyer* of that Name in the Time of the *Republick,* as *Pomponius* mentions, it must have been another Man. There is no notice taken in History what *Offices* he pass'd through, nor of any other Circumstance of his Life; but his Learned Writings sufficiently proclaim his Praise.

PAPINIAN, who study'd under *Scævola,* was *Master of Requests, Treasurer,* and *Captain of the Guard* to *Septimius Severus,* by whom he was highly esteem'd. He was called the *Asylum of Right* and *Treasure of the Laws:* He was the most Ingenious and Learned of all the Fraternity: Therefore *Cujacius,* who was better able than any Man to discover his Excellencies, says in his *Epistle Dedicatory* to the *Theodofian Code,* " That there never was so great a *Lawyer* before, " nor ever will be after him."

Antiquity also speaks of his sublime Genius, in the highest Terms of Commendation: And the Honour conferr'd upon him by *Valentinian* III. who order'd, that in case of an Equality of Opinions, *Papinian's* should turn the Scale; sufficiently teaches us, how great a Veneration we ought to have for his Memory.

The *Exactness* and *Perfection* which are in his Writings, and the great *Abundance* of them, would induce one to think, he exceeded the ordinary Term of Human Life: Yet, 'tis agreed by all Historians, that He was not *Eight and Thirty* when he was taken off by a Violent Death; which cannot be imputed to any other Cause than his *Virtue,* and the *Cruelty* of him who commanded it.

After

After *Caligula* had murther'd his Brother, he would feign have perfwaded *Papinian* to juftifie the Fact to the *Senate* and *People* ; but he anfwer'd, 'twas much eafier to commit *Parricide*, than to juftifie it : Which drew upon him the Emperor's Refentment, who order'd him to be Beheaded.

ULPIAN was at firft *Tutor* to *Alexander Severus*, afterwards his *Secretary*, and much favour'd by him. Having been of the *Council of State*, his Merit quickly rais'd him to the Office of *Captain of the Guard*, which was the moft confiderable of all the Empire. We have many of his *Laws* in the *Digeft*, and feveral *Fragments*, which are great Helps towards underftanding the *Law*. All his *Remains* fufficiently fhew, how greatly he had diftinguifh'd himfelf in the *Science* of the *Laws*. Many of the Emperors give him the higheft Commendations, as well as *Juftinian*, who in feveral Places fpeaks of his fublime Genius. But his over-great Attachment to the *Pagan Superftitions*, and his fevere Perfecution of the *Chriftians*, very much eclipfe the Glory of his Memory. He was Kill'd by the *Prætorian* Guards, in the Year of Chrift 226.

JULIUS PAULUS, *Papinian's* Scholar, was *Prætor*, *Conful*, and *Captain of the Guards*, to all which he attain'd by his fingular Merit : He lived in the Reign of *Alexander Severus*. His *Statue* is to be feen at *Padua*, where he was born. No *Lawyer* has wrote fo much as he ; his Stile is clear, and his Determinations Judicious. Some will have it, that he was not only an excellent *Lawyer*, but a very good *Poet :* *Aulus Gellius* fays thus of him, *Poeta vir bonus, & rerum literarumque veterum impensè doctus.* Lib. 19. Cap. 7.

POMPONIUS, who was brought up under *Papinian*, was one of the Council to *Alexander Severus*. He apply'd himfelf clofely to the Study of the *Law*, in which he had good Succefs. We have many of his *Laws* in the *Digeft*, among the reft, that *de Origine Juris, ff.* 2.

HERENNIUS MODESTINUS, was *Ulpian's* Scholar, or, as fome fay, *Papinian's* : He was a perfect Mafter of the Beauties of the *Greek* and *Latin* Tongues. Under *Alexander Severus*, who made him one of his Counfellors

fellors, he was rais'd to be *Consul* with *Probus*, in the Year
228 ; and was afterwards nominated for *Tutor* to the young
Prince, *Maximianus*. He made several Books of *Law* ;
among the rest Two *Greek* ones, of the *Excuses* of *Tutors*.

There is nothing remarkable in History of several other
Lawyers, whose *Laws* are to be seen in the *Digest* ; therefore
I shall only set down their Names, after having first ac-
quainted the Reader, that most of them liv'd under the
Antoninus's, and their Successors.

Such as TARUNTIUS PATERNUS, ÆMILIUS MA-
CER, TERENTIUS CLEMENS, ARIUS MEXANDER,
AURELIUS ARCADIUS, LICINIUS RUFINUS, PAPY-
RIUS JUSTUS, PUBLIUS FURIUS ANTHIANUS, MA-
XIMUS HERMOGENIANUS, FLORENTINUS, CLAU-
DIUS TRYPHONINUS, CALISTRATUS, VENULEIUS
SATURNINUS, JULIUS MAURICIANUS, JULIUS
AQUILIUS, and ÆLIUS GALLUS.

Having thus given an Account of all the *Lawyers*,
whose Writings have contributed to the Composition of the
Digest, I think I ought to say something of T R I B O N I A N,
who was particularly commission'd, to reduce them into
Order.

He was accounted one of the Brightest and most Skilful
Lawyers of his Time ; and to have had an universal Knowledge of all *Sciences*. His great Parts quickly rais'd him to
the highest Preferments, and won him the Esteem and
Confidence of *Justinian*. It was by his Advice, the Emperor undertook the Abridgment of the *Civil Law*, which till
then lay dispers'd in an infinite Number of Books. And
the Emperor's Success in that great Undertaking, was intirely owing to his Care and Labour.

Tribonian was not only a Man of a sweet and complaisant
Temper, but of strict Morals ; and his Life had been a
compleat Pattern of Virtue, had it not been for his too great
love of Riches ; which has made many of his *Laws* suspected
of *Self-Interest* ; and 'tis pretended, that *Money* has often
made Changes in the *Laws* of which he was the Author :
Eruditus erat admodum & indefessus sed habendi cupidior.
Suidas would have him pass for an *Atheist* and nauseous
Sycophant, whose only View was to govern the Empire, under

der *Juſtinian's* Name and Authority. But *Procopius,* a Grave and Cotemporary Author, ſpeaks of him in a quite different Strain, which ſeems to come nearer the Truth.

Tribonian was *Maſter of the Houſhold* ; the Emperor *Juſtinian,* in his Preface to the *Inſtitutes,* ſpeaks of him in theſe Terms ; *Triboniano viro magnifico magiſtro & exqueſtore ſacri palatii, noſtri & Ex Conſule.* (See my Explanation of the Word *Exqueſtor* in this Paſſage.)

Hitherto I have treated of the moſt remarkable Things in the ſeveral *Roman Laws.* I am now to give an Account of the chief Compilations of them, before *Juſtinian's* Time ; after which, I ſhall ſpeak of thoſe made by his Order.

C H A P. XVIII.

Of the Law-Books before Juſtinian's *Time.*

AS ſoon as there were any *Laws* eſtabliſh'd at *Rome,* care was taken to collect and reduce them to Order ; the Chief of which I ſhall give an Account of in this Place : Becauſe it will very much help towards underſtanding ſeveral Paſſages, wherein they are mention'd in our Books.

Under the *Regal* Government, they had *Two* Principal Compilations.

The Firſt conſiſted of the *Laws* made by *Numa Pompilius,* relating chiefly to *Religion* and *Divine Worſhip :* Theſe *Ancus Martius* took out of the *Pontiff's Regiſters,* put them into Order, and then hung them up in the Publick Places.

The Second was that of the *Regal Laws,* made by *Papyrius,* in the Time of *Tarquin* the *Proud :* This was called after the Author's Name, the *Papyrian Civil Law,* as I have obſerv'd before. During the *Republican* Government, all that remain'd in uſe of the *Regal Laws,* was collected with great Exactneſs ; to which the moſt Wholeſome *Laws* of the chief Cities of *Greece* were added : And our of them, the whole Body of the *Roman Law* contained in the *Twelve Tables* before ſpoken of, was taken.

After

After the *Law* of the *Twelve Tables,* the *Lawyers* compos'd certain Forms for regulating the Acts and Proceedings of the Court : Of theſe *Appius Claudius* made an exact Collection, which his *Secretary* ſtole from him, and publiſh'd as aforeſaid.

Let us now ſee what Compilations of *Law,* were made from the Time of *Julius Cæſar* to *Juſtinian*'s.

Firſt then; In *Julius Cæſar*'s Time, *Ofilius* the *Lawyer* undertook a Compilation of the *Prætors Edicts,* which a long time after were made into a Perpetual one, by *Julianus,* at the command of the Emperor *Adrian.*

Whilſt *Conſtantine* the *Great* Reign'd, *Gregorius* and *Hermogenius,* both excellent *Lawyers,* undertook each of them to collect the *Conſtitutions* of the *Pagan* Emperors, from *Adrian* to *Dioclefian* ; which Two Books were call'd by their Names; the *Gregorian* and *Hermogenian Code.*

About One Hundred and twenty Years after this, *Theodoſius* the *Younger* order'd a Collection to be made of the *Conſtitutions* of the Chriſtian Emperors, from *Conſtantine*'s to his own Time. He made alſo another *Code,* divided into Seventeen Books ; which was publiſh'd in the Year of Chriſt 438, and called the *Theodoſian Code.*

Thus the *Conſtitutions* of the *Roman* Emperors, from *Adrian* to *Theodoſius* the *Younger,* were comprehended in theſe Three Collections.

All that remains of the Two firſt of theſe Books, are ſome Fragments, which *Cujacius* has plac'd at the End of the *Theodoſian Code.*

This laſt *Code,* publiſh'd under the Name and by the Authority of *Theodoſius* the *Younger,* was receiv'd and follow'd, till it was ſuppreſs'd by *Juſtinian*'s Order.

It is a Work not altogether unworthy the Obſervation of the Learned, as containing the Deciſions made upon various Points of *Law,* by ſeveral Emperors from *Conſtantine* the *Great* to *Theodoſius* the *Younger* : Beſides theſe *Deciſions,* which are for the moſt part *Edicts* or *Reſcripts,* given by thoſe Princes to *Magiſtrates* who deſir'd their Advice ; there are many *Harangues* ſpoken in the *Senate, Ordinances* concerning their Proceedings, *Deliberations* of the Emperors Councils, and *Orders* hereupon, ſent to the Deputies in thoſe Provinces which depended on the Empire.

F

So

So that it was no ſooner finiſh'd, than publiſh'd and re-ceiv'd, both in the Eaſt and Weſtern Empire. The firſt *Novel,* which is at the Head of this *Code,* ſhews that the Emperor employ'd all his Authority, and how deſirous he was to bring a Work undertaken by his Orders, to a happy Concluſion.

Valentinian the Third, who govern'd in the Weſt, ſoon adopted this *Code,* which his Father-in-Law *Theodoſius* had order'd to be made, for the Advancement of the *Law.* Beſides this Conſideration of Alliance, and other Reaſons he had to reſpect *Theodoſius,* by whoſe Choice he was made *Ceſar,* and Heir to the Empire, there was another Motive which induc'd *Valentinian* to make this *Code* the *Law* of his Dominions, which he himſelf ſets forth in one of his *Novels*; *viz* That as the Empire obey'd Two Princes, whoſe Wills were inſeparable, ſo there ought likewiſe to be an exact Uniformity in their *Laws.*

If there be any that will diſpute the Authority of the *Theodoſian Code* in the Weſt, it would be an eaſie Matter to refute them by the Evidence of ſeveral Authors, either Cotemporaries or that have written ſince; their Names and Quotations are to be found in the Learned *Gothofredus's Prolegomena,* at the Beginning of his *Commentaries* upon this Collection of the *Imperial Conſtitutions.*

Sometime after the *Theodoſian Code* appear'd, about the Year 506; *Alarick* the Second, King of the *Goths,* made uſe of theſe Three *Codes,* and eſpecially the *Theodoſian,* to form a New Body of *Roman Law,* which he publiſh'd Twenty-three Years before *Juſtinian's Code* came out, by the Advice of his Biſhops and Nobles.

This was compos'd by *Amien, Refrendary* to *Alarick,* an Officer anſwerable to our Modern *Chancellor*; and publiſh'd under the Name of the *Theodoſian Code*; of which, properly ſpeaking, it was an Abridgment: This *Code* was for a long time, all the *Roman Law* that was known or uſed in *France.*

It were to be wiſhed that *Amien* had contented himſelf with making choice only of what was moſt uſeful in that *Code,* without altering the Texts which he has taken to make his Collection; but he has done quite otherwiſe, and very likely with a View of pleaſing *Alarick*: Some he has alter'd, others he has abridg'd, and to others added his own

Inter-

Interpretations; but one cannot avoid diftinguifhing his Language, which is not like the *Latin* of the Text of the *Roman Law*, but the Language of a *Chancellor* of a *Vifigoth*-King : However, in Confideration of what is taken out of the *Ancient Law*, his Work is not totally to be rejected.

It is not to be deny'd, that *Amien*'s Compilation was very favourably receiv'd by the *Goths*; it was not only called the *Theodofian Code*, but generally the *Roman Law* : And it is quoted by that Name in the *Capitulars* of our Kings, in *Marculfus*, in the *Laws* of the *Burgundians* and *Ripuarians*.

The Book called *Jurifprudentia Vetus anti Juftinianea cum Notis Schultingli*, has this whole Collection in it, and feveral Fragments of the Ancient *Lawyers*; it was printed at *Leyden*, in a Large *Quarto*, in the Year 1717.

Having given this brief Account, of the feveral Collections of *Laws* extant before *Juftinian*'s Time; I fhall now proceed to fpeak of thofe made by that Emperor's Order; and which form the Body of the *Civil Law* in its prefent State : But firft, let us confider the Motives which induc'd him to reform the *Law-Books*, and fet them in a new Light.

The *Three Codes* juft now mention'd, were rang'd in no kind of Order, and contain'd abundance of *Conftitutions* contradictory one to the other; which occafion'd a terrible Confufion in the Minds of thofe who confulted them : Befides, the Multiplicity and vaft Variety of the Writings of the Ancient *Lawyers*, render'd the Study of them equally tedious and difficult.

In truth, there was no Authentick Collection before *Juftinian*'s, of the *Anfwers*, and other Writings of the *Lawyers*, which lay fcatter'd in above *Two Thoufand Volumes*; and the Contradictions in them, were alone fufficient to render the Reading of them utterly ufelefs.

To remedy thefe Inconveniencies, and facilitate the Knowledge of the *Laws*, *Juftinian* undertook to make a general Compilation of the beft and moft ufeful *Conftitutions* of the Emperors his Predeceffors, and all his own to that Time : He form'd alfo a Project of collecting the beft of the Writings of the *Lawyers*, and by that means, making a Compleat Body of *Civil Law*; to which alone, recourfe might be had, without the trouble of confulting all thofe other Volumes, which had introduc'd fo much Confufion.

The

The Vaftnefs of this Project, tho' the Emperor had no other Merit than the putting it in Execution in the manner he did, ought to tranfmit his Memory to the moft remote Ages ; and the rather, becaufe before he undertook it, it was look'd upon as an impracticable and fruitlefs Attempt.

CHAP. XIX.

Of JUSTINIAN's *Code.*

THE Body of the *Law*, as it has been convey'd to us, is compos'd of the *Code*, *Digeft*, *Inftitutes* and *Novels*. The *Code*, which is to be the Subject of this Chapter, was the Firft of thefe Four Collections undertaken by *Juftinian* ; who in 528, being the Second Year of his Reign, fignified his Pleafure to *Tribonian*, and other celebrated *Lawyers* of the Time, to make choice of the beft and moft ufeful *Conftitutions*, pafs'd by the Emperors from *Adrian* to his Reign, and put them in better Order than they were in the Three *Codes* hitherto publifh'd ; which Order is fet forth in this Emperor's *Conftitution*, *De Novo Codice faciendo*, at the Beginning of his *Code*, and directed to the *Senate* of *Conftantinople.*

Tribonian foon comply'd with the Emperor's Defire ; the Compilation which he was order'd to make, came out the next Year, under the Name of *Juftinian*'s *Code* ; as appears by the Emperor's *Ordinance* to confirm this *Code*, intitled, *De Juftiniano Codice Confirmando*, and directed to the *Governor* of the City of *Conftantinople* : By this *Ordinance*, which is alfo at the Beginning of this Compilation, *Juftinian* gives every Thing therein the Authority of *Law* ; declaring, that he repeals all other *Conftitutions* not compriz'd therein ; and forbidding all Perfons whatfoever the Ufe of them : And then, to recommend them the more, tells how he has remov'd the Contrarieties in the *Gregorian*, *Hermogenian* and *Theodofian Codes.*

But

But tho' *Juſtinian's Code* is juſtly accounted an excellent Work, I cannot deny but the Order obſerv'd in the Succeſſion of the Titles, might have been more exact : Beſides, *Tribonian,* who (if one may ſay ſo) was at the Head of this Work, has been guilty of ſeveral Conſiderable Faults, that have been very hurtful to the Study of the *Law* ; and which would even extinguiſh the Knowledge of certain Principles, or render them very doubtful, if we could not have recourſe to the *Theodoſian Code,* for the Explanation of thoſe *Laws* which *Tribonian* has taken from thence, and tranſcrib'd into his Collection of *Imperial Conſtitutions.*

In effect, it is certain, as *Gothofredus* has very rightly obſerv'd in his *Prolegomena,* at the Beginning of his *Commentaries* to the *Theodoſian Code,* That *Tribonian* has mutilated ſome of the *Laws,* and even omitted Things in others, which were eſſential towards underſtanding them ; and paſs'd over in ſilence the Facts which gave occaſion to their being made : He has alſo ſometimes divided a *Law* into Two, and reduc'd Two into One ; and in ſhort, made no ſcruple to attribute many *Laws* to Emperors who were not the Authors of them, or had given quite contrary *Deciſions* ; which cauſe frequent Obſcurities, it might be wiſh'd, were not be met with in a Collection, that in all other Reſpects, deſerves to be highly prais'd. But by good Fortune, we have the *Theodoſian Code,* to compare with the Learned *Gothofredus's Commentaries,* which may be of great uſe towards the underſtanding abundance of *Laws* in *Juſtinian's Code.*

As to the *Imperial Conſtitutions* that make up this Collection, it muſt be acknowledg'd, the Stile of many of the *Laws* is not ſo conciſe, nor their *Deciſions* grounded on ſo good Reaſons as one could wiſh ; yet, we cannot ſufficiently admire in moſt of them the Wiſdom and Goodneſs of *God,* who made ſo many Wicked Princes his Inſtruments to eſtabliſh ſuch Juſt and Equitable *Laws* : *Nero, Domitian, Commodus, Heliogabalus,* and *Caracalla,* were no better than Wild Beaſts in Human Shape, full of Impiety and Cruelty ; as well as *Trajan, Valens, Decius, Galienus, Dioclefian,* and *Julian* ; yet their *Ordinances* are ſo juſt, that they are with great Reaſon admir'd by all Nations at this Day.

F 3

The

The great Care thefe took to find out Expedients for appeafing and pacif ing *Civil Commotions,* often hinder'd the moft declar'd Enemies of the Chriftian Religion, to refufe the Chriftians their Affiftance in fupporting the *Authority* and *Councils* of the *Bifhops* ; as *Ærodius* proves, *Lib.* 1. *rer. judica- tar. tit. de Hæreticis,* Cap. 2. wherein the wonderful Effects of D'vine Providence are vifible, which often makes ufe of the very Perfons to ftrengthen the Chriftian Religion, whofe only View was to fubvert it.

As long as the Seat of the Empire was at *Rome,* and dif- interéfted *Lawyers* were imploy'd by the Emperors in draw- ing up their *Conftitutions,* they were Short, Sententious, and Elegant; but after *Conftantine* had tranfported the Seat of the Empire to *Conftantinople,* where the *Latin* Tongue was in lefs Perfection, the Emperors employ'd none but their *Chief Officers* to frame their *Conftitutions* ; and as they were not always very expert *Lawyers,* and often biafs'd by Favour or Intereft, the *Imperial Conftitutions* carried but *little* in *abundance* of Words ; and are remarkable for a *Bombaft Stile,* fitter for an *Orator* than a *Prince* : In a Word, they come very fhort of the reft in *Eloquence, Prudence, Ex- actnefs* and *Majefty* ; this is plainly to be feen, by the *Confti- tutions* of *Marcianus, Leo, Zeno, Anaftafius, Juftin,* and of *Juftinian* himfelf.

Code, in *Latin Codex,* is what we commonly call *a Book in Sheets;* which comes from a Cuftom among the *Antients,* of writing upon the *Bark of Trees,* before the Invention of Paper ; w 'ch Name was given by way of Excellence to the Collection of the *Imperial Conftitutions.*

Juftinian's Cod is divided into *Twelve Books,* every Book into feparate *Titles,* and each Title into *Laws,* each Law containing feveral *Parts* ; the Firft is called *Principium,* be- ing the Beginning of the *Law,* and thofe which follow, *Pa- ragraphs* ; fo that the Part next the Beginning, is the Firft Paragraph : Upon which we muft obferve, that *Paragraph* is a *Greek* Term, fignifying a *Part* or *Section* of a *Law,* that contains one Article, the Sence whereof is compleat.

The Firft Book of the *Code* treats of the *Catholick Faith, Churches, Bifhops, Ecclefiaftical Perfons, Hereticks, Jews, Pa- gans, Church-Priviledges* ; then of *Laws,* and their different Kinds ; and laftly, of *Magiftrates.*

The

The Second Book explains the *Forms* to be observ'd in commencing a *Suit,* then it treats of *Restitutions.* and after that of *Compromises, Sureties* that are to be given, and the *Oath of Calumny.*

The Third Book speaks of those who may *stand in Judgment,* of *Contestation* in the Cause, of *Holydays,* of the *Jurisdiction* wherein we are to pursue our *Rights*; after which, it treats of *undutiful Testaments, undutiful Donations* and *Dowries,* of the *Demand* of *Inheritance,* of the real *Action* of *Services,* of the *Law Aquila,* of *mix'd Actions,* of *Actions* for *Crimes* done by *Slaves,* of the *Action ad exhibendum,* of *Gaming,* of *Burying Places* and *Funeral Expences.*

The Fourth Books begins with the *Explanation* of *Personal Actions* which are deriv'd from the *Loan* and *other Causes*; after which it speaks of *Obligations,* and *Actions,* with their *Effect,* in Relation to *Heirs,* and *other Persons* bound by them; then it treats of *Testimonial* or *Written Evidence,* of *Things borrow'd* for use, of the *Contract* by *Pledge,* and the *Personal Action* thereon, deriv'd from the *Senatus-Consulta Macedonianum* and *Velleianum*; of *Compensation, Usury, Deposites, Mandate, Partnership, Buying* and *Selling, Permutation, Hiring,* and *Mortgages.*

The Fifth Book treats of *Espousals, Donations* in *Contemplation* of *Marriage*; then of *Marriages, Womens Portions,* of the *Action* that lies for the *Recovery* of the *Dowry*; of the *Donation* made between *Persons join'd in Wedlock*; of *Estates* given in *Dowry*; of *Alimony,* due from *Fathers* to their *Children,* and from *Children* to their *Fathers*; of *Concubines*; of *natural Children,* and the Ways of making them *Legitimate.* After which, it treats of *Testamentary, Legal* or *Dative Tutorships*; of those who have a Power to appoint, or be appointed *Tutors*; of the *Administration* of *Tutors,* and the *Action* arising thereon, as well against *them,* as their *Heirs* and *Bondmen:* Then it shews after what manner the *Office* of a *Tutor* ceases; and lastly, it speaks of the *Alienation* of *Minors Estates.*

The Sixth Book, first treats of *Slaves,* and the *Theft* of *Freemen,* and the *Rights* their *Patrons* have over *them* and *their Goods*; then it explains at large the *Prætorian Possession,* called *Bonorum Possessio*; after which, it lays open the whole Matter of *Testaments,* as *Institutions* and *Substitutions, Preteritions* and *Dis-inherisons*; the *Right* of *deliberating* the *Refusal fufal* of an *Inheritance* ; the *opening* of *Wills* ; of *Codicils,* of *Legacies,* and *Fiduciary Bequefts* ; and laftly, of *Succeffions* to *Inteftates.*

The Seventh Book begins with *Manumiffions,* after which it treats of Matters relating to *Prefcriptions* ; and then of *Sentences* and *Appeals,* of the *Ceffion* of *Eftate* or *Goods,* of the *Seizure* of the *Debtor's Goods,* and *fale* thereof ; and laftly, of the *Privileges* belonging to the *Exchequer,* thofe of *Dowries,* and the *Revocation* of *Goods aleniated* to *defraud Creditors.*

The Eighth Book begins with *Poffeffory Judgments* in *Law,* called *Injunctions* ; then of *Pledges* and *Pawns* ; of *Stipulations. Novations* and *Delegations,* of *Payments, Acceptilations* and *Evictions* ; after which, it treats of *Paternal Power, Emancipation* of *Children* and their *Ingratitude* ; then it explains the *Right Poftliminii* ; what is meant by *Cuftom* or *unwritten Law* ; *Donations,* their *different Kinds,* and their *Revocation* ; and laftly, of taking away the Penalty of *Celibacy.*

The Ninth Book treats of *Criminal Judgments,* and the *Punifhment* of *Crimes :* The Firft Title explains what relates to *Accufations,* Publick or Private *Prifons* ; how the *Accufation* drops by the Death of the *Accufer* or *Accufed* ; the following Titles fpeaks of *Criminal Judgments,* which are *Treafon* ; *Adulteries,* and other *unlawful Copulations,* Publick and Private *Violence, Ravifhing, Homicide* ; and under this laft Head, of the *Correction* of *Slaves.* The reft of the Crimes which come under *Criminal Judgments,* and are explain'd in this Book, are *Parricide, Maleficium,* which comprehends *Poyfoning, Sacrilege, Juggling, Sorcery* and *Witchcraft.* The *Robbing* of *Sepulchres,* making *falfe Certificates* or *falfe Wills, Extortion, Cheating* the *Publick, Sacrilege,* and raifing *Sedition* and *Tumults :* Afterwards this Book treats of *Judgments* commenc'd for *Private Offences* ; fuch as *ftealing* or *taking away* any thing out of another Man's *Inheritance,* before *Adminiftration* be taken ; *Rapine, Cozenage,* called *Crimen ftellionatus, Injury,* and fome others ; then it fpeaks of *Abolition of Accufations,* which proceed either from the *Accufed* or the *Accufer* ; and laftly, of the *Explanation* of *Punifhments,* in which Number is the *Confifcation* of *Goods.*

The

The Tenth Book treats of the *Rights* and *Prerogative* of the *Exchequer*; of *vacant Goods*, and how the same may be united to the Princes *Domain*; of those by whose means the *vacant Goods* are discover'd: After which it speaks of *Treasurers*, *Tributes* levy'd upon the *People*, *Tolls*, *Super-impositions*, *Magistrates* called *Decuriones*, and Matters relating to them; of the *Freedom* of *Citizens*, of the *Inhabitants* of *Cities*; of the *Domicil*, or *place of Abode*; of *Publick Offices*, and the *Causes* which exempt Persons from bearing them; of *Embassadors*; of the different Kinds of *Publick Offices*, and *Functions* of *Officers*; and of those who were intrusted with the *Civil Government* and the *Reformation* of *Manners*.

In the Two last Books the Emperor speaks of the *Rights* that were common to the City of *Rome* and other *Municipal Towns*; Which were Four: The First is the *Right* of having *Bodies* and *Communities*; the Second consists in having *Publick Registers*, wherein every *Citizen's* Name and Condition were set down: The Third was in having *Dignities* and a *Militia*; the Fourth in having *Officers* for the Execution of *Judgments*, and the *Magistrate's Orders*. The two first of these are explain'd in the Eleventh, and the two last in the following Book.

C H A P. XX.

Of the Digests *or* Pandects.

IN the preceding Chapter it is said, that *Justinian* in the Year 528, gave Orders for compiling a *Code*, which should contain the most useful and best *Ordinances* of the Emperors, and that the said Work was publish'd the Year following.

As it was his Intention to make a compleat Collection of the *Roman Law*, he made an *Ordinance* in the Year 530, *De conceptione Digestorum*, directed to *Tribonian*; empowering him to chuse a certain Number out of the most eminent *Lawyers*; who, together with Him, were to make a Collection of the best *Decisions* of the Ancient *Lawyers*, and

to

to reduce them into *Fifty Books*, in such a Method as there should be no *Confusion* or *Contrariety* therein : *Sed his quin-quaginta libris, totum jus antiquum per millesimum & quadrin-gentesimum penè annum confusum, & à nobis purgatum, quasi quodam muro Vallatum, nihil extra se habeat.* §. 5. *de conceptione Digestorum.* He orders, that the Volume so composed, should be called *Digestorum vel Pandectarum Volumen* ; which were Names given by many of the Ancient *Lawyers* to their Works.

Then he proceeds to forbid all *Lawyers* making any *Commentaries* upon that Volume, lest they should introduce the same Confusion the Multiplicity of the *Lawyers* Writings, which were very often contradictory to one another, had occasion'd ; but he allow'd them to make *Paratitles*, or Summaries upon the Titles, to give a general Notion and serve for a Preliminary to the reading of that Work.

Lastly, He orders that every Word should be wrote at full length, and no Notes or Abbreviations made use of, which had caused so much Obscurity and so many Doubts in the Writings of the Ancient *Lawyers.*

In pursuance of this *Ordinance,* *Tribonian* made choice of Sixteen able *Lawyers,* who are nam'd in the last *Confirmation* of the *Digest* : They all apply'd themselves to take out of that Infinite Multitude of Volumes, which contained the *Writings* of the Ancient *Lawyers,* such *Decisions* as in their Opinions were the most Judicious and agreeable to Equity.

The Labours of these Great Men were crown'd with Success ; for in a very short time they finish'd the Work, notwithstanding it had been often before in vain attempted.

Suetonius, in the Life of *Julius Cæsar,* and *Cicero* in his Book *de Oratore,* report, that *Julius Cæsar* and *Pompey* had a Design to reduce the *Roman Law* into a Method ; which might have been done then with much more ease, considering the vast Number of Writings upon the *Law,* under the Emperors, down to *Justinian's* Time.

Some there are that affirm, the Emperor *Constantine* had projected such a Collection, but it proved abortive ; as if Providence had reserv'd the Honour of so great a Work for *Justinian's* Wisdom and Ability.

This

This excellent Collection of the *Writings* of the Ancient *Lawyers*, made by his Order, was not begun till 530; and was finish'd the Sixteenth of *December* 533: So that it was but Three Years in making; at the End of which, it was publish'd under the Emperor's Name and Authority, as may be seen by thofe *Ordinances* made for the *Confirmation* of this Work, to which he gave the Name of *Digests* or *Pandects*.

It was called the *Digest*, that is to fay, *A Methodical Compilation*; and it had the Name of *Pandects*, as containing *Decifions* upon moft of the Queftions that can arife in the *Law*: In fhort, παν in *Greek*, is *Omne*, and θεχομαι, *complector*; fo that *Pandecta* fignifies *a comprehenfive Collection.*

Altho' the great Diligence of *Tribonian* and the reft of the *Lawyers* employ'd in this Work was aftonifhing, and feem'd to be Praife-worthy, it has neverthelefs been found fault with by many; and indeed there was fome reafon to blame them for flubbering over with fo much Precipitation the important Bufinefs they had been intrufted with; in which they were fo much more inexcufable, as the Emperor had allow'd them Ten Years for the perfecting thereof: Nor was that too long a Term for reading over deliberately the vaft Quantity of Books in which the *Writings* of the *Lawyers* were then difpers'd. And therefore, many things in the *Pandects* are Imperfect, Obfcure, Uncertain and contradictory: Altho' the Emperor has affirm'd the contrary, 'tis certain there are many *Laws* in the *Digest* which contradict one another; and are no otherwife to be reconcil'd, than by faying, they are the Remains of the ancient Diffention between the *Sabinians* and *Proculeians.*

There are alfo many *Laws* which have been falfify'd by *Tribonian, Quæ manum Triboniani paffæ funt*, in order to accommodate them to the *New Law*. Nay, fome are of his own making, with a Defign to pafs them upon the World for Ancient ones; concerning which, *Cujacius* ufes thefe Words, *In fragmentis Pandectarum conftat ingentia Tribonianum admififfe flagitia, detortis fæpe, exempli gratia, Ulpiani verbis, in fententiam Juftiniani.*

It muft not however be imagin'd that *all* the Faults in the Body of the *Civil Law* are owing to *Tribonian*; for many Places have been alter'd by the Negligence or Ignorance of thofe employ'd in copying it over.

But

But be that as it will, it may be truly said, this Work is a Master-piece, exceeding all Commendation. Nor was it properly the Work of *Fifty* or a *Hundred*, but near *Six Hundred Years*; being compos'd of the *Writings* of the most Learned Men that had lived from the Times of the first *Roman* Emperors, to the Year 1282 of *Rome*; which was the Year of Grace 530, when it was first begun.

The *Stile* of it is the finest that possib'y can be, Elegant and Concise; all the Principles of *Law*, upon all kind of Matters are well establish'd; and the greatest part of the Resolutions are so exact, and at the same time so just, that it is impossible for the Mind of Man to go farther.

If the perusal of the *Digest* occasions so much Surprize and Pains, to those who are not yet in a Condition to understand it; what a Pleasure must it be to such as by their Study and Application, have made themselves able to comprehend and admire the Wise and Learned *Decisions* that are contain'd therein? The Advantage they reap, creates in them a particular Veneration for the Memory of those Great Men who were the Authors of it; and engages them insensibly to make it the chief Object of their Study, being perswaded, and with good Reason, that of all the Works produc'd by the Wit of Man, none can enter into Comparison with this.

Altho' the *Code* has its Merits, and contains abundance of excellent *Laws*, it is very far from being equal to the *Digest*: I have already taken notice that some of the *Laws* in the *Code* were made at *Constantinople*, where the *Latin* Tongue was not in Perfection; but there is a more general Reason to be given for the Inequality between the *Laws* of the *Code* and those of the *Digest*; which is, the different Characters and Employments of the *Authors* of both.

The *Laws* of the *Digest* are nothing else but the Meditations of *Lawyers*, who having no other Business to interrupt their Study, were greater Masters both of its Spirit and Language; and therefore, it is no Wonder if their *Decisions* comprehended much in a few Words, but very clear and decisive; and that the Nobleness and Shortness of their Stile, was suitable to the Elevation and Exactness of their Thoughts: For being wholly taken up with the Love of *Justice*, they had no other View but the *Publick Good*, and the Desire of giving substantial Marks of their Learning;

fo that their *Decifions* were neither grounded upon nor govern'd by the *Favour* of Great Men, or an immoderate Defire
of *Riches*, but by *Right Reafon* and *Equity*.

On the contrary, the *Laws* of the *Code* are often obfcure,
and contain but little in abundance of Words; becaufe the
greateft part of them were made by *Secretaries* or *Chancellors*
to the Emperors; whofe Heads being full of *State-Affairs*,
minded little elfe but to pleafe their *Mafters*, and advance
the Intereft of the *Exchequer* : So that being often byafs'd by
Favour, or their own *Intereft*, their *Decifions* were not always
agreeable to *Juftice*.

But if the *Laws* of the *Code* are for this reafon much inferior to thofe of the *Digeft*, the Collection of the *Imperial Conftitutions* is fo very Immethodical, that it is alfo on
this Account much inferior to the Collection of the *Writings*
of the Ancient *Lawyers*.

However Praife-worthy the Compilers of the *Digeft*
may have been, their Work, at leaft the manner in which
they perform'd it, has been blam'd by many Learned Men:
But I think, without being Partial, I may fay, it is without
Reafon or Foundation. All they can juftly be reproach'd
with, is the little Time they took for the Performance.

Many have pretended that this Work, containing only
the Fragments of the Ancient *Lawyers*, has been of very little ufe in the Study of the *Roman Laws*; and that it were to
be wifh'd, all thofe *Writings* had come to our Hands in the
Original Condition ; and the rather, becaufe there are many *Laws* which are not to be underftood, for want of having Recourfe to the Fountains from whence they are drawn:
For this Reafon, fome have accus'd *Juftinian* and *Tribonian*
of fuppreffing the *Twelve Tables* and *Writings* of the Ancient
Lawyers ; others fay, that *Tribonian* endeavouring to take in
all the *Roman Law* into the Fifty Books of the *Digeft*, has
confin'd it within too narrow a Compafs.

To this it is anfwer'd, that if the making of the *Digeft*
has been follow'd with fome Inconveniences, the Advantages the *Law* has thereby receiv'd, are far more confiderable: Befides, 'tis not certain whether we ought to afcribe
the Lofs of thofe Books to *Juftinian*. There is reafon
fufficient to believe, they were loft by the Misfortunes of
the Times, the Incurfions of the *Barbarians*, and by Accidents which could neither be forefeen nor prevented. Moreover,

over, the Choice which had been made of the beſt of theſe *Writings*, and which are plac'd in Order in the *Digeſt*, may very well compenſate for their Loſs ; which, all things conſider'd, is not ſo much to be lamented, in regard of the great Confuſion they had introduc'd.

The Truth is, that before the Publication of the *Digeſt*, the *Roman Law* was like a great Sea, without any Port of Safety ; it was diſpers'd in ſo many Volumes, that the Life of the moſt Laborious Perſon, would hardly ſuffice to read them over. Beſides, as they were the Works of particular Men, they had no abſolute Authority ; and as they contain'd many contradictory *Deciſions*, all the uſe they were of, was to occaſion Doubts, and keep Men in ſuſpence about Opinions they were willing to embrace.

But the Caſe is far otherwiſe with reſpect to the *Digeſt*, which comprehends the whole Matter of the *Law*, reduc'd into good Order, and compos'd of the beſt Part of all thoſe *Writings* : And as they are fortify'd by *Imperial Authority*, all its *Deciſions* are ſo many *Laws*, which have a Right of fixing the Judgment of thoſe who make it their Study. After this, I cannot conceive the Loſs of ſo many Books, which by the Publication of the *Digeſt* are become utterly uſeleſs, is ſo much to be regretted.

Hotoman blames *Tribonian* and his Fellow-Labourers, for not giving thoſe *Lawyers* a place in the *Digeſt*, who flouriſh'd in the Time of the *Republick* ; and confining themſelves only to thoſe who liv'd under the Emperors.

But this Reproach, upon the leaſt Reflection, falls of it ſelf : For it was not *Juſtinian's* Deſign to revive the ſuperannuated *Law* of the *Roman* People, but to methodize and reform the *Law* in uſe in his own Time : Beſides, whatever Reſpect *Hotoman* may pretend for thoſe Ancient *Lawyers*, it is certain they were too much addicted to Formalities and Punctilio's upon *Words* and *Syllables* : Beſides, the *Lawyers* who ſucceeded them, took out of their *Writings* whatever they thought beſt ; and made it uſeful to themſelves, by giving it a ſhorter and more elegant Turn.

In ſhort, ſome Commentators have affirm'd, that the *Digeſt* is not in good Order ; but others ſay, it could not be more Methodically diſpos'd, than by ranging the ſeveral Matters in the Order obſerv'd by *Salvius Julianus*, in his Compilation of the *Perpetual Edict*.

Cujacius

Cujacius fpeaks of it thus, in his *Paratitles* to the Title *Mandati* ; " Every thing therein is rang'd with wonderful " Art, not fo much by the Skill of *Tribonian*, as that of " *Julianus Hermogenianus*, and other Learned Men his Prede- " ceffors, whofe Steps he follow'd : Thofe who are defirous " of another Method, know not what they fay, and are " either Malicious, or ignorant of the Science of the " *Digeft*.

We have feveral Editions of the *Pandects*, that difagree in certain Places : The Firft is the *Vulgar*, which the Ancient Doctors made ufe of after *Jumerius*. The Second is that of *Holloander*, commonly called the *Noric* Edition ; which he made from the Books of *Bologuinus* and *Politianus*. The Third is that after the *Original*, which the *Pifans* had firft, and afterwards fell into the Hands of the *Florentines*, where it now is : Many are of Opinion, that this laft is the beft; and that it was a Copy from the Original, written intirely by *Tribonian*'s own Hand. And therefore, to decide all Doubts that may arife upon any Paffage, recourfe ought to be had to the *Florentine Pandects*.

The *Digeft* was divided by the Emperor into *Fifty Books*; each Book containing *feveral Titles*, divided into *Laws*, and the *Laws* generally into *feveral Parts* ; the Firft is called *Principium*, being the Beginning of the *Law*, the reft are called *Paragraphs*.

The Firft Book begins with laying down the *general Principles* of *Juftice*, and fets forth the different Kinds thereof ; after which it treats of the *divifion* of *Perfons* and that of *Things* ; then fpeaks of *Senators*, and laftly of *Magiftrates* ; and of their *Delegates* and *Affeffors*.

In the Second, we have an Account of the *Power* of *Magiftrates*, and their *Jurifdictions* ; how a Perfon is to be brought into *Judgment* ; and how it often happens that the Perfons *agree* after an *Action* is commenc'd : The Subject of the latter part of this Book, is *Covenants* and *Tranfactions*.

The Third Book explains in the firft Place, who thofe Perfons are that are allow'd to fue in *Law* ; and becaufe fuch as are *Infamous* are not admitted fo to do, the Second Title treats of *Infamous Perfons*: The following fpeaks of thofe whofe Miniftry fuch as go to *Law* are wont to make ufe of, as *Advocates*, *Proctors*, *Syndicks*, who ought all to abftain from *Calumny*.

The

The Fourth explains the different Caufes of *Reftitution* ; and becaufe it often happens that fuch as have *Difputes*, are willing to avoid the Trouble of a *Law-Suit*. The next Subject it treats of, is *Compromifes* and *Arbitrations* ; after which, it fpeaks of *Inn-keepers*, and others into whofe Cuftody we leave any thing.

The Fifth, after having fpoken of *Judgments*, explains who ought to give an *Affignation*; then it treats of the *Demand* of *Inheritance*, and of the *Complaint* againft an *undutiful Teftament*.

The Sixth treats of *Real Actions*, by which Private Perfons recover their own ; which *Actions* may be *Civil* and *Direct*, or *Prætorian* or *ufeful*.

The Seventh is of *Perfonal Services*.

The Eighth treats of *Real Services*, both in *City* and *Country*.

The Ninth fpeaks of *Perfonal Actions*, which are in Imitation of the *Real* ; as *Actions* for a Fault or Crime committed by a *Slave*, the *Action* of the *Law Aquilia*, and upon Occafion of this laft, at the End of the Book, of the *Action* againft fuch as throw out any thing into a *High-way*, by which any one is *wounded* or *damag'd* ; and of the *Action* againft fuch as hang any thing out of their *Window*, which may happen to damage fuch as pafs by.

The Tenth Book treats of *mix'd Actions* ; fuch as the Action of *Bounding* and *Buting*, the Action of *Partition* of an *Inheritance* or other particular Thing: After which, it treats of the Action called *Ad exhibendum*, which is preparatory to the *Real Action* above-mention'd.

The Eleventh Book fpeaks of *Interrogatories* upon *Facts* and *Articles* ; after that, of fuch Matters as are to be heard before the fame *Judge*: Then it treats of the *Slave* that is corrupted, or runs from his *Mafter*, or fuch as play at *Dice*, or fuch as *meafure Land* and make a *falfe Report* of the Quantity ; and laftly, of *Burials* and *Funeral Expences*.

The Twelfth Book explains thofe Perfonal Actions by which it is concluded, that the *Defendant* fhall be oblig'd to transfer the *Demefne* or *Inheritance* of any thing, fuch as the Action for a *Loan*, and fome others, which go by the Name of *Condictio*, in its proper Signification.

The

The Thirteenth Book speaks alſo of ſome of theſe *Actions*; and then of a Thing *lent*, and of the Action of *Pawning.*

The Fourteenth and Fifteenth Books, treat of Actions ariſing from *Contracts* by which we are bound, altho' they were made by other Perſons; and laſtly, of the *Senatus-Conſultum Macedonianum.*

The *Senatus-Conſultum Velleianum*, Compenſation, and the Action of Depoſites, are the Subject of the Sixteenth.

The Seventeenth treats of the *Mandate*, and of *Society.*

The Eighteenth explains the Meaning of the Contract of *Sale*, the Covenants that are generally us'd therein; the Reciſion of this kind of Contract, and for what Reaſons one may go from it; and upon whom the Gain or the Loſs of the Thing ſold is to fall.

The Nineteenth, in the Firſt Part treats of Actions of *Bargains* and *Sale*, of Actions of *Hiring*, of the Action called *Æſtimatoria*, of Permutation, of the Action called *Præſcriptis verbis*, proceeding from innominate Contracts.

The Twentieth Book treats of *Pledges* and *Pawns*, of the preference of **Creditors**, and the Subrogation of the *Rights* of the *Oldeſt*, of the Diſtraction or Sale of Things *engag'd* or *pawned*, and the Extinction of the *Pledge* or *Pawn.*

The Twenty firſt contains an Explanation of the *Ædile's Edict*, concerning the Sale of *Slaves* and *Beaſts*; then it treats of *Evictions*, *Warrantees*, and the *Exception* of the Thing bought and deliver'd.

The Firſt Part of the Twenty ſecond, treats of *Uſuries*, *Fruits*, *Dependencies*, *Acceſſaries* to Things; then of *Proofs* and *Preſumptions*, and of Ignorance of the *Law* or *Fact.*

The Twenty third is upon *Eſpouſals*, *Marriage-Dowry*, *Agreements* made upon that Subject, and *Lands* given in *Dowry.*

The Twenty fourth goes upon *Donations* between Huſband and Wife, *Divorces*, and recovery of the *Marriage-Portion.*

The Twenty fifth treats of *Expences* laid out upon the *Dowry*; of Actions for the Recovery of Things carry'd away by a *Wife* or other Perſon, againſt whom there is no Action of *Theft*; of the Obligation to acknowledge *Children*, and provide for their Maintenance; and laſtly, of *Concubines.*

G The

The Twenty fixth and the Twenty feventh Books, treat wholly of *Tutorfhips* and *Curatorfhips* ; of the Actions which refult from *Tutorfhips*, of Excufes of *Tutors*, and the Alienation of Goods belonging to *Pupils* and *Minors*.

The Twenty eighth Book is employ'd on the Subject of *Teftaments*, the Inftitution and Difinheriting of *Children*, of the Inftitution of an *Heir*, of *Subftitutions*, of Conditions required in *Inftitutions*, and of the Right of *Deliberating*.

The Twenty ninth Book treats of the *Military Teftament*, of the Acquifition of an *Inheritance*, opening of *Wills*, &c. and of *Codicils*.

The Thirtieth, Thirty firft, and Thirty fecond, treat of *Legacies* and *Fiduciary Bequefts* in general.

. The Thirty third, and likewife the firft Titles of the Thirty fourth, treat of particular *Legacies* ; after which follows the *Catonian Regulation*, concerning *Legacies* reputed never to have been made, and thofe that are taken away from unworthy Perfons.

The Thirty fifth fpeaks of *Legacies* left upon Condition, and of the *Law Falcidia*.

The Thirty fixth Explains the *Senatus-Confultum Trebellianum*, made for the fake of *Fiduciary Bequefts* ; then it treats of the Time when *Legacies* and *Fiduciary Bequefts* become due, and of the *Caution* the Heir is oblig'd to give for the Security of *Legacies* and *Fiduciary Bequefts* left upon Condition ; and of the *Seizure* thereof, for want of fuch *Caution*.

The Thirty feventh Book, fpeaks firft of *univerfal Succeffion* to a deceafed Perfon's Eftate, to which any one is called by the *Prætor*, and goes by the Name of *Bonorum poffeffio* ; after which it treats of the Collation of *Goods* and *Dowry*, and the Right of *Patronage*.

The Thirty eighth Book begins with the Explanation of the Services, due from *Freed Men* to their *Patrons* ; then it treats of Matters which relate to to the Succeffion of *Freed Men* ; after that, of the Succeffion of *Inteftates*, appointed by the *Prætor* ; and laftly, of Domeftick and Legal *Heirs*, and of the *Senatus-Confulta Tertullianum* and *Orphilianum*.

The Thirty ninth Book, firft explains the Means which the *Law* or the *Prætor* furnifhes to prevent any ones receiving Damage, where a *Perfonal*, *Real*, or *Mix'd Action* will not lye ; thefe means are, Complaint of a New Work, *Cautio Damni*

Damni infecti, and the Action *De Aqua pluvia arcenda* ; after which, it ends with the Explanation of *Donations*, that take Effect during the Life of the *Donor* ; and such as are made in View of *Death*.

The Fortieth Book relates only to *Manumissions*, by which *Slaves* were set at Liberty.

The Forty first treats of the different Ways by which the Property of Things are acquir'd, according to the *Law* of Nations, and of the Acquisition of *Possession* ; then of *Prescriptions* ; and lastly, of *Lawful Causes* which authorize a *Possession*, and consequently make it capable of *Prescription*.

The Forty second treats in the first Place of Things *adjudg'd*, of definitive and interlocutory *Sentences*, of Confessions in *Judgment*, of the *Cession* of Goods, of the Causes of *Seizure*, and their Effects ; and of the Privileges of *Creditors* : After that, it speaks of a *Curator* appointed for the Administration of Goods, and of the Revocation of *Acts* done to defraud Creditors.

The Forty third treats of *Injunctions* and *Possessory* Actions.

The Forty fourth, first treats of *Exceptions* and *Defences*, and then of *Obligations* and *Actions*.

The Forty fifth of *Stipulations*.

The Forty sixth of *Sureties*, *Novations* and *Delegations* of *Payments*, and *Discharges* of *Acceptilations*, *Stipulations*, and some *Cautions*.

The Forty seventh, is of Private *Faults* or *Offences*.

The Forty eighth begins with *Publick Judgments*, then follow *Accusations*, *Inscriptions*, *Prisons*, and all *Publick Offences* ; from thence it passes to the *Senatus-Consultum Turpillianum*, and Abolition of *Crimes* ; and lastly, it treats of the *Torture*, *Punishments*, *Confiscation*, *Relegation*, *Deportation*, and of the Bodies of *Malefactors* executed.

The Forty ninth treats of *Appeals*, and Matters relating thereunto ; after which, it gives an Account of the Rights of the *Exchequer* ; of Matters relating to *Captives*, *Military Discipline*, *Soldiers* and *Veterans*.

The Fiftieth Book treats of the Rights of *Cities* and *Citizens*, of *Magistrates* and their *Children* ; of *Publick Offices*, and the Causes which exempt Persons from them. And also of the Right of *Immunity* : After which, it speaks of *Deputies* and *Embassadors*, of the Administration of Things

G 2   be-

belonging to *Cities*; of *Publick Works, Fairs, Pollicitations;* Judgments given in extraordinary Cafes by *Magiftrates*; of *Brokers* and *Factors*, of Taxes laid upon the *Provinces*; and laftly, it ends with the Interpretation and Signification of the *Terms*, and with the Rules of the *Law*.

Befides this Diftribution of the *Digeft* into Fifty Books, of which we have here given an Account, this Work was again divided into *Seven Parts*; but the Reafon that induc'd the Emperor to make this Divifion is not known: Some pretend it was done to feparate the different Matters, and take in all that related to one Subject into one Part, confifting of feveral Books. Others attribute it to the Superfti:ious Refpect of the Ancients to the Number *Seven*, as the moft perfect; [Vide *Macrobium in fomnium fcripionis.*] However that be, the Firft Part, containing the *Commencement of Suits*, makes up the firft Four Books.

The Second begins at the Fifth, and ends at the Twelfth.

The Third goes from the Twelfth to the Twentieth.

The Fourth confifts of Eight Books, and ends at the Twenty eighth.

The Fifth begins at the Twenty Eighth, and ends at the Thirty feventh.

The Sixth takes in Eight Books, ending at the Forty fifth.

The Seventh is compos'd of the Six laft.

There has been another Divifion of this Work, made fince the Emperor *Juftinian*'s Time, into the *Old Digeft*, the *Infortiate Digeft*, and *New Digeft*.

According to this, the *Ancient Digeft* goes as far as the Third Title of the Twenty fourth Book, where the *Infortiate* begins, and ends at the Thirty ninth Book; and the *New Digeft* comprehends the Twelve laft.

This Divifion had not the Emperor's Sanction, is imperfect, and without any Foundation: Neverthelefs, it has been obferv'd in thofe Editions of the *Digeft*, which have Gloffes. This is thought to be owing to fome Writers, who not ⸱ ⸱ able to write the whole Work in one Volume, divid⸱ ⸱ into Three, without care to make an exact Divifion, according to the Subject Matters and Titles; and the Names they have given them, would make
one

ône believe, that they were not compos'd and publish'd all at the same Time ; and contain'd the *Answers* of the *Lawyers*, with regard to the Order of the Matter, but not according to the Order of Time.

CHAP. XXI.

Of JUSTINIAN'S *Institutes.*

WHILE the *Digest* was composing, the Emperor laid his Commands upon *Tribonian, Theophilus* and *Doratheus*, to make an Abridgment of the first Principles of the *Law*, for the Benefit of young Students, who should have a Mind to apply themselves to that Science.

These Three Persons were so diligent, that in the Year 533, this Collection was publish'd, under the Title of *Institutes*. It came out about a Month berore the *Digest* ; the *Institutes* being publish'd the Twenty first of *November*, 533 ; and the *Digest*, not till the Sixteenth of *December* following : Which has given occasion to *Zoezius* and some other Doctors, to be of Opinion, that the *Law* of the *Digest*, being publish'd after that of the *Institutes*, ought always to prevail whenever any contrariety appear'd.

The *Institutes* then, which are only the first *Elements* of the *Roman Law*, were compos'd at the Command of the Emperor JUSTINIAN, by *Tribonian, Dorotheus,* and *Theophilus*, who took them from the *Writings* of the Ancient *Lawyers* ; and chiefly from the *Institutes* and other Writings of *Gaius* ; especially from his Books called *Aureorum*, that is, *Of Important Matters.*

They had the Force of *Law*, given them by the same Emperor's *Constitution*, which is plac'd at the Head of the Work by way of Preface.

Why these first *Elements of Law* are called *Institutiones,* is obvious enough : I have translated the Word *Institutes*, because the French Word I... s, is not expressive enough of the Signification of ... Latin ; the Reason whereof is, that by *Institutes* is naturally understood

the

the firſt Principles of a Science : So that as the *Latin* Word
Inſtituta, which ſignifies the *Cuſtoms* or *Laws* of a Country,
is not us'd in this Sence ; ſo the *French* Word *Inſti*+*uts*, is
never made uſe of to ſignifie the firſt Principles of a Science, which are not to be expreſs'd but by the Word *Inſti-*
tutes, or *Inſtitutiːns*.

This Work, as well as the *Digeſt*, is a Maſter-piece in
its kind, which cannot be too often read, or too diligently
ſtudy'd, by thoſe who have already made ſome Progreſs in
the *Law*: Nay, even ſuch as are far advanc'd in it, always
reap great Advantage by the peruſal thereof, becauſe it contains an Abridgment of the firſt Principles of that vaſt and
ſublime Science. Therefore it is a common Saying, that *He*
who is Maſter of the Inſtitutes, *bids fair to be a great* Lawyer.
There is another thing, which is, That as it is impoſſible
to retain all one reads, ſo 'tis a very great Advantage to
one that Studies the *Law*, to have ſo preciſe and exact an
Abridgment thereof. When once one underſtands it thoroughly, 'tis no hard Matter to retain it ; provided it be
carefully read over from time to time, which the ableſt
Judges and beſt *Lawyers* do, being perfectly ſenſible of
the uſe it is to them, to be converſant in the Principles
of the *Roman Law*, which, as we ſhall ſhew hereafter, are
the Baſis and Foundation of ours.

The *Inſtitutes* are divided into *Four Books*, each Book into ſeveral *Titles*, and every Title into ſeveral *Parts* ; the
Firſt is called *Principium*, as it is the Beginning of the Title, and thoſe which follow, *Paragraphs*.

The Firſt Book of the *Inſtitutes* has Twenty ſix Titles,
the Second Twenty five, the Third Thirty, and the Fourth
Eighteen. Before I enter upon the Order of the *Titles* of
this Work, it is to be obſerv'd, that the *Law* has Three
Objects, PERSONS, THINGS and ACTIONS, which
make up the Subject Matter of the Four Books of the *In-*
ſtitutes. The firſt Book treats of the Right of *Perſons* ; the
Second, Third, and Five firſt Titles of the Fourth, of
Things ; and *Actions* are the Subject treated of, from the
Sixth Title of the Fourth Book, to the End.

The Firſt Book treats of PERSONS, but it is from the
Third Title only ; for the Two firſt, which are by way of
Preliminaries, explain what *Juſtice*, *Law*, and *Right* are ;
after which, the meaning of the *Right* or *State* of *Perſons*,

is

is explain'd under Two Diviſions, which make up the remaining Part of the Firſt Book.

According to the chief Diviſion of Perſons, treated of
from the Third Title of the firſt Book to the Eighth; Men
are either *Free* or *Slaves.*

The Condition of all *Slaves* is the ſame, but it is not ſo
with *Freemen*; whereof ſome are Free by *Birth*, others are
made ſo by *Emancipation*, which is null, when contrary to
Law.

The Second Diviſion of Perſons, begins at the Eighth
Title of the Firſt Book, and is explain'd in the following
Titles of the ſame. It is of Perſons independent; and of
ſuch as are under the Power of another, that is, a *Maſter*
or a *Father.*

The Emperor therefore, firſt ſpeaks of the Power of *Ma-*
ſters over their *Slaves*, then of *Fathers* over their *Children*;
after which, he ſhews the manner of acquiring Paternal
Power, *viz.* by *Marriage, Legitimation*, and *Adoption* : And
then, how that Power may be diſſolv'd.

From the Thirteenth Title, to the End of the Firſt Book,
He ſpeaks of Perſons that are Independant, I mean, *Pupils,*
or ſuch as have *Tutors*; of *Minors*, or ſuch as have *Curato*
appointed them; and laſtly, of Perſons that are of Age,
ſubject to no body, and Maſters of their own Rights :
Wherefore, all the Remainder of this Book turns upon *Tutor*
and *Curatorſhips.*

The Emperor particulary explains Three things which
concern *Tutorſhip*; the Firſt is the Definition or Diviſion
thereof into *Teſtamentary, Legal*, and *Dative*; the Second,
is the Effect of the *Tutorſhip*, which conſiſts in putting the
Pupil under the Care of his *Tutor*; ſo that he may do nothing that will bind him, unleſs the Authority of his *Tutor*
intervenes at the very Inſtant when the Act is paſs'd by the
Pupil : The Third thing concerns the manner how *Tutor-*
ſhips end or expire.

After this, in the Twenty third Title, He treats of Matters
relating to *Curators*; and in the three laſt of this Book,
ſpeaks of three things common to *Tutors* and *Curators*;
which are the Security they are oblig'd to give, to indem-
nifie *Pupils* and *Minors*; the Lawful Cauſes exempting
them from being *Tutors* or *Curators*; and laſtly, thoſe for
which they may be depriv'd of their Offices.

From

From *Perſons*, the Emperor paſſes to *Things*; of which he treats, from the Firſt Title of the Second Book, to the Sixth Title in the Fourth.

He explains three Points concerning Things, their *Diviſions*, the ways of *acquiring* them, and *Obligations* that are the Means by which Things become due to us.

As to the *Diviſions*, he makes them principally Two; by the firſt, Things are either *in Commerce* or *out of Commerce*; by the ſecond, they are *Corporeal* or *Incorporeal*.

In Relation to the Second, we ſhall obſerve, that the Property of *Things* is acquir'd either by the *Law of Nations*, or the *Civil Law*.

The ways of acquiring introduc'd by the *Law of Nations*, are explain'd in the Firſt Title of the Second Book.

The Second Title explains the Second *Diviſion* of things; which are either *Corporeal* or *Incorporeal*; upon which, the Emperor takes occaſion to treat of *Real* and *Perſonal Servi-ces*, as being Incorporeal Things.

From thence he paſſes to the Ways of *acquiring*, introduc'd by the *Civil Law*. Whereupon we are to obſerve, that the Property of Things, according to the *Civil Law*, is acquir'd either by *Particular* or *Univerſal Title*.

The Means of acquiring in the *Civil Law* by Particular Title, are *Adjudication, Uſucaption*, or *Preſcription*; and the Expreſs Diſpoſition of the *Law*, which transfers the full Right of a Thing, as a *Donation* in proſpect of Death, re-ſembling a *Legacy*, the Property whereof paſſes to the *Donee* without Delivery. Then the Emperor in the Sixth Title ſpeaks of *Uſucaption*, or Juſt *Uſurpation*, and the Conditions which it requires; and in the Seventh Title, of *Donations.*

After that, He goes upon *Perſons* who have the Power of *Alieniating*, and ſuch by whoſe Means *another* may *acquire* any thing.

The Ways of acquiring the Property of Things, accor-ding to the *Civil Law*, by Univerſal Title, are *Inheritance*, the *Prætorian Succeſſion*, called *Bonorum Poſſeſſio*, Acquiſition by *Adrogation, Adjudication* of the Goods of a deceas'd Per-ſon, in Favour of Liberty beſtow'd upon *Slaves*; Suc-ceſſion by *Publick* and *Open Sales*, and the Succeſſion called *Miſerable*; theſe Six Ways are explain'd from the Tenth Title of the Second Book, to the Fourteenth of the Third.

As

As every Succeffion is either *Teftamentary* or *Legal*, and the *Legal* takes place only in defect of the *Teftamentary* : The Matter of *Teftaments* is explain'd from the Tenth Title of the Second Book to the End thereof, and may be reduc'd to Three principal Articles.

The Firft relates to the Four Conditions requir'd to make a *Teftament* valid ; whereof the firft is, that it be made in the Form prefcrib'd by the *Laws* ; from which, however, the *Military Teftament* is exempt : Secondly, the *Teftator* muft be intitled to the Power of making a *Will* ; Thirdly, He muft either Inftitute or Difinherit thofe Children that are under his Power ; Fourthly, He muft inftitute an *Heir* ; for without that, there can be no *Teftament* : Now the Inftitution may be to the firft, fecond, or third Degree : That in the Firft, is called properly *Inftitution* ; that in the Second or other Degree, is termed *Subftitution* ; and it is divided into *Vulgar, Pupilary,* and *Quafipupilary.*

The Second Article fhews, how many Ways a *Teftament* duly made, may afterwards become null ; which is the Subject Matter of the Seventeenth and Eighteenth Titles of the Second Book.

The Third fhews how a *Teftament* made in the Form prefcrib'd by *Law*, and not invalidated may have its Execution ; which is done by the *Heir's* entring to the Succeffion : Now this may be done feveral ways, according to the different Qualities of the *Heir* ; for fome are *neceffary Heirs*, others are both *neceffary* and *fui Hæredes,* and others *extraneous Heirs.*

The entring to Inheritance, makes the *Heir* liable not only to the Debts of the Deceas'd, but to the Deliverance of *Legacies* and *Fiduciary Bequefts* ; which are therefore the Subject of the Second Book, from the Twentieth Title to the End.

In the firft Place, the Emperor explains the Meaning of a *Legacy* ; what Actions a *Legatee* may have on Account of the *Legacy* left him ; what things may be difpos'd of by *Legacy*, and to whom : Then he fhews how *Legacies* are taken away or transferr'd ; and laftly, what Diminution they receive by the *Law Falcidia.*

As

As to *Fiduciary Bequefts,* He treats of them in the Twenty third and Twenty fourth Titles: In the Firft of thefe, He explains the Nature of the univerfal *Fiducia·y Bcqueft,* called *Inheritance* by *Fiduciary Bequeft* ; and in the other, He explains what a particular *Fiduciary Bequeft* is : After which, in the laft Title of the Book, He fpeaks of *Codicils.*

Teftamentary Succeffions, which take place before all others, being explain'd in the Fifteen laft Titles of the foregoing Book; the firft Titles of the third Book, treat of *Legal Succeffions,* which are admitted only in default of *Teftamentary.*

According to the Ancient *Law,* there were but two kinds of *Legal Heirs :* For by the Difpofition of the *Law* of the *Twelve Tables,* the *Legal,* or Succeffion to *Inteftates,* fell only to two forts of *Heirs ;* which were , firft *Hæredes fui,* or *Domeftick Heirs,* and in default of them, to the next of Kin by the *Father ;* which makes the Subject Matter of the two firft Titles of this Book.

In procefs of time, there came to be another *Legal Succeffion,* appointed by the *Senatus-Confulta Tertullianum* and *Orphitianum,* of which mention is made in the Third and Fourth Titles.

The Fifth treats of the Succeffion of *Inteftates,* to which the *Cognati* were called by the *Prætorian Law ;* every one according to the Degree of Parentage : This leads the Emperor to fpeak of the Degrees of Kindred in the Sixth Title ; after which, He confiders thofe which were excluded from this *Prætorian Succeffion,* becaufe they were no otherwife ally'd to the deceas'd, than by a fervile Relation.

The *Succeffion* of *Freemen,* is the Subject of the Seventh Title ; and the *Affignment* of *Freemen,* that of the Eighth.

After the Emperor has explain'd the Matter of *Succeffion,* which, according to the *Civil Law,* is the firft way of acquiring the Property of Things by *Univerfal Title,* He proceeds to the other Five ; which are the *Prætorian Succeffion,* called *Bonorum Poffeffio,* Acquifition by *Adrogation, Adjudication* of the Goods of a deceas'd Perfon, in favour of Liberty conferr'd upon *Slaves,* the Succeffion which accrues by *Publick Sales,* and that called; *Miferable :* All which are treated of, from the Ninth to the Fourteenth Title.

Then

Then he comes to the laſt Point relating to *Things,* viz. OBLIGATIONS; which are the Means whereby Things become due to us: Firſt he ſhews what an *Obligation* is, and the Cauſes that produce a *mix'd Obligation*; that is, partly Natural and partly Civil; as a *Contract, Quaſi-Contract, Crime* or *Offence.*

As touching *Contracts,* ſome are called *Nominate*; that is, diſtinguiſh'd by certain proper Names, authoriz'd by the *Law,* which allows them a particular Action; others are called *Innominate* Contracts, having no ſpecial Name or particular Deſignation, and are form'd only by one of the Parties, fulfilling the Agreement.

Nominate Contracts are form'd Four ways, by *delivery* of the Thing agreed for, by *ſolemn* and *formal Words,* by *Writing,* and by the ſole *Conſent* of the Contractors.

Nominate Contracts, made by the Delivery of any thing, are the *Loan, Depoſite* and *Pawn,* which are treated of in the Fifteenth Title.

Contracts made by *Words,* are called *Stipulations*; the general Principles of which, are firſt unravell'd, in order to come to the chief Diviſions of that kind of Contract.

The Firſt is of the *Stipulation* made between the Perſon who Demands, and him that Promiſes; and of that made between ſeveral that ſtipulate or promiſe.

The Second is of the *Stipulation* made by *Free Perſons* or *Slaves.*

The Third of *Stipulations* that are called *Judicial, Prætorian, Common* or *Conventional.*

The Fourth of *Stipulations* called *Uſeful,* or good in *Law*; and of *Stipulations* that are *Unuſeful.*

The Fifth is of Principal and Acceſſary *Stipulations,* called *Sureties* or *Cautions.*

The Twenty ſecond *Title* treats of *Written Contracts.*

The Five following *Titles,* explain Contracts made by the *ſole Conſent* of the contracting Perſons; which are the Contract of *Purchaſe,* of *Hire,* of *Partnerſhip,* and of the *Mandate.*

The Twenty eighth *Title* treats of *Quaſi-Contracts*; the next ſhews how *Obligations* are to be acquir'd; and the laſt, after what manner they may be exſtinguiſh'd.

Having

Having fpoken of *Obligations,* which arife from *Contracts* or *Quafi Contracts,* the Emperor proceeds in the Five firft *Titles* of the Fourth Book, to treat of *Obligations,* that fpring from *Faults* and *Quafi-Faults.*

The reft of the Book, from the Sixth *Title* to the Six-teenth, is employ'd in treating of *Actions.*

It begins with the *Definition* of an *Action,* which is fol-low'd by feveral *Divifions,* explain'd in the Sixth *Title,* ac-cording to the Chief and Principal of which, Actions are either *Real, Perfonal,* or *Mix'd.*

The Second is, of Actions deriv'd from the *Civil Law,* and fuch as have their Foundation in the *Prætorian.*

The Third is, of Actions by which the *Plaintiff* only purfues the Right of a thing belonging or due to him, and of thofe by which the Punifhment of the *Offender* is only aimed at; and of fuch Actions by which both are intended.

The Fourth Divifion, is of Actions by which the *Plaintiff* fues for the Single, Double, Treble, or Quadruple Value of the Thing he would recover.

The Fifth is of Actions of *Good Faith, Strict Law,* and *Arbitrary* Actions.

The Sixth is of Actions in which the Total of what is due is fued for, and in which the *Defendant* is either not fued for the whole, or in Confequence of which, he is condemn'd to pay only as far as his Circumftances will al-low.

After thefe Divifions of Actions are explain'd in the Sixth *Title,* the Seventh treats of certain *Prætorian Actions* which Men are liable to, and which proceed from *Contracts* made by *Slaves* or *Children* under their Power, or elfe by fuch Perfons to whom they have committed the Management of their Affairs.

The Eighth *Title* fpeaks of Actions that may be brought againft a *Mafter,* for a Fault done by his *Slave.*

The Ninth, of Actions to which the Owner is liable, for the Hurt or Damage done by a Beaft.

The tenth, directs what Perfons are to be employ'd in carrying on *Law-Suits.*

The Eleventh *Title,* treats of the Security requir'd of the Parties to a Suit, or fuch as appear for them.

The

The twelfth fets forth the Nature of temporary or perpetual Actions, and what Actions the *Law* affords to or against *Heirs* ; what thofe are which lye in their Favour, and not against them ; and laftly, thofe which are neither allow'd for nor against them.

The thirteenth treats of *Exceptions,* and the Fourteenth of *Replies.*

The Fifteenth of *Injunctions,* or *Actions* to put the Party injur'd into *Poffeffion.*

The Sixteenth declares the *Penalty* of fuch as commence Vexatious Suits.

The Seventeenth prefcribes Rules to be obferv'd by Judges, in the feveral Suits brought before them.

And the Eighteenth and laft, fhews what were the *Roman Publick Judgments,* wherein every one had free Liberty of profecuting; and of which, the Penalties were eftablifh'd by the *Laws,* called *Judiciorum Publicorum Leges.*

C H A P. XXII.

Of the Second Edition of JUSTINIAN's *Code.*

FROM what has been faid, it follows, that in 533, the Body of the *Civil Law,* compos'd by *Juftinian*'s Order, confifted only of the *Inftitutes, Digeft* and *Code ;* but the *Code* came out afterwards, with fome Alterations : Befides, abundance of New *Conftitutions* publifh'd by this Emperor, produc'd in procefs of time, a Fourth Part of that Body of *Law* now in ufe ; of which I fhall give an Account in this and the following Chapter.

In the Year of Grace 534, the Emperor *Juftinian* publifh'd another *Code,* and fupprefs'd that which was put out by his command in the Year 529. He was fenfible that in the firft, there were many ufelefs *Laws,* which decided the fame Matter ; others contrary to the prefent *Ufage,* and that fince the Publication of it, he had been oblig'd to make feveral *Ordinances,* which it was proper to infert in this Volume : And therefore, thinking it not below his Majefty

to

to correct his own Work, He reform'd the firſt, and publiſh'd an *Ordinance, De emendatione Codicis Domini Juſtiniani, & ſecunda ejus editione* ; which he directed to the *Senate* of *Conſtantinople,* to receive his *New Code* ; declaring therein his Pleaſure, that his laſt *Code* ſhould have the Force of *Law,* and intirely rejecting the former : This laſt was intitled, *Codex repetitæ prælectionis* ; that is, *Revis'd, Corrected,* and *Augmented.*

The Additions and Alterations in the *Second Code,* naturally lead me to ſpeak in this Place, of thoſe Two Sects of *Lawyers,* who began to be taken notice of in the Reign of *Auguſtus* ; and continu'd till that of the Two Brothers, *Marcus Aurelius,* and *Lucius Verus.*

Altho' this Matter was touch'd upon in the Seventeenth Chapter, I thought it the beſt way to refer to this Place the particular Explanation thereof, which I ſhall now give ; and the rather, becauſe it diſcovers the Reaſons of the greateſt part of the Alterations made by *Juſtinian* in his *Code.*

Theſe Sects were not diſtinguiſh'd by any particular Name, till long after they had carry'd their Diſputes to a great length : Thus one was called the Sect of the *Sabinians,* from *Sabinus,* who was a Favorite of the Emperor *Tiberius* ; the other had the Name of the Sect of *Proculeians,* from *Proculus,* who liv'd under *Veſpaſian.* 'Tis held, that *Atteius Capito,* who was extreamly attach'd to *Precedents* and *Old Cuſtoms,* was the Head of the *Sabinians* ; and that *Labeo,* who did not confine himſelf to Rules, but follow'd the Dictates of Reaſon and his own Underſtanding, was the Head of the *Proculeian* Sect.

Thus the *Sabinians* choſe rather to ſtick to the Deciſion of the *Law,* than any Equitable Interpretation that might be drawn from it ; and gave their *Anſwers* and *Deciſions* according to the Rules and Principles they had learnt.

The *Proculeians,* on the other Hand, without ſticking cloſe to the Rules and Principles of the *Law,* carefully examin'd all Queſtions propos'd to them ; and being rather inclin'd to follow natural Equity, than the rigorous Deciſion of the *Law,* grounded their *Anſwers* upon their own Reaſon and natural Equity ; thereby endeavouring to eſtabliſh abundance of *New Principles,* contrary to the Rules of the *Ancient Law.*

How-

However, this was not fo general, but that it frequently happen'd otherwife ; and *Juftinian,* affirming the Opinion of the one, and fometimes of the other Sect, fufficiently demonftrates, both were often agreeable to the Rules of Equity. *Atteius Capito, Mafur, Sabinus, Caffius Longinus, Cæ- lius Sabinus, Javolenus Prifcus, Aburnus Valens, Tufcianus, Salvius Julianus,* were all of the *Sabinian* Sect.

Antiftius Labeo, Nerva the Father, *Nerva* the Son, *Pega- fus, Cèlfus* the Son, and *Neratius* the Elder, were of the Sect of *Proculeians.*

Thefe two Sects continu'd till the Reign of the two Bro- thers, *Marcus Aurelius* and *Lucius Verus,* fo that all the Stu- dents of the *Law,* generally follow'd the Principles and Opi- nions either of the *Sabinians* or *Proculeians.* But the *Lawyers* who flourifh'd under thefe two Emperors, affected neither of thefe Parties ; and fome who had gone before them had done the fame, following their own Judgments, with- out any regard to either of the two Sects.

Thefe *Lawyers,* who read the Writings of the *Sabinians* and *Proculeians,* without prejudice to either, agreed with the Opinions of either Side, as they feem'd to carry in them more Reafon and Juftice ; nay, fometimes they en- deavor'd by an equal Temperature to avoid the two Ex- tremities, into which the the two Sects, thro' too great Ob- ftinacy, had fallen ; and this got them the Name of *Erifcundi,* which comes from *Erifco,* to Divide : Becaufe they made ufe of the Opinions of both Sides, in order the better to form their own.

As neither of thefe Sects wanted ftrong Reafons to fup- port their Opinions, it often happen'd, that the Judge being hard put to it to determine between them, apply'd himfelf to the Emperor for his Decifion ; and feveral Emperors have decided Queftions, upon which thefe two Sects had given contrary Opinions : But notwithftanding, there re- main'd fo great a number of Cafes contefted by the two Sects, that whilft the *Digeft* was compofing, the Emperor made feveral *Ordinances,* to decide part of them ; thefe being Fifty in number, were called *Juftinian's Fifty Decifions :* And as he thought it proper to infert them in his *Code,* fo he refolv'd at the fame time to correct it, and retrench fome *Conftitutions* which feem'd ufelefs ; ad-

ding

ding thereto thefe Fifty Decifions, and fome other 'Conftitutions, which were not in his Firft *Code.*

This new Edition of the *Code,* was publifh'd in the Year
of Chrift 534, under the Title of *Codex Juftinianeus repetitæ
prælectionis,* as is before obferv'd ; and is the fame that is
now in ufe.

As to *Juftinian's* Fifty Decifions, they being mix'd with
the reft of the *Laws,* 'tis not an eafie Matter to diftinguifh all
of them, nor are our Authors agreed upon that Point : [*See
the Treatife written by* Merillus *upon that Subject.*]

But we muft not forget that the *Inftitutes* came out in
533, and confequently before the *Code* juft now mention'd ;
which is the Reafon, that altho' the *Fiduciary Tutorfhip* of
Brothers was abolifh'd by the laft *Law, §. 1. Cod. de Legit.
hæred.* there is no notice taken of it in the *Inftitutes,* under
the Title *De Fiduciaria Tutela ;* that *Law* being pofterior to
them, and not publifh'd till 534.

C H A P. XXIII.

Of Juftinian's *latter Conftitutions, called* Novels.

DUring *Juftinian's* Life, the Body of the *Civil Law* confifted only of Three Parts, the *Inftitutes, Digeft,* and
Code ; but after his Death, the Fourth Part was compos'd
out of his *Conftitutions,* called *Novels.*

So that this Emperor's *Novels* are his laft *Conftitutions,* made
after the Publication of the Second *Code ;* and which compofe the Fourth and laft part of the *Civil Law.*

This Emperor then, made feveral *Laws* pofterior to his
Second Code, at feveral times, and upon divers Subjects, as
Occafion requir'd.

Some Interpreters have thought thefe *Conftitutions* were
called *Novels,* as introducing a *New Law,* contrary to
that of the *Digeft* and *Code :* But they have no ground
for this Opinion, fince all the *Novels* are not repugnant
to the *Laws* of thofe Two Collections ; we muft fay
with **Cujacius,** that they were fo called, *Quafi Novæ Con-
fitutiones*

ſtitutiones & poſt Codicem Juſtiniani, repetitæ prælectionis pro-
mulgatæ. In the ſame manner, ſome of the *Conſtitu-*
tions of the Emperors *Theodoſius, Valentinianus, Martianus,*
Leo, Majoranus and *Severus,* were alſo called *Novels,* becauſe they were made after the *Theodoſian Code;* in Imitation of which, *Juſtinian* gave the ſame Name to certain
Conſtitutions by him made, between the Publiſhing of the
Two *Codes; L.* 1. §. *Sed cum Novellæ C. de emendat. Cod. 1.*
Siquis filium in fine C. de inoff. Teſtam. And in ſhort, this
Name has been given to the *Conſtitutions* of ſeveral Empe-
rors who came after *Juſtinian.*

As to thoſe made by the Emperors who preceded him, it
is to be obſerv'd, they had not the Authority of *Law,* af-
ter the Collection made by his Order; He having in his
Edict for the Confirmation of the *Digeſt,* declar'd, that no
Laws or *Ordinances* which were not comprehended in the
Collection publiſh'd by his Authority, ſhould be of any
Force; forbidding all *Lawyers* to quote or make uſe of
them, and the *Judges* to have any regard thereto.

Nevertheleſs, theſe *Novels* are not altogether uſeleſs; for
as *Juſtinian's Code* was chiefly compos'd of the *Conſtitutions*
taken out of the *Theodoſian,* and the *Novels* of ſome of *Ju-*
ſtinian's Predeceſſors, they may be of great ſervice towards underſtanding thoſe of which *Tribonian* has reported
only a Part.

To return to *Juſtinian's Novels,* it is to be obſerv'd, that
this Emperor after having made his *Code,* which has in it a
vaſt number of his own *Ordinances,* was oblig'd to make
New *Laws,* upon occaſion of ſome *Caſes,* not been decided; or to abrogate the Old ones, according to the Circumſtances of the Times: For all *Laws* have their Original in the Publick Advantage, which alters according to
the preſent Variety of Circumſtances.

In ſhort, many of theſe *Novels* were made only to confirm and inforce the Ancient *Laws,* that were become obſolete, by the Alterations to which all Human Affairs are
ſubject.

Thus amongſt this Emperor's *Novels,* ſome were deſign'd
to eſtabliſh a *New Law,* others to confirm the *Law* whereof
the Uſe was uncertain; and ſome to correct the *Ancient*
Law, or reform the Whole or in Part.

H   Altho'

Altho' *Tribonian* was often employ'd in making of the *Novels*, there is room to believe, *Juſtinian* made uſe of ſeveral other Hands on thoſe Occaſions ; which is to be perceiv'd, by the Difference of the Stile they are writ in : However that be, 'tis certain he reap'd great Advantages from ſeveral of thoſe which were of his Compoſition ; and it is believ'd, He very much enrich'd himſelf by introducing a *New Law* contrary to the *Old* ; or by deciding Diſputes, upon which Suits had been before commenc'd ; which is the Reaſon that many of the *Novels* are rejected in our *Provinces*, where the *Civil Law* is receiv'd.

All theſe *Novels* were either directed to *Magiſtrates, Biſhops,* or *Citizens* of *Conſtantinople,* and were of equal Force and Authority ; foraſmuch as by thoſe directed to *Private Perſons*, they are enjoin'd to have them proclaim'd, and ſee them executed according to their Form and Tenour.

After *Juſtinian's* Deceaſe, which happen'd in the Year of Chriſt 566, in the Eighty ſecond of his Age, and Thirty ninth of his Empire, ſome part of his *Novels*, which were diſpers'd here and there, were collected and reduc'd into one Volume, together with Thirteen of his *Edicts* ; all which make up the Fourth and laſt Part of the Body of the *Civil Law.*

The greateſt part of theſe *Novels* were written in *Greek,* becauſe the Seat of the Empire was then at *Conſtantinople,* where few or none ſpoke the *Latin* Tongue in Perfection : Yet, ſome of them were publiſh'd in *Latin,* and have been taken notice of by *Antonius Auguſtinus.*

There are Four *Latin* Tranſlations of the *Novels.*

The Firſt, whoſe Author is not known, appear'd juſt after *Juſtinian's* Death, as *Contius* proves in the Preface, which he made in 1559, at the Beginning of this Collection.

Contius Alciatus and many others, call this a *barbarous Tranſlation* ; and the Famous *Du Moulin,* in his Treatiſe of *Uſury,* Q. 1. *Number* 67. ſays, That *the Author of it was not very expert in the* Latin *Tongue.* Nevertheleſs, *Cujacius* in his *Obſervations, lib.* 4. *cap* 38. commends him very much, ſhews his Learning in many Paſſages, and ſays, that his Tranſlation is better than any ſince undertaken ; He allows that many Faults have ſlipp'd into the ſeveral Editions, but imputes them to the Preſs, and not to the Tranſlator.

Leun-

Leunclavius, in Notis *ad* Parat. Autor. Græcor. *Lib.*2. Not.244. Verf. *multis in locis,* alfo proves, that this Tranflation is in many Refpects, more ample and correct than the others.

But be that as it will, 'tis no wonder this Tranflation abounds with Barbarous Expreffions and unpolite Terms, for it is made Word for Word ; which way of tranflating will not allow the Language to be either very Elegant or Polite : *Habet omnis lingua fua quædam propria genera locutionum, quæ cum in aliam linguam transferuntur videntur abfurda.* " Every Language, fays St. *Auguſtine,* has its Idioms, which " when tranflated into another feem abfurd." *Lib. de vera Relig. cap.* 50.

The Second Tranflation, which came out almoſt at the fame time as the Firſt, is a *Latin* Paraphrafe, made by *Julian,* Profeffor of *Law* at *Conſtantinople ;* who liv'd under *Juſtinian,* and feveral other fucceeding Emperors : This Abridgment, called *Julian's Novels,* confiſts only of the Decifions contained in *Juſtinian's Conſtitutions,* by way of Paraphrafe ; but is fo much the more valuable, as the Author liv'd in *Juſtinian's* Time ; and was in great Reputation at *Conſtantinople,* for his exquifite Knowledge in the *Laws.* 'Tis true, He did not follow *Juſtinian's* Order, in the Second *Law* of the *Code, De veteri Jure enucleando ;* which was to tranflate the *Laws* Word for Word, and not otherwife : Yet certainly he is very excufable, for having omitted all that was ufelefs, and kept only to the Emperor's *Decifions,* which he often explains after the beſt manner, without deviating from their genuine Sence. So that when there is any Difficulty in a *Novel,* recourfe muſt be had to this Paraphrafe, which has the Character of being very Faithful and Exact.

The Third Tranflation is that of *Haloander,* printed firſt at *Norimberg* in the Year 531, and fince re-printed at feveral Places.

The Fourth and laſt, which is very much valu'd, is that made after *Seringer's Greek* Copy, printed at *Baffe* by *Hervagius* in the Year 1561.

The Firſt, commonly called the Vulgar, is printed in the *Civil Law* Courfes, either with or without Gloffes ; the Antiquity whereof, and unanimous Confent with which all the Interpreters of the *Law* have generally receiv'd it, renders it very valuable : Befides, as all Nations acknowledge it for *Law*, when any Doubt arifes upon the Text, there is no need to have recourfe to the *Greek* Original; becaufe, as *Contius* obferves, this *Latin* Verfion was made from a *Greek* Copy, much more correct and perfect than that which we have.

The unhappy Wars and Incurfions of the *Goths* into *Italy* and *Greece,* occafion'd the utter Lofs of *Juftinian's Law*; but it was recover'd at *Malfi*; and *Irnerius*, by the Authority of *Lotharius* the Second, in the Year 1130, reftor'd the *Digeft, Code,* and *Latin* Verfion of the *Novels:* Upon which, we are to obferve, that it was very defective, and many *Novels* wanting, either becaufe they could not be found, or were quite out of Date; as being calculated for particular Places, and therefore no part of the Common or General *Law.*

This Firft Verfion, contain'd only Ninety eight *Novels*; but *Holoander* and *Seringer* made up the Number One Hundred and Sixty five, out of the *Greek* Book of *Novels*; and *Cujacius* added the Three laft, which make in all the prefent Number of One Hundred Sixty eight. *Mathew* the Monk, in his Preface, *Coll. Conftit. Eccl. Græc.* affirms, that *Juftinian* made One Hundred and Seventy; if fo, there muft have been Two loft. *Juftinian's Epitomy* contains only One Hundred and Twenty eight; amongft which, there are Four of the Emperor *Juftinus*, and Three of *Tiberius*.

This Volume was called *Authentick*, becaufe *Juftinian's* laft *Conftitutions*, therein, are of greater Authority than the reft; according to the Maxim, that when Two *Laws* are contrary one to the other, the laft Repeals the firft.

'Tis believ'd that about the Year 1140, fome Interpreter chang'd the Order they were firft plac'd in, and divided them into *Nine Collations*; which Word fignifies a Heap or Jumble of feveral things together: But what Reafon he had for making this Divifion does not appear, fince there are *Conftitutions* upon very different Matters, that have no Relation one to the other, in the fame *Collation*; and which are in no other Order, than as he that divided them pleas'd. It were to be wifh'd he had obferv'd the order of Time, by which we might have eafily diftinguifh'd thofe that made others Void; but he has thought fit to put them into Nine *Collations.*

Every

Every *Collation* is divided into feveral *Titles:* and the Number of the *Titles* of a *Collation,* do not continue in the following *Collation;* fo that the laft *Title* of the Firft, is the Sixth *Collation;* and the Second *Collation* begins with the Firft *Title,* and is not the Seventh. But all thefe *Titles* are diftinguifh'd by the Number of *Novels;* for Inftance, The Firft *Title* of the Second *Collation,* is the Seventh *Novel.*

Moft part of thefe *Novels,* confift of a *Preface,* feveral *Chapters,* and an *Epilogue.*

In the Beginning or Preface, the Emperor explains the Reafons and Motives that induc'd him to make that *Conftitution;* which is the Method obferv'd in moft of our *Royal Edicts.*

The Chapters contain feveral Decifions upon the Matter in queftion; and thefe Chapters are divided into many *Paragraphs.*

Laftly, in the Epilogue, the Emperor enjoins a ftrict Obedience to his *Conftitution,* according to its Form and Tenour; in which manner, our Kings alfo conclude their *Ordinances.*

As the *Novels* are the laft *Conftitutions* and *Laws,* they are confequently not only of very great ufe, but abfolutely neceffary to fuch as defire a compleat Knowledge of the *Roman Law. Holoander,* in his *Epiftle Dedicatory* to the *Senate* of *Norimberg,* which is at the Front of his Tranflation, amongft other things in Praife and Commendation of this Work, fays, *That he prefers it before all the Riches of Kings and Princes.*

Towards the Year 1130, a *German,* called *Irnerius,* who had ftudy'd at *Conftantinople,* re-publifh'd the firft Tranflations of the *Novels;* in the clofe perufal whereof, finding fome *Decifions,* which might relate to feveral *Laws* in the *Code;* which he compos'd *Summaries* or *Extracts* of feveral of thofe *Novels,* and inferted them in fuch Places of the *Code,* as thofe Extracts had any Relation to.

Thefe, this Author plac'd at the End of fuch *Laws* as they wholly or in part Repeal'd, or to which they made any Addition, or gave any Explanation: Thefe Summaries were called *The Authenticks,* by which Name they go at this Day. And to hinder thefe *Extracts* of the *Novels* being confounded with the *Laws* of the *Code,* they are printed in a different

Cha-

Character. Nothing can better fhew the Variations of the *Law* ; for by their means, we may at once fee the Amendments and Abolifhments of the *Laws* of the *Code*, made by the *Novels.*

From what has been faid, it follows, there is a wide Difference between the *Authentick* and *Authenticks* : The firft being applicable only to the Collections of *Juftinian's Novels,* the latter, to the *Extracts* of thofe fame *Novels* : So that when any Difficulty arifes about thefe *Authenticks*, it will be neceffary to go back to the Fountain-head from whence they fpring, in order to remove it.

The particular Account I have given of the Four Parts which compos'd the *Roman Law,* in the State it now is ; and the Care I have taken to fet down the exact Time when each of them was publifh'd, fufficiently fhew, that the *Novels* were not put out till after the other Three Collections : And therefore we ought not to be furpriz'd, there is no mention of them in the Preface to the *Inftitutes* ; which was defign'd to give an Account, of how many Parts the Body of the *Roman Law* confifted : But *Juftinian* could fay nothing of a Work, He had not then fo much as projected.

Some of thefe *Novels* are not obferv'd in *France*, even in thofe Provinces where the *Written Law* is followed ; fome, becaufe they relate to particular Matters, which being quite out of ufe, or to which we are utter Strangers, are therefore intirely ufelefs ; others, becaufe they are not agreeable to the Rules of Equity, and are thought to be dictated by *Tribonian*, as well as feveral *Laws* which bear *Juftinian's* Name ; inferted in the *Code* thro' a Spirit of *Avarice*, which the Antients lay to his Charge.

I have not here given the *Analyfis* of this Work, as of the other Parts of the *Law*, becaufe it is impoffible to make a Methodical Succeffion of the Titles which compofe it : Befides, that the fame *Novel* contains feveral Matters which have no Coherence, there is no manner of Order obferv'd in the Collection. And *Gothofredus* was oblig'd to make an Abridgment thereof, in order to put the Subject Matters of which it treats, into the fame Order with the *Code* ; which Abridgment is to be feen at the Head of his Edition of the *Novels.*

The

The Order I have propos'd, requiring I fhould fhew what Authority the Body of the *Civil Law* was of in the *Eaft* and *Weftern* Empires after *Juftinian's* Death ; the fame fhall be the Subject of the following Chapters.

CHAP. XXIV.

Of the Law obferv'd in the Eaft, *after* Juftinian's *Death.*

THE Body of *Law* compos'd by *Juftinian*, kept its ground in the *Eaft* for Three Hundred Years after his Death, without fuffering any other Alteration, than being tranflated into other Languages.

The *Digeft* and *Code* were put into *Greek* in *Juftinian's* Time ; and after the Emperor's Death, one *Theophilus* (not he that compos'd the *Inftitutes*) made a *Greek Paraphrafe* upon the fame *Inftitutes*. The *Novels* alfo, written originally in *Greek*, were tranflated into *Latin*, as is obferv'd in the preceding Chapter.

But Three Hundred Years after *Juftinian's* Death, the Body of *Law* made by his Order, with fo much Pains and Succefs, receiv'd feveral Changes, and was no longer fol-low'd in the *Eaftern* Empire.

The Bafenefs of the Emperors, and their Jealoufie of *Juftinian's* Fame, made them ftudy for a Pretence to deftroy it ; at firft they gave out, that *Juftinian's* Books were not alone fufficient, to anfwer all Difficulties that daily arofe ; and that the Method obferv'd in compiling them wanted Exactnefs : After that, they made feveral *New Ordinances*, contrary to the *Roman* Law, and introduc'd particular *Cuftoms*, with a View of abolifhing it totally.

Thefe *New Ordinances* and *Cuftoms*, furnifh'd the Emperor *Bafilius* with a Handle to make a new Body of Law, which he fet about towards the Year of Grace 880, but did not live to finifh it. *Leo*, Sirnam'd the *Philofopher*, brought it to Perfection, and divided it into Sixty Books, which he publifh'd in 886, under the Title of Βασίλικα ; in Honour,

as

H 4

as ſome think, of his Father, who was the firſt Projector; but others believe, they were ſo called, becauſe they contain an *Imperial Law*, taken partly from the latter Emperors of *Conſtantinople* ; the Word Βασιλικὸς, ſignifying *Royal* or *Imperial.* [*See the Firſt and Seventieth of* Leo's Novels, *and* Cujacius*'s Sixth Book of his Obſervat.* Chap. 9.]

    Conſtantinus Porphyrogeneta, Leo's Son, corrected, augmented, and put the *Baſilicks* into better Order : About the Year 920 he publiſh'd them ; and then they began to be in full Authority among the *Greeks* ; the Truth whereof is ſo undeniable, that *Cujacius* ſays in the Seventeenth Book of his *Obſervations,* Chap. 31. *The* Conſtitutions *of the Emperor* Leo *were of no force, but as they agreed with the* Baſilicks.

    From that time, the *Baſilicks* alone, with ſome *Epitomies* and *Abridgments* of the *Law,* and a few *Conſtitutions* of the Emperors who ſucceeded *Baſilius,* made up the whole *Law* of the *Eaſt* ; and continu'd ſo till the Reign of *Conſtantine* XIII. the laſt Emperor of the *Greeks,* in whoſe Time, *Conſtantinople* was taken by *Mahomet,* Emperor of the *Turks,* in the Year 1453 ; which put an End both to the *Eaſtern* Empire and its Laws.

    But *Juſtinian's Law* was quite laid aſide, long before, upon the Introduction of the *Baſilicks* and *Epitomies* before-mention'd ; and ſo deſirous were the Emperors of *Conſtantinople,* to give a Currency to their own *Conſtitutions,* and encourage the Vulgar Tongue of the Countrey, in which the *Baſilicks* were written, that *Juſtinian's* Books were utterly neglected, and ſcarce any Copies of them to be found in the *Eaſt,* for a long time before *Conſtantinople* was taken by the *Turks.*

    Yet, ſome impute the Loſs of *Juſtinian's* Books, to the Burning of *Conſtantinople,* under the Emperor *Zeno,* when above Six Thouſand Volumes were deſtroy'd.

    There are Two Things be remark'd of the *Baſilicks* ; The Firſt, that they were partly compos'd of *Roman Laws,* tranſlated into *Greek,* the uſe whereof had been preſerv'd in the *Eaſt* : The Second, that after the taking of *Conſtantinople* by the *Turks,* they lay hid a long time.

    Hervetus firſt publiſh'd Seven Books of them, then *Cujacius* Three more, and 'tis ſaid he had them all ; laſtly, M. *Tabrot* put out a *Greek* and *Latin* Edition of Seven Volumes in *Folio,* which is held to be compleat enough.

                                                                    The

The *Grecian Lawyers* made many *Remarks* and *Commentaries* upon the *Basilicks*, which I have made use of, as well as of those by *Accursius*.

As to the *Novels* set forth by *Leo* the *Philosopher*, there are One Hundred and Thirteen of them, which are to be found translated into *Latin* at the End of the Body of the *Civil Law*, and we make use of them in *Cases* omitted by *Justinian*.

Besides, the *Basilicks* and *Novels* of *Leo* the *Philosopher*, the *Grecians* had many *Abridgments* of their *Laws*, which were more in Credit than the *Basilicks*: The First is the Manual of *Basilius*; the Second, *Michael Ataliatus*'s Abridgment, called *The Abridgment abridg'd*; it came out in 1070. The Third is *Michael Psellus*'s Abridgment, publish'd about the same Time: The Fourth is, *The Epitomy of the Universal Law*, by *Harmenopulus*, put out about 1150. The Fifth, is the *Basilicks* of *Leunclavius*, which appear'd in 1570.

CHAP. XXV.

Of the Law observ'd in the West, *after Justinian's Death.*

THE Body of *Law* compos'd by *Justinian*, was at first only receiv'd by part of the *Western* Empire; for, except the City of *Rome*, *Sclavonia*, and some other Provinces, the *Roman* Empire had been swallow'd up by different Nations, to the most of which the *Roman Laws* were unknown; yet, in some Places, they were adopted by the *Goths*, *Burgundians*, and *Franks*; who having divided *France* among them, continu'd the use of the *Roman Law*, with a Mixture of *Laws* of their own making, suitable to their Manners and Genius; which Mixture remain'd after the Establishment of that Kingdom.

Alarick the Second, King of the *Goths*, perceiving the *Gauls* unwilling to submit to the *Gothick Laws*, order'd a Collection of the *Roman Laws* to be made for their use, which he publish'd in 506. under the Title of the *Theodosian Code*.

And

And this is the *Code* mention'd by *Agathias*, when he ſays, The *Franks* and *Germans*, regulated *Contracts* and *Marriages* by the *Roman Law* ; and that they were wont to make uſe of it in all Caſes not decided by the particular *Laws* of *France*.

The Body of *Law* compos'd by *Juſtinian*, was in a manner wholly unknown to the greateſt Part of the Weſtern Empire, till the Time of *Lotharius* II. who found the *Pandects* at *Malſi*, about the Year 1130.

But ſince that, it has been receiv'd with great Applauſe by all *Europe*, quoted at the Bar, and taught publickly in the Schools ; which ought not to be wonder'd at, being ſo agreeable to Right Reaſon and Equity, that 'tis look'd upon as the Rule of all good *Laws*, and Fountain of the true Principles of that Science : Therefore, ſeveral Nations are wholly govern'd by it, and others have recourſe to it, when their own *Laws* or *Cuſtoms* fail. But all the Nations of *Europe* agree, in admitting no other *Law* to be taught in their Univerſities ; and in ſeveral of them, the Degrees of *Doctor* or *Licentiate* in the *Law*, are indiſpenſable Qualifications to intitle Men to be *Advocates* or *Judges* ; as being the only Road to all Preferment in the Profeſſion of the Long Robe ; which ſhews the Value all Nations ſet upon this Body of *Law*, as ſoon as ever it came to their Knowledge.

This was the Fate of the *Roman Law*, after the Deſtruction of the Empire : It ſeems as if Providence had been particularly careful, in the Downfal of ſo vaſt and flouriſhing an Empire, to preſerve this perfect Model of Juſtice and Human Prudence, for the good of Mankind. Herein one cannot ſufficiently admire the Goodneſs of God, who in ſubverting the Throne of Emperors, ſtill ſupported the Empire of the *Laws* ; the very People who had ſhaken off the *Roman* Yoke, yielding to be govern'd by their *Laws* ; and even thoſe whom the *Roman* Arms had never reach'd, acknowledging the Power and Authority thereof.

Natural Equity, therefore, being the Foundation of this *Law*, inclin'd People to receive and have recourſe to it ; not thro' a Neceſſity of obeying, but Reaſon, which engag'd them voluntarily to follow it : *Non quidem ratione Imperii, ſed imperio rationis.* In effect, this *written Reaſon*, drawn from the *Law of Nature* and *Nations*, ought not to be regarded ed as the particular *Law* of the *Romans*, but as the Common *Law* of all Nations.

But tho' *Justinian*'s *Law* was unknown in the Western Empire, till the Time of *Lotharius* the Second, it must unquestionably have been known before in other Places ; of which here are some uncontestable Proofs.

In the *Capitulars* of *Charlemagne*, we find the very Terms of *Justinian*'s Seventh *Novel. De rebus Ecclesiæ alienandis vel non. Charles* the *Bald*, in his Answer to Pope *Adrian* the Second's Letter, makes use of the very Expressions in *Justinian*'s Hundred and Thirteenth *Novel.* To conclude, *Ives* of *Chartres*, in his *Decree*, quotes the *Pandects*, and gives the Definition of *Marriage*, in the very Words of the Fifth Paragraph of the Title upon that Subject in the *Institutes.*

C H A P. XXVI.

Of the Use of the Roman Law *in* France.

BEfore I explain how far the *Roman Law* is admitted in *France*, it will be proper to shew how it was first receiv'd in this Kingdom.

After the *French* had subdu'd those People who were govern'd by the *Roman Law*, they suffer'd them still to continue the use thereof: And it is observ'd of the Kings of *France*, that they were not so Ambitious of having the Title of *Glorious Protectors of Liberty*, as of deserving it : Therefore, when the *Gauls* were intirely reduc'd to their Obedience, they permitted such as were govern'd before by the *Roman Laws*, to make use of them still.

Nay, it is held, that every one who commenc'd a Suit, was oblig'd by the *Ordinances* of our first Kings, to declare at the Beginning of the Process, by what *Law* he design'd to pursue it. And it is also pretended, that certain Forms were prescrib'd by order of those Kings, to govern all Actions either according to the *Salick* or the *Roman Law* ; and that *Judges* Learned in both, were appointed to determine
Dif-

Difputes, by the Rule of that *Law* to which the contending Parties were fubject.

The *Roman Laws*, which at firft were known only in a few Places in this Kingdom, in time fpread themfelves over other Provinces, which, till then, were wholly govern'd by their own particular *Laws* and *Cuftoms*, by reafon of the few *French Laws*, and their infufficiency to decide all Cafes that arofe: And as the *Roman Law* at all times had that great Authority which it deferves, and was even follow'd by many of the Nations the *French* had conquer'd, it was eafily communicated to the reft, fo that it was univerfally receiv'd in this Kingdom, but the ufe of it, in the feveral Provinces, has varied very much.

The Kingdom of *France* is divided into Provinces, fome of which are called the Country of the *Written Law*, and thers that of the *Cuftomary Law*.

Thofe of the *Written Law*, are fuch as being in the Neighbourhood of *Italy*, were firft conquer'd by the *Romans*, and laft by the *French*, and had no other *Law* but the *Roman* at the Time they were fubdu'd.

The Neighbourhood of *Italy*, not only gave them the Conveniency of ftudying, but alfo an Inclination of conforming themfelves to them. We reckon in the Number of thefe Provinces *Guyenne, Provence, Dauphiné*, and others; in a Word, all thofe which are Dependant upon the Parliaments of *Tholoufe, Bordeaux, Grenoble, Aix*, and *Pau*, and feveral Provinces which depend upon the Parliament of *Paris, viz.* the *Lyonnois, Forreft*, the *Bauiolois*, and a great part of *Auvergne*.

As the People of thefe Provinces, were unwilling to fubmit to other *Laws*, than thofe to which they had been accuftomed; they obtain'd, thro' fpecial Favour of our Kings, the Liberty of following the *Roman Law*, in Matters not determin'd by the *Ordinances*; and tho' many *Cuftoms* that were different from the *Roman Law* have been introduc'd among them, they are not very Oppofite, nor of very great Extent: Befides, thefe *Cuftoms* are only obferv'd in thofe Places where they were inttroduc'd, and none of thefe Provinces have any other *Common Law* but the *Roman*.

But

But this is thro' the Prince's special Grant ; for every one knows, conquer'd Nations can have no other *Law* but that of the Conqueror ; nor any Power to make, adopt, or even retain their own *Laws,* without his leave : From whence it must be concluded, that the *Roman Law* does not derive its Authority in these Provinces from the Authors thereof ; but from the Grant of our Princes, who have thought fit to indulge their Subjects the Use of it. It is the same with *Customs,* which have not the Force of *Law* in the other Provinces, but by virtue of the Royal Authority, from whence they receive their Virtue.

In the Provinces of the *Written Law, Contracts, Wills,* and all kind of Affairs, are intirely regulated according to the *Roman Law :* And altho' some of them have been dismember'd from the Parliament of *Bordeaux,* and brought under the Jurisdiction of that of *Paris,* they have still had their *Law* preserv'd ; and all Disputes relating to them, altho' in the Parliament of *Paris,* are decided according to the *Roman Laws.*

The *Customary* Country, is the Provinces where the *Roman Law* is not receiv'd as *Law* ; being govern'd by their own particular *Usages,* which in process of Time, were reduc'd into Writing, by the Authority of our Kings. They are called *Customary,* because their *Customs* are their *Common Law* ; and the *Roman Law* is consider'd by them, only as *written Reason.*

In effect, the *Roman Law* not having been brought into those Provinces, till after a long time, was not adopted by them as a *Law,* which they were oblig'd to follow, but admitted as *written Reason,* to which they had recourse, when their own *Customs,* and the *Royal Ordinances* were silent.

The *Roman Law,* notwithstanding, is of very great use in the *Customary* Provinces ; and the Study of it there, no less requisite for a *Judge* or *Advocate,* than in the Countrey of the *Written Law :* For in Cases omitted by their *Customs* or *Ordinances,* they are oblig'd to consult and take their Measures from the *Roman Law,* in order to make their Determinations Just and Equitable : So that 'tis a Mistake to imagine, when the *Ordinances* and *Customs* have made no Provision, the Judge may give what Sentence he pleases ; and besides, it is contrary to the Nature of *Judgments,* which are to be govern'd by Certain and Uniform Rules ; and to
the

the Practice of many Ages, as well as the Opinion of our best Authors.

Such an Arbitrary way of proceeding, would introduce a dangerous *Ignorance* into our Courts, and disconcert the the whole *Judicature* : And indeed, to what can we more properly have recourse, than the *Roman Law*, which is the *Civil Law* of all well-govern'd Nations ; and the Light that informs our Understanding ; without which, our natural Faculties in most sorts of Business, would be nothing but Darkness and Confusion : Therefore, a Judge should be well stock'd with *Right Reason*, I mean, the *Roman Law*, which is the true Source thereof.

The Judicious *Coquille*, one of the most Learned Interpreters of our *Customary Law*, says in his Preface to the *Customs* of *Nivernois*, " That the *Roman Law* ought only to " be regarded as *Reason* ; He adds, That the *Romans* excell'd " both in *Arms*, and making *Good Laws*, for Govern- " ing their People in time of Peace : And therefore, we " ought to make use of them, in default of our *Ordinances* " and *Customs*." Which is also the Opinion of *Mornac*, one of our most celebrated *Lawyers* ; who says, " That where " *Custom* has determin'd nothing, *Tunc ad jus commune &* " *Romanum confugimus*.

Loyseau, a very famous Author, in his Treatise upon Forfeitures of Copy-hold Estates, says, That the *Roman Law* is the *Common Law* of *France* ; and it was a Maxim in his time, That Cases omitted by the *Customs*, ought to be decided by the *Roman Law*. So that before the *Custom* of *Paris* be extended to others, we ought first to examine, if the Question be not decided by the *Roman Law*.

M. *le Pretre* says, " That as the Emperor *Antoninus* said, " the Earth was govern'd by his *Laws*, and the Sea by " those of the *Rhodians*, as far as they were not repugnant " to his ; so the *Roman Law* governs in *France*, when the " *Customs* and *Ordinances* are not contrary thereto.

Charondas, in his *Answers*, the famous *Argentre*, and M. *Ricard*, all say, " We do not consider the *Roman Law* as " an absolute *Law*, which of Necessity we are to obey ; " but we admit the Reason therein contain'd ; and be- " cause of its great Equity, make use of it in default of " our *Customs* and *Ordinances*, to govern our Determinati- " ons as far as our *Usage* will allow.

But

But befides the Solidity of the Principles, and Equity which is obferv'd to be in all the *Roman Laws,* and from which it would be dangerous to deviate, there is another Reafon, that makes the Study of it abfolutely neceffary even in the *Cuftomary* Countries ; which is, that the *Roman Law* is univerfal, and comprehends the Decifion of almoft every Cafe that can poffibly arife ; whereas, the *Regulations* of the *Ordinances* and *Cuftoms,* are confin'd to fo narrow a Compafs, that they are fcarce fufficient to determine one Fourth of the Cafes that arife : So that the Decifion of the reft, which are without Comparifon far the greateft part, depend abfolutely upon the *Civil Law* ; by which the Judges ought to give their Decifions, when it is conformable with Equity and Reafon ; elfe it would be ufelefs, to oblige Officers of Judicature to anfwer upon *Law-Queftions,* before they can be admitted ; and to qualifie themfelves with that Science, if the Study thereof would be of no ufe to them, in the Exercife of their Employments, nor obferv'd as *Law* in their Determinations.

By the *Ordinances,* our Kings are contented to lay down general Rules for the Good Government of their Kingdom, to regulate the Power and Duty of their Officers, and cut off the dilatory Courfes of the *Law,* by prefcribing certain Rules for the Proceedings : So that the greateft part of the *Ordinances,* relate rather to the manner of carrying on the Procefs, than the Decifion thereof.

Our *Cuftoms* are almoft all limited, to particular Matters, of which the *Roman Laws* take no cognizance ; as *Fiefs, Seignoral Rights,* the Community of *Goods,* between married Perfons ; the *Right* of *Redemption, Noble* and *City Ward,* and fome others.

On the other Hand, the *Roman Law* directs all Matters relating to *Contracts, Tutorships, Reftitution* to the *firft State, Obligations, Actions,* and a vaft Number of other Matters, which are either not at all mention'd, or very lightly touch'd upon in the *Ordinances* and *Cuftoms.*

Befides, it cannot be deny'd, but that in the Matters treated of both in the one and the other, there are many Articles borrow'd, or in Imitation of the *Roman Law:* From whence it follows, that neither the *Cuftoms* nor *Ordinances* can be rightly underftood, without the Help of the *Roman Law;* in refpect of the Relation moft of them have thereto.

thereto. Therefore, all our *French Lawyers* have fill'd their Commentaries with *Roman Laws*, to fupport their own Opinions ; and it was not poffible for them to do otherwife, becaufe both *Ordinances* and *Cuftoms*, are for the moft part taken from thofe *Laws*.

It is alfo certain, the *Roman Law* is the Model by which the beft *Ordinances* of our Kings have been made ; and to which, confequently, recourfe muft be had for their Explanation. And, as they always employ'd the ableft Men in that *Law*, to draw up their *Ordinances*, 'tis no wonder they have fuch a Refemblance of that which their Authors were fo full of.

It muft alfo be agreed, that our *Cuftoms* have been partly taken from the Principles of the *Roman Law* ; for in the Method they are at prefent, one may eafily obferve, they are nothing elfe but a Mixture of different *Laws*, which our Kings of the *Firft Race* fuffer'd their Subjects to ufe, as they faw beft. Now amongft thefe, the *Roman Law* was follow'd in many Particulars, and all the reft had a great deal borrow'd from it ; from whence it is called, the *Mother of the Laws* : And our *Interpreters* have always made ufe of it in their *Commentaries* upon our *Cuftoms*, as the only Means to difcover their true Sence ; whether it be upon Account of the Footfteps of the *Roman Law*, which are to be obferv'd in moft of them, or Exactnefs of the Principles which is peculiar to it.

It muft then be agreed, that our *Cuftoms* have been taken partly from it ; and that it is always made ufe of to interpret them : Wherefore, thofe who are moft skill'd in the *French Law*, confefs, that the greateft Part of our *Cuftoms*, are nothing elfe but *Confirmations, Extenfions, Derogations*, and *Reftrictions* of the *Roman Law* ; to underftand which, a perfect Knowledge thereof is abfolutely neceffary, in regard our *Cuftoms* touch but very lightly upon Matters determin'd by the *Roman Law*.

For Inftance, the *Cuftom* of *Paris* fays, in *Article* 185. That *Compenfation takes place in a clear and liquid Debt, of another equally clear and liquid* ; which agrees with the *Roman Law* : But it does not treat of the *Queftions* that may arife upon that Subject. All the Sixth Title of that very *Cuftom* treats of *Prefcriptions* ; but there are a vaft Number of *Queftions* whereof it makes no mention, and which muft be be decided by the *Roman Law.* And if we obferve, thofe who were employ'd in reducing or reforming our *Cuftoms,* have treated at large of thofe Matters only, which are unknown to the *Roman Law* ; taking very little notice of what is decided therein : By that means, pointing out to us, that we are to look for the *Decifion* thereof in the *Roman Law.*

The fame Obfervation holds good in the *Ordinances,* when they fpeak of Matters decided by the *Roman Law,* 'tis only *En paffant* : For Example, the *Ordinance* of *Lewis* the Twelfth, of the Month of *July,* 1510. mentions the Caufes of *Reftitution* introduc'd by the *Civil Law* ; but gives no Explanation thereof, which we are to look for there : And indeed, if *Reftitutions* to the *Firft State,* are the mere Invention of the *Roman Laws,* Why fhould we not have re- courfe to the fame in Matters of this kind ; fince it would be often impoffible to decide them as we ought, if we va- ry'd from them ?

'Tis true, as I have taken notice in another Place, our Kings in this Cafe, order us to feek our Remedy by *Royal Letters* ; but they do not require the Judge to obey them, without Cognizance of the Caufe, unlefs the *Damage* fugge- fted, upon which the faid *Letters* were granted, appears ve- ry plain. But pray, what Damage ? Why the very fame that is deduc'd and pronounc'd by the *Roman Laws.*

There was formerly a Famous Difpute between Mr. *Pe- ter Lizet* and Mr. *Chriftopher de Thou,* concerning the Au- thority of the *Roman Law,* in the *Cuftomary* Countries of *France* : The firft maintain'd, it ought to be receiv'd as *Common Law,* where the *Cuftoms* were filent ; and that the defect of a *Local Cuftom,* ought not to be otherwife fup- ply'd. On the contrary, the other was of Opinion, that the *Roman Law* ought to have no other Force than as *Written Reafon,* which might be follow'd, or not, as was convenient ; and that for want of a *Decifion* of any Cafe, recourfe was to be had, rather to the Neighbouring *Cuftoms* than to the *Roman Law.*

But to fpeak impartially, this was a Queftion rather a- bout the Name than the Thing it felf ; fince *Reafon* is the Soul of the *Law,* and the Rule of all *Determinations* : So that altho' the *Roman Law* were not to be regarded in the *Cuftomary* Countries, as a *Law* to which we were abfolute y

I   oblig'd

oblig'd to submit; if it be receiv'd as a Rule to guide our *Judgments*, does it not follow that a Judge ought to have recourse thereto, so far as it is agreeable to Equity, and may serve to determine the Dispute in Hand?

As to the Question, whether upon failure of the *Custom* of a Place, we should have recourse to Neighbouring *Customs*, or to the *Roman Law*, I think there is a Medium to be observ'd therein: In Matters that are merely *Customary*, the Neighbouring *Customs* or that of *Paris* may be consulted; but in such as are directly deriv'd from the *Roman Law*, there can be no difficulty in the *Customary* Countries to have recourse to the *Civil Law*; not as the *Common Law*, since it is not so in those Parts of *France*, but as *Written Reason*, and as the Opinions of the most Learned and Wisest Men that ever liv'd; to whose Judgments that Deference is due.

Thus, as the *Roman Law* treats of abundance of Matters, not at all or but very lightly mention'd in our *Customs*, we may well say, that in such Matters the *Roman Law* is the *Common Law* of the *Customary* parts of *France*; but improperly, because the Judges are not oblig'd absolutely to follow it; and if they do, 'tis thro' *Reason* and not *Necessity*: Which has made *Brodeau* say, in his *Preface* to the *Customs* of *Paris*, " That the *Custom* of *Paris* is not easily ex-" tended to others, in Matters that have their Original " and Foundation in the *French Law*, or partake of the " *Common* or *Universal Law*: Such as the *Formality* in ma-" king of *Wills*, the *Legitime*, and others of the same Na-" ture, not thoroughly discuss'd by our *Customs*; in which " Case, this Author says, recourse must be had to the *Ro-* " *man Law*.

We may also say, that our *Customs*, out of their own *Districts*, are not properly the *Common Law* of the *Customary* Parts of *France*, in *Customary* Matters; especially in the Neighbouring Provinces: Nor are the Judges absolutely oblig'd to make it the Rule of their Determinations, in Cases that are omitted by the *Customs* of the Place, for any other Reason, than that the *Proximity* of *Places*, and near *Scituations* and *Climates*, naturally produce a *Similitude* of *Inclinations* and *Manners*.

Let us therefore conclude, that as to Matters of the *Roman Law*, tho', from what we have faid before, the Judges are not abfolutely oblig'd to make it their Guide; neither ought they to deviate from it, when it agrees with Reafon and Equity: For not to make ufe of it as a *Common Law*, to fupply the Defects of the *Municipal Laws*, would be to leave moft Caufes undecided; and by that means, intrdouce a kind of ambulatory and fluctuating Juftice.

A more proper Occafion, doubtlefs, could not offer, to fet forth the Excellence of the *Roman Laws*, and the Neceffity all *Judges* and *Advocates* are under to make themfelves Mafters thereof, even in the *Cuftomary* Countries; but this Subject deferves a feparate Treatife, wherefore I fhall make a particular Chapter of it, after having explain'd the *Decretal Super-fpecula, titulo Decretalium Privilegiis;* and the Sixty ninth *Article* of the *Ordonnance* of *Blois.*

CHAP. XXVII.

The Decretal Super-fpecula *explain'd.*

AS fome have upon very flender Grounds advanc'd, that teaching of the *Civil Law* publickly in the Univerfity of *Paris*, was prohibited for a confiderable Time; I thought it would be proper to fhew they are miftaken, and that the Publick Exercife of the Study of the *Roman Law*, was never difcontinu'd in this Chief Univerfity of the Kingdom; either after the *Decretal Super-fpecula*, or even after the *Ordonnance* of *Blois:* This was a Point that feem'd to challenge a Place in this Work; wherein I propos'd to infert every thing that any ways regarded the Hiftory of the *Roman Law*, and fully fatisfie the Curiofity of the Reader in that particular.

No fooner were the *Pandects* difcover'd, than they were admir'd by all Nations; and from that time, the *Law* compos'd by *Juftinian* has been publickly profefs'd in the City of *Paris.*

Irnerius

Irnerus was the Firſt, who read Publick Lectures upon. it at *Bologna* in *Italy* ; from which Place, abundance of *Lawyers* diſpers'd themſelves all over *Europe.*

In *France*, it was firſt taught at *Paris*; where, about the ſame Time, there appear'd Three Great Men, who reduc'd the Study of Three of the moſt uſeful Sciences into a certain Method ; *viz. Peter Lombart, Theology* ; *Gratian,* the *Canon-Law* ; and *Peter Comeſtor,* or the *Eater,* the *Sacred Hiſtory* : All theſe Sciences were greatly encourag'd in that Capital City, from their firſt Appearance ; and probably, were the Occaſion of founding the Univerſity of *Paris.*

So that notwithſtanding there can be no *Act* produc'd before the Year 1199, from whence the Incorporation of *Doctors* into a *Community* in this City may be prov'd; it cannot be doubted, but theſe Sciences were long before cultivated, and even from the Time of *Lewis le Gros,* who began his Reign in 1108.

Rigord, Chaplain to *Philip* the *Auguſt,* remarks, that in his Time, the Number of Learned Men was greater than ever it had been, either in *Rome, Athens, Alexandria* or *Egypt,* which were the moſt famous Theatres of Learning ; as he mentions the *Civil Law,* we may conclude, not only that, but the *Canon Law,* was allow'd by the Prince to be taught in the Univerſity of *Paris,* from the Time of its Foundation.

Nay, the *Civil Law* had more Students than any other Science ; for not only the *Laity,* but abundance of *Churchmen* follow'd it with great Application : The Truth is, moſt of the Eccleſiaſticks and Religious Perſons, left the Study of *Divinity* and the *Canon Law,* to follow either the *Civil Law* or *Phyſick* ; under pretence of qualifying themſelves to manage the Affairs of their reſpective Societies, or the better to help and adminiſter to the Sick ; but they were often reproach'd with Inſincerity, and told that it was a Worldly View or Self-Intereſt, or a vain Affectation of Reputation, that made them ſo diligent in the Study of prophane Sciences.

To put a Stop to this Irregularity, which daily increas'd, the Council of *Tours,* where *Alexander* III. preſided, in the Year 1163. made an Order, *That no profeſs'd Religious Perſon, ſhould leave the Convent he belong'd to, with a Deſign of Studying either* Law *or* Phyſick; which *Deciſion* of the Eighth
Canon

Canon of that Council, is reported under the Title *Ne Clerici vel Monachi fecularibus negotiis fe immifceunt.*

After that, Pope *Honorius* III. thinking himfelf oblig'd to renew that Prohibition, in the Fourth Year of his *Papacy*, which was in 1219, made that famous *Decretal* beginning with thefe Words, *Super-fpecula.*

The Drift of this *Epiftle*, was to encourage the *Regulars* and other Ecclefiaftical Perfons, to read the *Holy Scriptures*, being, as the fame Pope often hints, the Study which beft. fuited their Profeffion ; but as it relates to Three Points, which are divided into fo many different Titles, in the *Decretal* of *Gregory* IX. the Sence of its Author has been in fome meafure mifapply'd.

The firft *Article*, which is in the laft *Chapter* of the *Decretal Titulo ne Clerici vel Monachi fæcularibus negot. fe immifceant*, orders, in explaining the Council of *Tours*, That the *Bifhops* fhould declare fuch Religious Perfons as ftudy'd *Law* and *Phyfick* in their refpective Dioceffes, to ftand *Excommunicated* ; and it extends the *Penalties* appointed by the Council of *Tours*, to *Arch-Deacons, Deans, Curates, Provofts, Chanters*, and other *Clerks* belonging to any *Chapter*, and even to *Priefts.*

In the Second Part, which is reported in the laft Chapter of the *Decretal Titulo de Magiftris, Honorius* orders, That in purfuance of the *Decree* of the General Council, that is, the Fourth *Lateran Council*, there fhould be in every Metropolitan Chŭrch a *Profeffor of Divinity*, with a Salary equal to a *Prebend*, to inftruct the Poor *Clerks* in that Science.

And to the End that fuch Ecclefiafticks might not be taken off from that Study, by following the *Secular Laws*, the Third Part of the *Epiftle*, which is the famous Chapter *Super-fpecula* 28. *Extra de Privilegiis*, prohibits the Study of the *Laws* in the City of *Paris*, and adjacent Places.

If this *Epiftle* had been preferv'd in it natural order, in the *Decretals* of *Gregory* IX. the Author's Intention by this laft *Article*, had been eafily underftood, by the Coherence thereof with the preceding Parts ; which is calculated only to regulate the Study of *Churchmen.*

But the Compiler, having divided this *Conftitution* into feveral *Articles*, according to the different Matters to which, in his Judgment, they relate, it has happen'd that the latter Part, which in reality refpects *Ecclefiaftical Perfons* only,

I 3   being

being feparately taken, paffes upon the World for a general
Prohibition, including all Ranks of Men.

For how is it poffible, if it be confider'd as belonging to the
Firft Part of the *Decretal*, not to perceive it no otherwife regards the *Civil Law*, than by extending the Prohibitions of
the Council of *Tours*, which reach only the *Religious*, to all
Ecclefiafticks in general, from applying themfelves to this
Study, to the neglect of thofe Sciences which feem to be their
proper Bufinefs : And the Reafon why thofe of *Paris* are
mention'd, is only becaufe the Sciences flourifh'd moft there
at that Time.

Befides, the Reafon of this *Decretal's* mentioning the
Univerfity of *Paris*, was, becaufe it was then the only one
in *France* ; for that at *Tholoufe*, which comes next to it in
Antiquity, was not founded till 1230 ; Eleven Years after the Promulgation of this *Conftitution* ; and all the reft
fince the Year 1300.

We have, befides, fubftantial Proofs to fhew, that this
Decretal, in the Article *Super-fpecula*, was only intended a-
gainft Ecclefiaftical Perfons.

For, the Pope, having no *Temporal Jurifdiction* within ano-
ther Prince's Dominions, how could his Prohibitions to read
or ftudy the *Civil Law*, extend to any other than *Ecclefiafticks*.
The Diftinction which the *Law of God* makes between the
Temporal and *Spiritual* Power, fhews evidently, that fuch a
Prohibition would have been an open Invafion of the *Royal
Authority*.

Befides, how could fuch a *Decree* be regifter'd in the
Reign of a Prince fo powerful and tender in thofe Matters
as *Philip* the *Auguft*: Every Body knows, that all *Bulls*
and *Conftitutions* from the *Holy See*, even thofe that relate to
Ecclefiaftical Matters, as well as the *Regulations* of *General
Councils*, are of no force in this Kingdom till they have been
duly confirm'd in Parliament, in purfuance of his Majefty's
Letters Patents.

But to remove this Difficulty, 'tis pretended, that Pope
Honorius had not made this Prohibition, but at the Requeft
of *Philip* the *Auguft*, forafmuch as the *Sovereignty* of the Kings
of *France* feem'd to be diminifh'd, by Reading the *Civil
Law* in the Univerfity of *Paris*.

To

To this it is anſwer'd, if the King had been of that Opinion, he needed not the Pope's Aſſiſtance, to make ſuch a Prohibition, which was abſolutely in his own Power.

Beſides, is it likely the Pope would excommunicate all the Laity, for Diſobedience in a Matter that is neither of a *Spiritual* or *Criminal* Nature ; eſpecially ſince that Puniſhment is reſerv'd for the moſt heinous Crimes ?

The Pope therefore, could not give this Prohibition in *Paris,* for any other than the Religious and Eccleſiaſtical Perſons, whoſe Duty it is, to make the *Holy Scriptures* and the *Canon Law* their principal Study, in order to acquit themſelves worthily in their reſpective Stations.

As the Matter in Queſtion was of great Importance, being to recal them to the Study of *Divinity* and of the *Canons,* which they had forſaken for *Phyſick* or the *Civil Law;* it was neceſſary for that End to make uſe of all the Severity of Eccleſiaſtical Penalties : But ſince the *Churchmen* betook themſelves of their own accord, to the Study of thoſe Sciences which ought to have the Preference with Them, our Divines have been ſo far from diſcouraging them to Study the *Civil Law,* that they have exhorted them to it, as a part of Learning which might not only be of great uſe to them, in examining Caſes of *Conſcience,* but alſo in underſtanding many of the *Canons.*

We need only read the Inſcription of the *Decree Super-ſpecula,* and join its Concluſion to the Beginning, to be convinc'd, that the Pope never intended his Prohibition ſhould extend to the Laity. It cannot be deny'd, that the Pope's *Epiſtles,* as well as *Letters* and *Reſcripts* of Princes, which are iſſu'd for the Explanation or Eſtabliſhing any thing, are generally directed to thoſe who are to look after the Execution, or are otherwiſe concern'd : From whence it follows, that if it had been the Pope's Intentions to oblige all Orders of Men by this *Decree* to abſtain from reading the *Civil Law* at *Paris,* He would have directed it either to the *King* or the *Magiſtracy,* who could have inforc'd the Execution of it among the *Laity ;* or elſe to the *Regent Doctors* who might have done it in their *Schools ;* yet it is addreſs'd to the *Chapter* of the Church of *Paris,* and other Prelates dwelling there, as *Conçius, Ciranius,* and the *Roman Correctors* report.

This

This Direction is to thofe only, who had Jurifdiction over the *Priefts* and *Monks*; and were themfelves under an Obligation of obferving the Prohibition, as well as making others do it; for the Word *Prelate* here, fignifies not only *Bifhops*, but *regular Abbats, Deans, Provofts,* and all others who had *Spiritual Jurifdiction.*

Nor is it lefs manifeft, from the Body of this *Epiftle*, that this *Decree* relates only to *Religious Perfons* and *Priefts,* if it be laid altogether, and the latter compar'd with the former Parts; which is a Rule the *Lawyers* prefcribe for interpreting all *Laws*: In fhort, to underftand the true Meaning of it, it muft not be taken by Scraps and Pieces, but confider'd intire, and in the Literal Coherence one Part has with the other; by which means, it will foon be difcover'd, that the *Decree* relates only to Ecclefiaftical Perfons, and that the latter Part thereof cannot be extended to the Laity.

The Motive alfo of the other *Conftitution,* is another Argument to fhew, that the Defign of it was to regulate the Study of the *Ecclefiafticks*; the Pope alledging no other Reafon for his making it, than to encourage the Study of the *Holy Scriptures.*

Now, methinks, it cannot be pretended that his Intention was to make the *Scriptures* the only Object of the Study of the Laity of *Paris.*

'Tis objected, that the Terms of this *Conftitution* are General; and enjoin *Ne quifquam,* That no Perfon whatfoever fhould prefume to Teach or hear the *Civil Law* read at *Paris.* To this it is anfwer'd, that *Verba intelligenda, funt pro fubjecta materia*: Thus the Terms, *Nullus, Quifquam, Omnis,* &c. tho' they feem General, and to comprehend all kind of Perfons and Places, are neverthelefs to be underftood conditionally; and with fuch Reftrictions as Reafon and Circumftances require: This is a Rule which the *Laws* themfelves teach. Now amongft thefe Conditions, the moft neceffary, is, that thofe who are comprehended in any *Law* or *Ordinance,* fhould be fubject to the Jurifdiction of him that makes it; and in that Point which the *Conftitution* goes upon: For no Man is oblig'd to obey another, who commands a thing out of his own *Diftrict,* or for which he has no competent Power. From whence it follows, that when the Pope faid *Ne quifquam prefumat,* His Intention by thofe General Terms, was only to bind all Ecclefiaftical

Perfons

Perfons mention'd in the former Part of his *Epiftle*, and over whom only he could exercife his Authority in that Particular.

Let us now fee if this *Decree* was ever obferv'd in refpect of the Laity, and whether the Prohibition it contains of teaching the *Civil Law* publickly at *Paris*, was put in Execution ; for every one knows that the Pope's *Decrees* have not the Force of *Laws* amongft us, till they are authoriz'd by *Ufage*, having firft been duly accepted and regifter'd.

Rigord, who was a Cotemporary Author, and out-liv'd *Philip* the *Auguft*, proves, that in his Time the *Civil Law* was not only allow'd by the King to be taught at *Paris*, as well as other Sciences, but with extraordinary Privileges.

We find in Hiftory, that the *Doctors* and *Scholars* of the Univerfity of *Paris*, having had fome Difguft given them by the *Townfmens* infringing their Privileges, in the Beginning of the Reign of St. *Lewis*, difpers'd themfelves into feveral Places both in *France* and the neighbouring Countries. Pope *Gregory* the Ninth, who thought it neceffary to preferve the Univerfity of *Paris*, contriv'd, in Conjunction with St. *Lewis*, to induce the greateft part of thofe Doctors to return to *Paris*, in the Year 1231 ; and amongft the reft, the Profeffors of the *Civil Law*. [*Videndus Navigius Bern. Guido. in Chro. Rom. Pontif. & Gregorium IX. in Epift. ad Raynaldum in Annal. Ecclef. ad ann.* 1228, & 1231.]

Several Authors make mention of an Oath of Fidelity taken to Queen *Blanche*, Mother of St. *Lewis*, as Regent, by the Univerfity of *Paris* ; and particularly, by the *Doctors of Law*, and *Batchellors*, who under them read the *Decretals* or the *Civil Law* : This was in the Year 1251, and confequently, Thirty two Years after the Publication of Pope *Gregory's Decretals*, and fo after his Death.

The *Statutes* of the *Faculties of Law* at *Paris*, prove alfo, that the *Decretal Super-fpecula* did not all interrupt the Study of the *Civil Law* in that *Faculty* ; they were made in the Year 1296, which was the Eleventh of *Philip* the *Handfome*, and renew'd upon reforming that Univerfity, a long time after.

It appears by thefe new *Statutes*, there were at that time *Batchellors* in the *Civil* as well as the *Canon Law*, and they prefcribe the fame Rules for both,

The ancient Regifters of the *Deanaries* of the fame *Faculty*, take

take notice of the Names of thoſe who were *Graduates in Jure Canonico tantum, vel in Legibus tantum, ſeu in Jure Civili, aut in utroque Jure.* Several old *Acquittances* of the Monks of St. *John de Lateran* ſhew, that they receiv'd from the *Faculty* the *Annual Stipend* allow'd them for ſaying Maſs in their Church.

All our Regiſters teſtifie, that ſince the *Decretal Super-ſpecula,* there have been continually Publick Lectures of *Civil* and *Canon Law* in our *Faculty*; and the Names of ſuch as underwent thoſe Laborious Functions being regiſter'd, we may eaſily obſerve, the greateſt part of them have been Perſons remarkable for their Birth, Perſonal Merit, as well as great Offices to which they were advanc'd. The great Number of them will not allow me to give an Account of all; but ſome I ſhall take notice of.

In our firſt Regiſter, amongſt others, we find the Name of *Miles de Irliers,* who was *Counſellor* to the Parliament, *Arch-Deacon,* and at length, in 1459, made *Biſhop* of *Chartres*; of *John Courcelles, Counſellor* to the Parliament, *Canon* and *Arch-Deacon* of *Joſas,* in the Church of *Paris*; of *Martin de Freſnes* alſo, *Counſellor* in the Parliament of *Paris.*

In the ſecond Regiſter, amongſt others, we have the Names of *Amboiſe de Cambray,* Maſter of *Requeſts,* Son of *Adam de Cambray,* Firſt-Preſident, who was employ'd by *Lewis* the Eleventh in ſeveral Embaſſies; of *Nicholas de Conty,* Precentor of *Amiens*; of *James Juvius, John du Plais, John Picard* and *Robert Luller,* all Four *Counſellors* in the Parliament of *Paris*; and of *John Seguyer,* who in the Year 1480, was made *Counſellor* of the Parliament of *Tholouſe.* The ſame Regiſter has alſo the Names of *Robert Gaguin,* afterwards Firſt-Preſident; of *Reguard de la Vaquerie,* alſo Firſt-Preſident; of *Claudius de Hangeſt, Counſellor* in the Parliament of *Paris*; and of *Nicholas d'Origny, Canon* of *Troyes,* and *Preſident* of the Parliament.

In the third Regiſter, among other *Regent-Doctors,* are *Martial Galiciere, Arch-Deacon* of *Meaux, Canon* of *Paris,* and *Preſident* of the Parliament in 1525; *Peter Parpas, Counſellor,* afterwards *Preſident* of the Great Council; *Philip le Boindre, Counſellor*; *Peter le Clerc, Embaſſador* of *Francis* I. at the Council of *Trent:* Theſe laſt were Collegues with *John Rebuffe, John Quintin, John Vadel,* and for ſome time of *Anthony le Conte,* all famous Men in the Profeſſion of the *Law.*

Beſides

Befides thefe, there were feveral other *Regent Doctors,* who were *Counfellors* in the Parliament, and whofe Names are fet down in the Regifter; as *Francis de Marillac, William de Boucherat, Charles le Fevre, Anthony le Cirier,* and many others.

We learn from the fame Regifters, that M. *Henry de Mefmes,* Deputy to one of the *Regent-Doctors,* read Lectures in the Schools upon *Juftinian's Inftitutes,* in the Year 1551 ; and that in the Year 1556, M. *John Chevalier,* who was afterwards Firft-Prefident of the Court of *Aids,* read Lectures there publickly, upon the Title *De Actionibus* ; having firft difputed, in order to be made Deputy to M. *Peter le Clerc,* Regent-Doctor.

And if *Rome* and *Conftantinople* have *Lawyers,* whofe Profeffions were adorn'd with the moft Eminent Offices of the Empire, fuch as *Conful, Governor* of the *City, Mafter* of the *Houfhold, Treafurer* or *Chancellor* ; The *Faculty of Law* at *Paris,* can alfo among its Profeffors, boaft of a great Number of Illuftrious Perfons ; not only by their Science, but the moft eminent Employments of the Long Robe, to which they have been advanc'd thro' their Merit, and fill'd the fame with fingular Capacity and Diftinction. But, if on one hand the *Law* was honour'd by the Dignity of thofe *Magiftrates* who taught it, on the other, the Splendor they added to the Profeffion, did them no lefs Honour ; being an infallible Token of their Application, Merit, and Capacity.

We have many other Proofs, that notwithftanding the *Decree Super-fpecula,* the *Civil Law* has been always publickly taught in the *Faculty of Paris.*

Bouchel, in his Book call'd *The French Law-Library,* under the Word *Univerfity,* mentions an Order or Letter, written by the Rector of the Univerfity of *Paris, Novemb.* 22. 1410. Directed and Signify'd to the *Regents* and *Deputies* of the Univerfity ; in which the Names of all the *Licentiates,* either in the *Canon* or *Civil Law* are exprefsly fet down.

In the third Regifter of the *Faculty,* there are Two Orders of the Court, one dated the Firft of *July,* 1542, the other the Firft of *September,* 1547. to forbid the Printing of any Books in *Paris* without Licence ; in which, the Right of Licenfing and Approving *Civil* and *Canon* Law-Books, is granted to the *Dean* of the *Faculty* of *Law,* as that of *Divinity* and *Phyfick,* was given to the Profeffors of thofe Sciences ;

ences; and that of *Grammar*, to the *Rector*; which has been since put in Execution, and renew'd on several Occasions. Now if the *Civil Law* had not been publickly taught in the Schools at *Paris*, could such a Knowledge of the *Civil Law*, as was necessary to pass a true Judgment upon the Books that treat of that Subject, have been reasonably requir'd ?

All that has been before said, makes it fully appear, that till the Publishing the *Ordinance* of *Blois*, the *Civil Law* was ever taught in the *Faculty of Paris* ; and therefore, it will be needless to add any other Proofs : It may not be amiss, however, to consult the Note made by M. *Charles Du Moulin*, upon the *Article* 273, of the Ancient *Custom of Orleans* ; *Rebuffe, in tractatu Nominat. Quæst.* 5. *Num.* 15. *& seq.* *Pasquier*, in his *Recherches*, Book 9. Chap. 35. and 37. and M. *Caseneuve*, in his Treatise of *Frankaloid*, Book 1. Chap. 5.

As to what remains, it will be no difficult Matter to prove, notwithstanding the *Ordinance* of *Blois*, the *Civil Law* has been continually read at *Paris* ; which shall be the Subject of the following Chapter.

C H A P. XXVIII.

The Sixty ninth Article of the Ordonnance *of* Blois *explain'd.*

THE *Ordonnance* of *Blois*, publish'd in *May*, 1579, was was drawn up by the *Journal of the States*, two Years before : In the Minutes by which that *Ordonnance* was form'd, there was no mention of prohibiting the Study of the *Civil Law* in the *Faculty of Paris*; yet, the Enemies of the *Faculty*, have had the Dexterity to get the Sixty ninth Article inserted, which forbids the *Regent-Doctors* of the *Faculty of Law* at *Paris*, to read, or confer Degrees in the *Civil Law*.

Let us briefly examine the Manner and Reasons upon which that Prohibition was grounded, and then see if the *Ordonnance* of *Blois* has been put in Execution in that particular.

I

I have juft now faid, there was no fuch thing mention'd in the *Minutes* from which that *Ordonnance* was taken ; but there is fomething more in it ; for that Prohibition was made without any Examination or Cognizance of the Caufe, and even without hearing the Parties concern'd.

This Article which was not touch'd upon in the *Affembly* of the *States,* was afterwards added to the *Ordonnance* by the Chancellor *Chiverny,* to favour the City of *Orleans,* where he was *Governor* and had a great Eftate ; this is a Fact related by feveral Authors, and not at all unlikely.

The Pretence for making this *Ordonnance,* was the *Decretal* of *Honorius* before fpoken of, to which it was hinted, Obedience ought to be paid.

And to give this Article the Colour of a *Reafon of State,* it was laid down for a Principle, that it was the King's Intereft to forbid the teaching of the *Roman Laws,* in his Capital City of *Paris*; becaufe it tacitly infer'd the Empire's Superiority over the Kingdom of *France*; which is abfolutely independant of any other : Their Argument run thus, " The *Civil Law* is the Work of the *Roman* Emperors, there- " fore, it cannot be admitted, without acknowledging in " fome meafure, that the Crown of *France,* which the King " holds of God only, and his Sword, is a Dependant of " the Empire, as a Superior Power.

If the Parties concern'd had been call'd upon, this Objection would have been eafily remov'd, by a very plain and natural Anfwer, which is, that the allowing the *Civil Law* to be read at *Paris,* derogates no more from the King's Sovereignty, than the Permiffion of reading it in any other Place of the Kingdom.

And indeed, what appearance is there, that the Sovereignty of a Prince fhould be in the leaft diminifh'd, by adopting the *Laws* of another Sovereign Prince, or giving his Subjects leave to follow and make ufe of thofe *Laws* ?

Our Kings, by approving the *Roman Laws,* have made them their own, as the *Romans* did the *Laws* of *Rhodes,* in *Maritime* Affairs ; and can it be faid, that the *Roman* Emperors fubmitted to that Ifland, becaufe they adopted fome of their *Laws* ?

The Book of *Fiefs*, which is generally thought to be the Compofition of fome *Lombard Doctors*, pafs neverthelefs for *Law* all over *Europe*, when *Cuſtom* is not contrary to it, yet no one ever concluded from thence, that all Chriſtendom was fubject to the Princes of *Lombardy*.

'Tis well known, the Kings of *Poland* and *Denmark*, fuf- fer their Subjects to make ufe of the *Roman Laws*, and that they are oblig'd to follow them, when their own *Municipal Laws* are defective ; the fame are alfo taught in their Uni- fities of *Cracow* and *Copenhagen*, yet they were never under any Apprehenfion, that this Permiffion would blemifh their Sovereignty in the leaſt Degree.

Has the *Turkiſh* Emperor diminifh'd his, by fubmitting to the Decifion of the *Roman Laws*, when the *Alcoran* is filent! And do fo many other Princes, who were never fubject to the *Romans*, or withdrew themfelves from their Obedience, all become Dependants of *Rome*, by obferving the *Laws* made there ? No certainly ; the voluntary Deference which they fhew them, is not an Effect of their De- pendance, but of their Reafon, which leads them to make choice of fuch *Laws*, as they could not reject, without ſtray- ing at the fame time from Equity and Right Reafon : And the Truth is, the *Roman Law* is now, not the *Law* of any particular People, but a General and Common *Law*, which, from the Deſtruction of the *Roman* Empire, has ever been regarded by all well-govern'd Nations, as a *Natural Law*, and a *Law of Nations*, which confequently ought to be uni- verfal.

Thefe are the Reafons, why after the Deſtruction of the *Roman* Empire, their *Laws*, inſtead of lofing their Authori- ty, fpread themfelves all over *Europe*, and moſt Nations were proud of following them.

The King of *France* therefore, who is a Monarch in his own Kingdom, and inveſted with all Imperial Privi- leges, does in no meafure fubmit to the Empire, by fuffer- ing the *Civil Law* to be taught, and his Subjects to make ufe of it : There is only one Obfervation to be made on this particular, which is, that in *France* the Nullities of the *Civil Law* are not allow'd ; that is, when the *Roman Law* an- nuls a *Contract*, by any Remedy or Benefit introduc'd by the Equity thereof, the Judges cannot pronounce Sentence upon that Nullity, unlefs the Party has firſt obtain'd *Letters* from

from the Prince for that Purpofe, in token of not acknowledging the *Roman* Emperor's Authority ; whereas they may pronounce definitively without fuch *Letters*, when the Nullity proceeds from the *Ordonnances* or *Cuftoms* : So that when we fay, the ways of Nullity are not admitted in *France*, it is for the Reafon aforefaid, to be underftood only of fuch as have their Foundation in the *Civil Law.*

But it may be faid, the *Civil Law* is not receiv'd as *Law* all over *France* ; 'tis true, yet this is no Reafon why it fhould not be taught there : Do thofe Nations of *Europe*, which follow it only when their own *Laws* are defective, fuffer any other *Law* to be taught in their Univerfities ? And is it not a Rule among many of them, not to admit any one to be a *Judge* or *Advocate*, before he is a *Doctor* or *Licentiate* in the *Civil Law* ? So true it is, that this *Law* is every where look'd upon as the perfect Model of all good *Laws*, and Source of all good Principles.

Befides, the *Decretals* are not admitted as *Laws* amongft us, till Cuftom has given them that Authority ; and when they are not repugnant to the Liberties of the *Gallican* Church, nor to our particular *Cuftoms* ; yet, there is no Univerfity in the Kingdom, wherein there are not Publick Lectures upon them.

Thus, as the Prohibition of reading the *Civil Law* publickly at *Paris*, contain'd in the *Ordonnance* of *Blois*, is againft all Rule, 'tis no wonder if it never was obey'd ; nor has it hinder'd the *Regent-Doctors* of the *Faculty*, to continue their Explanations of the *Inftitutes*, and other parts of that *Law* ; and to admit the *Licentiates* of the *Faculty of Paris*, to be *Judges* and *Advocates*, as they were before the *Ordonnance* of *Blois* came out.

The truth of this is fufficiently made out, not only by the Hiftorians of that time, but by the *Statutes* of the *Faculty*, which were reform'd by *Commiffaries* appointed by *Henry* IV. in 1598, and ratify'd in Parliament the Year following.

Thefe *Statutes* begin with an *Encomium* of the *Faculty*, which is called, The Seminary of Perfons defign'd to fill the moft eminent Employments both in Church and State ; the Words are thefe. *Juris Canonici fchola adhæc ufque tempora feminarium honeftiffimorum hominum, ad Ecclefiafticos gradu & Reipublicæ munia, tam Ecclefiaftica quam fæcularia promovendorum exftitit,* &c.

The

The Fifth Article of thefe *Statutes* provides, That all new Scholars in the *Faculty*, fhall begin their Studies of the *Civil* and *Canon Law*, by reading the *Inftitutes*; and learn by heart the *Rubricks* of both *Laws*. *Prolyta, à lectione & auditione Inftitutionum & Canonici & Civilis Juris ftudium exordiatur ac fedulam operam in eo collocet, ut utriufque Juris titulos memoriter teneat*.

Another Argument, and a very good one, might be added to all thefe Proofs, which is, that the *Faculty*'s Power of teaching the *Civil Law* at *Paris*, has never been call'd in queftion; from whence it follows, that it ought never to have been depriv'd of that Power: For whoever has the leaft Tincture of the *Canon Law*, will eafily judge of the Impoffibility of underftanding it rightly, without the Affiftance of the *Civil Law*. Indeed, as they are the two Eyes of Politick and Judiciary Prudence, the Strength of both ought to be united, to fee things in their true Light; and in a Word, ought both to operate at the fame Time.

In what manner foever we confider the Prohibition in the *Ordonnance* of *Blois*, againft teaching the *Civil Law* in *Paris*, 'tis plain, the Execution of it is Impracticable: Every one knows, the Univerfity of *Paris* is the Firft in the Kingdom; our Princes have honour'd it with the Title of their *Eldeft Daughter*, as having had its Birth in the Royal Palace: Befides, it claims a Place in the *States*, has fent Deputies to *General Councils*, been frequently confulted by our *Kings*, and often by the *Popes*; and Foreign Nations have chang'd the Advice they have had from thence into *Laws*; fo that one may fay, it is not confin'd to the Circle of *Paris*, but according to its Motto, is, *HIC ET UBIQUE TERRARUM*: From whence it follows, that it is fo far from being inferior to other Univerfities, it ought to have fome Prerogatives, and ferve as a Pattern for their Imitation.

This being laid down for a Certainty, as it really is, would it have been fit that this Univerfity fhould be defective, and want one of its moft Noble Parts, the *Civil Law*? How could it without that, have maintain'd either the Dignity or even the Name of an Univerfity, which is nothing elfe but a Collection of all the Sciences?

In ſhort, the City of *Paris* being the Common Countrey of all *Frenchmen*, the largeſt and moſt beautiful Theatre of *Europe*, it was neceſſary that all kinds of uſeful Learning ſhould be taught there, for the Advantage of our own Countreymen, as well as Strangers, who continually flock thither.

Now it cannot be deny'd, that there is no Study comparable to that of the *Civil Law*, and that the Science thereof is far above all others, as ſhall be ſhewn in the following Chapter ; but here we muſt firſt remark, that *Lewis* XIV. being inform'd of the Inconveniencies, which might ariſe from the *Ordonnance* of *Blois*, made an *Edict* in *April*, 1679. by which he orders, that for the future, the Publick Lectures of the *Civil Law*, jointly with thoſe of the *Canon Law*, ſhould be reviv'd and eſtabliſh'd in the Univerſity of *Paris*.

This *Edict* preſcribes the Time which all Students are to employ in that Science, before they are made *Graduates* ; with many other things relating to the Diſcipline of the Scholars, which till then had been mightily neglected, by all the *Faculties of Law* in the Kingdom.

There was an abſolute Neceſſity of applying ſome Remedy to this laſt Abuſe ; and the reſt of the Univerſities obſerving no Rules, and conferring Degrees on every one that ask'd, without examining whether they were qualify'd or not, it became the King's Wiſdom, to put a Stop to the Diſorder which this Irregularity had introduc'd.

Nor was the re-eſtabliſhing of the *Civil Law* in the *Faculty* of *Paris*, leſs neceſſary for the Preſervation of good Order ; for the Enemies of the *Faculty* complain'd continually, that the *Civil Law* was taught, in breach of the Prohibition contain'd in the Sixty ninth Article of the *Ordonnance* of *Blois* ; ſo that the Royal Authority was oblig'd to interfere, to ſupport the *Faculty* in a Right that had ever belong'd to them.

CHAP. XXIX.

Of the Excellency of the Roman Law.

IF there have been fome that have difputed the Excellency of the *Roman Law,* the abfurdity of fo extravagant an Opinion, may very well fave me the Trouble of refuting it : For tho' particular Miftakes often become general, there is no likelihood it will happen fo in this Cafe ; and the Merits of the *Roman Law* are eftablifh'd upon too good a Bottom to give way to a Prejudice, which in all likelihood proceeds from the Ignorance of thofe who fuffer themfelves to be led away by fuch an Error.

Neverthelefs, it cannot be deny'd, but the Number of Perfons who favour this Opinion, may very much increafe, becaufe it offers at firft fight an agreeable Profpect, in fparing fuch as embrace it a laborious Study. This, doubtlefs, is the only Advantage that can refult from it : But it will be no hard Matter to expofe the Fallacy of this pretended Advantage, and undeceive thofe, who having compleated the Time prefcrib'd for their ordinary Exercifes, content themfelves with taking their Degrees, and look no farther than to get the *Teftimonials* ufually given on that Occafion.

The Time allotted for ftudying the *Law,* by the King's Declaration, to intitle Students to take their Degrees, is not fufficient to acquire a compleat Knowledge of fo profound a Science.

It would therefore become thofe who have taken their Degrees, to make a better ufe than fome do of the Principles they are taught ; for the Publick are fenfibly interefted, that all who are *Magiftrates,* or take upon them the Profeffion of *Advocates,* fhould be fully inftructed in the Maxims of the *Roman Law,* without the Help of which, it will be impoffible for them to become eminent in *ours.*

What is before faid in the Twenty fixth Chapter, concerning the Ufe of the *Roman Law* in *France,* has a very near Relation to the Subject of this Chapter ; therefore I fhall
refer

refer the Reader to it. Let us now fee what new Evidence
we can bring of the Excellency of the *Roman Law.*

As there is no better Proof of the Excellency of any Science, than Reafon, and the unanimous Opinion of Perfons
who acknowledge it; that of the *Roman Law*, may be fully
juftify'd by Two Obfervations: The Firft is, that Reafon
alone ought to convince us thereof; the Second, that the
Excellency of the *Roman Law*, has ever been acknowledg'd
by the Great Men of all Ages, whofe Authority alone, fufficiently fpeaks its Praife: Thefe Two Points I fhall examine in a few Words.

Natural Reafon having implanted in the Heart of Man,
thofe Principles which govern him, both as a Private Perfon, and as a Member of the Society to which he belongs,
nothing ought to be more facredly obferv'd by him; and
methinks, he fhould want no other *Law* to engage him to
follow them: But as all Men are not fo prone as they ought
to be, to follow the Dictates of *Natural Reafon*, there was
a Neceffity of making *Laws* to keep them to their Duty.

Thus, after they were oblig'd by Neceffity to relinquifh
their firft Habitations, and were difpers'd into different
Countries, and had built Cities and eftablifh'd Kingdoms,
every Nation apply'd the Precepts of the *Law of Nations*
to their own Ufe and particular Benefit; and fo making
fome Additions to the Common *Law* of Mankind, or re-
trenching it, according to their different Genius, and the
Neceffities of the Countrey they liv'd in, they made *Laws*,
and eftablifh'd a *Right* peculiar to themfelves.

Afia had the Advantage of being reckon'd to have the
Wifeft and moft Equitable *Laws*. This was a Truth fo generally receiv'd, that the *Romans* notwithftanding their Haughti-
nefs, fetch'd the moft valuable Part of their *Laws* from thence,
and made ufe of it in the Compofition of a Body of Univerfal *Laws*; I mean, thofe of the *Twelve Tables*, which
were afterwards look'd upon as the Source of all *Laws*, both
Publick and Private; and which infinitely furpafs'd all that
the Sages of *Afia* had made before.

All thefe Precautions taken by the *Romans* to make a perfect *Law*, and the infinite Pains which their greateft Men
were at, to give Juft Interpretations to that *Law*, are un-
conteftable Proofs of the Excellency of the *Roman Law*; nay,
even the Emperors had this always in view, and encourag'd

their

their *Lawyers* to give a new Splendor to the *Roman Laws*, by their Labour and Application.

So that *Rome* was the Countrey of *Laws*; and the Body of the *Roman Law*, as we have it at this Day, is a Collection of the beft *Laws* that were made in *Rome :* This valuable Treafure of Antiquity, contains the refin'd Doctrine of the Precepts of the *Law of Nature* and *Nations*, as well as all the principal Points of Morality ; wherein alone the Principles of Equity, and Rules of Univerfal *Law* are to be found ; and no doubt, if all this Nation were fo happy as to live under the fame *Law*, there would be no need of any other for the Regulation of the Condition and Manners of all its Subjects ; and indeed, where elfe fhall we find certain Maxims for the Regulations of *Agreements* and *Contracts*, for eftablifhing *Penalties* upon thofe that are guilty of *Crimes* and *Offences ?* In fhort, where fhall we find Principles to govern the moft Ordinary, as well as the moft Important Affairs, but in the Body of the *Civil Law*, whofe *Decifions* are fo Equitable and Judicious, that they may be apply'd to Matters quite different from thofe for which they were originally made ?

The Science of the *Roman Law*, has not only the Advantage of informing the Underftanding, but fetting the Heart upright ; it communicates at the fame time Light to the Mind, and Righteoufnefs to the Soul, and teaches us how to conduct our felves as well in a Private as Publick Capacity ; and furnifhes the *Magiftrate* with Rules to give every Man his due : In a Word, the *Roman Law* is a Mafter-piece of Wifdom, Honefty, Politicks, Prudence, Juftice and Equity.

It was called *The Law*, by way of Excellence, as if there was none other Confiderable in the World ; and altho' the *Roman* Power has been quite loft for many Ages, the *Roman Law* is ftill preferv'd over all *Europe*. But it is no wonder if its Excellency has been perceiv'd by all People, and at all Times ; and tho' it was made for the Subjects of the Empire only, there are few Nations that have not adopted it ; and even thofe whofe Inclinations and Manners were the moft oppofite to the *Romans*, were the firft that embrac'd the *Laws* made by them.

Let it not therefore be faid, this was an Effect of the Univerfal Monarchy acquir'd by the *Romans* : The great Equity which all Nations obferv'd in the *Roman Laws*, was the only Caufe of the Deference paid to them, and of their readinefs to follow them ; *Servatur ubique jus Romanum non ratione imperii fed rationis imperio.* In fhort, moft of the Nations conquer'd by the *Romans*, admir'd and cultivated the Equity of their *Laws* ; altho' their Tyranny feem'd infupportable : And when, upon the Declenfion of the *Roman* Empire, they recover'd their Liberty, that Revolution did not at all diminifh the Refpect they bore to the *Roman Laws.*

I cannot in this Place , pafs over an Obfervation which prefents it felf ; Whatever Glory *Rome* might have acquir'd, by the Number and Extent of its Conquefts, that which gave it the greateft Luftre, was, without doubt, its being acknowledg'd by all the World to be the *Mother of the Laws.* The fubduing the greateft Part of the Univerfe, muft be allow'd to be owing, either to their great Strength or mafterly Skill, or to particular good Fortune ; of all which there are fome other Examples : But the Credit of making fuch Wife *Laws*, fo generally receiv'd by all Nations, is peculiar, and what the *Romans* only can boaft of.

Befides, how much has the Efteem of the *Roman Laws* furviv'd the Empire ? All thofe Nations who had freed themfelves from the *Roman* Bondage, continu'd voluntarily in that of their *Laws*, which they preferr'd to thofe of their own Countries. Can this Concurrence be the Effect of Flattery, that Power which was the Object of it fubfifting no longer ?

The *Romans* equally fubdu'd the Univerfe, by their *Arms* and *Laws* ; but that Empire which was gotten by Force, is gone to ruin ; whereas, they ftill continue to govern by their *Laws :* This Dominion is fo much the more glorious, as it is not owing to Force, and is over the Minds and Hearts of Mankind ; and as 'tis founded upon Reafon and Equity, nothing can deftroy it. The *Wars* of the *Romans* were often unjuft ; but their *Laws* feem to have been dictated by *Juftice* her felf : Therefore, they ought never to ceafe being obferv'd by Mankind, unlefs they will utterly banifh from Society, that Vertue which is the ftrongeft Support of it.

K 3

To

To this, let us add, that the invincible Stubbornnefs of the *Jews*, has yielded to the Excellency of the *Roman Laws*; who have recourfe to no other, in default of their own: And as great as the Antipathy of the *Turks* is, to every thing that is of Chriftian growth, yet it has not hinder'd them from tranflating the *Roman Law* into their own Language, nor from following its Decifions, in Matters to which the *Alcoran* cannot be apply'd.

Nothing could be eafier, than to add a Thoufand other Obfervations of this kind, to fhew the Excellency of the *Roman Laws*; but Truth has the Prerogative of Self-Perfwafion. Befides, all that I could fay, would not be Equivalent to the Encomiums which the Great Men of all Ages have ever given the *Roman Law*. Let us therefore hear what they fay, and run over the moft Famous of them who have mention'd it; upon whofe Credit, every Man of Sence will without Scruple ground his Judgment.

St. *Auftin*, * in his Book *De Civitat. Dei*, fays, that " Providence made ufe of the *Roman* People, to fubdue " the Univerfe, and to govern it the better by their *Laws*, " after it had utterly deftroy'd that Empire.

St. *Jerom*, † fpeaking of the Declenfion of the *Roman* Empire, fays, " The Ruins and Shadow thereof, were yet to be " feen in *Germany*; but tho' nothing at all of it had re- " main'd, we have ftill their *Laws*, which all Nations have " admitted with great Applaufe.

Zonaras, upon the *Conftitutions of the Apoftles* ‡, fays, " God " made Choice of the *Romans*, to give the World a fample " of his Juftice.

Peter Pech ‖ fays, " The *Roman* is the Sovereign *Law*, " univerfally receiv'd for fo many Ages.

D. *Gothofredus*, ** fays almoft the fame, and adds, " That the *Laws* and *Regulations* of other Nations do not " come near it; and that all their *Cuftoms* and *Ordonnances* " are comprehended in it.

---

* Chapter 22. Book 18.
† Epift. 10. of *Monogamy*, Tom. 1.
‡ Book 7. Chap. 27.
‖ *De Regulis Juris*, Chap. 28.
** *In praxi rerum Civil*, Lib. 2, Tit. 1.

Baldus,

Baldus, upon the *Law*, *Nemo C.de sentent. & interlocut. omnium Judicum*, says, " The *Roman Law* has the same command " in all Nations as *Reason*.

Contius, *Lectionum Juris*, cap. 9. says, " There is no *Law* " more just or conformable to Reason, than that which is " contain'd in the Books of the *Roman Law*.

Baro, *lib.* 3. *de jur. Benef. tit.* 2. *& ad legem si reus C. de pactis*, says, " That *Justinian*'s Books are valu'd like fine " Pictures sav'd from a great Shipwreck.

Baldwinus, in his *Prolegomena* upon the *Institutes*, says, " The Study of the *Law* was ever in great repute among " the *Romans*, and spread it self afterwards over all Nati- " ons, with universal Approbation.

Charles Du Moulin, whose great Reputation was wholly owing to his adding a perfect Knowledge of the *Roman Law* to that of our *Ordonnances*, says, in his *Preface* to the *Custom* of *Paris*, that the *Roman Law* is so just, and so agreeable with Reason, that all Christendom has receiv'd and approv'd of it, as the *Common Law* of Nations : His Words are these ; *Mutuamur à jure Romano quod & æquitati consonum, & negotio de quo agitur congruumque invenitur, non quod nusquam subditi fuerimus Justiniano magno, aut successoribus ejus, sed quia jus illo autore à sapientissimis viris ordinatum tam æquum est, tam rationabile, ut omnium ferè Christianarum gentium usu & approbatione, commune sit effectum.*

Cujacius, in his *Epistle* to his *Son*, tells him, " No Nation " can be well govern'd, without the Help of the *Roman Law* ; and adds, that " without the Knowledge of that Divine " Science, the most Prudent, Wise, and Fortunate Man, " will have but a very imperfect Idea of the Rules of " Equity and true Justice.

Mornac, upon the Title of the *Code*, *De veteri Jure enucleand.* says, " That in Matters not determin'd by the Cu- " stoms, recourse must be had to the *Roman Law*, as to a " Sheet-Anchor, and the most secure Means to come to " Equity ; because the Precepts and Duties of Civil Life, " are no where else so well establish'd.

Leuvius, in his *History of the Law*, says, " The Books of " the *Roman Law*, contain the most Religious and Just De- " terminations that ever were made, as well as the most " perfect Idea of Right and Justice : Therefore, says he, " all Nations acknowledge the *Roman Law* for their Com-

K 4 " mon

" *mon* Law ; not becaufe it is *Roman*, but that it is the
" Law *of Nations*.

Albericus Gentilis, Book 1. *De Jure belli*, Chap. 5. carries
it fo far as to fay, " All Sovereign Princes are oblig'd to
" be govern'd by it, in the Difputes that happen between
" them.

Coquille, in his *Queftions*, Chap. 306. fays, " The *Roman*
" *Laws*, by the wife and politick Reafons, upon which they
" are grounded, were receiv'd by us in aid of our Royal
" *Conftitutions*, and of our *Cuftoms*, when they either are
" deficient or want Explanation. He adds, That the great
" Events of the Politick Government of *Rome*, fhew, that
" God endow'd that People with a fingular clearnefs of
" Judgment, and opennefs of Heart.

Charondas in his *Anfwers*, Book 3. upon the *Edict* of *Second-
Marriages*, and in his *Pandects*, Book 3. Chap. 9. fays, " 'Tis
" a general Cuftom amongft us, to obferve the *Roman* as
" the *Common Law* ; to which we have recourfe in default
" of the *Ordonnances* and *Cuftoms :* Not that the *French* any
" ways acknowledge the Emperor of *Rome*, but becaufe the
" *Laws* of no Nation or Government are more juft, better
" contriv'd, or more agreeable with Reafon, than thofe in
" the Body of the *Roman Law*.

Loyfeau, in his Treatife of *Surrendry of Copy-hold Lands,*
Book 2. Chap. 1. N. 17. *Rebuffe*, upon the Title *De Confue-
tud.* *Tiraqueau*, in the Preface to his Treatife called, *Le
mort faifit le vif.* *Chaffanée*, upon the *Cuftom* of *Burgundy ;*
Pontanus, upon that of *Blois ; Chopin*, upon that of *Paris*, in
his Preface upon that of *Anjou*, and his Treatife of the *Do-
maine ; Ricard*, upon the Hundred and Sixty firft Article of
the *Cuftom* of *Senlis*; all fay almoft the fame thing.

M. *Colombet*, in his *Abridgment* of the *Roman Law*, Tit. 3.
fays, that " the Body of the *Roman Law*, is not the Work
" of one Man, nor of a few Years, but of feveral Nations
" and Ages ; brought to Perfection by long and labori-
" ous Obfervation of Human Affairs, which Men of the
" beft Underftanding in that flourifhing Nation, fully in-
" ftructed by the Exercife of inferior Offices, and from
" thence rais'd to the higheft Employments in the Empire,
" have made ; and reduc'd to practife, by certain Principles and
" General Maxims. He adds, that this Work was found to
" be fo excellent, that even after the Fall of the *Roman* Em-
                                                        " pire,

" pire, it was embrac'd by the best govern'd Nations of
" the World ; which still continue to make use of it in
" deciding their Disputes, and cause it to be publickly
" taught for that purpose.

M. *Servin*, in one of his *Pleas*, says, that " The *Civil*
" *Law* of the *Romans*, surpasses in Natural Equity all other
" *Laws* ; and that all of them have recourse thereto.

M. *le Maître*, so famous for his Eloquence and extraordinary Parts, in his *Twelfth Pleading*, calls the *Roman Law*,
" The wonderful Collection of the Wisdom of so many
" Wise Men, who did not confine themselves to particular
" *Usages*, but to Justice in general ; and have establish'd
" such *Laws*, as they thought most useful to Mankind ; and
" who have written the Rules of Government for all Nati-
" ons, as *Solomon* did those of Divine Wisdom.

It cannot be objected, that these Proofs are liable to any
Exception, being for the most part taken from *French Lawyers*,
who have studied our *Customs*, and could not forbear taking
notice, how preferable the *Roman Laws* are to those of their
own Countrey ; in which, they have shewn both their good
Sence and Judgment.

The particular Veneration which most *Kings* in the
World have had for the *Roman Law*, is not a slender Indication of its Excellency ; they have given it the Force of
Law in their Dominions, and order'd it to be publickly
taught ; which is a peculiar Privilege belonging to the *Laws*
of *Justinian's* Collection : For hitherto, there has been no
Attempt that we know of, to teach *Solon's Laws*, how much
soever they are cry'd up, or any others, publickly in the
Schools.

But to confine my self to *France* ; Our Kings have not
only taken care it should be taught in those Provinces where
'tis in full force, but even in those govern'd by *Customs*, as
appears by the *Ordonnance* of *Moulins*, made in *August* 1546
and 1566, Article 10 ; and that of *Blois*, in 1576, Article
108.

Our Kings have upon all Occasions commended it, and
made many *Ordonnances*, to enforce its Observation in their
Dominions.

Clotarius, in his *Ordonnance* of 560, commands, that all
Matters relating to the *Romans*, that is, the *Gauls*, should be
regulated according to the *Roman Law*.

As

As for the Second Race of our Kings, we have the *Conſtitution* of *Charles* the *Bald*, dated the 25th of *June*, 864. in which he declares, that neither he nor his Predeceſſors ever intended to order any thing in oppoſition to the *Roman Law*.

But as the Difficulty does not fall upon the Times of the Two firſt Races, let us paſs to the Third.

I ſhall begin with St. *Lewis*, who, for his great Care to promote Religion and maintain Juſtice in all his Dominions, may be a Pattern for all our Kings. He order'd in his *Edicts*, that all Matters ſhould be decided by the *Roman Laws*, which, by way of Excellence, he calls *The Law*.

Philip the *Handſome*, as well as *Francis* I. ſpeaks of it in the ſame manner.

Henry IV. in his Declaration of 1607, made to empower *Mortgagées* to enter into the Succeſſion of old *Creditors*, without *Ceſſion* or *Subrogation* ; ſays in expreſs Terms, *He alwaysapprov'd of the* Roman Law, *as it agreed with Reaſon and Equity.*

All our Kings have expreſs'd themſelves upon it almoſt in the ſame Terms ; and 'tis from thence they have taken their beſt *Ordonnances*.

Lewis XIV. in his *Edict* of 1679, for re-eſtaliſhing the Publick Profeſſion of the *Civil Law* in the *Faculty of Paris*, begins by ſaying, " that altho' the Wars had not hinder'd him " from publiſhing ſeveral *Ordonnances* for the Reformation " of *Juſtice*, yet, enjoying at that time a glorious Peace, " he was more diſengag'd, and in a better Condition to " provide for the due Execution of Juſtice, thro' all his Do- " minions." He goes on, and ſays, " that he believ'd he " could do nothing that would more contribute to the Hap- " pineſs of his Subjects, than the affording ſuch as were " deſign'd for the Adminiſtration of it, the Means of qua- " lifying themſelves as they ought : Therefore, having un- " derſtood that the Uncertainty of Judgments, ſo prejudici- " al to his Subjects, was chiefly owing to the utter Neglect " of the Study of the *Civil Law*, for above an Age, all over " *France* ; and that the Publick Profeſſion thereof had been " diſcontinu'd in the Univerſity of *Paris* ; He orders, That " from thenceforward, the Publick Lectures of the *Roman* " *Law* ſhould be reviv'd ; any thing in the Sixty ninth
Article

" Article of the *Ordonnance* of *Blou* to the contrary not-
" withstanding.

To see to the Execution and Continuance of this *Edict*,
his Majesty commission'd Four *Counsellors of State, viz.* Mr.
le Pelletier, Bazin de Bezons, Boucherat and *Bignon* ; whose
Characters being capable of no Addition by any thing I
can say, I have only mention'd their Names, to shew the
Importance of the Affair, as well as to encrease, if possible,
the Respect which Posterity ought to have for the Memory
of such illustrious Restorers of the Study of the *Roman Law* ;
for one may say, all Discipline was at that time utterly
lost, and there never was more Occasion for reviving it.

But these Commissioners, by their great Application, restor'd the Study of the *Civil Law* ; and the Success which
attended their Endeavours, is a further Proof of the Excellency thereof ; and of the Necessity every one is under,
to make himself Master of it, who intends to be an *Advocate,* or aims at the Office of a *Judge.*

From all I have said, it follows, that notwithstanding the
the *Roman Law* is not of equal force in the *Custumary* Countries, as in those of the *Written Law,* its Decisions are of
great weight, in those Parts which are called *Custumary* in
France, since it is there receiv'd as *Written Reason* ; to which
every Judge ought to have recourse, in Cases omitted by
the *Customs* of the Place : What is said upon this Subject in
the Twenty Sixth Chapter, to which I refer the Reader,
will save me the Trouble of enlarging further upon it in
this Place.

I shall only observe, that if all our *Law* was confin'd to
the *Ordonnances* and *Customs,* their would be very little Difference between the *Judges, Advocates,* and *Practitioners* ;
nay, sometimes, the latter would be more able than either of the others, for where the Learning of an *Advocate*
goes no farther than *Tritura fori,* or *Practice,* 'tis impossible
he should defend a Cause with Success ; which made *John
Fauvre* say, *Ad.* 23. *Instit. tit. de Legat. Quod appellamus pra-
xim, non est in patrono nuda & circumforanea praxis, cujusmo-
di est procuratorum forensium, sed juris scientiam applicare negotiis.*

In ſhort, Experience ſhews, that whatever good Diſpoſitions young Men may have, it will be no eaſie Matter for them to learn the Sciences, unleſs they are directed by a *Method, and general Principles ; the future Application of which, depends upon their own good Underſtanding. Now it is in the *Roman Law* only, theſe Principles are to be found ; which are ſo much the more valuable, as they are the Opinions of the wiſeſt Men among the Ancients : Whereas the Deciſions of our *Cuſtoms,* have no other Foundation than certain *Uſages,* introduc'd frequently without any Reaſon or Principle at all, or of which the Reaſon is unknown, even to thoſe, who by good Obſervation are the beſt Judges of what is the Common *Uſage.*

This made *Cujacius* ſay, Tit. 14. of his Book of *Fiefs,* That we muſt judge of moſt Things ordain'd by the *Cuſtoms,* as *Neratius* did of the *Law* introduc'd by *Uſage* ; who adviſes, not to look too diligently after the Reaſon of it, leſt we ſubvert the Authority of the whole. The Words of *Cujacius* are theſe ; *Multa ſunt in moribus Galliæ, diſſentanea multa ſine ratione, ut quod de jure recepto Neratius ſcripſit, non eſſe ejus rationem anxiè inquirendam ne multa ex his quæ certa ſunt, ſubvertantur id Galliæ moribus aptari veriſſimè, poſſit quod plerumque omni ratione deſtituantur petiti, partim ex jure Gallico, partim ex imperitorum ſententiis malè cohærentibus.*

'Tis true, the Reformers and Reducers of our *Cuſtoms,* have corrected abundance of unjuſt Things, which Uſe had introduc'd ; but it was impoſſible for them to make a perfect *Law* from the bad Principles they had to work upon ; and therefore, the *Oracle* of the *Cuſtumary Law,* when he undertakes to explain ſome of the Articles of our *Cuſtoms,* exclaims in many Places, *O the unjuſt Cuſtom ! O the extravagant Cuſtom !* He ſhews how it came to paſs, that ſo many unjuſt and odious Diſpoſitions remain among our *Cuſtoms,* and imputes it partly to the *Attornies* or *Practitioners,* who made the *Regiſters* of which the *Cuſtoms* were form'd ; and partly to the *Commiſſioners,* who did not allow themſelves Time, nor take the Pains a Work of that kind requir'd.

Chopin, de Comm. Gall. conſuet. Part I. N. 4. aſcribes it wholly to the Officers of the ſeveral Places, whoſe Buſineſs it was to draw up the Subſtance of the *Cuſtoms* in Writing: He ſays, they inſerted Aricles for their own, or the Intereſt and Conveniency of their Friends.

Mornac,

Mornac, Ad Leg. 2. §. 5. *ff, de Origin. Juris,* fays, "There
" are many obfcure Things in our *Cuftoms,* which are ow-
" ing to the Negligence of thofe who reduc'd them ; and
" that they were often put in by Defign.

The *Commiffioners,* whofe Names are at the Head of
the Proceeding, were too precipitate in the Execution of
their Commiffion, and often did nothing more than hear
the *Cuftom* read in their Prefence, and refer contefted Matters to the Court, which never decided them : Befides,
'tis impoffible that Order or Method fhould be thought of,
in fuch tumultuous Affemblies : So that in the manner our
Cuftoms have been reduc'd, 'tis hard to believe, the *Magiftrates* who were intrufted with it, were Men of great Underftanding.

All thefe Circumftances and Reflections, are but too
ftrong Arguments, to fhew the Difference we ought to make
between the *Roman Law* and our *Cuftoms* ; nor is there any
one but knows, in how many Refpects the *Roman Laws* are
fuperior to our *Cuftoms.*

Thofe *Laws* were made with all the Precaution imagi-
nable, and were the Work of the greateft and moft learned
Men of thofe Ages ; on the contrary, the *Cuftoms* were reduc'd in hafte, upon the Report of Practitioners, who were
unable to give any Reafon for the *Ufages* they obferv'd were
then in vogue.

The greateft part of the *Roman Laws,* are in an eafie elegant Stile, and put under Titles fuitable to the Nature of
them : But our *Cuftoms* are generally immethodical, and
the Stile of them harfh and obfcure, and confequently, hard
to be underftood and remember'd.

All kind of Matters, as well of an Ordinary as Extraordinary Nature, are explain'd in the *Laws* ; but our *Cuftoms*
are confin'd to a few particular ones, as has been before obferv'd.

In fhort, the Decifions of the *Roman Law* are fo Judicious,
that they infinitely furpafs every thing that has been done
by the *Legiflators* of other Nations ; but the greateft part
of our *Cuftoms,* are the Production of mere Chance, or of
the Fancy of thofe who have fuffer'd themfelves to be led,
rather by certain *Ufages* than Reafon.

There-

Therefore, the *Cuftoms* are reckon'd as fo many Facts, of which the *Judges* are prefum'd to be ignorant ; altho' they are at this Day reduc'd to Writing, as *Fontain* has obferv'd, in his Additions to M. *Bourdin*'s *Paraphrafe*, Art. 42.   And perhaps, this is the Reafon, that when an *Advocate* reads an Article of the *Cuftoms* to the Audience, he is uncover'd as if he were reading a Play ; becaufe the *Cuftoms* are particular *Ufages*, which no one is oblig'd to know : But if he is to quote any Text of the *Laws*, he is not uncover'd ; nor is he allow'd to read it out of the *Digeft* or *Code*, but having it written on a Paper, is to recite it as it were by Heart ; becaufe the *Judges* and *Advocates*, are fuppos'd to know the Difpofitions of the *Common Law.*

Let no one, therefore, any longer pretend, that the Study of the *Roman Law* is ufelefs : So bold a Paradox, ought at leaft to be fupported by fome Colour of Reafon ;   But what do all the Reafons that are brought to maintain this Affertion, amount to ?   Why, they fay, the Science of the *Roman Law*, is a Matter of mere Curiofity, which recompences thofe who are at the Pains to obtain it, with nothing but a Confufion of Maxims ; without the Help of which, they might make as good a Progrefs in the Study of our *Law* ; to prove which, they fay, that this *Law* treats of feveral Matters not in ufe amongft us.

This Objection is eafily anfwer'd ; for, granting that the *Roman Law* does contain fome Matters which are not in ufe with us, muft it from thence be concluded, that the Science of that *Law* is ufelefs ?   It treats of other Matters that are in ufe with us, and which relate both to the Prefervation of the *State*, and the Order of *Civil Society* : Muft we then reject a Work which in general is fo ufeful, becaufe fome Things in it are not applicable to the prefent Ufe ? Befides, in the *Cuftumary* Part of *France*, the *Roman Law* is obferv'd no farther than as Reafon :   Now it happens every Day, that the Reafons, upon which the Principles of Matters not in ufe amongft us are grounded, may be very fitly apply'd to thofe which are frequently in ufe.

In fhort, having thefe ftrong Reafons and Authorities on our Side, may we not fay, that if any one attacks the *Roman Law*, 'tis for want of knowing its Beauty and Solidity ? How often does it happen, that the beft and moft ufeful Sciences are rejected thro' Ignorance ? Nothing is more common,

mon, than to fee Men, thro' Weakneſs or Indolence, declare againſt a thing that requires Pains and Application; either they have little hopes of Succeſs, or rather, ſtrange Apprehenſions of the Difficulties which inſeparably attend all Beginnings; and fanſie, they can excuſe their Caprice in deſpiſing what they are ignorant of, or juſtifie their Idleneſs, in crying down what ought to have taken them from it.

But if there are ſome at the *Bar*, who are prejudic'd againſt the *Roman Law*, there are, without Compariſon, a far greater Number, who looking upon it as the Source of indubitable Maxims, adhere to it with the utmoſt Attention; which is what all our able *Magiſtrates* and *Advocates* have ever done; nor have they fail'd of a Reward, for making it the principal Object of their Application.

To conclude, is there any likelihood, that Men of Sence, who have not, as one may ſay, a Moment's time they can call their own, would take ſo much Pains as they do, in a Study that could be of no advantage to them?

C H A P. XXX.

Of the moſt celebrated Interpreters of the Roman Law.

MEthinks, this *Hiſtory of the Roman Law*, would be in ſome meaſure imperfect, if I ſhould ſay nothing of thoſe, who by their Works have contributed to the better underſtanding thereof; wherefore, I thought my ſelf oblig'd to give ſome Account of the principal *Interpreters* of this *Law*. The Reader muſt not expect here an Hiſtorical Library of every Author that has wrote upon that Subject; my Deſign being only to ſhew Beginners, thoſe who have moſt ſignaliz'd themſelves in that way, and whom they will find mention'd at every turn.

AZO,

AZO, was one of the firſt who took any Pains in the Study of the *Roman Law* ; his *Summaries* upon the Titles thereof, are an excellent Work. He was born at *Bologna* in *Italy* ; 'tis held, that he profeſs'd the *Law* about the Eleventh Century : The Enemies which his Merit rais'd him, oblig'd him to leave his Countrey, and go to *Montpellier*, where he profeſs'd the *Law* ; afterwards, he came back to *Bologna*, where having taught the *Law* ſome time, he died in 1200, or as others ſay in 1225. There goes a Story of his being Hang'd, for killing *Bulgarus* in the Heat of a Diſpute ; but 'tis not warranted by any Writer of thoſe Times.

ACCURSIUS, a Native of *Florence*, began to ſtudy the *Law* when he was Forty Years old, under the famous *Azo* ; in which he made ſo ſwift a Progreſs, that he ſoon out-ſtripp'd his Maſter. He profeſs'd the *Law* publickly at *Bologna*, and after that retir'd, in order to write upon the Explanation and Concordance of the *Law* : This Work, which coſt him Seven Years hard Labour, prov'd ſo uſeful; and anſwer'd his Expectations ſo well, that he deſtroy'd all the Gloſſes he had before made ; yet, he ſometimes reports *Laws* that are nothing to the Purpoſe, and gives others a very wrong meaning ; but all that, as well as the Contradictions for which he is blam'd, proceeds, poſſibly, from his having too haſtily collected an Heap of his Predeceſſor's Opinions: Beſides, there are many Deciſions taken to be his, which are reported from others ; which Miſtake is owing to his making uſe of the firſt Letters only of the Authors Names in his Quotations ; thoſe Letters, thro' the Negligence of Copyiſts, having been often omitted : However that be, he was formerly of ſo great Authority, that he was called *The Advocate's Idol.* Certainly he was a Man of great Parts, and the Barbariſms we meet with in his Writings, ought to be imputed to the Unpoliteneſs of the Times. *Cujacius*, who finds fault with him in ſeveral Paſſages, even to ridicule him, could not forbear praiſing him in his *Obſervations*, Book 3. Chap. 11. and Book 12. Chap. 16. And thoſe who have Judgment enough to compare *Accurſius*'s *Gloſſes* with *Cujacius*'s *Explanations*, will find them to be the very ſame, excepting the Order and Stile. He died in the
Year

Year of Chrift 1229, Aged 78. His Tomb is to be feen in the Church of the *Francifcan* Friers, at *Bologna*, with this Infcription, *Sepulchrum Accurfii Gloffatoris Legum & Francifci ejus filii.*

BARTOLUS was born in 1300, in a Village of the Province of *Umbria* in *Italy*; He was Profeffor of *Law* at *Pifa*, at the Age of Twenty five; after that, he taught it at *Perouze*, in 1350. He was a Man of a very bright Wit and Penetration, and fo ftudious, that nothing could divert him from his Books. His furpaffing Merit, made him reckon'd the beft Interpreter of the *Laws*, next to *Accurfius*. He was of the Council to the Emperor *Charles* IV. who permitted him to bear the Arms of *Bohemia*; but having no Children, that Honour died with him. He was fo fevere and ftrict a Follower of the Letter of the *Law*, that being a *Magiftrate*, he executed his Office with fo much rigour, that he drew upon himfelf the Hatred of the People, which oblig'd him to retire into the Countrey, where he compos'd fome part of his Works, that are now extant: His Writings are full of Learning, but very Unpolite. He wrote upon the *Inftitutes*, fome Books of the *Code*, and a good part of the *Digeft*, and made a Book of the Councils. He died in 1355, Aged 56.

BALDUS, was the Son of a Learned Phyfician of *Perouze*; He ftudied the *Law* under *Bartolus*, and with fo good Succefs, that he was thought to have improv'd that Science, more than any that went before him; which made *Jafon* frequently fay, that *Bartolus* knew every thing. Some have reported, that he did not begin to apply himfelf to the *Law*, till he was Forty; which feems to have little Truth in it, becaufe *Pancirole* proves, that when he was but Fifteen, he rais'd a very puzzling Objection againft his Mafter *Bartolus*; and at Seventeen, read Publick *Law-Lectures*. He was *Praceptor* to Pope *Gregory* XII. His great Skill in the *Law*, got him fo much Reputation, that *John Galeas Viceconti*, Duke of *Milan*, brought him to the Univerfity of *Pavia*, where he continu'd Profeffor of the *Law* for Fifty fix Years. He was much talk'd of for a quick Repartee, when he firft enter'd the Schools at *Pavia*; For, being a very Diminutive Perfon,

L   fome

ſome of the Auditors upon his Entrance ſaid, *Minuit præ-*
ſentia famam ; to which he inſtantly reply'd, *Augebit cætera*
virtus.

He often pleaded againſt his Maſter *Bartolus,* and the
Emulation between them, turn'd at laſt to perfect Hatred.
He got a great Eſtate, and wrote ſeveral Books. His Writings, which favour very much of the Barbarity of the
Times, are not altogether free from other Faults : He
advances a Thouſand Singularities, without the leaſt Authority, and ſome that are quite contrary to the common
Opinion. He has little or no Order in any thing he treats
of ; he often quotes *Laws* that are foreign to the Purpoſe ;
is very large upon uſeleſs Matters, and paſſes ſlightly over
thoſe which are moſt neceſſary. He ſays nothing upon Caſes that ariſe every Day, and is very Learned upon thoſe
that ſeldom or never happen, and often confounds himſelf with his own Subtilties.

He died *April* 28. 1400 ; there is ſomething melancholy
in the Nature of his Death, He was bit in the Lip by a little favourite Dog, which turn'd to an incurable Diſtemper.

PAUL, called DE CASTRO, becauſe he was born at
Caſtro, a Town in the Kingdom of *Naples,* flouriſh'd in the
Fifteenth Century : He profeſs'd the *Law,* in ſeveral Univerſities of *Italy,* for Fifty Years, his Explanations upon
the *Laws* of the *Digeſt* and *Code,* are in ſo great Eſteem, that
Cujacius ſays, *Qui non habet Paulum de Caſtro, tunicam ven-*
dat & emat. He died in a very advanc'd Age, in 1437.

BUDEUS, was of a Noble Family, and born at *Paris,*
1467. He ſpent Three Years at *Orleans,* and after that,
ſome at *Paris,* in the Study of the *Law,* but made no great
progreſs therein : At laſt, his Inclination to Learning
got the better of his Pleaſures ; and tho' his Friends repreſented to him the Danger of deſtroying his Health, by his
cloſe Application to Study, no Perſwaſions could draw him
from it ; and that he might follow it without Interruption,
he retired to the Village of *Hieres,* in the neighbourhood of
Paris ; where, in a very ſhort time, he acquir'd as much
Learning, as if he had had the beſt Maſter, and the moſt
worthy Competitors to animate and inſpire him with Emulation.

He

He foon gave Publick Marks of his Improvements, and after having tranflated fome *Greek* Authors, put out his *Obfervations* upon the Books of the *Roman Law*. *Francis* I. made him his *Library-Keeper*, and *Mafter of Requefts*. The exceffive Heats in the Year 1540, having oblig'd the King to retire for Air towards the Coafts of *Normandy, Budeus* went with him; but being feiz'd on the Road with a violent Fever, he return'd home, and died the Twenty third of *Auguft*, 1540; leaving behind him a numerous Family, of Four Sons and Eight Daughters.

JOHN PAUL ALCIAT, a *Milaneze* Gentleman, was the firft, as Mr. *de Thou* fays, who united the Study of the *Law* with polite Learning, and the Knowledge of Antiquities. His Works upon the *Law*, and his *Emblems*, are Proofs of his great Capacity and Judgment. *Francis* I. brought him into *France*, where he taught the *Law* at *Avignon* and *Bourges*; after that, paffing the *Alps*, he profefs'd it at *Bologna, Ferrara*, and laftly, at *Pavia*, where he Died, in the Year 1550. His *Epitaph*, which I have here fet down, is to be feen in the Church of St. *Epiphania*: *Andreæ Alciato Mediolanenfi Jurifconfulto, Comiti, Protonotario Apoftolico Cæfareoque Senatori, qui omnium doffrinarum orbem abfolvit primus Legum ftudia antiquo reftituit decori, vixit annos 58. menfes offo, dies quatuor, obiit pridie Idus Januarias, anno* 1550.

FRANCISCUS CONNANUS, Sieur *de Coulon* and *de Rabeftan*, was a *Parifian*, and Son of one of the *Judges* of the *Exchequer*, or *Mafters* of *Accompts*. He ftudied the *Law* at *Orleans*, under *Peter Stella*, and at *Bourges*, under the famous *Alciat*, who was fo taken with his Wit and great Parts, that he fhew'd him all poffible Marks of his Efteem. At his return to *Paris*, he follow'd the Bar, and was afterwards a *Mafter of Accompts*; and at length, preferr'd by *Francis* I. to be *Mafter of Requefts*, in 1544. He was fo zealous to improve this Study that he undertook to reduce it to a Method; but the Tendernefs of his Health, prevented his finifhing it: He was but Forty three, when he died, which happen'd in *September* 1551.

BARONIUS, a Native of *Leon* in *Britany*, profefs'd the *Law* with *Duarenus*, at *Bourges* ; the Emulation between thefe Two Learned Men, fet them at Variance. We have a *Commentary* upon *Juftinian*'s *Inftitutes*, fome *Interpretations* upon the other Books of the *Law*, and a Treatife of *Benefices*, and fome other Matters, written by the firft. He died *Auguft* 22. 1550. Aged 55.

DUARENUS, was born at *Brien* in *Britany*, where his Father was a *Judge*, and whom, tho' very young, he fucceeded in his Office. He came to *Paris*, in the Year 1536; where he read Lectures upon the *Pandects*, I fuppofe, as Deputy to fome Profeffor : He was intimately acquainted with the Learned *Budeus*, who imparted to him much of his Knowledge of the *Greek* Language, and *Roman* Antiquities : He took great Pains whilft he was at *Paris*, to improve *Budeus*'s Three Sons in the *Law* ; being willing thereby to repay the Obligations he ow'd their Father.

He was fent for to *Bourges*, in 1538, Three Years after *Alciat* left that Place ; that he might join the Practice with the Theory of the *Law*, he quitted his Profefforfhip, and came to the Bar at *Paris*, where he ftaid only Three Years or thereabouts. *Baudwinus*, who fucceeded him in the Faculty at *Bourges*, prevail'd upon his Collegues to recal him ; and to remove all Obftacles, yielded to him the Point of Precedency.

The Dutchefs of *Berry*, Sifter to *Henry* II. increas'd his Penfion, as Chief Profeffor of the *Law*, and made him her *Mafter of Requefts* : So that no Body, except *Alcitatus*, acquir'd fo much Reputation in that Univerfity. His Writings, which are perfectly free of the Barbarifm of the Gloffaries, contain nothing but the pure Sources of the *Roman Laws*. The defire he had, not to fhare this Honour with any Man living, made him jealous of his Collegue *Baronius* ; but that ended with *Baronius*'s Death, and turn'd into fo paffionate an Efteem, that he endeavour'd all he could, to perpetuate his Memory, by erecting a Monument in honour of him, which he adorn'd with an Epitaph. This kind of Behaviour, which is very common between Men of the fame Profeffion, feems to be elegantly defcrib'd by *Horace* in this Verfe ;

Urit enim præfens, extinctus amabitur idem.

Dua-

Duarenus had other Collegues, who reviv'd his Difquiet; He could not with any Patience fee *Bodwinus* out-ftrip him; and his Death, inftead of eafing him of his Pain, did but encreafe it, when he found *Cujacius*, who had more Merit, fucceeded him : The Quarrels that arofe between them, would have ruin'd the Univerfity of *Bourges*, had not *Cujacius* given way, by retiring to *Valence* to teach the *Law* there. *Duarenus's* Works were always in great Efteem among the Learned, and *Cujacius* himfelf valu'd them exceedingly; for notwithftanding their frequent falling out, he us'd to fay, he was much oblig'd to his Collegue, for making him double his Pains, which had greatly contributed to his Advancement. However, it is to be obferv'd, that the Works of *Duarenus* upon the *Canons*, infinitely furpaffes all that he has wrote upon the *Civil Law*. He died in 1559, Aged Fifty Years.

DU MOULIN, defcended from a Noble Family, was born at *Paris*, towards the latter End of the Year 1500: He came to the Bar at Twenty five; and follow'd the Study of the *Roman, Canon*, and *French Law*, with fuch Application, that his Name foon became famous all over *Europe*. He us'd to fay of himfelf, *That he would neither yield to, nor be taught by any one*; which Saying would have become any other better than him. He had a vaft and tranfcendent Genius, more than is to be exprefs'd; his Learning was not to be equall'd, and he had the Theory, join'd with the Practice of the *Law*, in the higheft Perfection. But how great foever his Knowledge of the *Roman Law* might be, he was infinitely more Learned in the *Canon*, in our *Ufages* upon *Beneficial Matters*, and in the *French Law*.

He was ever at Work, and had read fo many Books, that 'tis incredible : He lov'd ftudying fo much, that he refus'd to be made a *Counfellor* in the Parliament of *Paris*, left it fhould take him from his Reading. Yet, there is one Fault in this great Man's Works, that is, his Style; which he form'd after the Model of the *German* Authors, having read a prodigious Number of them : He feems to have borrow'd from them that harfhnefs of Expreffion, and confufed manner which appears in all his Queftions; but his Penetration and Exactnefs, in ftarting all the Queftions that can poffibly arife upon the Subject he handles, is fo

L 3   won-

wonderful, that not one escapes him. He examines them with such a Depth, and states the Reasons of doubting with so much Skill, that the Reader is puzzled which Side to take: Then he determines with so much Judgment, and such convincing Proofs, that one cannot help condemning the very Uncertainty, which those Reasons of Doubting had occasion'd: So that one may liken him to the Sun, which still casts Light, notwithstanding the Opposition of the Clouds. In short, there never was in *Europe*, nor ever will be, a Man of so deep and penetrating a Genius, and so laborious, as Monsieur *Charles Du Moulin*.

His Life was chequer'd with good and bad Fortune: He died at *Paris*, in 1566.

BALDWINUS was born at *Arras*, the First of *January*, 1620. His Father was a *Counsellor*, and the King's chief *Advocate*. He studied *Latin* and *Greek* at *Louvain*, and afterwards turn'd to the *Law*, of which he render'd himself Master the more easily by living with *du Moulin*. Afterwards he profess'd the *Law* at *Bourges*, for Seven Years; and then at *Strasburg*, *Heidleberg*, *Douay*, and *Besançon*; from whence *Henry* III. then King of *Poland* only, sent for him, and made him one of his *Counsellors* of *State*: As he was preparing to follow that Prince into *Poland*, a violent Fever carried him off, on the Twenty fourth of *October*, 1523. his Body was buried in the Cloyster of the *Mathurins*, in the College of *Arras* at *Paris*. We have several of his Works that are in pretty good Esteem; amongst the rest, a *Commentary* upon the *Institutes*, and another upon the *Laws* of *Romulus*, and the *Law* of the *Twelve Tables*.

Mr. *de Thou*, calls him a *Lawyer* of a *sure Judgment* and *exact Diligence*; and *Cujacius* us'd to say of him, *That he had a better Head for the* Law *than himself, if he would but have taken a little more Pains*: However that was, *Baldwinus* was not insensible of the Emulation that reign'd then among the chief *Lawyers* of his Time; so that by endeavouring to make himself able to contend with them, he acquir'd a great Knowledge of the *Law*, of which the Books he left behind him, as well as the great Esteem *Margaret* Dutchess of *Savoy* and *Berry* had for his Worth, are uncontestable Proofs. He died at *Bourges*, in 1586, and was buried in the Church dedicated to St. *Hypolitus*, near the famous

mous *Duarenus*, who was his Adverſary. Thus Providence was pleas'd, that thoſe Two who could never agree together in their Lives, ſhould reſt together after their Deaths.

HOTOMANNUS, originally deſcended from a *German* Family, was born at *Paris*, *Auguſt* the Twenty third, 1524. He begun about Fifteen to ſtudy the *Law* at *Orleans*, and after Three Years ſpent therein, obtain'd a Doctor's Degree. His Father, who was a *Counſellor* in the Parliament of *Paris*, put him to the Bar, with a Deſign of bringing him into his own Employment ; but the young Man, had more Mind to follow the Study of the *Roman Law*, and other polite Learning : 'Tis ſaid, he read Publick Lectures in the Law-Schools in *Paris*, at the Age of Twenty five. He was afterwards Profeſſor of *Law* at *Strasbourg*, and then at *Valence* ; the Credit of which Univerſity was very much increas'd by his Merit. He was call'd to *Bourges* Three Years after, by *Margaret* of *France*, King *Henry* the Second's Siſter ; from whence he went to *Geneva*, and after teaching the *Law* there for ſome time, he went to *Baſle*, where he died in 1590, Aged Sixty five Years. He left Two Sons, and Four Daughters : The Eldeſt *John Hotoman*, Author of the Burleſque Piece called *Antichopinus* ; and of *Anticolaſon*, which is an Apology for his Treatiſe of the *Ambaſſador*.

The Father, who is here ſpoken of, was ſo famous a *Lawyer*, that St. *Marthe* makes him almoſt equal to *Cujacius* ; yet, 'tis certain, he minded the *Antiquities*, more than the Deciſions of the *Roman Laws*.

CUJACIUS, the moſt celebrated of all the Interpreters of the *Roman Law*, was born at *Tholouſe* ; his Parents were of the Scum of the People ; but Nature made him amends for the Baſeneſs of his Extraction, by endowing him with a Gènius, next to a Prodigy : He learnt the *Greek* and *Latin* Languages, without the Aſſiſtance of any Maſter. He was better qualify'd than ever any Man was, to be an excellent Profeſſor of the *Law* ; I mean, by the Uprightneſs of his Heart, the Clearneſs of his Underſtanding, his ſound Judgment, accompany'd with polite Learning, and an exquiſite Diſcernment ; to all which, he added an indefatigable Application.

Theſe

These extraordinary Qualifications, one would think, should have procur'd him a Professorship; yet, his ungrateful Countrey, after putting him to the Trouble and Fatigue of a Dispute, preferr'd his unworthy Competitor; which crying piece of Injustice, made him leave *Tholouse*; and 'twas, perhaps, on this Occasion that he said, *Ingrata patria non habebis offa.*

M. *de l'Hopital*, afterwards Chancellor of *France*, fetch'd him to *Bourges*, from *Cahors*, to which Place he had retir'd: He profess'd the *Law* near Forty Years; sometimes at *Tholouse*, sometimes at *Cahors*, then at *Bourges*, and *Turin*; and lastly, again at *Bourges*, to which he retir'd at the pressing Instances of the *Magistrates*.

He had every where a full Audience, his Scholars follow'd him up and down, and his great Reputation, got him every day new ones: He never gave an Opinion, which he did not think infallible; nor made any scruple to require time, if he was in the least doubt of answering the Question propos'd to him, with that Confidence and Certainty, which usually attended his Determinations: And tho' his Penetration was very great, whether he undertook to interpret or reconcile the seeming Contrarieties of the *Law*, He always spent Seven Hours in preparing for every Lecture; and by that means, was able to personate all those great Men, whose *Decisions* compose the most valuable Parts of the Body of the *Law* In short, his Writings have the majestick Gravity of *Papinian*, the rich Abundance of *Ulpian*, the Sweetness and Chastness of *Paul*, and the Concisenefs and Sententiousness of *Affricanus.*

In a Word, 'tis easie to perceive, that he had united in himself, all those different good Qualities, which were distributed among those great Men, and made them admir'd by the World: But that which is most to be esteem'd, and agreeable to Civil Society, is, that none of these Perfections were eclips'd by any of those Blemishes which Learned Men are often subject to. His deep Meditations had not sowr'd his Temper; nor was his vast Knowledge accompany'd with the least Pride: He was Affable and Modest to all the World, heard every one kindly that address'd themselves to him, instructed them with Patience, talk'd to them with the utmost gentleness, and always sent them back charm'd with his Treatment, and made of

them

them fo many Friends. A Learned Man, may by Skill in his Profeffion, attract the Admiration of the World ; but if he would be beloved, he muft add Mildnefs and good Manners to his Learning, which *Cujacius* has fhewn us are not incompatible.

The prodigious Quantity of his Works, and the Correctnefs in all of them, are invincible Arguments of the Beauty of his Mind, and unwearied Application : He has explain'd, *ex profeffo,* moft of the *Roman Laws* ; and there are fcarce any that may not be underftood by the help of his Works.

Pope *Gregory* XIII. appriz'd of his great Worth, and knowing that he had penetrated farther into the Myfteries of the *Roman Law,* than any other, endeavour'd to bring him to *Bologna,* by offering him a very confiderable Salary.

He was *Honorary Counfellor* of *Grenoble* and *Turin* ; but his Infirmities and Bufinefs, did not often allow him to make any Advantage thereby.

M. *de Thou* fays, that *Cujacius* was the Firft and the Laft, fince the Antient *Lawyers.*

He died at *Bourges,* in the Year 1590, Aged Sixty eight or Seventy Years. All the Orders of the Town, in feveral Bodies attended his Funeral ; and the next Day after his Burial, M. *Marefchal, Counfellor* in the Parliament of *Paris,* who had formerly been his Scholar, publickly made his Funeral Oration.

Papirius Maffon, who wrote the Abridgment of this great Man's Life in *Latin,* has collected abundance of Epitaphs made in honour of his Memory.

When he was dying, he forbad the publifhing of any of his Works but what he had already put out ; yet, all that could be got of his Writing, has been fince printed : He alfo order'd, that his Books fhould be fold by Detail ; with a Defign of difappointing fuch as might collect his *Annotations* on the Margins, and publifh them at the Expence of his Reputation ; having made them only for himfelf, without that Order or Method that is requifite in Writings defign'd for the Prefs.

I cannot omit mentioning here a kind of Difpute, between fome of the Learned, which ought to have the Preference *Cujacius* or *Du Moulin.*

Du Moulin, by conſent of the beſt Judges, has been allow'd to be the Prince of the *French Lawyers*; and certainly,
he would ſurpaſs all the Writers upon the *Law*, if there
could be any one ſuperior to *Cujacius*.

If I may be permitted to give my Thoughts in ſo nice a
Matter, I think, both of theſe great Men have excell'd each
other : *Du Moulin* is more inventive, and has a deeper and
more tranſcendent Genius : *Cujacius* is clearer, more uniform, and perfect. *Du Moulin* handles Matters with more
Vivacity and Extent ; *Cujacius* with greater Order, Exactneſs, and Elegancy ; is more eaſily underſtood, and never
goes from his Point.

Thoſe who have moſt envied the latter, pretend that he
is Dull ; but at the ſame time allow, his Works upon
the *Law*, are ſo exact and correct, that there is nothing
wanting.

Anthony Favre ſays, *Nihil ferè intactum in Jure reliquit & aſ-
ſiduo labore vicit tarditatem ingenii.* But *Du Moulin*'s greateſt Admirers, admit that he has neither Order nor Method ;
and that it were to be wiſh'd, he had wrote with *Cujacius*'s
Politeneſs, Plainneſs and Brevity.

But let us end the Parallel of theſe two great Men, by
ſaying, that *Cujacius* made the *Roman Law* his particular
Study ; of which he acquir'd ſo compleat a Knowledge,
that he has ſurpaſs'd all that went before, and ought to be
a Guide to thoſe that come after him.

Du Moulin, who did not apply himſelf particularly to the
Study of the *Roman*, excell'd in the *Canon* and *Cuſtuma-
ry Law* ; but in ſo tranſcendent a meaſure, that no one
could ever come near him : Therefore, as one is beyond
Contradiction the Prince of the *French Lawyers*, the other is
unqueſtionably the Prince of the *Interpreters* of the *Roman
Laws* ; and both incomparable in their different Ways and
Manner.

BRISSONIUS, Preſident in the Parliament of *Paris*, was
born at *Fontenay le Comte* in *Poitou* : He was firſt *Advocate-
General.* *Henry* III. us'd to ſay, that no Prince in the World
could brag of ſo Learned a Subject as *His* BRISSON,
as he call'd him by way of Excellence : Therefore he employ'd him in ſeveral Negotiations of Peace, and to collect
his *Ordonnances*, and thoſe of his Predeceſſors. He was
the

the Author of Two Pieces upon the *Roman Law*; one, *De verborum quæ ad jus pertinent significatione*; and the other, *De formulis & solennibus populi Romani verbis*, which are full of exquisite Learning: He had given hopes of other Works, when he was kill'd at *Paris* in a shameful manner: Some of the *Leaguers* being angry that he was not of their Party, broke in upon him, and hurried him to Prison, where they strangled him on the Fifteenth of *November*, 1591; but they paid for it with their Lives a few Days after, by order of the very Heads of the *League*. His Body is interr'd at St. *Cross de la Bretonnerie*.

DION. GOTHOFREDUS was born at *Paris*, in 1549; where, in process of Time, he acquir'd great Reputation. The Civil Wars having oblig'd him to leave *France*, he profess'd the *Law* in some of the Universities of *Germany*: After the Death of *Cujacius*, no means were left unattempted, to persuade him to accept of his Chair, but he was otherwise engag'd in *Germany*. He died in 1622, Aged Seventy three, leaving behind him most excellent *Notes*, and some other Works upon the *Law*, *History*, and other parts of polite Learning.

There was another *Dion. Gothofredus*, known more particularly by his *Histories*, who was Son to *Theodorus*, the Eldest Son of *Dionysius* of whom we are now speaking: This *Theodorus* was also remarkable for his great Learning; but he wrote nothing upon the *Law*.

JAC. GOTHOFREDUS, second Son of *Dion.* settled at *Geneva*, where he was preferr'd to the Chief Offices of the Government; he was a Man of universal Learning, understood *Greek*, *Chronology*, the *Fathers*, *Councils*, and *Ecclesiastical History*: The best of his Works, is his Learned *Commentary* upon the *Theodosian Code*. He did not live to publish any of his own Works; but *Anthony Marville*, Professor of *Law* at *Valence*, having purchas'd his Library of the Executors, gather'd from it that vast Work, which he printed at *Lions*, in Four Volumes in Folio, in the Year 1665; the rest of his Writings have since appear'd.

ANTO.

ANTONIUS FABER, a Native of *Bourg* in *Breſce*, was a long time the Chief *Magiſtrate* there : After the Exchange of the Province, the Duke of *Savoy* being unwilling to loſe ſo uſeful a Man, made him Preſident of the Council at *Geneva*, and afterwards of *Chambery*.

This able Magiſtrate, in the midſt of all his great Employments, dedicated ſome of his private Hours to the Publick ; He made ſeveral *Commentaries* upon the *Law*, which are printed in Eight Volumes in *Folio*. He has carry'd his Notions a greater length than any of the Moderns. He had a vaſt Underſtanding, which was never diſcourag'd by the greateſt Difficulties ; but he is juſtly accus'd of deciding too Magiſterially, contrary to the receiv'd Opinions ; and of taking too great a Liberty, in adding to or clipping the *Laws* : He carries his Niceties too far, and a Man muſt be aware, left he be miſled by them ; for in going from the common Opinions, he alſo frequently leaves the Principles. In a Word, 'tis impoſſible to expreſs the Subtilty of this Author, but he is very far from being ſure.

Bachovius, a *German* Author, has wrote againſt the Second Part of his Book, *De Erroribus Pragmaticorum* ; and *Jer. Borgias*, of *Naples*, has cenſur'd his Treatiſe *De Conjecturis* ; but it muſt be allow'd, their Criticiſms are not all of them juſt. His *Code* is reckon'd the beſt, and leaſt faulty of his Works, in that he does not ramble, but generally keeps to adjudg'd Caſes : But notwithſtanding all the Faults in his other Works, it were to be wiſh'd he had lived to finiſh Two ; that is, his *Rationalia*, which goes no farther than the Twenty ſixth Book of the *Digeſt*, and his *Juriſprudentia Papiniana*, wherein his Deſign was to have comprehended all the *Law*, according to the Order of the *Inſtitutes* ; but he made only the Firſt Book. He died in 1622, Aged Sixty ſeven Years.

ANTHONY MORNAC, *Advocate* in the Parliament of *Paris*, was one of the moſt famous *Lawyers* of his Time, remarkable for his great Probity and Learning : To his Skill in the *Roman Laws*, he added that of the Practice of the Bar ; and had undertaken a Compariſon between the *Roman* and the *French Law*, a Work that deſerves the higheſt Commendation, but he did not live to finiſh it ; what we have of it, is enough to make us regret the Loſs

of

of the reft, it were to be wifh'd fome able Hand would
continue, and might have the Happinefs of finifhing it.

I could here mention feveral other *Lawyers*, whofe Writings have contributed to facilitate the Study of the *Roman*
Laws; but it would be an endlefs Work : And I gave the
Reader to underftand in the Beginning of this Chapter,
that my Defign was only to mention the moft renown'd of
them ; thofe who are defirous of knowing the reft, need
only confult the Book intitled, *Le Bibliotheque des Interpre-*
tes du droit; written by M. *Simon, Counfellor* in the *Prefidial*
Court, and *Affeffor* in the *Marfhalfea* at *Beauvois.*

C H A P. XXXI.

Of the Dispositions requir'd for the Study of the Roman Law.

IF it be true, that nothing can be more ferviceable to fuch
as embrace the Profeffion of the *Law*, than the Study of
the *Roman Laws*; it is alfo neceffary they fhould bring
thofe Difpofitions with them, which are requifite to make
them full fuccefs therein.

It is with the *Roman Law* as with moft other Sciences ; I
mean, that fuch as defire to be Proficients in it, muft befides
Natural Talents bring with them a fincere Defire of Learning.

Among thefe Natural Talents, we muft reckon firft, a
found Judgment, good Memory, and *clearnefs* of *Expreffion.*

And if it be certain, that all Men ought to labour as much as
poffible to form their Judgments ; it is yet more incumbent upon thofe who follow the *Law*, to have their Judgments
form'd before they begin : And indeed, as the *Laws* are
nothing elfe, but the Refult of the Meditations of a vaft
Number of wife and underftanding Men, is it poffible their
Beauty fhould be perceiv'd, by fuch as have not Difcern-
ment enough to follow that which is moft Reafonable ? The
Principles of the *Civil Law*, being only an Emanation from

the

the *Law of Nature* and *Nations*, we muſt firſt learn theiṙ Principles, before we enter upon the *Civil Law*.

A right Conception is no leſs neceſſary in Studying the *Law* ; for by that means, we are enabled to diſcover the Circumſtances, which make the Difference in two Caſes, that at firſt ſight appear to be intirely the ſame.

To ſoundneſs of Judgment, and a right Conception, we muſt add a good Memory ; *We know nothing,* ſays the *Roman* Orator, *but what we remember* : Therefore, it would be in vain to take Pains to learn the Definitions and Principles of the *Law*, unleſs the Student can retain them ; beſides, as the Number of the *Roman Laws* is vaſtly great, and have either a great Conformity, or a very apparent Oppoſition, 'tis not ſufficient to have a lively Memory, but it muſt be ſtrong and unconfus'd.

Memory is generally reckon'd a mere Gift of Nature, altho' Experience ſufficiently juſtifies, how much it may be improv'd, by Care and Vigilance ; this muſt be done by daily Exerciſe. Nature is generally more liberal to us, than we are grateful to her, and ſeems to require nothing more in return for the Talents ſhe beſtows upon us, than the neceſſary Exerciſe for their Cultivation and Increaſe ; yet, how many are there that never think of this Matter ? And whilſt ſome neglect to improve the Gifts they have receiv'd, we ſee others by Care and Pains repair the Injury Nature has done them, by her Parſimonious Hand.

Let not thoſe who complain of a bad Memory, ever deſpair of mending and making it more happy ; Let them know, that as it may be quite loſt for want of Exerciſe, 'tis ſtrengthen'd by employing it ; 'tis true, if it be over-burden'd, 'twill be difficult for it to anſwer our Expectation ; but when manag'd prudently, will acquire more ſtrength. A continual Exerciſe, with Moderation, accuſtoms it inſenſibly to what we expect from it ; but Experience has put this Matter beyond Doubt, and therefore, I ſhall not enlarge thereupon.

Clearneſs of Expreſſion is another Qualification, requiſite in ſuch as would ſucceed in the Study of the *Law* ; becauſe without it, it would be impoſſible to unravel the nice Diſtinctions, in which the Point of Deciſion often lies.

I

I agree, that all Men are not born with thefe Difpofitions, and that 'tis very feldom they are all found, in any eminent Degree, in the fame Perfon ; but to begin the Study of the Sciences, 'tis fufficient that Nature promifes thefe Accomplifhments, and fhews an early Difpofirion, which by Care and Application, will with Time, infallibly ripen and come to Perfection.

After thefe Natural Talents, we have already obferv'd, all Students in the *Law*, ought to be animated by a ftrong Inclination for Study ; for the Mind and Memory are averfe to Burthens that are difagreeable to them.

Laftly, The Study of the *Law*, ought to be preceded by a perfect Knowledge of all kind of polite Learning, efpecially the *Roman* Hiftory.

As to polite Learning, if it be requifite for making a Progrefs in all other Arts and Sciences, 'tis much more abfolutely fo in the Study of the *Roman Law* ; the Proof whereof is eafie : The *Roman Laws* were compos'd, as I have already often faid, by the moft Learned and Wife Men that flourifh'd in different times at *Rome* ; and therefore, were conceiv'd in fuch proper and apt Terms, that it would be very difficult to put others in their Places of equal Energy, and confequently are to be underftood only by fuch as by their Studies, have contracted a Familiarity with the Expreffions made ufe of in the pureft *Latinity*.

In regard to Hiftory, I have fpoken fo fully in the Beginning of this Work, concerning the Relation of the *Roman Laws*, to the *Hiftory of that People*, by whom they were made, that I need fay no more here on that Subject.

It may therefore be fafely concluded, that fuch as have reap'd no other Benefit from their Studies, than the Duft of the Schools, are in no Capacity to undertake the Study of the *Roman Law* ; which fublime Science will not difcover it felf, but to thofe, who by improving the Endowments Nature has given them, have laid in a great Stock of Learning : Befides, they muft employ in Study a fufficient time every Day, for many Years ; for how diligent foever a Student in the *Law* may be, it will be a great while before he is fenfible of the Progrefs he has made therein.

And

And tho' thefe Difficulties that arife from the vaft Extent of the *Roman Law*, may intimidate young Beginners, they will find in themfelves Motives to fpur them on, if they have improv'd as they ought, by their Leffons in the Claffes.

The Glory of Succefs, is proportion'd to the Pains and Labour that attends it; and the Difficulties, how great foever they may be, when we are able to furmount them, difcourage none but thofe, who either have no Ambition for Glory, or want Perfeverance to deferve it.

Whatever Pains the Application which the Study of the *Law* requires, may coft, the Advantages that accrue by it, are more than a fufficient Recompence ; which Confideration, ought to encourage Youth to employ their whole time in a Study, the End whereof is not fo much to obtain Degrees, as to improve their Underftanding, and refine their Reafon.

By what is here faid, 'tis evident I have not been over-ftudious to conceal the Difficulties of the Study of the *Law*, and the Time it requires. In the next Chapter, I fhall fhew the fhorteft and moft eafie way to fucceed therein ; whch I think my felf the more oblig'd to do, the End of this Work being to point out to Youth, the Courfe they are to obferve in the purfuit thereof.

CHAP. XXXII.

Of the Method to be observ'd in studying the Roman Law.

EVERY one knows, that to be in a Condition to make any Progress in the Study of the *Law*, *Justinian's Institutes* must be the first Book we read, they are the first Elements of the *Law*, made by Order of that Emperor, for the Benefit of the Youth who have a mind to apply themselves that way: They cannot be too often read, nor too perfectly learn'd, since they contain an Abridgment of the whole Oeconomy of the *Roman Law*.

To succeed herein, the *Definitions* and *Titles* are first to be learn'd by heart; then the *Text* is to be read over carefully, with the *Notes* made by *Vinnius* thereupon; after which, it will be very easie to reap the Advantage of the *Commentaries* made in the Schools; the *Paraphrase* of *Theophilus* will be of great help towards a right Understanding of the *Text*, by means of the several Cases therein reported upon most of the *Paragraphs*.

As to the Text of the *Institutes*, we must not be satisfy'd with once reading it; we must turn it over and over, and as far as possible retain it: For it is the Text that is the chief Object of their Application, who desire to make any Progress in the Study of the *Law*; the right Sence of which cannot be taken, unless the very Terms are known. The Style, in the Body of the *Roman Law*, especially in the *Institutes* and *Digest*, is so fine and pure, the Terms are so proper and well chosen, that there is no making use of any other, without running the Hazard of forsaking their true meaning, or at least rendring them obscure.

One thing, which Beginners ought especially to take Care to avoid, is the reading of abundance of Books: We ought to make choice of the Best, read them often, and endeavour to understand and retain their Substance; above all, we ought not to meddle with large Commentaries, which are rather apt to confound than help Beginners: A plain and

easie

eafie way is what Youth is pleas'd with; by which Means, being encourag'd with the Progrefs they make, they are infenfibly accuftom'd to a noble Emulation and Exactnefs, that leads them by Degrees to all fublime Learning.

The reading the *Inftitutes,* ought to be follow'd by that of the the Two laft Titles of the *Digeft,* which it is fit alfo to get by heart ; one of them contains the Explanation of thofe *Laws,* in which there is any *Ambiguity,* the other the Rules of the Ancient *Law* ; that is, certain General *Deci-fions,* taken from the *Lawyers Writings.* The next to be ftudied, are the *Paratitles* of the *Digeft* and the *Code* ; after which, the Student will be in a Condition to come at the true Sence of the *Laws* themfelves ; having firft pro- pos'd the Cafe, and deduc'd the Reafons for doubting and deciding according to our common practice, in the Exerci- fes which our Profeffion obliges us to make every Day.

I cannot help obferving in this Place, that if their Pri- vate Studies are of great ufe to forward them in the *Law,* the Inftructions which they receive in the Schools, when they are follow'd as they ought to be, are incomparably of more Service : Thofe who are oblig'd to make Publick Le- ctures, are under a Neceffity of doing their utmoft, to make the moft abftrufe and obfcure Things clear and per- ceptible to the dulleft Underftanding : Befides, as St. *Je-rom* fays, *Habet nefcio quid latentis energiæ vivæ vocis actus & in aures difcipuli de autoris ore transfufa fortius fonat.*

Another thing which muft not be forgotten, is to look out and make good the Quotations we find in the Books of the *Law,* and carefully to examine their Application : The reading over the *Laws* that are quoted, gives us a better Conception of the Sence : And therefore, thofe who have any skill in this profound and fublime Science, agree, that it is the only means to fix the Principles of the *Law* in the Memory ; and even the greateft Difficulties, which, with- out fuch Affiftance, would but too eafily efcape us : There- fore, we muft be particularly careful in reading over and underftanding the Texts that are made ufe of by thofe Au- thors, which we make ufe of to direct us in our Study.

'Tis

'Tis not sufficient to read over the Texts of the *Institutes*, and the *Laws*, which are brought to explain some Principles; we must be able to understand what we read, and to retain it, in order to make a just Application thereof to such Questions as may offer. *Scire Leges non est verba earum tenere, sed vim ac potestatem, L. 17. ff. de Legib.* For which Reason, I thought my self oblig'd to set down here in a few Words, the Method to be observed therein.

The true Sence of a *Law*, is generally taken first from the *Law* it self; that is to say, the Terms in which it is conceiv'd: Secondly, from the Circumstances which may be suggested by the true Sence; to come at the Knowledge of which, we must first know, by whom the *Law* in question was made, upon what Occasion, and what was the Motive, and to whom it was directed. An Abstruseness in these Points is very disagreeable; and it is losing almost all ones Time, not to examine with Care, those Circumstances, which often serve to unravel the Difficulties that at first seem unsurmountable.

When we meet with *Laws* that are not to be understood by bare reading, we must have recourse to *Cujacius*, who is indisputably the best Interpreter of the *Roman Laws*, and most to be rely'd on; and as we may happen to meet with some *Laws* not explain'd by him, the *Gloss*, and other Interpreters are then to be consulted.

I shall here lay down a few Rules, by which those that have already made some Progress in this Study, may know how to reconcile those *Laws* that seem contradictory.

The first is, when one *Law* is oppos'd to another, to be certain of the true Reading of both; for the Texts of many *Laws*, have been corrupted by the Ignorance of Scribes, employ'd to write over the Body of the *Law*, before the Art of Printing was discover'd; they often transpos'd Words, Stops, and Comma's, and even whole Periods: Which Omissions or Transpositions, have frequently given the *Law* a quite different, and sometimes a contrary Sence.

It was the same formerly with the Abbreviations made use of by the Writers; which had introduc'd into the *Laws* a prodigious Obscurity: Therefore, the Emperor *Justinian*, to take away that Inconveniency, commanded *Tribonian* and the rest of the Compilers, not to make use of them in the Composition of the *Digest*.

M 2   *Antoninus*

Antonius Augustinus has made a Book, *Emendationum*, in which he has corrected the *Laws* that have been corrupted by Omiſſion, Addition, or Tranſpoſition of Notes, Stops, Comma's or otherwiſe. *Cujacius* and *Faber*, have alſo corrected ſeveral defective Paſſages in the Body of the *Law*; but the Corrections of the latter, are ſometimes too bold, and therefore not to be blindly followed.

The ſecond Rule is, to take notice whether the Terms of the Two *Laws* that ſeem oppoſite to one another, are not capable of receiving different Significations; for if a Word in a *Law*, be taken in a different Sence from the Author's meaning, we ſhall find abundance of Contrarieties, where in reality there are none.

The third is, to ſee if One of the Two *Laws* which ſeem contradictory, does not contain an expreſs *Deciſion*, in the moſt rigorous Sence, and the other an Equitable Temperature.

The fourth is, to obſerve the Authors of thoſe *Laws* which ſeem contradictory, and examine if they were not of different Factions: For the *Lawyers*, who were of different Schools and Sects, were alſo frequently of contrary Opinions, upon the ſame Queſtion. I ſhall here inſtance ſome *Laws*, which are the Remains of their Diſſentions, and can be reconcil'd by no other means, than ſaying their Authors were of different Factions; *Vide L. 22. ff. de Jurejurando juncta. L. 5. ff. de Peculio, L. 9. §. 2. ff. de Acquir. rer. Diminio juncta. L. 23. §. 3. ff. de rei Vendicatione, L. 7. §. 7. ff. de Acquir. rer. Dominio juncta, L. 61. ff. de rei Vendicatione, L. 35. ff. de Peculio,* cum *L. 1. §. 10. ff. de dote Prælegata juncta, L. 1. §. 7. ff. Quando de peculio Actio Annalis eſt,* cum *L. 18. ff. de peculio Legato.*

The fifth is, to take notice of the Inſcriptions of the *Laws*, and the Titles under which they are placed; for there are many *Laws*, which are not to be underſtood, but by the Relation they bear to the *Titles* whence they are taken, and which cannot be apply'd to Matters of another kind: *Multa generaliter accepta incautos fallerent & reſtringi debent ad Argumentum libri unde deſumpta ſunt. Vide L. 2. §. 1. ff. de ſuis & Legitime hæredibus juncta, L. 3. ff. de ritu Nuptiarum, L. 153. ff. de Verborum ſignificatione, juncta epigraphe ejuſdem Legis, L 197. ff. eodem titulo juncta, L. 3. §. 14 ff. de Senatus-Conſulto Silaniano.*

The

The sixth is, to obferve the Time when the Two oppofite *Laws* were made ; *Sæpe enim diftinguenda funt tempora
ut confilientur jura* ; for that which was the laft made, repeals the former : And herein we muft take great Care to
diftinguifh betwixt the Ancient and the New *Law* ; for
many *Laws* in the *Digeft*, have been mutilated by *Tribonian*, in order to accommodate them to the *Law* obferved
in his Time, which makes it impoffible to reconcile them
any other ways than by faying, *Paffæ funt manum Triboniani.*

The feventh, is to examine carefully the State of the
Queftion propofed ; that is, whether it be *De genere an de
aliqua fpecie* ; for as the Orator fays, *Lib.* 2. *De inventione
Si ex contrariis Legibus controverfia nafcatur cum inter fe duæ
videntur, aut plures Leges difcrepare, confiderandum eft utra
Lex de genere omni utra de parte quadam, utra communiter in
omnes, utra in aliquam certam rem fcripta videatur* : The Queftions, *De genere atque univerfo infinitæ funt* ; but thofe, *De
fpecie funt finitæ* : Wherefore, *Semper generalibus fpecialia infunt, fed fpecialibus non infunt generalia* : For Example, a
Legacy of *Alimony*, does include *Meat, Drink, Cloathing* and
Lodging ; becaufe the Body cannot be fupported and maintain'd without them, *L. 6. ff. de Aliment. legat.* But not on
the contrary ; for a *Legacy* of *Cloathing*, does not comprehend
either *Alimony* or *Habitation.*

The eighth is, to examine whether the *Law* that is oppofite to another, does not give a different Decifion for
fome particular Reafon or Circumftance, which induc'd
the Maker to go out of the common Road ; *Quod jure fingulari contra communes juris regulas introductum eft non debet
trahi ad confequentias.*

The ninth is, to endeavour to find out the true Caufes
of oppofite *Laws*, which is often the Way of refolving the
greateft Difficulties, that we meet with in the Explanation
of the *Laws* ; *Ex facto enim jus oritur* : To this End, the
Terms of the *Law* are to be well examin'd ; the right Underftanding whereof, does not only lead us to the Fact and
the Cafe upon which the *Lawyers Anfwer* or Emperor's *Refcript* was made, but alfo to difcover the Rules and Principles of *Law*, by which the Queftion was determin'd.

If

If, notwithstanding all these Precautions, there still remains some Contrariety in the *Laws*, we must agree, that they are *Antinomies*, overlook'd by *Tribonian*, thro' Inadvertency ; *Etenim contra Justiniani mandatum nonnulla contraria, & pugnates Jurisconsultorum sententias in Pandectarum libris reliquit. Vide L. 1. ff. de usufructu accrescendo, juncta L. 20. ff. de Legatis 2°. L. 15. ff. de rebus creditis, juncta L. 34. ff. mandati, L. 18. ff. de rebus creditis, juncta L. 36. ff. de Acquir. rer. Dominio. L. 82. ff. de Legat. 2°. juncta L. 5. ff. ad Legem falcidiani, L. 22. ff. de Jurejurando, juncta L. 5. ff. de Peculio, L. 6. & 7. de servis exportandis. Vide etiam* Cujacium, *L. 8. Observat. cap. 9.*

In short, *Tribonian* has reported in the *Digest, Laws* that were utterly abrogated, or contrary to *Usage, Vide L. 41. ff. De pigneratitia Actione juncta, L. 22. de Pignoribus & Hypothecis, L. 122. §. 2. ff. de Verborum obligationibus, juncta L. penult. ff. Qui sine manumissione*, &c. *L. 9. ff. ad municipalem, juncta L. 5. ff. de statu Hominum.*

CHAP. XXXIII.

Of the Quotations and Abbreviations.

AS it is necessary in the first Place, to know how to make use of the *Quotations* which we meet with in the Books of the *Civil Law* ; and to find out the several *Laws* quoted by Authors : I thought it my Business to lay down some Rules for that purpose.

The Body of the *Civil Law*, as we said before, is compos'd of Four Parts, the *Digest, Code, Institutes*, and *Novels.*

The *Laws* of the *Digest*, are generally quoted by the first Word, and Number of the *Law* ; for Instance, *Lege siquis tertia Digestis de jure Codicillorum* ; sometimes the Number only, or the first Word of the *Law* from whence the Quotation is taken, is set down.

When a *Law* is divided into several *Paragraphs*, after the Number of the *Law*, that of the *Paragraph*, or the first Word of it, is set down ; for Example, *Lege 32. §. 11. Digestis de Donationibus inter virum & uxorem.*

Some-

Sometimes a *Law* of a Title in the *Digest*, is quoted by the firſt Word only, with the *Title*, without mentioning whether it be out of the *Digest* or *Code* ; and in that Caſe, it is an Indication that the *Law* quoted is in the Collection before ſpoken of ; that is, in the *Digest* or *Code*, according as they were before mention'd.

The *Laws* of the *Code*, are quoted after the ſame manner as thoſe of the *Digest*.

The *Paragraphs* of the *Inſtitutes*, are quoted after the ſame manner as the *Laws* of the *Digest* or *Code* ; thus a *Paragraph* of the *Inſtitutes* is quoted, by ſhewing the Number, and mentioning the firſt Word of the *Paragraph*, or by either ; but the *Title* under which the *Paragraph* is, muſt always be mention'd, as thus, *Paragrapho teſtes* 15. *Inſtitutionibus,* or elſe *apud Juſtinianum de Teſtamentis ordinandis.*

The *Novels* are quoted by their Number, with that of the *Chapter* and the *Paragraph* : For Example, *Novella Juſtiniani* 185. *Capite* 2. *Paragrapho* 4. or elſe a *Novel* is quoted by the *Collation*, and by the *Title*, *Chapter*, and *Paragraph*, after this manner, *In Authentiço, Collatione* 1. *Titulo* 1. *Cap.* 281.

As to the *Authenticks*, they are quoted by the firſt Words of them, after which is ſet down the *Title* of the *Code* under which they are placed ; for Example, *Authentiça cum teſtator Codice ad Legem falcidiam.*

This being laid down, let us now ſee how we ſhall go about to find out a Quotation in the Body of the *Law*.

If the Paſſage quoted is taken from the *Digeſt* or the *Code*, it will be beſt for Beginners to turn to the Alphabetical Table, of the *Titles* at the Beginning of the Body of the *Law* ; where having found the *Title* mention'd in the Quotation, they muſt then look in it for the *Law* ; by the Number or firſt Word.

If the Quotation is taken the *Inſtitutes*, they muſt likewiſe have recourſe to the Table of *Titles* ; and after having found the Book in which it is, look after it there, and then the *Paragraph* which is quoted.

If we would find out a *Novel*, there is nothing more to be done, than to look after it by the Number it is under.

If it be an *Authentick*, we muſt look in the Table of the *Code*, for the *Title* under which it is plac'd : It is ſo much the more eaſily found, becauſe all the *Authenticks* are inſerted in the *Code* in a different Letter.

M 4 To

To conclude, as thofe who have a Mind to look after any *Law,* wafte a great deal of time in turning over the the Table or Index, they may fave themfelves that Trouble, by rendring the Titles of the Body of the *Law* familiar, and getting them by heart, by which means, they will acquire a general Notion of the Places where every particular Matter is treated of, and without the leaft Difficulty, be able to find out any *Law* they have occafion to confult.

To compleat thefe Inftructions for young Students how to find out the Quotations in our Books, it remains only that I explain the Abreviations.

A B R E V I A T I O N S.

AP. JUSTIN. *Apud Juftinianum,* in *Juftinian's Inftitutes.*

ARG. or AR. *Argumento,* by an Argument drawn from fuch a *Law.*

AUTH. *Authentica,* in the *Authentick* ; that is to fay, the *Summary* of fome of the Emperors *Novel Conftitutions* inferted in the *Code* under fuch a *Title.*

CAP, *Capite* or *Capitulo,* in the Chapter of fuch a *Novel.*

C. or COD. *Codice,* in *Juftinian's Code.*

C. THEOD. *Codice Theodofiano,* in the *Theodofian Code.*

COL. *Columna,* in the firft or fecond Column of the Book quoted.

COLL. *Collatione,* in the *Collation* of fuch or fuch a *Novel.*

C. or CONT. *Contra,* this is generally us'd to denote a contrary Argument.

D. *Dicto* or *Dicta,* that is, the aforefaid, or *Law* or *Chapter* before quoted.

D. *Digeftis,* or in the *Digeft.*

E. or EOD. Under the fame Title.

F. *Finalis,* the laft or latter Part.

ff. in the *Pandects* or *Digeft.* The *Grecians* having made ufe of the Letter ᴨ, to fignifie *Pandects,* the *Romans* chang'd them into Two *f*'s join'd together. *Digeftorum liber ideo duplici ff. fignatur, quod Græci Pandectas per ᴨ cum accentu circumflexo notabant, fub quibus, & Digeftorum libri comprehenfi funt, unde facili litura ᴨ in ff. latine inolevit,* fays *Calvin* in his *Lexicon Juris.*

GL. *Gloffa,* the *Glofs.*

H. *Hic,* here, in the fame Title, *Law,* or *Paragraph.*

H. TIT.

H. TIT. *Hoc titulo,* in this Title.

I. or INF. *Infra,* beneath or below.

J. GLO. *Juncta Glossa,* the Glofs joined to the Text quoted.

IN AUTH. COLL. 1. *In Authentico, Collatione* 1. in *Justinian's Novels,* Part or Section 1, *&c.*

IN F. *In fine,* at the End of the *Title, Law* or *Paragraph* quoted.

IN PR. *In principio,* in the Beginning, and before the firft *Paragraph* of a *Law.*

IN F. PR. *In fine Principii,* toward the End of a Beginning of a *Law.*

IN SUM. *In fumma,* in the *Summary.*

L. *Lege* in fuch a *Law.*

LI. or LIB. *Libro,* in the Firft or Second Book, *&c.*

NOV. *Novella,* in fuch a *Novel.*

PAR. *Paragrapho,* in fuch a *Paragraph* or *Article* of the *Law,* or of a *Title* in the *Institutes.*

PR. or PRIN. *Principium,* the Beginning of a *Title* or a *Law.*

π. *Pandectis,* in the *Pandects.*

Q QU. or QUÆS. *Quæstione,* in fuch a Queftion.

RU. or RUB. In fuch a *Rubrick* or *Title.* The *Titles* were called *Rubricks,* from their being formerly written in Red Letters.

SC. or SCIL. *Scilicet,* that is to fay.

SOL. *Solutio,* the Anfwer to an Objection.

SUM. *Summa,* the *Summary* of a *Law.*

§. *Paragrapho,* in fuch a *Paragraph.*

T. or TIT. *Titulus, Titulo,* Title.

V. or *V. Verficulo,* in fuch a Verfe, which is a Part of a *Paragraph.*

ULT. *Ultimo, ultima,* the laft *Title, Paragraph* or *Law.*

O F

OF THE
USE and AUTHORITY
OF THE
CIVIL LAW
IN THE
Kingdom of *England*.

BRITAIN, as it is feparated by the Ocean; fo in the Ufe of the *Civil Law* it differs from all other Nations in *Europe*, the Kings thereof not allowing the *Roman Laws* fo great Authority within their Dominions, as the reft of the *European* Princes. Hence it is commonly reported amongft them, that we make but very little ufe of the *Civil Law*. And fome of the beft *French* Authors who are neareft to us, have affirm'd, that the *Englifh* make no ufe at all of the *Civil Law*; into which Miftake they have been led, by obferving, that none of our Countrymen have taken the Pains to Explain and Illuftrate it, as the Learned of other Nations have done: For it was impoffible, by the Books written in *Englifh*, they fhould underftand what *Ufe* and *Authority* the *Civil Law* was of among us.

But, in order to Treat more diftinctly of the Authority of the *Roman Laws* in *Britain*, it muft be firft confider'd, what Princes and Governments this Nation has been unde

der from the earlieſt Times; firſt, under the *Romans*, then the *Saxons*; after that, the *Danes*; and laſtly, the *Normans*. From which ſeveral Tranſmutations we ſhall clearly diſtinguiſh what Laws the *Britains* have from time to time been govern'd by; how far the *Civil Law* has been received, and of what Authority it ought to be at this time among us.

     Britain being bounded by the Ocean, was never attempted by any Foreign Power, till the time of *Julius Cæſar*: For neither *Hercules*, nor *Bacchus*, nor any other of thoſe Antient Princes (ſays *Diodorus Siculus*, who wrote the Hiſtory of the Reigns of *Julius Cæſar* and *Auguſtus*) carried their Conqueſts ſo far. *Polybius* reckons what is related by the *Roman* Hiſtorians of the *Britains*, to be Fabulous; and *Dio Caſſius* likewiſe ſays, neither the *Greeks* nor *Romans* were at any Certainty concerning *Britain*; but that all they reported of it was Gueſs-work. The firſt *Roman* who came over into *Britain* with an Army, was *Julius Cæſar*; who having conquer'd all *Gaul*, made an Expedition into *Britain*, under pretence of revenging the Affront the *Britains* had offer'd him, by ſending Supplies to the *Gauls* during the Courſe of his Wars; or rather excited by Ambition, and Deſire of Enlarging the Limits of the *Roman* Empire: And after ſome Advantages obtained, and Hoſtages receiv'd for the Payment of an Annual Tribute, return'd into *Gaul*: Wherefore *Tacitus* obſerves, He rather Diſcover'd than Conquer'd *Britain* for the *Romans*.

     After the Death of *Julius*, the Imperial Power ſhifting from the People to the *Cæſars*, the ſucceeding Emperors ſtrenuouſly labour'd to make a Conqueſt of *Britain*. *Auguſtus* was upon the Point of coming hither with an Army, but was prevented, firſt, by the Revolt of the *Pannonii*, then of the *Cantabri*. *Tiberius* contented himſelf with the *Britains* Annual Tribute; which, when they refus'd to pay under *Claudius*, he Invaded *Britain*; and with the Aſſiſtance of *Aulus Plautius Veſpatianus* and *Oſtorius Scapula*, gave them a ſignal Overthrow, leading their General *Carractacus* in Triumph to *Rome*, and aſſuming the Title of *Britannicus*. But *Nero*, who was his Succeſſor, was like to have loſt this new Acquiſition, had not *Suetonius Paulinus* made a brave Reſiſtance: Nor could the *Romans*

mans

mans render themfelves abfolute Mafters of *Britain*, till *Ve-ſpaſian*'s and his Son *Domitian*'s time. During which Interval of One hundred and thirty Years the *Romans* and *Britains* contended for the Sovereignty with equal Fortune; But then being embroil'd in Factions and Civil Wars among themfelves, were eaſily overcome by the *Roman* Generals; and, to their great Misfortune, never having been under the Adminiſtration of One Perſon, became an eaſie Prey to the *Roman* Eagle.

For both the South and North *Britains* and *Caledonians* were fubdu'd under *Veſpaſian* and *Domitian*; and the *Britiſh* Iſlands, under the Conduct and Bravery of *Petitus Cerealis* and *Julius Agricola*, added to the *Roman* Empire and all *Britain*, then firſt reduc'd into the Form of a *Roman* Province: From which happy Loſs of Liberty they learnt the *Roman* Manners, Laws, Language, Eloquence, Architecture, Art of making High Ways, and all other Sciences in which the *Romans* excell'd; and, as good Luck would have it, the Memory of theſe Tranſactions has been preſerved to us by *Tacitus*, Son-in-law to *Agricola*, and other *Roman* Hiſtorians, which otherwiſe would have been forgotten, and buried among the Ruins of the *Druids* fuperftitious Laws and Ceremonies.

BRITAIN being thus made a *Roman* Province, the following Emperors feem'd more careful of it than of the reſt of the Provinces depending upon the Empire; and to quiet the Diforders and Inſurrections that happen'd, viſited *Britain* oftener than any other part of their Dominions; affecting, above all the reſt of their Titles, to be called *Britannici*. Under the Emperor *Adrian*, when the North *Britains* were in Arms againſt his Lieutenant *Cn. Trebellius*, the Emperor coming into *Britain*, put them to flight; and to prevent the Incurſions of the *Picts* and *Scots*, built a Wall of Stakes and Turf of Eighty thouſand Paces long: But the *Scots* breaking thro' the fame, again invaded the South *Britains*: To whoſe Affiſtance *Helvius Pertinax* was fent by the Emperor *Antoninus Pius* and *Commodus*, who kept them in Awe for fome time, till under *Septimius Severus*, *Virius Lupus*, then Governour of *Britain*, being oppreſs'd by the Revolt of the *Britains*, implor'd the Emperor's Affiſtance, who came hither, accompany'd by *Baſianus* and

Geta,

Geta his Sons, and *Papinian* the Chief Juftice, and continued here for Three Years, built *Adrian's* Stone Wall, fubdued the *North Britains* and *Caledonians*, but not without
great flaughter on his part, and at length dyed at *Tork*: This
Emperor is by *Herodian* extoll'd, as more skilful than any of
the reft in Warlike Affairs. He had the Title of *Britannicus
Maximus*.

After *Severus* and his Son *Caracalla*, the fucceeding Emperors could fcarce keep *Britain* in obedience ; not being
a Match for them, by reafon of the frequent Infurrections
in other Provinces, which drew their Forces another way,
and many of the *Roman* Commanders, ufurping the Imperial
Power, Lorded it tyrannically over the *Britains*; among
whom was *Carausius* and *Alectus* in *Dioclefian's* Time; againft
whom *Conftantius Chlorus* being made Governor, and fent
into *Britain*, reftor'd the Ifland again to the Imperial Dominions : And being declared *Cæfar* by *Dioclefian*, begot
Conftantine upon *Helena*, Daughter to *Coel*, one of the
Britifh Kings ; which *Conftantine*, after his Father's Death,
was faluted Emperor by the *Britifh* Legions, and by their
Power and Bravery, fubduing his Rival *Maxentius*, made
himfelf fole Mafter of the *Roman* Empire.

This, the moft Illuftrious of all *Britains*, not only honour'd
Britain with his Birth, but by introducing a new kind of
Provincial Government, under the *Prætorian* Lieutenant of
Gaul, together with the Duke and Count of *Britain*, the
Count of the *Saxon* Shore, and the Lieutenant or Vicar of
Britain, who had the Adminiftration of Affairs both in
Peace and War committed to them : And was the firft *Ro-
man* Emperor that encourag'd the Chriftian Religion, and
favour'd the Light of the Gofpel.

Now that *Conftantine* the Great was born of his Mother
Helena in *Britain*, not only the Writers of our own Hiftory,
but Strangers do affirm ; and the fame is ftrenuoufly afferted againft *Julius Firmicus* and *Juftus Lipfus*, by the Moft
Reverend *James Ufher*, Archbifhop of *Armach*, who for his
great Learning, is defervedly reckon'd an Ornament of the
Britifh Nation.

In this Particular only our Emperor *Conftantine*, in all
other Refpects without Controverfie the greateft of all the
Emperors, was unhappy ; that thro' an Over-Ambition of
extending the *Roman* Empire, he tranflated the Seat thereof

of to *Byzantium*, a pleafant and ftrong place, fcituated almoft in the midft of the World : For the *Barbarians*, tempt-
ed by the Abfence of the Emperors, quickly invaded the
Empire ; *Italy* was feiz'd by the *Goths* and *Lombards*, *Spain*
by the *Goths* and *Vandals*, *France* by the *Franks*, and *Britain*
by the *Scots* and *Picts*; after which, the total Extinction of
the Eaftern *Roman* Empire immediately enfu'd.

Conftantine the *Great* being dead, his Sons *Conftantinus*
and *Conftantius*, and after them, the Emperor *Gratian* kept
Poffeffion of *Britain*, till *Valentinian*'s Time ; whofe Lieutenant *Theodofius*, once more delivered *Britain* from the
Oppreffions of the *Scots* and *Picts*, and put the Countrey into fo peaceable a Condition, that the Emperor order'd, the
Part which was fubdued by *Theodofius*, fhould be called *Va-
lentia*: The fame *Theodofius* being afterwards rais'd to the
Empire, was fucceeded by his Son, the Second of that
Name ; and after him, by *Honorius* a *Minor*. The Government, during his Minority, being by his Father committed
to *Stilicho*, who alfo reliev'd the *Britons* from the Invafions
of the *Picts* and *Scots*.

But afterwards, under the fame *Honorius* and *Arcadius*,
the *Picts*, *Scots*, and *Attacots* invading *Britain*, now quite
exhaufted, and the *Roman* Forces employ'd in defending
other Provinces againft the *Barbarians*, the poor *Britons*,
whofe Sighs are defcribed by *Gildas*, the moft Ancient of
our Hiftorians, and after him by *Beda*, in vain implor'd
the Emperor's Affiftance ; driven, fay they, by the *Barbarians* to the Sea, and then back to the *Barbarians*, they met
with Death every where. Nor was *Honorius* or *Valentinianus* III. ever in a Capacity to defend them from the Infults
of their Neighbours: So that *Britain*, about Five Hundred
Years after *Julius Cæfar*'s firft Entrance, became a Derelict.

Thus the miferable *Britons*, unable to refift the Fury of
the *Scots* and *Picts*, firft by them, and then by the *Saxons*,
were forced to fly for Safety, fome into *Bretany* in *France*,
and others into *Wales* and *Cornwal* ; and the few *Anglo-
Saxons* that remain'd, apply'd to their Neighbour the *Germans*, for help to expel the *Scots* and *Picts*.

Britain was deferted by the *Romans*, about the Year of
Chrift 1455 ; and *Julius Cæfar* firft entred it, Sixty Years
before Chrift's Nativity.

The

The *Saxons*, who were called in to help and protect the *Britons* against the *Scots* and *Picts*, after having subdued them, turn'd Traitors to their *British* Masters: Charm'd with the Fertility and Sweetness of the Countrey, they complain of not being paid their Wages, and sufficiently rewarded by the *Britons*: Wherefore, *Hengist* and *Horfa* undertake to satisfie their own Demands, by pillaging the People; to whom other *Saxon* Forces afterwards joining, they subdued the *Britons* in several Parts of the Island, created new Kingdoms and Principalities, and at length form'd the *Heptarchy*.

The first of the Seven Kingdoms was that of *Kent*, over which *Hengist* the *Saxon* made himself King, in the Year 445; the second was of the *South Saxons*, whose first King was *Ella*, who began his Reign in 488; the third was of the *East Angles*, first erected by *Offa*, in 575; the fourth of the *East Saxons*, began by *Erchwin*, in 527; the fifth of the *Mercians*, was first ruled by *Creda*, a *Saxon*, who began to Reign in 582; the sixth Kingdom was that of the *Northumbrians*, first possess'd by *Ida*, in the Year of Christ 588; the seventh and last, of the *West-Saxon*, was first govern'd by *Cerdicus*, in the Year 521; whose Successors, either by their own Bravery or the Strength of their Subjects, which were reckon'd the most Warlike of all the *Britains*, conquer'd the rest of the *Saxon* Kings, extinguish'd the *Heptarchy*, and brought all their Dominions under the sole Power of *Egbert* King of the *West Saxons*, in the Year 800; and he first impofed the Name of *England* upon *Britain*, and by his Edict, order'd the *Britons* to be called *Englishmen*; from which time, all Nations have diftinguifh'd us by that Name.

After *Egbert*, who out of the Spoils of the *Saxon* Kingdoms had erected the Monarchy of *England*, succeeded *Ethelwolf* and his Descendants, for a Hundred and Seventy five Years; during which time, they suffer'd great Slaughter and Damages by the Incurfions of the *Danes*, who poffefs'd the Kingdom for fome time, till the *Anglo Saxons* recover'd it, and were themselves in a fhort time, oblig'd to quit it to the Dukes of *Normandy*, whose Pofterity enjoy it to this Day.

But in the Time of *Ethelwolf*, the *Danes* invaded and plunder'd the Countrey of *Kent* ; and under *Etheldred*, that of *Northumberland* ; and afterwards, under *Elred*, *London* and *Exeter*, exacting Tribute from the *English* : At length *Swain* King of *Denmark* got Possession of the whole Kingdom, in the Year 1014 ; and with his Son *Canute* after him, enjoy'd it for Twenty eight Years. Upon the Death of *Canute*, the *English*, out of hatred to the *Danes*, recall'd *Edward Etheldred*, at that time an Exile in *Normandy* ; who, by the Assistance of *William* the *Bastard*, Duke of that Countrey, being made King of *England*, reign'd Twenty four Years, with great Piety and Justice ; and enacted several *Laws*, so just and agreeable to the Temper of the Nation, that his Memory is still venerable on that Account, and at length was canoniz'd.

Edward dying without Children, *Edgar Etheling* Grandson to *Edmond*, commonly called *Ironside*, and a Favourite of the People, endeavour'd to possess himself of the Kingdom ; but being under Age, and unfit to govern, *Harold*, Son of Earl *Godwin* by King *Canute*'s Daughter, seized the Throne, and got himself inaugurated by the Archbishop of *York*, in the Year 1046.

William Duke of *Normandy*, by his Embassadors, requir'd the Restitution of the Kingdom ; first, because he was the nearest of Kin to St. *Edward*, as being the Son of *Robert*, by *Emma* Daughter of *Richard* Duke of *Normandy*, who was St. *Edward*'s Mother ; and because St. *Edward* had by Promise made him Heir to the Kingdom, in case he died without Children ; and also *Harold* had by Oath engag'd himself, to assist *William* in getting the Kingdom after St. *Edward*'s Death.

William came with an Army, to vindicate his own Right and punish *Harold*'s Perfidy ; who being slain, he was proclaim'd King in 1067 : After a Reign of Twenty one Years, he was succeeded in *England*, in 1088, by *William Rufus* his second Son ; who dying without Children, the Crown fell to his Brother *Henry* I. youngest Son to the Conqueror ; in whom, after a Reign of Thirty five Years, and leaving no Children, the Male Line of *William* the First was extinct. He was succeeded in 1136, by *Stephen* of *Blois*, Son of *Adela*, *Henry* the First's Sister. To *Stephen* succeeded *Henry* II. and to him his Son *Richard* I. with

whom

whom ended the *Norman* and Foreign Government ; for
Richard and his Succeſſors were born in *England*, and ac-
cuſtom'd to the *Engliſh Laws:* And it is much for the Honour of the *Engliſh* Nation, that tho' the *Normans,* who
hated the *Engliſh,* endeavour'd all they could to abrogate their *Laws,* and introduce the *Norman Manners* and
Cuſtoms ; yet they ſtill preſerv'd, and have tranſmitted the
Engliſh Name to Poſterity.

From what is premiſed, the ſeveral Changes of Princes
and Governments which *England* has ſuffered, ſufficiently
appear : Let us now return to the different *Laws* made under thoſe ſeveral Changes and Revolutions, and ſee how
far the *Civil Law* obtain'd among them, and what Authority
it is of at this Day in *England.*

There is no Hiſtorical Account either of the *Laws* or Government of the *Britons,* before the Entry of *Julius Cæſar,*
except what we find in the *Roman* Authors : *Cæſar* relates,
that in *Britain* and *Gaul,* the *Druids* were both Prieſts and
Judges, and decided all kind of Publick and Private Con-
troverſies ; if Murther or any other Crime was committed,
or Diſpute happen'd about Inheritance or the like, they
determin'd it ; and ſuch as refus'd to ſtand to their award,
were forbid to appear at their Sacrifices : But of their
Laws and their *Holy Ceremonies,* there is no Account extant ;
not being permitted to commit any thing to Writing. But
Cæſar made no Alterations in the *Laws* of *Britain* ; He ſuffer'd them to be govern'd by their own *Kings* and *Laws* ;
only requir'd Hoſtages and a Tribute : And *Seneca* ſays,
Britain before Claudius's *Reign was SUI JURIS.*

But *Claudius* ſubduing a part of the Iſland, introduc'd the
Roman Laws ; and by his *Edict,* ſilenc'd the *Druids :* Which
made *Seneca* ſportingly ſay,

Ille Britannos　　　　*Colla Catenis*
Ultra noti　　　　　*Juſſit & ipſum*
Littora ponti　　　　*Nova Romanæ*
Et cæruleos　　　　*Jura ſecuris*
Scuta Brigantes　　*Tremere oceanum.*
Dare Romuleis,

'Twas

'Twas He, whofe All-commanding Yoke
   The fartheft *Britains* gladly took ;
Him the *Brigantes* in blue Arms ador'd :
   When fubject Waves confefs'd his Power,
   Reftrain'd with *Laws* they fcorn'd before ;
And trembling *Neptune* ferv'd a *Roman* Lord.

And *Tacitus* writes, that *Claudius* planted a Colony at *Doncafter*, to keep the Rebels in awe, and teach his Allies the Study of the *Roman Laws* ; and *Jof. Scaliger* underftands the ancient Poet, of the Times of *Claudius*, when he fays,

   Cernitis ignotos Latia fub lege Britannos
   Sol citra noftrum flectitur Imperium.

Tacitus alfo relates the Complaints of *Britain* under *Nero* in thefe Words ; *That whereas in former times they had only one King, now they were govern'd by Two ; the* Lieutenant *to fuck their Blood, the* Procurator *their Subftance.*

But *Britain* being intirely fubdued by the Prudence and good Conduct of *Agricola*, was reduc'd into the Form of a Province by *Vefpafian* and *Domitian* ; who, as well as their Succeffors govern'd it by the *Roman Laws*, and adminiftred Juftice to the *Britons* by *Roman Magiftrates* ; fuch as Proconfuls, Prefidents, Legates, Prætors, and latterly by Earls of *Britain*, or their Deputies ; the *Britifh Laws* being intirely abrogated.

Under *Domitian*, the *Roman Laws* had taken fo deep root in *Britain*, that *Agricola* exhorts them to build Temples, Market-Places, and Houfes after the *Roman* Manner ; and they accommodated themfelves fo well to the *Roman* Arts, that they learnt the *Roman* Eloquence, and Art of Pleading from the *Gauls*. And *Ariftides* the *Grecian* Orator, in the time of *Mark Anthony*, places it among the Encomiums of *Rome*, that fhe had rendred her *Laws* common, even to *Britain* ; and extended the Ufe of them as far as her Empire : And *Rome* is by *Claudian* called the Mother of *Arms* and *Laws* ; and by *Sidonius Apollinaris*, the Abode or Place of Refidence of the *Laws*.

N 2   The

The Use and Exercise of the *Roman Laws* in *Britain* appears also from this ; that under *Septimius Severus*, *Æmilius Papinianus* sat at *York*, as *Præfectus Prætorio* or Chief-Justice, which was the most eminent Degree in the Empire, and pronounc'd Judgment there ; concerning which, *Dio Cassius*, who wrote the Life of *Severus* is to be credited, altho' there is no mention of it in any of the other *Roman* Writers.

Severus, to wean his Sons *Antoninus*, *Caracalla* and *Geta*, from the Debaucheries of *Rome*, and keep his Legions from Idleness, came over into *Britain* ; and leaving his Son *Geta*, with some of his Counsellors and intimate Friends to govern the Inland Parts, subject to the *Romans*, went himself with *Antoninus*, at the Head of an Army against the *Caledonians* : In which Expedition, as they were riding together, *Antoninus* stopping his Horse, of a sudden drew his Sword, with intent to kill his Father ; but was prevented by the Interposition and Clamour of the Soldiers. *Severus* pass'd this over, and stifled his Resentment till he came to his Quarters, where he order'd his Son, together with *Papinian* and *Castor*, his intimate Friends, to come to him ; and having commanded a Sword to be laid before him, reprimanded his Son for making so villainous an Attempt, in the Sight of the Allies and Enemies ; and said, *If thou art desirous to put me out of the way, now kill me with thy own Hand ; or there is* Papinian, *who if thou commandest will obey thee.* This *Papinian* was made First Minister to the Emperor *Severus*, as well for his superlative Skill in the *Laws*, as that he was nearly related to the Emperor by a Second Marriage.

The *Caledonians* being subdu'd by *Severus*, he return'd to *York*, where he made the Edict, whereby it is provided, That if a Man had a Slave, which he bought, or came otherwise honestly by, and believed himself to have a good Title to him, tho' he proved to belong to another ; yet all Acquisitions made by that Slave, either with the present Master's Money, or by his own Work and Industry, should stand good in Law. And, on the contrary, if the Master knew the Servant to belong to another. This Edict was made in the Year when *Faustinus* and *Rufus* were Consuls, in which *Severus* died at *York*; and was wrote
by

by *Papinian :* For our Commentators are of opinion, that all the Laws both of *Severus* and *Antoninus* were written by *Papinian* with great Care and Deliberation : And the Learned think, that not only *Papinian*, but *Paul* and *Ulpian*, were both in *Britain* as Affeſſors to *Papinian*, and Coadjutors to *Geta* in the Adminiſtration of Affairs. All which is much for the Honour of our Nation : For there never was, nor ever will be, as *Cujacius* ſays, a Lawyer that excell'd, or can equal *Papinian* in that Science.

Ulpian and *Javolenus* alſo, bear witneſs in the *Pandects*, that the Government of *Britain* was under *Roman* Laws. The *Britiſh* Children were ſubject to Paternal Authority *ex Jure Romano, by the Roman Law*. And Fathers made Pupillary Subſtitutions ; but not unleſs they had firſt conſtituted their Heir by Will. And *Ulpianus* reports of *Severus*, that he gave the ſame Anſwer to *Vinius Lupus*, Governour of *Britain*. And *Javolenus*, in the Caſe of *Sejus Saturninus*'s Will, gives his Opinion, that the Eſtate ought to be reſtor'd by the Fiduciary Heir, if the Perſon to whom he was by the Diſpoſition of the Will to ſurrender it, happen'd to die before the time for the Reſtitution expir'd.

But the *Britons* not only conformed themſelves to the *Roman* Laws, but affected their Manners, Language, Dreſs, Eloquence and other Arts, which by Divine Povidence ſpread over the whole Countrey, that otherwiſe had continu'd under its Native Barbarity : For they were no whit improv'd by the *Saxons, Danes* and *Normans*. So that whatever our Anceſtors boaſt of, either of Beauty or Splendor, was all owing to the Manners, Vertues and Government of the *Romans :* And the *Britons* at length, ſo adapted themſelves to the *Roman* Diſcipline, that *Gildas* reports, the Countrey was called *Romania*.

Nor did the *Britons* forſake the *Roman Laws*, till they themſelves were deſerted by the *Romans*, which happen'd in the Time of *Honorius* ; when a barbarous People inhabiting the other ſide of the *Rhine*, invading this Countrey and plundering it as they pleas'd, reduc'd the *Britons* to ſo great Streights, that obeying no longer the *Roman Laws*, they erected a Government of their own, as *Zozimus* ſays ; which, however, they did not maintain long, being conquer'd

quer'd by the *Saxons*, and by them oblig'd to follow their *Laws*.

But forasmuch as some of our most celebrated *Lawyers* have advanc'd, that the *Romans* never impos'd their *Laws* upon the *Britons*, but suffer'd them to use their own; upon what Foundation I cannot imagine, since it is repugnant both to the *Roman* and *British* History; and both *Camden* and *Selden*, two famous Men, maintain and prove the contrary by most evident Testimonies; of whom one has render'd our Nation illustrious, by his *Chorography* and Annals of Q. *Elizabeth*; and the other by his exquisite Skill in our *Common Law*, to which he added that of the *Mosaick* and other Nations, with a singular Knowledge of the Oriental Languages: To whom may be added, *Spelman* the famous Antiquary; all proving by substantial Reasons, that the *Romans*, having abrogated the *British Laws*, introduc'd their own, and administer'd Justice by them, as long as the *Roman* Emperors continu'd Masters of *Britain*. And we ought to be convinc'd by the Arguments of those who excell'd, both in all kinds of Learning, and in the Knowledge of the Antiquities of our Nation.

This Opinion, however, seems to be oppos'd, by the Epistle sent to Pope *Eleutherius*, from *Lucius* one of our *British* Kings; whereby he desires the Pope to transmit to him the *Roman Laws*; which would have been an Absurdity, if *Britain* had then been govern'd by them. This Epistle was first printed in the Reign of *Henry* VIII. and has been recited by some of our Modern Historians, byass'd by the Desire of doing Honour to our Countrey, in order to give it the greater Credit; in which also *Lucius*, the first Christian King, desires to be admitted by the Pope to the *Christian Faith*.

But this Epistle is liable to Suspicion, because our most ancient *British* Writers, who take notice of it, say not a Word of the *Roman Laws*; and our later *English* Historians, affirm upon many Reasons, that it is spurious; First, because it bears Date in the Year of Christ 159, whereas *Eleutherius* was not Pope before 1030; 2dly, Because many of the Words favour of the *Norman Latinity* and the *English Law*; and that the Scriptures are quoted in it according to St. *Jerom*'s Translation, who flourish'd about Two hundred Years after *Eleutherius*: 3dly, Because neither *Geofrey* of *Monmouth*, *Hoveden*, nor any other of our antient Historians,

take

take any notice thereof. There are befides feveral Pre-
fumptions, that help to deftroy the Credit of this Epiftle ;
as, that the Pope fpeaks to *Lucius* in the Plural, *Vos eftis Vicarius Dei* ; which manner was introduc'd by fome of the
later Princes ; that the Stile of the *Roman* Language in
thofe Days, did not allow of the Pope's Expreffion, *Se Leges
Cæfaris poffe femper reprobare* ; that the Words *Protectione*
and *Pace*, are not of *Roman*, but a modern *Englifh* Stamp ;
that in the ancient Copies of the *Conqueror's Laws*, this Epiftle is not to be found ; that the *Conqueror's Laws* and *Cuftoms* of *London*, in which this Epiftle has been publifh'd,
are fubject to many Objections ; and feveral other grounds
of Sufpicion, which the Learned Dr. *Gerard Langhbain*, *Pro-
voft* of *Queen's* College in *Oxford*, together with his learned
Obfervations upon the *Antiquities* and *Laws* of the *Romans* in
Britain, in which, as well as in Univerfal Hiftory, he is
moft skilful, has communicated to me.

From hence, 'tis evident, the *Britons* were govern'd by
the *Roman Laws*, as long as it made a Part of the Empire ;
'till forfaken by the *Romans*, they were oblig'd to ftoop to
the *Saxon* and *Danifh* Yoke.

Tho' there remains but little Appearance of the *Roman
Laws*, under the *Saxon* and *Danifh* Governments, as being
intent in propagating their own, the more eafily to keep
the *Britons* in Subjection ; yet it will appear, the beft
and moft religious of their Princes, often imitated the *Romans* in adminiftring Juftice to their Subjects.

Thus under the *Saxon Heptarchy*, *Beda* tells us, *Ethelbert*
King of *Kent*, about the Year of Chrift 613, with Advice
and Confent of his Wife Men, made certain *Decrees* to be
obferv'd in *Judgments* between his Subjects, according to
the *Roman* Model ; in which he provides in the firft Place,
againft *Robbers of Churches*, of *Bifhops*, and others ; and thefe,
Bede fays, were wrote in *Englifh*, and obferv'd in his time.
This was the firft of the *Saxon* Kings that made *Laws* : Afterwards *Ina*, King of the *Weft-Saxons*, enacted more *Laws*;
then *Offa* King of the *Mercians*, put out the *Mercian Laws* ;
and after thefe, *Alured* King of the *Weft-Saxons*, made feveral Additional *Laws* ; and his Succeffors *Edward* the Elder,
Athelftan, *Edmund*, *Edgar*, *Etheldred*, all *Saxons*, and *Canute*
the *Dane*, publifh'd their feveral *Laws*, which are yet extant,
and have been tranflated into *Latin*, by *William Lambard*.

But

But in all thefe, there are few Judgments agreeable with the _Roman Laws_, which after _Juſtinian_'s Time, were ſcarce known to the _European_ Nations ; and the _Saxon_ Kings were very active in eſtabliſhing their Power, altho' many of them were remarkable for their Religious Zeal ; and 'tis to their ſhining Piety, the Erecting and Founding ſo many Cathedral Churches, Monaſteries, and Colleges is wholly owing. But this could not be expected from the _Danes_ ; who being Heathens, and invading _England_ in the Year 800, not only deſtroy'd Cities, Towns, Churches and Monaſteries, but Laws, Sciences, and all kinds of Learning. Theſe being expell'd, St. _Edward_, Sirnam'd _the Confeſſor_, form'd one _Common Law_, out of thoſe of the _Engliſh_, _Danes_, and _Mercians_, which are ſtill called _the Confeſſor's Laws_ ; and of which the _Engliſh_ afterwards grew ſo fond, that in the _Norman_ Times, whenever the People, oppreſs'd by the Severity of the _Norman Laws_, murmur'd and grew tumultuous ; the Kings uſed to ſooth and pacifie them, by promiſing a Reſtitution of the _Confeſſor's Laws_ : And in thoſe Days, our Kings at their Coronations, oblig'd them-ſelves by Oath to obſerve St. _Edward's Laws_.

When the _Saxons_ and _Danes_ were Maſters of _England_, the _Britons_ who had fled from their Fury into _Wales_, were govern'd by their own Kings ; yet none of their written _Laws_ are extant, before their King _Howel Dha_ ; who, about 940, having called his Biſhops and the moſt Learned of the Laity together, corrected the _Ancient_ and made _new Laws_ ; which he commanded _Blegaridus Longuaridus_, a Learned Man for thoſe times, to put into _Latin_ and Pub-liſh ; amongſt which, the Eighty fifth Article highly com-mends the _Roman Law_, for providing, that where the Num-ber of Witneſſes is not defin'd, _Two_ ſhall ſuffice ; and for not admitting he Teſtimony of _One_ : Yet that very _Law_ men-tions ſeveral Perſons, whoſe ſole Evidence is to be taken, as of the _Lord_ between two _Tenants_, of an _Abbat_ between two _Monks_, of a _Father_ between two _Children_, of a _Prieſt_ in a Matter atteſted before him, of a _Virgin_ in a Rape, of a _Thief_ impeaching his Accomplices at the Gallows ; and ſome others. Nor can we expect much Light concer-ning the _Roman Laws_ in theſe Ages, when _Juſtinian_'s Books lay buried, and there was ſuch an amazing Neglect of the Sciences over all _Europe_. The _Danes_ eſpecially deſtroy'd all

kind

kind of Literature in this Nation ; and thofe few *Roman* Remains which are to be feen in the Time of the *Saxons,* were taken from the *Theodofian Code,* and Fragments of *Gaius, Paulus,* and *Ulpian,* which with fome Parts of the *Pandects,* were then extant in *Europe.*

Let us therefore proceed to the *Norman* Period, in which the firft Kings made many Alterations in the Government, abrogating former *Laws* and enacting feveral new ones ; and laid the Foundation of the Government under our pre-fent Kings, who derive their Title and Succeffion from him. Now that the *Normans* introduc'd the *Ufe* and *Authority* of the *Civil Law* in feveral Cafes amongft us, is plain from what follows.

William Duke of *Normandy,* having got Poffeffion of the Crown of *England,* tho' he gave out he was Lawful Heir by *Edward's* exprefs Promife, and as his Kinfman ; yet he was not fo nearly allied to *Edward* as *Edgar,* Sir-nam'd *Etheling,* which fignifies the Peoples Darling : And therefore, to ftrengthen his Caufe of making War, he added another Reafon, *viz.* the Death of *Alfred, Edward's* Brother, and Banifhment of *Robert* Archbifhop of *Canterbury* ; from all which Caufes, he concluded his War to be juft againft *Harold* and the *Englifh.* But as foon as he had got the Crown upon his Head, he made feveral Alterations in their *Laws,* and inftituted new Forms and Methods in the Courts of Juftice ; turning many of the *Allodial* Lands belonging to the *Englifh* into *Feudal* Te-nure, and impofing many Taxes and Tributes, to which the *Englifh* had been Strangers till his Time : At length dying, and difinheriting his Eldeft Son *Robert,* he made his Second Son *William,* Sirnam'd *Rufus,* Heir to the Crown of *England.*

This *William,* commonly call'd the *Conqueror,* in the Be-ginning of his Reign, was prevail'd upon by his Nobles to command *Edward* the *Confeffor's Laws* to be obferv'd, with fuch as he fhould add thereunto. But the Kingdom being quieted, when he applied himfelf to make *new Laws* out of thofe obferved by the *Mercians, Danes,* and *Eaft Saxons,* which were the chief People in this Nation, he preferr'd thofe of the *Danes,* becaufe they came neareft to the *Laws* of the *Normans,* who were originally defcended from the *Danes* ; thefe he mix'd with the *Laws* of *Normandy,* and then publifh'd them in his

his own Name ; and many of them are ſtill in force among us. And notwithſtanding his Succeſſors, *William* II. *Henry* I. *Stephen*, *Henry* II. and others after them, always pacified the People when they grew uneaſie on account of the *Norman* Innovations, by promiſing to obſerve St. *Edward's Laws*; yet they never were ſo good as their Word, only the Barons got from K. *John* and *Henry* III. the Charter of *Liberties*, by which the Severity of the *Laws* before in uſe was moderated ; which they call'd the *Great Charter*, and which is to this time highly valued by us.

The *Conqueror's Laws* at firſt ſeem'd harſh to the *Engliſh*, and they often attempted to ſhake off the Yoke, till Time and Cuſtom made them eaſie and familiar, and by Degrees, acceptable to the People ; for the Force of a received Cuſtom, is very great in all Places ; and therefore, a *Law* is compared to a Tyrant, but a *Cuſtom* to a good King : And *Laws* which are given by *Preſcript*, have a kind of Servitude in them ; whereas *Cuſtoms* receiv'd by Conſent, govern thoſe that are ſtill free.

But above all, the Hardſhips introduc'd by the *Laws* of the *Conqueror*, This ſeem'd the moſt intolerable to the *Engliſh*, that whereas under their former Kings, the *Laws* were writ either in *Latin* or the *Saxon* Language, he order'd all his Laws and Proceedings in the Courts of Juſtice, to be writ in the *Norman* Dialect ; which neither the *Engliſh* nor *French*, many of whom were his Subjects, could underſtand : And moreover, that Children ſhould be taught the ſame in the Schools ; which St. *Auguſtine* charges the *Romans* with as a Hardſhip, they having order'd the Nations they conquer'd, to make uſe of the *Latin* Tongue in all their Judicial Proceedings : Yet this continu'd here till *Edward* the Third's time, when a *Law* was made, that all Actions and Pleadings in the Royal Courts of Judicature, ſhould be in the *Engliſh* Tongue.

That the *Cuſtoms* of *Normandy* were mix'd with thoſe of *England* by the *Conqueror*, is evident in many particulars ; and this the *French* ſay, was the Reaſon that *Charles* the VI. and VII. Kings of *France*, after recovering *Normandy* from *Henry* VI. whoſe Anceſtors had held it from the *Conqueror's* Time, did not immediately reform the *Cuſtoms* of *Normandy*, as he did thoſe of other Provinces, becauſe they had not been alter'd by the *Engliſh*, as agreeing with their

own

own native *Cuſtoms* ; the firſt that reform'd the *Cuſtoms* of *Normandy*, was *Henry* III. King of *France*, in 1583, till which time, the ancient *Cuſtoms* of that Countrey continu'd in force.

The *Conqueror* making uſe of his Abſolute Power, introduc'd ſeveral new Forms, and either chang'd the Old, or erected New Courts of Juſtice : There is indeed ſome mention of *Chancellors* in the *Saxon* Times, but the Court of *Chancery* was inſtituted under the *Conqueror*, and continued by his Succeſſors ; in which, a *Chancellor* appointed by the King preſides, and from him all Original Writs and Patents iſſue : It is the firſt in Dignity of all the great Offices. Out of this Court alſo come *Feudal Inquiſitions* ; and the *Chancellor* has Power of moderating the Rigour of the *Law*, and granting Relief in all Caſes of Fraud and Deceit cognizable before him, in the ſame manner as the *Prætor* aided, ſupplied, and corrected the *Roman Law* : And tho' ſome Learned Men amongſt us, have been of Opinion, that this Power was not granted in ſo full extent to the *Chancellors* by the *Conqueror*, but that it came to its preſent Grandeur by Degrees, in the Courſe of ſeveral Ages ; yet, 'tis certain the *Chancellors* had the ſame Power under *Henry* II. from what *John* of *Salisbury*, Contemporary with *Thomas à Becket*, ſays in his Book,

Quærendus Regni tibi Cancellarius Angli
  Primus ſollicita mente petendus erit
Hic eſt qui Regni Leges Cancellat iniquas ;
  Et mandata pii Principis æqua facit,
Siquid obeſt populo, vel moribus eſt inimicum ;
  Quicquid id eſt, per eum deſinit eſſe nocens.

And *Alexander Neckham* ſays of *Becket*, That he was prais'd for cancelling unjuſt *Laws*.

In the *Conqueror*'s Reign, the Court of *King*'s *Bench*, for determining Criminal and Civil Cauſes between the King and the Subject was erected ; and likewiſe the Court of *Common Pleas*, for judging of Matters between the Subjects ; as alſo the Court of *Exchequer*, in which all Matters relating to the Treaſury, Fines, Taxes, Confiſcations, and the like, are examin'd and determin'd : And tho' ſome have thought that theſe Courts, eſpecially the King's Bench,

were

were of an older Date ; yet 'tis moft certain they have
fubfifted among us from the *Conqueror*'s Time.

But the *Conqueror* exerted his Power in nothing more
than appointing the Terms for diftributing Juftice, and regulating the Method of Evidence, for whereas in other
Parts of *Europe* the Courts of Juftice are always open, except in Harveft and Vintage Seafons, and Holidays ; the
Conqueror eftablifhed Four ftated Terms of the Year, of fo
many Days each; out of which, no Profecution could
be carried on in any of thefe Supream Courts : He alfo
appointed all Evidence of Facts, to be heard and determin'd
by Twelve fworn Men, whom we call *the Jury* ; the Points
of *Law*, if any fhould arife, being left to the *Judges* : Of
which kind of Judgment, altho' there be fome faint Appearance under the *Saxon* Government, long before the
Conqueror's Time, yet it was by him reduc'd to a Method,
and continues in the fame to this Day.

The *Conqueror* alfo diftinguifh'd the Ecclefiaftical from
the Lay Courts ; for when under the *Saxon* Adminiftration,
the *Alderman* or Prefident together with the *Bifhop*, held a
Monthly Court of Juftice, called the *Centenary* or *Hundred*.
He commanded the *Bifhops* and *Archdeacons*, not to interfere
any more in the *Hundred*, but to confine themfelves to fome
Place appointed by the *Bifhops*, and there to judge according to the *Canon* or Epifcopal *Laws* ; and all were oblig'd
to obey their Sentence upon Pain of Excommunication,
and the King's Difpleafure : The *Sheriffs* and other Officers
being charg'd not to take Cognizance of any Matter belonging to the Spiritual Jurifdiction.

During the *Conqueror* and his Son *William Rufus*'s Reigns,
the *Civil Law* was not heard of in *England* ; for the *Pandects* were not reftored by the Emperor *Lotharius* till the
Year 1128, which was the Twenty eighth of our *Henry* I.
and *Irnerius*, after long teaching the *Civil Law* at *Bononia*,
died there in 1190. At the very fame that he began to
profefs it in *Italy*, *Vacarius* did the fame here ; for fo *Ger-
vafs* of *Dover*, writes in the Life of *Theobald* Archbifhop of
Canterbury under *Henry* I. *Tunc Leges & Caufidici in Angliam
primo vocati funt quorum primus Magifter Vacarius hic in Oxen-
fordia Legem docuit.* Now *Vacarius* read *Law* in the Year
1149, which was the Fourteenth of King *Stephen*, as appears from the *Norman* Hiftory, written by *Andrew Querce-
tanus*

tanus, where he fpeaks thus of *Vacarius*; *Magifter Vacarius gente Longobardus vir honeſtus & juris peritus cum Leges Romanas, anno ab Incarnatione* 1149; *in Anglia Diſcipulos doceret & multi tam divites quam pauperes, ad eum cauſa diſcendi confluerent ſuggeſtione pauperum de Codice & Digeſtis exćerptos novem Libros compoſuit, qui ſufficiunt ad omnes Legum lites quæ in Scholis frequentari ſolent, ſiquis eos perfecte noverit.* And the *Civil Law* was profeſs'd here by *Vacarius,* before *Placentinus* profeſs'd it in *France,* who after *Vacarius's* Death began to read upon it at *Montpellier,* in the Year 1196.

The Learned Mr. *Selden* fpeaks very much in Commendation of this *Vacarius,* believing him to be the *Rogerius* who is reckon'd amongft *Irnerius's* Scholars, and who wrote the Treatife *De Præſcriptionibus,* ſo highly efteem'd and prais'd by the Interpreters; and that he was the Author of that *Summary,* which excited *Placentinus* to make his after him; and *Azo* another, which all the Writers allow to be the beſt *Summary* of the *Civil Law.* Befides, 'tis plain this *Vacarius* was a Perſon of repute, from his being afterwards made Abbat of *Bech* in *Normandy,* and then upon the Death of *Theobald,* elected Archbiſhop of *Canterbury;* which See, either out of Religion, or fondneſs of a Monaſtick Life he refus'd, and died in the Monaſtery of *Beck,* in the Year 1180.

In the fame Reign, *Theobald* Archbiſhop of *Canterbury* fent *Thomas Becket* to *Bologna* in *Italy,* there to Study the *Civil Law,* in order to qualifie himſelf for Publick Buſineſs; who, upon his return was made *Doctor of Law* at *Oxford,* and is reckon'd one of the principal Civilians of that Univerſity: He was afterwards fent by the fame *Theobald* to Pope *Celeſtine,* to move him for the Revocation of the Legatine Power granted to *Henry* Biſhop of *Wincheſter,* the King's Brother; and Three Years after King *Stephen's* Death, by the Intereſt of *Theobald,* made Chancellor of *England,* by *Henry* II.

But foraſmuch as almoft all the Clergy and Laity in King *Stephen's* time, applied themſelves to the Study of the *Civil Laws,* and the Number of Students became incredible; the Divines, and Mafters of Arts, either moved by Envy, or a View of ingratiating themſelves with the Biſhop of *Wincheſter,* who was *Theobald's* declar'd Enemy, prevail'd with King *Stephen* by an Edict, to forbid teaching the *Civil Law*

in

in *England*, and making use of Law-Books; so *Vacarius* was silenced: Which Prohibition some will have to be understood of *Gratian*'s Decree, at that time not publish'd, nor did *Vacarius* read upon the *Decree*, but the *Laws*, which *Salisbury* says *Theobald* brought into *England*. But *Stephen*'s Prohibition was of little Signification, for *John* of *Salisbury*, who was famous in those Days, writes, that the greater Opposition the Study of the *Law* met with from the Wicked, the more it flourish'd and grew into repute; and immediately after King *Stephen*'s Death, the Study of the *Roman Laws* began to revive, and *Becket* was made Chancellor upon *Theobald*'s Recommendation.

In those Days, every one that affected Learning, both Civil and Ecclesiastical Persons, eagerly pursu'd the Study of the *Civil Law*, as the High Road to Rewards and Preferments; and the Authors of those Times, as *Jo. Sarisburiensis*, *Pet. Blessensis*, and *Girald. Cambrensis*, all shew by their Writings, that they were skill'd in the *Civil Law*; which is the Reason that the Professors of Divinity, Philosophy, and Arts of that Age have left grievous Complaints against the *Roman Laws*, the Admission of which, had extinguish'd all other Studies; that those who applied themselves to the *Law*, did not qualifie themselves for it as they ought, by the previous Knowledge of other Arts; and that the Clergy were over diligent in following it: All these Faults, *Giraldus Oxonienfis* blames in the Students of his time; and tells us of a certain Clerk called *Martin*, who reprehended the *Oxonians* in a Publick Assembly, for suffering the Imperial *Laws* to smother the rest of the Sciences, as *Minervius* a famous Orator of *Paris* had foretold: All which, *Giraldus* wrote under *Henry* II. for he Dedicated his Works to *Baldwin*, Archbishop of *Canterbury*, who held that See in his Reign. And *Daniel Morley*, who travell'd first into *Portugal*, and then to *Tholouse* to Study; after he return'd to *Oxford*, where he says the Study of the *Civil Law* was in great vogue; complains, that *Aristotle* and *Plato* were shut out of Doors for *Sejus* and *Titius*, and *Ulpian*'s Traditions deliver'd in Golden Letters: And *Roger Bacon*, a great Philosopher and Mathematician of the same Age, blames the Prelates for neglecting the Study of Divinity, and that the Cavils of the *Law* had obscur'd Philosophy; putting them in mind at the same time of King *Stephen*'s

Pro-

Prohibition ; and that the *Regulars, viz.* the *Franciscans* and *Dominicans,* tho' otherwise very ignorant, were famous for their great Skill in the *Law* ; and the Secular Priests, out of Covetousness and a Desire of Preferment, had for Forty Years addicted themselves to the Study of the *Law* ; and not wrote one single Treatise in Divinity all that time.

In the Reign of *Henry* III. *Stephen Langton,* a celebrated Professor of Philosophy and Divinity in *Paris,* and afterwards Archbishop of *Canterbury,* rattles off the Monks of his time, for affecting to be called *Lawyers* and *Decretists,* and forsaking the Field of the true *Booz,* that is, the Holy Scriptures, and betaking themselves to Secular Knowledge for Worldly Interest. And *Robert Holcot,* of the Order of Preachers at *Northampton,* complains of the vast Numbers that flock'd to the Study of the *Civil Law* ; *Leges & Canones istis temporibus innumerabiliter sunt fœcundæ, concipiunt divitias & pariunt dignitates ad illas confluunt, quasi tota multitudo Scholarum his diebus.* Now *Morley* flourish'd in the Reign of *Richard* I. *Neckhamus* and *Longtonus* under *Henry* III. and *Holcot* under *Edward* III. And *Eatred* Abbat of *Ri----,* in the Diocess of *York,* and *Hugo de St. Victoire,* writing of the Abuses in Monasteries, reckon up Twelve, in which *Monacus Causidicus,* or a *Monk-Lawyer,* has the Fifth Place.

But the flourishing State of the Civil Law at *Oxford* at that time, is sufficiently evident from the Professors of it, whose Memory is preserv'd to this day : For soon after *Irnerius,* there were many famous Professors of it at *Oxford,* who were in great reputation, even with the *Italians.*

Amongst them is *Aldricus,* Professor of Laws at *Oxford,* whose Sayings are often quoted by *Accursius* in his Glosses, and who was the Author of many Learned Books upon the *Civil Law.*

After him, *Richard,* firnamed the *Englishman,* and *William de Dororeda,* were, according to *Jo. Andreas,* Professors of Laws at *Oxford.* The first of them wrote a Copious Treatise, entituled, *Summa Ordinis Judiciorum* ; the latter, another *De Ordine Judiciorum,* and is by *William Dorochius* and others called *William* of *Drogheda.*

After these, came *Alanus, Gulielmus, Jo. Severleus,* Professor of Laws at *Oxford,* who publish'd Lectures upon the *Civil Law, Stephanus Anglus* and the Famous *Mylius,* with many

many others : And the Univerfities fo abounded with Students of the Law, that *Matth. Paris* reports a Conftitution of Pope *Innocent* IV. then publifh'd, forbidding the Admiffion of any Advocate or Profeffor of Laws to any Ecclefiaftical Dignity, and the reading of the *Civil Law* for the future in the Kingdoms of *France, England, Scotland, Spain* and *Hungary*, notwithftanding the refpective Kings and Princes fhould confent thereto : But thefe Princes ftill preferved the Imperial Laws ; and our Kings, efpecially *Edward* I. and *Edward* III. were great Friends and Favourers of the Students and Profeffors thereof.

In *Edward* the Third's Reign, when the Chapter of *Winchefter* had elected *William de Raleigh* for their Bifhop, againft the King's Inclinations, he appeal'd from their Eleletion to the *Roman* Pontiff, and fent his Appeal to the Readers of the Law, and other Men fkilful in that Science at *Oxford* for their Opinion, who approved of it.

In the fame Reign, when *Mafters* and *Batchelors in Divinity* and *Arts* at *Oxford*, trufting in their Numbers, made certain Statutes againft the *Doctors* and *Batchelors* of *Laws*, relating to the Anfwers of the *Batchelors* in both Faculties, and had proceeded to a Sentence of *Profcription* againft fuch as refufed to fubmit to them, the King, upon Complaint of the *Doctors* and *Batchelors of Laws*, appointed the Bifhops of *London* and *Ely*, and others his Delegates, to examine the matter ; who having heard the Parties, avoided the Statutes, and revoked the Sentence ; and the fame was afterwards ratified by the King's Charter, wherein he promifes his fingular Favour and Protection to the *Doctors* and *Students* of the *Civil Law.* All which was afterwards confirmed by the Charter of *Richard* II.

But the Lawyers of other Countries relate, that our King *Edward* I. out of his Care to have the *Civil Law* taught in *England*, (a Circumftance omitted by our own Authors) invited *Francis Accurfius*, Son of the Famous *Accurfius* who wrote the *Gloffes*, from *Bologna*, where he profefs'd the *Law*, into *England* to teach it at *Oxford* ; who taking *Tholoufe* in his Way, read Publick Lectures there upon the Famous Law. *L. unic. C. de Senten. quæ pro eo quod intereft.* Of which *Bartolus* takes notice in his Commentaries upon the fame ; and he was called the

King

King of *England's Advocate* by him, and was fent to read *Law* at *Oxford* ; and there is ftill extant a Precept to the Sheriff of *Oxfordſhire* to put him in Poffeffion of the Royal Mannour at that Place , for him and his Family to dwell in. He had accordingly the Mannour of *Marlegh* given him for that purpofe, which then was in the King's hands, by reafon of the Minority of *Hugo Le Difpenfe* Son of *John* deceas'd, who held the fame *in Capite* ; in which Precept the King calls *Francis Accurſius* his *Trufty and Well-beloved Secretary* : And the fame *Accurſius* feems to be defcribed in another Letter, wherein he is called *Francis* of *Bologna, Doctor* of *Laws*, and *Counſellor to the King of* England. But whether he taught the *Law* at *Oxford*, is not certain : For all that the *Italian* Authors fay of him, is, that fearing his Goods fhould be confifcated, he return'd to *Bologna*.

The fame King *Edward*, when, upon the Death of *A-lexander* King of *Scotland*, there arofe that arduous Queftion between the *Engliſh* and *Scotch*, concerning the direct Dominion of all *Britain*, and the Parliament was fummon'd to meet at *Norham* upon *Tweed* ; fent for all the *Canoniſts* and *Civilians* throughout his Dominions ; becaufe he look'd upon them to be the moft proper Judges of the Affair in Difpute.

Another remarkable Monument is the Letter of King *Henry* to the other Univerfity of *Cambridge* ; wherein he commands the Students in the *Civil* and *Canon Law*, diligently to attend the Publick Lectures in their refpective Faculties ; and to pay the *Ordinaries* and *Beadles* belonging to the fame their Annual Salaries.

This Letter, *Caius*, in his Defence of the Antiquity of this Univerfity, fays, was wrote by *Henry* I. in the Year 1101, and is ftill preferv'd in their Regiftry : But it is utterly inconfiftent with the Hiftory of thofe Times : For *Juftinian's* Books were not then recover'd by *Lotharius* ; nor had *Gratian* publiſh'd his Edict ; nor did any of our Kings take upon them the Stile and Titles of *Lord of* Ireland, before *Henry* II. nor of King of *France*, before *Edward* III. So that this Letter muft have been from *Henry* V.

From what has been faid, it is plain, the Study of the *Civil Law* has flourifh'd in this Kingdom from the Reign of King *Stephen*; that our Kings have ever had it in their Royal Protection, and fince the Reign of *Henry* VIII. allow'd an Annual Salary for the Maintenance of *Royal Profeffors* of the *Civil Law*, who before were fupported by Contributions from their Audience. And in the Univerfity of *Oxford* King *James* I. befides the Yearly Stipend, added a *Prebendary* in the Church of *Salisbury* towards the Support of the *Profeffors* of the *Civil Law* in that Univerfity : Befides which, feveral of the Founders of Colleges in both Univerfities have appropriated many Fellowfhips for the Maintenance of Students in the *Civil Law*.

When the Epifcopal Power decreas'd, the Revenues of the Church began to be diminifh'd, and the Study of the *Civil Law* languifhing for want of Encouragement, *Edward* the Sixth, a Prince endow'd with all kinds of Royal Vertues, and a great Encourager of Learning, took care to to revive it : For in the fecond Year of his Reign having appointed the Earl of *Warwick*, the Bifhops of *London*, with *Rochefter* and Lord *Paget* Comptroller of his Houfhold, and feveral other Great Men, to vifit both Univerfities, he gave them Inftructions, That whereas it had been reprefented to him, that the Study of the *Civil Law* in both Univerfities did not only flacken, but was in danger of being totally extinguifh'd ; therefore they fhould ufe all their Power to revive and encourage the fame.

So much for the *Civil Law* in the *Schools* and *Univerfities*. It remains, that we fhew, of what Ufe and Authority it is in the Courts of Juftice.

The Kings of *England*, above all other Princes of *Europe*, boaft of their Independency of the *Roman* Empire and its Laws ; becaufe the *Romans* had no other Right, but that of Arms, to *Britain* ; which, at laft, they relinquifh'd to the Natives. Hence it is, that the *Italian, Spanifh*, and Lawyers of other Countries commonly affert, that our Kings acknowledge the Emperor neither in Law nor Fact, have no Superior in their Dominions but God alone ; exercife all Rights of Sovereignty ; are Monarchs, and, as Sovereign

reign Princes, no Appeal can lie from them ; that since *Conſtantine* the *Great,* they have Power of wearing the Imperial Crown, and in the Ceremonial Books of the Church of *Rome,* are ſet down among the few Kings who are Crown'd and anointed by their own *Laws :* Therefore *Cujacius* had no Foundation for ſaying, the Kings of *England* were once *Feudataries* to the Emperor, but thoſe of *France* never ; whereas both *France* and *England* ſhook off the Imperial Yoke in the ſame Age. But the *Britons* make another Title, that is, of a Derelict ; for they were utterly abandon'd by the *Romans,* whoſe Aſſiſtance they implor'd againſt the *Scots* and *Picts,* and that they might be intirely a free People, did not permit the *Roman Laws* to be mix'd with their own.

For this Reaſon, perhaps, our Interpreters ſay, that when other Princes or Private Perſons mention the *Law* in *Bargains, Contracts, Statutes, Compromiſes, Wills,* or other Acts whatſoever, it is to be underſtood of the *Roman Civil Law,* which is common to all Nations ; but when the King of *England* mentions the *Law,* his own, that is, the *Law* of *England,* is always intended : And therefore, *Edward* II. made a *Law,* that the Imperial *Notaries* ſhould not exerciſe their Office in the Kingdom of *England,* left he ſhould thereby ſeem to acknowledge a Dependence upon the Empire.

But our *Lawyers* do not allow the Kings of *England* the ſame Independency in relation to the Pope, to which See they ſay they are *Feudataries,* and that King *John* ſurrendred and acknowledg'd himſelf to be a Vaſſal of Pope *Innocent* III. Wherefore, when *Alexander* III. allow'd the Queſtion concerning Poſſeſſion of Lands in *England* to be determinable by *Henry* II. *Johannes Hoſtienſis* obſerves, that if it had happen'd in King *John's* Reign, the Pope, without derogating from the Royal Authority, might have taken upon him to decide the Queſtion ; becauſe that King had made his Kingdom *Feudatory* to the See of *Rome* : And therefore, all *Engliſh* Malefactors apprehended in *England,* were not to be ſent to *Rome,* but puniſh'd here by the Pope's *Marſhal.* But theſe are vain Pretenſions ; for the Popes have no other Proof than the Grant or Promiſe of a certain Tax by *Ina* one of our *Saxon* Kings; and *John,* from whence they pretend our

Kings

Kings are tributary to them : Befides, there is a wide
Difference between being Tributary and Feudatary ; for
Cujacius himfelf allows, that *Charles* King of *France* paid a
Tax to the Pope, and yet all the *French Lawyers* affert their
Kings are more independant than any, of Foreign Jurifdi‑
ction : But our Kings could in neither of thefe Cafes oblige
their Succeffors nor any ways impair their Rights, without
the Confent of Parliament.

The *Englifh* have ever preferv'd their *Laws* with the
utmoft Exactnefs ; and when any Attempt has been
made in Parliament to change or moderate them with
the Equity of the *Roman Law*, it has been ftrenuoufly op‑
pos'd, of which there are feveral Inftances in the Journals ;
Thus when the Bifhops in *Henry* the Third's time, moved
for an Act to Legitimate Children by fubfequent Marriage,
as *Juftinian* has, upon very good and fufficient Reafons fet
forth, in the *Conftitution* for that purpofe, and the Church
allow'd the fame ; the Earls and Barons unanimoufly an‑
fwer'd, *Nolumus Leges Angliæ mutari, quæ huc utque ufu funt
approbatæ : We will not fuffer the Laws of* England, *hitherto
approved by ufe, to be changed.* In the Parliament under
Richard II. when *Thomas* Duke of *Glocefter*, and others of
the Nobility accufed *Alexander Nevil* Archbifhop of *York*,
Robert de Vere Duke of *Ireland*, and others of Treafon, and
the Common *Lawyers* and *Civilians* were requir'd to give
their Opinion; they anfwer'd, that the Complaint or Accu‑
fation was not regular, either according to the *Law* of *Eng‑
land* or the *Civil-Law* : But the Earls and Barons faid it
was according to the *Ufage* of Parliament, and protefted
they would never fuffer the Kingdom of *England* to be go‑
vern'd by the *Roman Law*. And tho' 'tis not unlikely this
might have been the Effect of Paffion, and the Heat of thofe
factious Times, yet it has been ever fince duly obferv'd ;
and all Authority and Ufe of the *Civil Law*, utterly exclu‑
ded from the Courts of Juftice, wherein the *Law* of *Eng‑
land* is practifed.

The Courts of Juftice in this Kingdom proceed different‑
ly, fome according to the mere *Law* of *England*; as the
Court of King's Bench, Common Pleas, and other inferior
Courts depending on them ; others do not follow the mere
Law of *England*, but proceed according to Equity and good
Con‑

Confcience ; as the High Court of *Chancery,* and Court of *Requefts* ; of which I fhall fpeak feparately.

The Courts which follow the mere *Law* of *England,* have nothing in them common with the *Roman Civil Law* ; for they admit of no Proof but what is given by the Evidence of living Witneffes in Court ; of which our Jury of Twelve Men, who are fometimes ignorant both of *Law* and *Letters,* are Judges ; the Points of *Law* only arifing upon the Fact, being left to the Direction of the Judges.

Now the *Law* of *England* confifts of certain *Cuftoms,* (and therefore is called *Cuftomary* and *Unwritten,*) and the *Statutes* enacted by the King, in and with the Advice of his Parliament ; wherein, if any Cafes are omitted, or Difficulties arife from the Ambiguity or Obfcurity of the *Laws,* which may require Explanation, the Judges have not recourfe to the *Civil Law,* as in other Nations of *Europe,* but are left to their own Judgments and Confciences, unlefs the Difficulty be very great, and then it is referr'd to the Parliament.

To this *Law* of *England,* we add the Writings of certain famous *Lawyers* ; as *Glanvil, Bracton, Britvn, Thornton,* and *Fleta,* who have explain'd the *Cuftoms* and *Laws* of *England* in their Works, as *Papinian, Ulpian,* and *Paul,* did thofe of the *Prætors Edicts* and *Conftitutions* ; to which afterwards were added the Yearly Reports of adjudged Cafes, in the Royal Courts of Juftice under our Princes, from the Time of *Edward* III. wherein the Arguments and Reafonings of the feveral Judges are reported, very often with great Accuracy and Judgment ; and thefe have fince been enlarg'd, by the Reports of *Dyer, Plowden* and *Coke,* all celebrated *Lawyers,* of Cafes adjudged in their Times : And thefe Books of *Reports,* are now ufed as *Commentaries* and *Interpreters* of the *Law* of *England.*

The firft Writer upon the *Englifh Law,* is *R. Glanvil,* who was Chief Juftice under *Henry* III after him, *Henry Bracton,* likewife Chief Juftice under *Henry* III. then *John Briton,* Juftice of *England.* And under *Edward* I. *Gilbert Thornton,* Chief Juftice of *England,* abridged *Bracton* ; about which time, an uncertain Author, called *Fleta,* lately publifh'd by the celebrated *Selden,* reviv'd the Name of *Thornton,* almoft buried in Oblivion. Yet neither the Writings

of

of thefe Learned Men, nor the Reports before mentioned, have the Authority of *Law* ; for thefe Treatifes were written by Men that had no Power of making *Laws* ; nor are the Judges for the time being, oblig'd to follow the Opinions of their Predeceffors, unlefs they find the Cafe agrees in all Points with that before them : For no one has a Power over his Equal ; nor a preceding Judge, any Right or Authority over his Succeffor ; their Powers being in all things alike, and their Judgments to be directed by the the *Laws*, not by Precedents, as *Juftinian* has obferv'd.

All thefe Common *Lawyers*, were excellently well verfed in the *Civil Law*, from whence they have borrow'd a great deal, both to explain and illuftrate the *Law* of *England*. *Bracton* was Profeffor of *Civil Law* at *Oxford*, and *Briton* Doctor of *Laws* ; and both *Glanvil* and *Bracton* began their Books in the fame Words and Method, as *Juftinian* does his *Inftitutes* ; and their Treatifes often quote the *Civil Law*, and apply the Authority thereof, not only in deciding Private Matters, but fuch as relate to the Publick Adminiftration. And fo much was the Study of the *Civil Law* in fafhion for the Space of Two hundred Years, between the Reigns of *Stephen* and *Edward* III. that it was frequently cited, not only in the Univerfities, but at the Bar, in Pleadings, Reports, and Judgments of Caufes, which *Selden* has fhewn by many Examples in his Writings upon *Fleta* ; the Profeffors of the *Civil Law* were in fo high Efteem in thofe times, that under *Henry* II. there were feveral famous for their Skill therein, who were alfo Clerks ; as *Simon de Patfhull* Dean of St. *Paul's*, *Philip Lovell*, *John Manfell*, and many others, advanc'd to be Judges in the Supream Courts of Juftice.

The Courts which do not proceed by the mere *Law* of *England*, but according to Equity and Confcience, are firft, the High Court of *Chancery*, in which there are many Things that agree with the *Civil Law*. In this Court, Actions are carried on by Petition or Bill, Witneffes fecretly examin'd, the Acts or Decrees of Court written in *Englifh*, not in *Latin* or *French* ; there is no Jury, but all Sentences are pronounc'd by the *Chancellor* ; the greateft part of whom, fince *Tho. Becket*, under *Henry* II. were *Bifhops* or *Clerks*, and learned in the *Civil Law*, till the

Reign

Reign of *Henry* VIII. when Lord *Rich*, the firſt Common *Lawyer*, was by him made *Chancellor*; after whom, ſome *Biſhops* Civilians, but chiefly Common *Lawyers* were by our Kings advanc'd to that High Office.

The *Aſſeſſors*, or *Maſters* in this Court, were alſo generally Doctors of the *Civil Law* ; and 'tis plain the *Clerks* were all well skill'd therein, from the Book of Original Writs, which is deſervedly called the Foundation of the *Laws* of *England*, and Regiſter of the High Court of *Chancery*, reſembling the Book of *Actions*, publiſh'd for the Benefit of the *Roman* People by *Cneius Flavius* ; who, as a Reward for his Service, from the Condition of a manumitted Freeman, was made Tribune of the People, and a Senator.

That theſe Writs and Reſcripts were written with great Brevity, Accuracy, and Judgment, by Perſons skill'd in the *Roman Laws*, is obvious to any one that reads them, and is what our late Attorney-General *Noy* has often obſerv'd to me : The Care of making theſe, is by Statute committed to the Clerks of this Court; who being all *Civilians* and *Clerks*, and therefore prohibited to marry, a *Law* was afterwards enacted in their Favour, for enabling them to enjoy their Employments, and reap the Benefit of their Studies after Marriage.

The *Keepers of the Privy Seal* alſo, in the Court of *Requeſts*, were formerly all Biſhops or Prelates, learned in the *Roman* or both *Laws* ; and the *Maſters of Requeſts*, who by the Juriſdiction of the ſaid Court, had Power of judging and determining according to Equity and good Conſcience, were alſo Profeſſors of the *Civil Law* ; for there is no *Law* ſo well adapted to the Practice of all Courts, where *Cuſtomary Law* is not obſerved, as the *Civil Law* of the *Romans* ; which contains the moſt ample Rules about *Contracts*, *Wills*, *Offences*, *Judgments*, and all Human Actions.

To be ſhort, our Kings have ever caſt a favourable Eye upon the *Biſhops*, *Clerks*, and Profeſſors of the *Civil Law* ; preferring them generally to the chief Offices of the Government, as our Hiſtorians do witneſs : And in the Reign of *Edward* III. all the great Employments, as *Chancellor*, *Treaſurer*, *Keeper of the Privy Seal*, of the *Rolls*, of the *Wardrobe*, and *Chancellor* of the *Exchequer*, were all in their Hands. But

But to return to my purpofe : The Courts, in which, by the Cuftom of *England*, they proceed by th♦ *Civil Law* only, are reducible to Three Heads ; *viz*. the Court of *Chivalry*, or *Military* Court, under the *Conftable* and *Marſhal* of *England* ; the Court of *Admiralty*, and the *Ecclefiaftical* Courts, under the *Archbiſhops*, *Biſhops*, and *Archdeacons* ; which have all hitherto continued in the Hands and Direction of *Civilians*.

In the Military Court, the *Judges* are the *Conftable* and *Marſhal* of *England* ; who are of equal Authority as to giving Judgment : But the Executive Part is wholly in the *Marſhal*. There is no Appearance of thefe Officers under our *Saxon* Kings ; they were introduc'd after the Conqueft by the *Normans*, in Imitation of the *French*, who copied after the *Romans*, and anciently had their *Conftables* and *Marſhals*, from the time of *Charlemagne* ; much refembling the *Maſters of Horſe*, and *Captains of the Body Guards* among the *Romans*, as the *French* Hiftorians do teftifie.

Thefe, with us, were always reckon'd Offices of the higheft Honour, that of the Conftable being generally conferr'd upon the King's Brethren, Uncles, or fome other of the chief Nobility ; and the fame was Hereditary in the Family of the *Staffords*, Dukes of *Buckingham*, till it ceafed in the Time of *Henry* VIII. So great was the Conftable's Authority, that it became fufpected by fome of our Kings ; and Chief Juftice *Finex*, being ask'd by *Henry* VIII. how far the Conftable's Power reach'd, declin'd giving a direct Anfwer, and faid, The Decifion of that Queftion belong'd to the *Law* of *Arms*, and not to the *Law* of *England*. And from thence forward, that Office was feldom given to any by our Kings, and then only *pro hac vice*.

The Office of *Marſhal* of *England*, has likewife antiently been fill'd by many of the Chief Nobility ; but *Thomas Moubray*, Duke of *Norfolk*, was the firft that had the Grant of it under the Title of Earl *Marſhal* of *England*, from *Richard* II. and the fame Family is in Poffeffion of it at this Day.

The Conftable and Marſhal, in the Military Court, have Cognizance of Crimes committed out of the Kingdom, of Contracts made beyond Sea, and Matters relating to War and Arms, either within or without the Kingdom of *England*.

If

If one *Englishman* accuse another of Treason acted in Foreign Parts, the Trial is before the Constable and Marshal ; and the Proof by Witnesses, or according to the Ancient *Usage* of this Court, by single Combat.   If one of the King's Subjects kill another in *Scotland*, or any other Countrey, he cannot be tried in any of the Courts which use the *Law* of *England*, but before the Constable and Marshal ; nor are these Matters cognizable by the Parliament. Therefore, when the famous Sea-Captain, Sir *Francis Drake*, had commanded *Dourish* to be put to Death in *America*, in the Twenty fifth of *Eliz.* the said *Dourish*'s Brother and Heir petition'd the Queen for Justice ; and the Judges being consulted thereupon, were of Opinion, that the Fact was cognizable only before the Constable and Marshal : But the Queen, for weighty Reasons, refusing to appoint a Constable for that purpose, the Prosecution dropt.   And lately, when *William Holmes*, an *Englishman*, killed *Wife*, another *Englishman*, in the Island of *Terra Nova* in *America*, *Anno* 1632, and *Wife*'s Widow had leave to prosecute for the Death of her Husband ; the Earl of *Lindsey* constituted Constable for that Occasion, and Earl *Arundel*, Earl Marshal of *England*, condemn'd *Holmes* by Sentence publickly pronounc'd in the Court Military, in the Month of *April* 1633, to suffer Death, which had been put in Execution, if the King had not thought fit to grant him a Pardon.

If an *Englishman* wounds another of the same Countrey in *France*, and he dies of his Wounds after his return to *England*, the Criminal cannot be tried by the *Law* of *England*, but the Prosecution must be in the Constable's Court ; and tho' some Statutes have brought Treason in certain Cases, under the Cognizance of the Judges of the *King's Bench*, or *Commissioners* specially appointed by the King ; yet the Jurisdiction of the Constable and Marshal are not understood to be taken away thereby.

The Cognizance of Contracts made in Foreign Countreys, belongs also to this Court.   *Pountney*, in *Henry* the Fourth's time, brought his Action in this Court against *Borney*, for one Thousand and twenty Pounds *English*, lent him at *Bourdeaux*, in *Gascoigny*, as may be seen in our *English* Law-Books ; and amongst the Records in the Tower, are abundance of Instances of Judgments given in this

Court,

Court, upon Civil Contracts made beyond Sea, especially in the Reigns of *Edward* III. *Richard* II. *Henry* IV V. and VI. when our Kings were in Possession of *Normandy, Aquitain, Gascoigny, Anjou,* and several other large Pro inces in *France* ; all which are taken notice of by our *Lawyers.* And 'tis an Opinion generally receiv'd, that the Cognizance of all Foreign Contracts belongs to this Court, as that of those made in the Kingdom of *England,* does to the Common Law Courts.

But this was afterwards chang'd, and the Cognizance of these Matters brought into the Courts of *Common Law,* by a Fiction declaring such Contracts to be made within the Kingdom : For now the *Law* is, that if one *Englishman* robs another beyond Sea, or enters into Covenants there, the Matter may be tried in any of the King's Courts, by supposing the Crime to have been committed, or the Contract made in some Place within the Kingdom ; in the very same manner as the *Romans* preserv'd the Validity of those Persons last Wills who were taken Captive b the Enemy, by the Fiction of *Postliminy* and of the *Law Cornelia:* For when a *Roman* by falling into the Hands of the Enemy lost his Liberty, with all the Rights of a *Citizen,* and his Will, if he had made any, became void thereby ; if he happen'd to return Home, he was by this Fiction suppofed never to have been taken Captive, but to have been all the while in the City : But if he died in his Captivity, then the Fiction of the *Law Cornelia* came in to his Aid, and suppofed he d 'd before he was taken, and was a Citizen in full Possession of all his Rights at that time. Yet there was this Difference between those and our Modern Fictions, that theirs were introduc'd by the *Roman Laws,* in favour of the Laft Wills made by their Citizens ; not by the Practice alone of *Lawyers.*

All Controversies relating to War and Arms, are determin'd in the Conftable's and Marfhal's Court. If a Foreigner, coming into *England,* raifes a War againft the King, he is not punifhable by the *Law* of the Land, but by a *Court Marfhal :* And for that Reafon they are called the *Keepers of the Common Peace of the Kingdom* ; which in Matters of War and Arms is committed to their Charge.

        And

And as there are but two Degrees of Nobility with us; *viz.* those of the first Rank, as Dukes, Marquisses, Earls, Viscounts, and Barons; and the second, as Knights and those we call Gentlemen: So these are distinguish'd from the common People by Arms and Ensigns, concerning which, all Controversies are cognizable in the Military Court; and there have been frequently very warm Disputes in this Court about the Right of Arms, when Two Families have claim'd the same, and one endeavour'd to exclude the other from that Right. Such were those Causes between *Reginald Grey,* of *Ruthin,* and *Edward Hastings;* between *Richard Scrope* and ----- *Grovener,* between *Thomas Bodwin* and *Nicholas Singleton,* and many others; which after long Strife have sometimes been decided by Sentence of the Judges, and sometimes by Combat: For when Two or more assume the same Arms and Ensigns, or any one pretends another has no Right to bear Arms, not being a Noble or Gentleman, or if any Man complains of Injury done him, by Diminution of his Honour, and calling his Right of bearing Arms in question. All these Matters are to be tried in the *Constable's* Court; the Dignity of which is very much augmented, by the ministerial Officers of the same; namely, *Garter King at Arms,* who regulates the Solemnities of the august Order of the Garter; *Clarencieux King at Arms,* for the South; and *Norroy King at Arms* for the North: And under them, Six inferior Officers, whom we call *Heralds,* whose chief Business it is, to be the Messengers of Peace or War, to adjust the Order of Precedence, make out Genealogies, and Arms of Families, to Order the Solemnities at the Coronations of our Kings, and of Duels before the Constable and Marshal; to lead up the Funerals of Noblemen and Gentlemen who are bury'd publickly; besides many other Things incumbent upon them by their Office. And all these are associated in one College, endow'd with many Privileges by our Kings; and exercise their Offices under the Power and Jurisdiction of the Constable and Earl Marshal.

Now the Use and Authority of the *Civil Law* in this Court, is allow'd by all our Common *Lawyers;* and therein is termed the *Law of the Kingdom,* the *King's Law,* and the *Law of the Land:* And it is confess'd, that the Causes cogni-

cognizable in this Court, are to be tryed by the *Civil Law* and *Cuſtom of Arms*, and not by the *Common Law* of *England* : For which Reaſon, ſuch Criminals as are condemn'd in this Court, neither forfeit Eſtate, nor Blood.

When the Conſtable and Marſhal are otherwiſe employ'd by the Publick, ſome Doctor, or other expert Civilian, is appointed to preſide in this Court; and under *Edward* IV. there was a *Promoter of Royal Cauſes* conſtituted in this Court; which Employment, King *Charles* in the Seventh Year of his Reign was pleas'd to confer upon *Me*, by his Letters Patent under the Great Seal of *England*; for all Cauſes therein, are proſecuted according to the Form preſcribed by the *Civil Law*, that is, by Libel or Petition, Witneſſes ſecretly examin'd, Exceptions, Replications, and all other Things, done according to the Rules of the *Civil Law*; Sentences and Appeals put into Writing : And for the Honour of this Court, when any Declinatory Exception is made to the Juriſdiction thereof, the ſame is made to the Privy Council; and all Appeals from Definitive Sentences, to the King himſelf, and not to the *Chancellor*; who generally appoints ſome of the Peers, and Doctors of *Civil Law* for his Delegates. All this is to be made out by the Publick Acts of this Court, which are to be ſeen amongſt the Records in the Tower; in which we may alſo meet with ſeveral learned Quotations out of the *Civil Law*.

Secondly, In the *Admiral Court*, the High Admiral of *England* is Judge, or his Lieutenant or others delegated by him : Now the *French* affirm, that this Office of Admiral had its Original from them, and from thence grew in faſhion in other Countries; it does not indeed appear that we had any Admiral under the *Conqueror*, and ſeveral of his Succeſſors Reigns, till *Edward* the Firſt's Time; from which Date, our Kings have generally made ſome of the chief Nobility Admirals of *England* : Becauſe in a Kingdom almoſt ſurrounded by the Ocean, it was neceſſary his Power ſhould be very great, to whom the Safeguard of the Sea, and Coaſts thereof, are committed : For all Crimes done upon the Sea, and Civil or Marine Tranſactions there, are cognizable in this Court; the Sea being without

out the Dominion of the *Common Law*, and under the Power of the Admiral, as our Common *Lawyers* themfelves acknowledge.

In this Court, the Admiral adminifters Juftice according to the *Civil Law* and *Cuftoms* of the Court; for the Common *Lawyers* do themfelves allow, the *Civil*, exclufive of the *Common Law* to be in ufe here: And therefore, Offenders condemn'd therein for Murder, Theft, Piracy or other Crimes, except Treafon, forfeit neither Blood nor Eftate. But becaufe the judging of Crimes in this Court by the *Civil Law* proved inconvenient, the accufed Perfon not being fubject to Conviction, but by his own Confeffion, or Eye-Witneffes of the Fact, which can feldom be expected in Matters done at Sea; by which means, Offenders of the moft criminal Nature often efcap'd with Impunity: It was therefore enacted under *Henry* VIII. that the *Civil Law* fhould be fo far laid afide, and Matters of Fact, in criminal Cafes fhould be determin'd by a Jury of Twelve Men, as in the *Law* of *England*.

Befides the *Civil Law* in the Admiral Court, the *Laws* of *Oleron*, made by *Richard* I. who was in Poffeffion of that Ifland, are in ufe; and alfo the *Marine Conftitutions*, publifh'd by feveral Princes at *Rome, Pifa, Genoa, Marfeilles, Barcelona, Meffina*, and other Places; together with the *Cuftoms* fet down in the Publick Acts of that Court. And laftly, under this Court may be reckoned the *Court-Merchant*; in which all Controverfies about Contracts between Merchants, are determin'd in Equity and good Confcience, according to the Rules of the *Civil Law*.

Thirdly, In the *Ecclefiaftical Courts*, the *Archbifhops. Bifhops, Archdeacons* or *Vicars-General, Commiffaries* or *Officials* appointed by them, are Judges; whofe diftinct Power is deriv'd from the *Conqueror*, who feparated the Epifcopal from the Secular Jurifdiction: Thefe, by the Indulgence of our Kings and *Cuftom* of *England*, have the Cognizance of many Caufes both Criminal and Civil; as Blafphemy, Apoftacy, Herefie, Schifm, Simony, Inceft, Adultery, Whoredom, Fornication, Chaftity attempted, Sacred Orders, Inftitutions to Ecclefiaftical Benefices, or Relinquifhment of the fame; Performance of Divine Service, Matrimony, Divorce,

vorce, Tithes, Offerings, Mortuaries, repairing of Churches, Dilapidation of Parfonage-Houfes, Penfions, Procurations, Wills, Codicils, Legacies, Succeifion to Inteftates by Adminiftration, and feveral other Matters which are exactly taken notice of by our *Lawyers* : All thefe are determin'd in this Court by the *Civil* and *Canon Law*, together with the Provincial *Conftitutions* of *Canterbury*, and thofe of the Pope's Legates fent hither to our Kings ; from all which our Ecclefiaftical Law is taken, and by which it is allowed, all thefe Caufes are to be decided.

As to the *Civil Law* there is no difpute, for it has been receiv'd by the Confent of all, and in this Court is called the *Law of the Land* ; but for the *Canon Law* there has been fome Difficulty, ever fince the Reign of *Henry* VIII. The Power of the Bifhops and Prelates before his time, and the Deference of our Kings to See of *Rome* was fo great, that moft part of the Decretal Epiftles contain'd in the *Canon Law* were directed to the *Englifh*.

But after *Henry* VIII. had thrown off the Pope's Supremacy, it was propos'd in Parliament to abrogate the *Canons*, and make a new Ecclefiaftical Law ; the Care thereof being committed to Thirty Perfons, of the higheft Characters and Reputation in *Divinity*, *Civil* and *Common Law* ; who, either finding themfelves unequal to the Task, (for 'tis not the Work of a few, nor of one Age,) or for other Reafons, went no farther than drawing the Plan or Project of a new *Law*, which was rejected ; fo the old *Canon Law* was confirm'd by a *Statute*, excepting fuch Articles thereof as were repugnant to *Holy Writ*, the *King*'s *Prerogative*, the *Law*, *Cuftoms* and *Statutes* of *England* ; and the fame is ftill in ufe, as in the Dominions of other Princes.

After this *Canon Law*, we receive the Archbifhop of *Canterbury*'s *Conftitutions*, made in his Provincial Councils ; of which, thofe that *Stephen Langton* directed to *Henry Chichley*, have been illuftrated with learned *Commentaries*, by Doctor *William Lynwood*, made Official by Archbifhop *Chichley* ; who was alfo a great *Lawyer* in the Court of *Canterbury* ; and he deferves the more to be remember'd, becaufe he was the firft of the few *Englifh* Writers that have written upon the *Civil Law*. Whilft he was *Official*, he was fent Embaffador by *Henry* V. to the Kings of *Spain* and *Portugal* ; from

from whence he return'd, after the King's Death, to his Place of *Official*, and was made Keeper of the Privy-Seal, and Bishop of St. *David's*.

Next are the *Legatine Constitutions*, made by the Pope's Legates: First by *Otho*, and then *Othobon*, sent hither by *Clement* IV. whom also he succeeded in the Papal Chair; upon which, *John de Atho*, Doctor of both *Laws*, has given us *Glosses* and *Commentaries*.

By all these they proceed in the Ecclesiastical Courts, according to the Rules of the *Civil* and *Canon Law*; the Action is propounded by Libel, after Suit contested; the Witnesses are examined in private, Exceptions and Replications are given, and the Terms of Causes prescrib'd by both *Laws* obferv'd; the Sentences are in Writing, and Appeals lye from the Bishop to the Archbishop, from the Archdeacon to the Bishop, or directly to the Archbishop; from whom, as it was usual to Appeal to the Pope till the Reign of *Henry* VIII. so ever since Appeals are carried to the King in Chancery; where Delegates being appointed, either confirm or revoke the Sentence by the *Civil* and *Canon Law*; and the *Common Lawyers* acquiefce in such Sentences, and do not take upon them to examine the same, unlefs they find Caufe for a Royal Prohibition.

And to encourage the Study of the *Civil Law* among us, after the Pope's Supremacy was abjur'd, the Doctors of *Laws* were allow'd to exercife Ecclefiaftical Jurifdiction, tho' not in Orders, or married, which is contrary to the *Canon Law*.

Among the Courts of *England*, wherein Juftice is adminiftred by the *Roman Laws*, we muft not forget the Two Univerfities of *Oxford* and *Cambridge*, honour'd by our Kings with great Privileges; from whence the Students cannot by any Profecution be drawn to the Court of *Common Law*, but are to be judg'd by the Chancellor of the Univerfity or his Commiffary, in all perfonal Actions of Debt, Accompts, Contracts, Injuries, and any Crimes, except Murther and Mahaim. And the same Privileges are granted to the Chancellor of *Oxford*, by *Richard* II. within the Liberties of the Univerfity; if either of the Parties be a Student, or any ways belonging to them: This Univerfity had many other prior Privileges, granted by King *John*, *Henry* III. *Edward*

ward I. and *Edward* III. with a Power from the Popes and Archbishops of *Canterbury*, to Imprison, Proscribe, Excommunicate, and Suspend all Contumacious Persons. And the University of *Cambridge*, have the same; altho' most of their Charters have been lost or consum'd in the War under *Henry* III. and Fire set to the University by the Townsmen, in *Richard* the Second's Time: In all these Matters the *Chancellor* determines according to the *Civil Law*, and *Custom* of the University; which Privilege is specially granted to that of *Cambridge*, by the Statutes thereof, made in Q. *Elizabeth*'s Reign: From whom there lies an Appeal to the Regents, and then to the King.

Lastly, I cannot forbear mentioning, to the Honour of the *Civil Law*, that after *Lotharius* had restor'd it, the same began to be taught under King *Stephen*; and the succeeding Kings, upon Embassies, sent Professors of the *Law*, either by themselves, or as Collegues with Noblemen; to make Alliances, Contracts, and transact other Business with Foreign Princes; it being a Rule with them, to employ *Civilians* on those Occasions: Nor indeed are others so fit for that Purpose, the *Civil Law* being common to all Christian Princes; which is evident from the Instruments of these Publick Treatises still to be seen among the Records. And Q. *Elizabeth* also employ'd *Civilians*, as her Secretaries of State, Privy-Counsellors, Embassadors, and in other Publick Offices: But in the latter End of her Reign, her Chief Ministers chose rather to use an *Amanuensis*, in transcribing Leagues and Contracts, than the Assistance of skilful *Civilians*; which continu'd also in the succeeding Reigns: Having, perhaps, fallen upon that Ancient Caution in relation to Wills, *A testamento dolus Malus & Jurisconsultus abesto*. Thus are the *Civilians* excluded both from Publick and Private Business.

As for my self, I have done my Part in shewing how highly the *Civil Law* was once esteem'd and regarded by the *English*; and that both the *English* and *French Lawyers*, *Forcatulus* and *Chopinus*, were true Prophets; in foretelling, That one time or other, the *Civil Law* would be no longer in use in this Kingdom.

F I N I S.

THE
HISTORY
Of the ORIGINE of the
FRENCH LAWS.

Tranſlated from the FRENCH.
By *J. B.* Eſq^r;

With a PREFACE and NOTES,
ſhewing, The ANALOGY of the LAWS
of the Antient *GAULS* and *BRITONS*.

LONDON,

Printed for D. BROWNE, at the *Black Swan,*
and F. CLAY, at the *Bible,* without *Temple-Bar.*
MDCCXXIV.

To the Right Honourable

D A V I D,

Lord *MILSINTOWN.*

MY LORD,

Mong all the Improvements and Accomplishments which young Noblemen acquire in their Travels, none is more instructive or serviceable in

A 2   the

the Conduct of their Lives,
(whether we confider them
Abroad or at Home, in
Publick or Private Capa-
cities,) than a competent
Knowledge of the Laws of
Foreign Countries, and the
Principles upon which they
are grounded.

For this Reafon, I doubt
not, but your Lordfhip,
while you were in *France,*
made it a Part of your
Study and Obfervation, and
added it to thofe Endow-
ments which naturally a-
dorn your Mind, and fhew
you are defcended from
Noble and Wife Parents.

This

This is not a Place for your Lordſhip's Pedigree, or the Hiſtory of your Anceſtors: Let it ſuffice, that as you are derived on your Mother's Side, from a very Antient Family, remarkable for Wit, and a refin'd Underſtanding; ſo by your Noble Father's, you inherit Prudence and Valour : Many of his Anceſtors having, with the greateſt Reputation, fill'd very conſiderable Military Employments in the *Low-Countries*, from the Time of the Emperor *Charles* V. down to this Day.

A 3 　　　But

But, my Lord, You have
no need to look fo far back
for Examples, to excite you
to the Purfuit of Honour
and Vertue: Your Father
is before your Eyes; whofe
Titles of *Baron* and *Earl*,
are the Rewards of a long
Series of Brave and Honourable Actions, conferr'd upon him by our Two laft
Princes.

To thefe, my Lord, You
are Heir, and your own good
Sence and Inclinations af-
furedly promife, that You
will give an Additional Luftre to your Noble Family,
by

DEDICATION.

by the Brightneſs of your own Character.

Your Lordſhip will pardon the Liberty I have taken, in prefixing your Name to this little Treatiſe, which may ſerve to Amuſe you with a ſhort View of what you have already gone over.

And I beg you will be perſuaded, that I have no other Deſign in it, than to publiſh the Sence I have of the many Favours conferr'd upon Me by the Earl of *Portmore* and your Self; and the Ambition I have

A 4
of

of being always confider'd,
as I really am,

My Lord,

Your Lordſhip's moſt Obedient, and

Moſt Humble Servant,

J. Beaver.

THE

THE

PREFACE.

HE Original of the ensuing Discourse, (being an Histori-cal Deduction of the French *Laws, from* Cæsar's *Conquest of the* Gauls, *to the Modern Times) was first publish'd in* French *about the Year* 1708. *and obtain'd the Esteem and Applause of all Knowing and Judicious Persons, as a Work full of exqui-site and admirable Learning, and highly ne-cessary for a right Understanding of the* French *Laws.*

'Tis true, it at first appear'd without a Name, as those exquisite Institutes *of the* French *Laws, composed by* Monsieur Argout, *also did: But seeing since his Death, it has in divers Impressions, been constantly prefix'd as a Preface or Introduction to those Insti-tutes, we may well presume, both were com-*

posed

poſed by the ſame Hand : And indeed, not only the ſubject Matter, but the Style and Connection of both Tractates, do manifeſt an Identity of Thought and Language.

Now, as this Treatiſe is by all acknowledg'd to be of admirable Uſe, as an Introduction to the Knowledge of the French Laws *in particular ; ſo it muſt be confeſs'd, with re- ſpect both to the* Civil *and* Canon Law *in general. The Reader may here trace them from their very Fountains and Originals ; whereby the ſeveral Authors who have writ- ten Syſtems or Inſtitutes of thoſe Laws, (as Monſieur* Domat *and others) and in ſhort, the whole Body of the Civil and Canon Law, may be better illuſtrated and explained.*

But what chiefly induced the Publiſhing hereof in Engliſh, *was the great Analogy or Conformity obſerved herein, between the Laws or Cuſtoms of the Antient* Gauls *and* Francs, *and thoſe of our* Britons *and* Saxons, *many of which will here appear to be derived from the ſame Original. As for Inſtance,*

We here find the Antient Gauls *to have been governed by certain* * Uſages *and* Cu- ſtoms, *not by any written* Law. *So we read*

---

* Cæſar de bello Gallico. *Lib.* 5. & 6.

of the Britons, *they had no written Law, but were govern'd by certain Traditional* Ufages, *preferved by means of their* Bards *and* Druids, *who were* Priefts *and* Judges, *as well amongft the* Britons *as the* Gauls : *For we have it from good Authority, that in both* Nations, *the* Druids *had originally the fole Power of deciding of Rights, and determining Controverfies.* Which *Power continued here, till the time that the Emperor* Claudius, *having abfolutely conquered* Britain, *by his Edict prohibited the* Druids *any longer to exercife their Religious Rites* *, &c.

And hence, as Selden *obferves, it came to pafs the* † Druids, *being prohibited the Exercife of thofe Rites, fuch Nations as were govern'd by them in point of Law,* viz. *the* Gauls, Britons, *&c. grew regardlefs of their Authority ; and not refpecting them as before, became prone to receive and embrace the* Roman *Law. And this occafioned that Obfervation of the Poet,*

> Gallia, Caufidicos, docuit facunda Britannos.
> *Juvenal.* Sat. 15.

As if he had faid, Whereas heretofore the Britifh Druids, *taught thofe of* Gaul *the*

---

* *Suetonius* in Vita Claudii. Cap. 25.

† *Not.* ad Fortefc. p. 12.

Know-

Knowledge of their Law ; *now the* Gauls *do inftruct the* Britons *in the* Roman Law: *And for this Reafon, he elfewhere calls* Gaul Nutricula Caufidicorum.

Sat. 7.

As for the Office of the Britifh Bards, *efpecially of the Chief, called* Penkert, Penbeirt *or* Penbeirdh, *the Reader may confult the Laws of* Howel Dhaa, *i. e.* The Good, *which, we hear, will fhortly be publifh'd by the Reverend Dr.* Wotton.

But to return to the Roman Law. *We find the fame fully eftablifhed in this Ifland, in the Reign of the Emperor* Severus : *For he kept his* Prætorian Court *at* York ; *wherein the fam'd* Papinian *for fome time fat as Judge, having thofe two great Civilians,* Paul *and* Ulpian *for his Affeffors*[*]. *And in the* Code *of the* Civil Law [†], *we have a Refcript or Decree, made at* York, *in the Name of that Emperor and his Son* Antoninus.

Pag. 10. and 11.

'Tis alfo obferved by our Author, That the fame Magiftrates, Language and Laws, were at the fame time ufed at York, Cologn, Lyons, Cordoua, *and* Carthage ; *and we may well add, in moft other eminent Towns*

---

[*] Dion. Caffius, in Vita Severi.

[†] Cod. Lib. 3. Tit. 32. Cap. 1.

and

and Cities, where there were Roman Colonies *settled: For which the Reader may consult* Lipfius de Magnitudine Romani Imperii, *Lib.* 1. *cap.* 6. *and* Velferus de Antiquit. Augustæ Vindelicor. *Lib.* 2.

And we have no Reafon to doubt that the Roman Law *was received, nay ftudied and practifed in* Juftinian's *Time, in moft Parts of the* Roman *Empire : But from his Death, which happened about the Year* 565. *to the Year* 1125. *it became fo neglected and difufed in the Weftern Empire, that we don't find any Perfon during all that time, that there profefs'd it : Nor indeed, could it be otherwife while the Body of it was loft.*

But as our Author takes notice, the Emperor Lothair, *after near* 600 *Years, taking* Amalfi *in* Apulia, *found an Old Copy of the* Digefts *or* Pandects, *and gave it to the* Pifans : *whence 'tis called,* Litera Pifana; *which being afterwards carried to* Florence, *is to this Day carefully preferved in the Great Duke's Palace, and never brought forth or produced without Lighted Torches and other great Ceremonies* *.

---

* *Selden's* Preface to his *Titles of Honour*, Edit. Prim.

And

And whereas Juſtinian *had by an Ediɛt commanded, that the* Civil Law *ſhould not be read or taught but at* Rome, Berytus, *and* Conſtantinople : *So* Lothair *by a like Ediɛt enjoined, That* Bologna *ſhould be* Legum & Juris Schola una & ſola *; *Yet, neither of theſe Ediɛts were obſerved.*

For as Irnier *taught the Civil Law at* Bologna, *without any regard to the Firſt;* *ſo* Aro *and* Placentinus, *who immediately ſucceeded him, read and taught it publickly at* Montpellier *and* Tholouſe, *contrary to the Second Ediɛt.*

As to the Univerſity of Paris, *our Author indeed ſays, that Pope* Honorius III. *about the Year* 1200. *expreſly forbad the Study of the Civil Law there ; but adds, that his Decree thereupon deſerves Examination, which has lately been done by Monſieur* Claude Joſeph de Ferriere, *who has ſhewn beyond Contradiɛtion, that the* Pope's *Prohibition related only to* Prieſts *and* Monks, *who were too much addiɛted to that Study, and apt to negleɛt their proper Buſineſs, the reading and ſearching of the Holy Scripture.*

---

* Ibid. *See* Paul Merulas, *Coſmog.* p. 1. lib. 4. c. 23.

And tho' this Decree was not then pub-lished, the very same Reason induced our King Stephen *to put out an Edict against the Study of the* Civil Law *at* Oxford, *and to silence* Vicarius, *who began to profess and teach it in that University, about the Four-teenth Year of his Reign. But his Orders were not followed; for* John of Salisbury, *a Man of great Note who lived at that time, says,* Parum valuit Stephani prohibitio, nam eo magis invaluit virtus Legis, Deo favente, quo eam amplius nitebatur impietas fub-vertere.

This may serve in general, to shew how far the Roman *or* Civil Law, *was antiently regarded both Here and in* France. *As for particular Laws mention'd in the ensuing Treatise, the Analogy between them and our* Saxon Laws, *will more fully appear from* Dr. Wilkins's *Notes on those Laws, lately published; wherein he has compared those Laws with the* Burgundian, Ripuarian, Sa-lick, *and other Laws mention'd by our Au-thor; and shewn, that they all help to con-firm and illustrate the Laws of this Nation.*

THE

[1]

THE
HISTORY
Of the ORIGINE of the
French LAWS, *&c.*

HE Inhabitants of * *Gaul* (for *The Deſign of this Treatiſe.* near 500 Years) before the Irruption of the *Francs* into that Countrey, were wholly govern'd by the Antient *Roman* Laws, and which afterwards continued to be obſerved under the Kings of the Firſt and Second Race; but mix'd with ſome Barbarian Cuſtoms, and the Capitularies of thoſe Kings.

---

* Touching the Antient *Gauls*, &c. ſee Monſieur *Peʒron*'s Book *Of the Antiquities of Nations* : Wherein he ſhews , the *Gauls*, and *Britons* or *Welſh*, to have ſprung from the ſame Original, *i. e. Gomer* the Eldeſt Son of *Japhet* ; and that there was an entire Conformity between them in their Language, Laws, Manners, Habits, *&c.* [*See alſo* Verſtegan, p. 190,*&c.*] who makes the *Germans, Gauls* and *Britons*, to have been originally the ſame People.

B   THE

[2]

THE † Troubles that happen'd in the Tenth Century fo confounded all thofe anti- ent *Laws*, that at the Beginning of the *Third* * *Race*, there was no other Law in *France*, but a very uncertain *Ufage*; which the Learned having afterwards improv'd by the Study of the *Roman* Law, their Decifions, mix'd with that *Ufage*, formed thofe *Cuftoms*, which in Procefs of time were reduced into Writing by Publick Autho- rity. But of later times, the *French* Kings have Enacted feveral *New Laws*, by their Ordinances or Edicts.

THESE are the Heads I defign to treat of in this Difcourfe; and I hope to be excus'd, if fometimes I make ufe of pro- bable Conjectures, confidering how little

---

† 'Twas in the Tenth Century, That the *Danes* and other Northern Rovers over-ran both *France* and *England*; at which time *Jus fepultum, & Leges fo- pitæ funt, &c.* [*See the* 16th *of* Edward the Confeffor's *Laws.*]
* The Three Races are the *Merovingian*, the *Car- lovingian*, and *Capetian*: The Firft fo call'd from *Me- rovée*, who came out of *Germany*, and fettled in *France* about the Year 448 : The Second, from *Charles* the Son of *Pepin*, called *Charlemagne*, who began his Reign about the Year 770 : The Third, from *Hugh Capet*, who *Anno* 987, fucceeded *Lewis the Idle*, being the laft Male of the *Carlovingian* Race. From this *Hugh* the prefent King of *France* is defcended in an Uninterrupted Line. [*See the Hi- ftories of* Du Haillan, Mezeray, *&c.*

has

has been hitherto faid or done, to clear up thefe Points.

I fhall call that the *Antient Law*, which was obferv'd till the Tenth Century; be-caufe fince that time the Practice of it has been fo interrupted and difcontinu'd, that there are hardly any Footfteps of it now remaining; and I fhall give that the Name of *New Law*, which follow'd under the Kings of the Third Race: Becaufe tho' it underwent great Alterations, there ftill remains a Traditional Succeffion of Laws and Maxims, which may be trac'd down to our Times.

I queftion whether it will be worth while to look fo far back as the Original *Gauls*; and whether it be probable, that after fo many Changes, we have any Law left that comes immediately from them.

However, I fhall here give the Reader out of *Cæfar's Commentaries*, an *Idea* of their Antient Manners or Cuftoms, and Civil Government; in which, perhaps, fome may difcover a great Conformity with thofe of the latter Times. *Comment. Book 6. of the Wars in Gallia.*

" The whole Countrey of the *Gauls*
" was originally canton'd into petty States,
" independent on each other: (moft of
" whofe Names are ftill continu'd in thofe
" which were then their * Capital Cities, as *Antient Govern-ment of the Gauls de-fcribed.*

* *Vide* Mezeray, Tom. 1. P. 2.

B 2

Pa-

[4]

" *Paris,Sens,Tours*, and many others.) The
" Perſons of greateſt Account among them
" were the *Druids*, and the *Knights :* The
" reſt of the People liv'd in a ſort of Bon-
" dage, could undertake nothing of them-
" ſelves, were never ſummon'd to any Pub-
" lick Debate; nay, many, oppreſs'd by the
" Severity of their Creditors, or the Ty-
" ranny of the Nobility, ſurrender'd them-
" ſelves their Abſolute Slaves.

Druids.　" THE *Druids* had the Management of
" all that concerned Religion and Learn-
" ing, and even the Adminiſtration of
" Juſtice in Criminal Matters, in their
" great Annual Aſſemblies : Their Power
" was very great, and they were exempted
" from attending the War, or paying any
" Taxes : The Penalty inflicted upon ſuch
" as diſobeyed them, was a kind of Excom-
" munication: They were thereby excluded
" from their Sacrifices and Publick Aſſem-
" blies, and eſteemed as Impious and Profli-
" gate Miſcreants : All Men avoided their
" Converſation; and they were incapable of
" any Degree of Honour, or even of Proſe-
" cuting their Rights in Courts of Juſtice.

Knights.　" THE *Knights*, for their Parts, were all
" Soldiers, and attended the Wars, which
" between thoſe Petty States happen'd al-
" moſt every Year.　Their greateſt Glory

The Reader may here obſerve the great Analogy
between the antient Cuſtoms of the *Gauls* and *Britons.*

" con-

" confifted in being courted by a vaft Num-
" ber of Vaffals and Dependants, who fol-
" low'd them as occafion requir'd. They
" never allow'd their Children to appear
" publickly in their Prefence,till they were
" of Years fit to bear Arms." All this, and
much more, may be feen at large, in the *Intituled,*
Collection of *German* Laws made by *Gol-* Colleĉtio
daſtus; wherein the Cuftoms of the *Gauls* Confuet.
and *Germans* are recited in the exprefs Legum
Words of *Cæſar* and *Tacitus*, and ranged Franco-
under different Titles. Imper. furti,1613

As the *Romans* extended their Conquefts *The Ro-*
over the *Gauls*, their Language, Manners, *man Law*
and Laws eftablifhed themfelves among *brought*
them *. as in other Countries : For the *firſt into*
the whole *Roman* Empire was but One Gaul.
Great Body, aĉtuated by the fame Spirit,
and agreeing in all its Parts in an exaĉt Symmetry, by the mutual Dependance
each had upon the other. All the Go-

---

* Notwithftanding what is here faid, we muft
obferve, That the *Romans*, as to Civil and Perfonal
Rights, left every Nation they conquer'd the Liberty of ufing their own Laws; except in fuch
Cafes only, as immediately refpeĉted the Government. And therefore our Author's Meaning here
muft be, That the *Gauls*, as well as other Conquer'd
Nations, finding the *Roman* Laws more Exaĉt in the
Decifion of Rights, and more Equitable than their
own, voluntarily embraced the *Roman* Law. [*Sed
vide poſt.*]

vernours

vernours of Provinces, and Publick Officers, down to the *Apparitors*, were natural-born *Romans*, not to mention the reſt of their Retinue, which they called the *Cohort*, and was always very numerous; and their ‑Employments laſted ſo ſhort a time, that their Reſidence in the Provinces could not work any conſiderable Alteration in them. The Farmers of the Publick Revenues were *Romans*, and ſome, of the Degree of Knighthood. The Legions were made up of † *Romans :* And beſides all theſe, who were in the Provinces upon Publick Service, many *Romans* ſtaid there on their own private Account ; as Bankers, Merchants, Husbandmen and Graſiers, eſpecially where there was any Colony or Settlement : Nay, abundance, without ever ſtirring out of *Rome* or *Italy*, got Conſiderable Fortunes out of the Provinces by the Induſtry of their Slaves.

O N the other hand, the Natives of the Provinces often went to *Rome*, either as Deputies, to tranſact Publick Buſineſs , or to manage their Private Affairs, or to make their Court, or out of Curioſity; and thoſe of Chief Note

---

† *i. e.* Either Native or Emancipated.

a-

among them, claimed a Right of Ho-
fpitality from the Principal Citizens, or at
leaft were under their * Patronage and Protection.

———————————

* We may obferve from *Cicero*, *Livy* and *Tacitus*,
That 'twas ufual for the Nations and Provinces fubdued by the *Romans*, to have the *Patronage* of fome
Eminent *Roman* Citizen ; who refiding at *Rome*,
and being a Member of the Senate, might, in cafe
of any Oppreffion of their Governors, apply to
fuch *Patron* for Relief, who was obliged to repre-
fent the Matter to the Senate, and to endeavour a
Redrefs of their Grievances. [*See* Tacit. *Hift.
lib.* 1, *&c.*]
  But as to the *Roman* Cuftom of *Patrons* and *Clients*, that was practifed among the *Romans* themfelves, even in the Infancy of *Rome*, by virtue of a
Law made by *Romulus* ; as *Paulus Manutius* in his
Book *De Senatu Romano*, has truly obferv'd ; whofe
remarkable Words affording us an evident View
of the Original of the *Feudal Law*, (which is generally, tho' without any Foundation, attributed to the
Lombards ;) I fhall therefore give the Curious Reader
the Subftance of them, *viz*.

  Romulus, *ut erat fingulari confilio, &c. cum verere-
tur ne quid injuriæ* Plebs, *per infcitiam circumventa, à*
Senatoribus *ferret ; indeque* Concordiam *fine qua diu-* Patrons
turnum nihil eft, exorta Seditio *diffolveret ;* univerfæ and Cli-
Civitatis *animos quafi* neceffitudinis vinculo *conjun-* ents *like*
xit, *conftituit enim* Clientelas & Patrocinia : *quod* our Lords
erat hujufmodi, ut Plebeii Patronum *fibi deligerent è* and Te-
Senatoribus, *quem quifque vellet, &* Senatores Ple- nants.
beiis *in* clientelam *receptis* Fidem *fuam ac ftudium
benigniffimè præftarent ; Erat autem hæc inter utrofque
officiorum viciffitudo, ut* Patricii Plebeios *ab ufu rerum Their reci-
urbanarum* imperitos, *confilio* erudirent, accufatos procal Du-
defenderent, &* præfentes, & abfentes *omni ope tue-* ties.
                                                rentur----
B 4

tection. Some, who settled at *Rome*, enjoy'd, not only the Freedom of the City,
but also were chosen Senators and Magistrates;

Like our *rentur*----- *E contrà,* Clientes *ad collocandas* Patrono-
Aids pur rum filias, *si* Parentibus *copiæ non suppeterent, de suo*
Fille mar- conferrent : *in æris inopiam gratuitam pecuniam eroga-*
rier, *&c.* rent : *ab* hostibus *in* bello captos *redimerent ; in Ma-*
& ad re- *gistratibus & honoribus (petendis) officiosa sedulitate de-*
dimen- *ducerent. Etiam, Quod si* Clientem Patronus, *aut* Pa-
dum cor- tronum Cliens *accusasset, contráve* Testimonium *dix-*
pus Do- *isset, aut* suffragium *tulisset, is* Proditionis Lege *tene-*
mini, *&c* *batur, eúmque qui occidisset, piè fecisse, & infernè Jovi*
hostiam mactásse putabatur.

Here you have, not only the Original of *Patrons*
and *Clients,* but also the Duties incumbent on each ;
the Breach whereof seems to be *Capital,* and no less
than *Treason.*

After which, *Paulus Manutius* immediately adds a
Passage, which more fully explains the Sence of our
Author, as to the whole Provinces and Nations putting themselves under the Patronage and Protection
of some Eminent *Roman, viz.*

Atque hujusmodi Clientelæ *quanquam ab initio potis-*
simùm Urbanæ Plebis *causæ sunt institutæ, tamen per*
ea quæ consecuta sunt tempora, aucta jam Urbis Diti-
one, *ita* (Clientelæ) *sunt amplificatæ, ut non* Coloniæ
solùm, sed Gentes *etiam, aut* Bello *victæ, aut* Societate
Amicitiáque *Populo Romano conjunctæ, sese* Civium Ro-
manorum *in* Patrocinio *contulerint :* Sic M. Marcellum
Syracusani, Q. Fabium Allobroges, & alios alii, &c.

But as to the mutual Duties of *Lords* and *Tenants,*
the Reader may please to compare the *Grand Custumier*
of *Normandy. Cap.* 35. with our *Glanvil, Lib.* 9. *Cap.* 4,
5,6,8, *&c.* Bract. *Fol.* 78. Fleta, *Lib.* 2. *c.* 40. & *Lib.* 3.
c. 14. See also Co. *Lit.* 65. 76. 100.

ftrates; infomuch, that many of the Emperors were Defcendants of Provincial Families. In fhort, they were often made
Romans, without going out of their own
Countrey, by a Grant of the Freedom of
the City; which was not only beftow'd
on particular Perfons, but upon whole
Towns: And after the Emperor *Antoninus* had conferr'd that Honour upon all
the Subjects of the Empire, there were
Romans of all Nations.

'Tis true, this General Intercourfe did
not introduce equal Changes in all the
Provinces : The *Romans* made a vaft Difference between the *Greeks* and other
Nations, which they called *Barbarians*.
For, as they were beholden for all their
Politenefs to the *Greeks*, who alfo taught
them the Liberal Arts and Sciences; they
always very much efteemed them : So that
the *Romans*, contented with the Dominion or Superiority, fuffer'd them to live
according to their Antient Laws. They
learned the *Greek* Language, to fave the
Greeks the Trouble of fpeaking *Latin.*
They copied them in their Manners;
and fetting afide what related to the General Adminiftration of the Empire, alter'd more the *Romans*, than the *Romans*
the *Greeks:* Whereas they held the *Barbarians* in great Contempt, over whom
they had a double Advantage, of Politenefs

nefs and Power ; and they imagin'd that it was the greateſt Inſtance of Kindneſs, Quære of this, and ſee the Notes antè to oblige them to a Conformity with the *Roman* Way of living. On the contrary, the *Barbarians* did admire the *Romans*, and ſtrove to imitate their manner of Life, as being both more ſplendid and convenient than their own.

In this Diverſity of Manners was the whole Empire divided : All *Greece* and the Eaſt, that is to ſay, all that Part which devolved to *Alexander's* Succeſſors, uſed the *Grecian* Language and Cuſtoms ; the reſt ſpoke *Latin*, and followed the *Roman* Laws and Manners. This laſt Diviſion included almoſt all that which has ſince been called the Weſtern Empire, *viz.* *Africa*, *Mauritania*, *Spain*, the *Gauls*, Part of the *Britiſh* Iſles, a ſmall Portion of *Germany* , *Rhetia* , *Pannonia* , and *Illyrium*.

The Truth of the foregoing Remarks will be acknowledg'd by all Perſons who are well read in the *Roman* Hiſtory.

As for ſuch as are not, they will perhaps, hardly believe, that the ſame Language, Magiſtrates and Laws were at one and the ſame time uſed at *Cologn, York, Lyons,*

[11]

Lyons, *Cordoüa* and *Carthage*. But there
are fome Proofs peculiar to *Gaul*; which
fhew, that it became at laft intirely *Roman*:
If we confider, firft, the native Original
of feveral of the Emperors, efpecially
in the Fourth Century; next, the Writings of the *Gaulick* Authors, as *Aufo-
nius*, *Salvienus*, and *Sidonius*; then the
Names of the *Gauls*, and among the reft,
of their Bifhops, till about the Eighth
Century; as alfo, the Names of abundance
of Cities and Towns, as *Lagny*, *Latiniacus
ager* or *fundus*, *Percy*, *Patriciacus*, *Savigny*,
(or as others pronounce it, *Savigne*,) *Sabi-
niacus*, and many others, which ftill wear
the Badge of their *Roman* Mafters: And
laftly, the Language the *French* now fpeak,
which has infinitely a greater Mixture of
Latin Words, than of any other; notwithftanding the Variety of *Northern* People,
that fucceeded the *Romans* in *Gaul*.

But to keep clofe to my Subject: There
can be no doubt the *Roman Law* was obferved in *Gaul*, if we reflect, that one
of the Four *Prætorian Præfects* refided
there; that this Magiftrate had the fo-
vereign Adminiftration of Juftice in the
Emperor's Abfence, and was Superior to
all the Governors of the Provinces; and Cod.*l.*10.
that the Titles of feveral Laws in *Jufti-* *tit.* 38. *de*
nian's *Code*, fhew they were calculated *bus.* *Municipi-*

for

for *Gaul*, or the People of that Countrey.

To all which may be added, that the
Romans had peaceable Poſſeſſion of *Gaul*
for Five entire Centuries. *Cæſar* compleated his Conqueſts about Fifty Years
before the Nativity of our Saviour ; and
Merovée, who was the firſt *Frenchman* that
made any conſiderable Settlement in *Gaul*,
did not fix there till the Year 450. after the Incarnation. Five Hundred Years
were ſufficient to produce great Alterations in a Countrey, and what hath been
ſo long practis'd, is not eaſily aboliſh'd.

LET us then be aſſur'd, that when
the *Francs* ſubdu'd the *Gauls*, they found
them entirely *Romans* ; ſpeaking *Latin*,
and living according to the *Roman Laws*.

BUT here it will be convenient to
obſerve, what the *Roman Law* was at
that Time ; for 'tis plain, it could not
be *Juſtinian's*, which was compil'd only
for the Uſe of the Countries under his
Dominion, and almoſt a Hundred Years
after the *Francs* broke into the *Gauls*.

*What the
Roman
Law con-
ſiſted of.* Now the *Roman Law* of that time,
conſiſted of the ſeveral Conſtitutions of
the Emperors, and Writings of the Civilians : Theſe Conſtitutions were colle-
ćted

æed into Three *Codes* ; the *Gregorian,* the
Hermogenian, and *Theodofian,* publifh'd by
the Emperor *Theodofius* the Younger, in
435. which confirm'd the Two Former.
Afterwards, the *Novels* of the fame *Theodofius* and his Succeffors were added.

THE Writings of the *Civilians* were
fuch as the *Theodofian Code* authorized ; as,
thofe of *Papinianus, Paulus, Caius, Ulpianus, Modeftinus,* and others cited by them
namely, *Scævola, Sabinus, Julianus* and
Marcellus.

BY this Reftriction, it appears, the
Works of the reft of the *Civilians,* fome
Fragments of which, we meet with in the
Digeft, were either wholly unknown, or
of no Credit in the Weftern Empire. I
am farther of Opinion, that the Text of
the *Perpetual Edict, of the † Laws, of

---

* The Number of *Pretorian Edicts* growing too
great, and many Inconveniencies enfuing thereupon,
the Emperor *Adrian* employ'd *Julianus,* a Famous
Civilian, to make One Edict out of the whole, which
was to ferve for a Rule in all future Cafes. This
they called the *Perpetual Edict* ; becaufe the *Prætors* were never after permitted to publifh any.

† *Lex eft quod populus Romanus Senatorio Magiftratu interrogante (veluti Confule) conftituebat.*

the

the * *Plebiscita*, of the † *Senatus Consulta*, and particularly the Text of the || *Twelve Tables*, were at that time utterly loft, or rarely to be met with ; becaufe when *Ju-ftinian* had a mind, in the following Century, to form a compleat Body of all the Laws, he took all his Materials out of the Emperors Conftitutions, and Works of the *Civilians*. This alfo appears, by comparing the *Mofaick* Law with the *Roman*, as it was ufed in the Reign of *Theodofius the Younger :* For it contained only certain Decifions of the Civil Lawyers, and fome of the Conftitutions taken from the Three Codes , with a fmall Portion of the *Theodofian* Code, which then, perhaps, was only publifh'd.

---

* *Plebifcitum eft, quod plebs plebeio magiftratu in-terrogante (veluti Tribuno) conftituebat.*

† *Senatus Confultum eft, quod Senatus jubet aut con-ftituit.* Inftit. lib. 1. tit. 2. par. 4.

|| The Laws of the *Twelve Tables* are fo called, from Twelve Tables of Brafs, in which they were engraved. They confifted of the chief Maxims of Government, pick'd out of the *Grecian* Laws, the Laws of *Rome* under the Kings, and the Cuftoms of the Place : A moft excellent Compofition ; having in them (as *Cicero* in his Book *de Oratore*, fays) every thing that was ufeful and good, mentioned in the Books of the Philofophers.

THE

THE moſt conſiderable Part therefore of the *Roman Law*, was the antient *Theodoſian* Code, which had the good Fortune longeſt to ſurvive the Ruin of the *Weſtern* Empire ; and many believe, it was this only, that was abſtractedly call'd the *Roman Law* : And indeed, *Gregory de Tours* makes mention of one *Andarchius*, in the Service of *Sigibert* Son of *Clotarius the Firſt*, who, he ſays, was very expert in the *Theodoſian* Law.

THE *Francs*, and other barbarous conquering Nations, brought with them a New Law into *Gaul* : But as they had not the uſe of Letters in their Tongues, ſo their Laws were only writ in *Latin* by ſome *Romans*, after they had been ſettled and converted to the Chriſtian Faith.

AT the time of their firſt Incurſions, they were govern'd only by meer Cuſtoms, tranſmitted to them by their Anceſtors, which ſerved them for a Guide in all their Determinations ; and their manner of living affording little occaſion for Law-Suits, made them not very exact in their Forms.

The Laws of the Barbarians meer Cuſtoms.

ALL

ALL thefe Nations came from *Germany*, whofe Manners are defcribed by *Tacitus* in his Hiftory of that Country.

WAR and Hunting was their whole Employment; and as they had no fix'd Habitation, nor other Goods than Cattle, their common Difputes, arofe either from Perfonal Quarrels or Theft; and thofe were decided in the Publick Meetings, either according to the Depofitions of Witneffes upon the Spot, or in doubtful Cafes, by *Combat*, or the Trials of *Fire* and *Water*.

THE *Romans*, tho' conquer'd by thefe People, were far from imitating them in any thing, and fhew'd the fame Averfion to them, as we fhould to *Tartars* or *Coffacks*. Befides, the *Barbarians*, whofe End of Conqueft was not Ambition or Glory, but to Plunder and live more at Large than they could in their own wretched Countries, were contented with the Dominion, and fuffer'd the *Romans* to live as they had done before.

ON the contrary, they themfelves imitated the *Romans*, whom their Forefathers had long before valued and admir'd.

THUS their firft Kings gave their Officers the fame Titles as the *Romans*, they call'd the Governors of their Provinces, *Dukes,*

Dukes, *Earls*, and *Vicars* ; and thofe who ferved about their Perfons, *Chancellors*, *Refrendaries*, *Chamberlains*, and in general *Palatins* : They thought it Honourable to be ftiled *Confuls* and *Patricians*, and were fond of being called *Glorious* * and *Illuftrious* ; which laft, were no more than ordinary Titles, commonly beftow'd by the *Romans* upon certain Magiftrates, and thofe not of the higheft Diftinction.

THEY had the fame Species of Coin as the *Romans*, that is, Gold † Shillings, and Silver Pence ; and their Kings reprefented upon it, with much the fame Ornaments as the Emperors.

IN a Word, the Good Senfe and Politenefs of the Conquered, foon got the better of the Conquerors, efpecially where Arts and Sciences were concern'd.

---

* See for this the *Novellæ* of *Juftinian*, Coll. 2. Tit. 1. Nov. 7. Tit. 2. Nov. 8. & *alibi*. That the Titles of *Gloriofiſſimi*, *Illuſtriſſimi*, &c. were apply'd as well to the *Prætors*, *Quæſtors* and the Ordinary Judges, as the Emperors themfelves : And even their *Chartularies* or Secretaries, were ftiled *Excelſi* and *Magnificentiſſimi*, as in the fame *Novella*, Tit. 2. Nov. 8. cap. 7. *Magnificentiſſimo Chartulario*, &c.

† *Solidi ex auro, Denarii ex argento.*

C   A6

As this Conformity in Manners drew
on an Affociation and Confederacy; fo
it was much increafed by the Converfion
of the *Barbarians* to the Chriftian Faith,
who now began to reverence the Bifhops
and Priefts as Holy Men, whom they
before admir'd for their Learning and A-
bilities ; and from thence, the *Romans*
entertain'd better Thoughts of, and obey'd
their Conquerors with greater chearful-
nefs.

But ftill, they were Two different
Nations in Language, Habit, and Cuftoms;
which *Diftinction* feems to have lafted in
France, through the Two firft Races of
their Kings ; but it chiefly appear'd in
their Laws : And as it was incumbent
on the Magiftrate, to render Juftice to
every Man, according to the Law under
which he was Born, or had made Choice
of, (for that was allow'd;) it was thought
adviſable, to reduce the Laws, or rather
the Cuftoms of the *Barbarians* into Writing.

These Laws are ftill extant, in a
Volume entitled, *A Code of the Ancient
Laws* † ; containing thofe of the *Viſgoths,*

---

† By *Frederick Lindenbrogius.*

an

an Edict of *Theodofius* King of *Italy*, the
Laws of the *Burgundians*, the *Salick* and
Ripuarian (which are properly the Laws
of the *Francs*;) the Law of the *Germans*,
that is, of the Inhabitants of *Alfatia* and
the Upper *Palatinate*; the Laws of the
Bavarians, *Saxons*, *Englifh* and *Frifons*;
the Laws of the *Lombards*, (which are
far more confiderable than the reft;) the
Capitulars of *Charlemagne*, and the Conftitutions of the Kings of *Naples* and
Sicily.

It would be an endlefs Labour to give
a particular Account of each of thefe
Laws: I fhall therefore confine my felf
to thofe that have the neareft Relation
to *France*; obferving by the way, that
there are none of them, even thofe made
for the moft diftant Nations, but may be
of fome ufe, either in Hiftory or the Civil Law; many of them being lick'd
into the Shape they are now in by the
Command of the *French* Kings. Befides,
all thofe *Northern* People, fwarming from
the fame Hive, and keeping a frequent
Correfpondence together, obferv'd a great
Conformity of Manners, as before is remark'd.

I fhall

I fhall fpeak of thefe Laws, according
to the Order of Time wherein they were
committed to Writing, that is, as the
feveral Nations were conquer'd and eftablifh'd.

Laws of the Vifi-goths. THOSE of the greateft Antiquity, are
the Laws of the *Vifigoths*, who poffefs'd
Spain, and a great part of *Aquitain* in
Gaul. And as their Kingdom was the
firft eftablifhed; fo it feems, their Laws
were written before any of the other
Barbarians.

THEY were firft digefted by *Evarix*,
who began his Reign in 466. but being
adapted only to the *Gothick* Conftitution,
his Son *Alarick* commanded *Avien* his
Chancellor, to abridge the *Theodofian* Code
for the ufe of the *Romans*, which he
publifhed at *Aire* in *Gafcony*. This A-
bridgment *Avien* illuftrated with Notes,
by way of Glofs; or at leaft, put his
Name to them for their greater Credit;
for we have no fufficient Proof that he
was the Author of them. However, we
may depend, that this Abridgment was
authoriz'd by the Bifhops and Nobles in
506; and was defign'd to comprehend all
the *Roman* Law then in ufe, which was
taken,

taken, as we have obferv'd, both out of the *Three Codes*, and the Writings of the *Civilians*.

ANOTHER *Abſtract* was afterwards made of this *Code*, conſiſting only of *Avien*'s Remarks, with the Title of *Scintilla*.

THE *Gothick* Law being much enlarged by fucceeding Kings, when fufficient Proviſion was made for moſt Cafes, it was put into *Twelve Books*, in imitation, as fome fay, of *Juſtinian*'s Code, altho' there is no refemblance in the Difpoſition of the Materials; and it was ordained, That this Collection ſhould be the only Law obferved by the Subjects of the *Go-thick* Kings, of what Nation foever they were.

BY this means, the *Roman* Law came to be extinct in *Spain*, or rather blended with the *Gothick* : For it was from the *Roman*, they took the greateſt Part of what was added to their own Antient Laws. This Collection was called the Book of the *Gothick Laws*; and King *Egica*, who reigned till 701. about Twelve Years before the *Moors* invaded *Spain*, got it confirm'd by the Biſhops in the Sixteenth Council of *Toledo*, held in the

C 3   Year

Year 693. It has the Names of several
Kings prefix'd; but all since *Recaredus*,
who was their first Catholick King.

THE Laws in use before, were called
the *Antient Laws*, but without the Sanction of any King's Name, not even of
Evarix; and probably they were all
suppressed in Detestation of *Arianism*. These
Antient Laws separately taken, bear a
great Analogy with those of the other
Barbarians; and comprehend all the *Gothick*
Customs, reduced into Writing by order
of King *Evarix*; but considered with the
Improvements they receiv'd, are undoubt-
edly the most Copious, as well as most
Wholesome, of all the Laws in use among
the Barbarous Nations, and point out the
Judicial Forms observed in *Justinian's* Time,
better than his own Books. This is the
Ground-work of the *Spanish* Laws, and
it prevail'd in *Languedoc*, long after the
Dissolution of the *Gothick* Government
there, as is manifest by the Second
Council of *Troyes*, held under Pope *John*
the Eighth, in the Year 878.

Laws of the Bur-gundians. THE *Burgundian* Laws were reform'd by
Gondebaud, one of their last Kings, and
published at *Lions*, the Twenty ninth of
March, 501. the Second Year of his Reign;
and

and from his Name they are called *Gombettes*, altho' he was not the firſt Inventor, as he himſelf confeſſes : And to confirm it, *Gregory de Tours* ſays, *Gondebaud* introduc'd more gentle Laws, to protect the *Romans* from being miſus'd by the *Burgundians*. There are ſome *Addenda* that reach up to 520 or thereabouts, Ten or Twelve Years before the Expiration of the *Burgundian* Government.

THIS Law of *Gondebaud* makes mention of the *Roman Law :* From whence 'tis plain, the Name of *Barbarian* was then no Reflection, ſince the *Burgundians* themſelves, for whoſe ſake it was made, are therein ſo call'd, by way of Diſtinction from the *Romans*. But as the Countries under the Dominion of the *Burgundians*, were near a Fourth Part of *France*, ſo no doubt, this was ingrafted into the Body of the *French* Laws.

As to the *Salick Law*, which was peculiar to the *Francs*, the Preface thereto ſays, it was wrote * before they paſs'd the

Laws of the Francs.

---

* But this is very much doubted, and directly contradicted by our *Engliſh* Hiſtorians. *Vide infra.*

Rhine;

Rhine; and the † Places of their Meetings, with the Names of the *Four* || *Sages* who were its Authors, are therein mention'd: And tho' the Veracity of this History is called in queſtion, I thought it the ſafeſt way to ſtick to the Edition we have, without taking the Pains to examine, whether this Law was *then* firſt digeſted or projected.

Vide *the* Notes antè

It is therein ſaid, to have received its Authority under *Childebert* and *Clotharius*, Sons of *Clovis* : And it expreſsly declares, that every thing in the antient Cuſtoms of the *Francs* reliſhing of Paganiſm, ſhould thereby be utterly aboliſhed.

Of this Law we have Two Copies, the ſame in Sence, but very different in Words. The Oldeſt, which was alſo the firſt printed, has in moſt Articles ſome Barbarous Words, denoting the Place of

---

† In Places called *Salehaim, Bodohaim, Widohaim,* on the other Side of the *Rhine*. [*See the Preface to the* Salick Law.]

|| Having out of many choſen Four, namely, *Wiſogaſtus, Bodogaſtus, Salogaſtus, Widogaſtus*. [*See the Preface to the* Salick Law, *and* Quære *if theſe* Names are not forg'd.]

every

every particular Decifion, or the Sum of the Fines adjudged upon each Cafe, as Monfieur *Vaudelin,* Official of *Tournay,* underftands it in his Treatife of the *Sàlick Law.*

THE other Copy, is the Edition of *Charlemagne,* and is in the Code of the Antient Laws; at the End of which are certain *Addenda,* intituled, The Decrees of *Childebert* and *Clothair* ; being the Refult of the † Solemn Meetings, held Annually on the Firft of *March.*

THE

---

† Thefe Annual Solemn Meetings feem to have been in Nature of our *Parliaments,* and were generally practifed by moft of the Northern Nations : Thus here in *England,* antecedent to the Conqueft, the Practice was to hold a General Solemn Affembly, called *Populi Conventus,* or *Folkmote,* twice yearly, *viz.* on the Kalends of *May,* and the Kalends of *October,* wherein Grievances were redrefs'd, and Laws and Provifions made for the good Government of the Kingdom ; and in them were elected and conftituted, all the great Officers of the Kingdom, both Civil and Military, as appears by the Laws of *Edward the Confeffor,* Cap. 35.

Befides which, we may obferve, That thefe Solemn Annual Affemblies, were ftated and certain, and did not depend on the King's Writ of Summons, or other Royal Mandate, (as Parliaments now do ;) and therefore the *Statute* of *Ed.* I. *Cap.---* which fays, *Parliaments fhall be held twice Yearly* ; feems to refpect this antient Practice, and the

common

Laws of the Ripuarians. THE *Ripuarian*, is in a manner, nothing elſe but a Repetition of the *Salick Law :* Both were made for the Uſe of the *Francs ;* the firſt, 'tis thought, for the People inhabiting between the *Loire* and the *Meuſe ;* and the latter, for thoſe between the *Meuſe* and the *Rhine. Theodorick,* being at *Chalons* upon *Marne,* cauſed the Laws of the *Ripuarians, Germans* and *Bavarians,* all under his Obedience, to be reform'd and corrected, eſpecially, as far as they were repugnant to the Chriſtian Religion. After him, *Childebert,* and then *Clothair* made farther Amendments ; and laſtly, *Dagobert* renew'd, and with the Aſſiſtance of *Four* ‖ *Eminent Men,* brought them to that Perfection in which they are.

Laws of the Barbarians in general. THESE were the Laws of the *Barbarians,* which properly relate to the pre

---

common Cuſtom of the Realm before the Conqueſt : And the following Words, [*or oftner if need be*] only gave the King a Power to call *other Parliaments* by *Summons* whenever the neceſſary Affairs of the Kingdom required it.

‖ *Claudius, Chaudius, Indomagnus, Agilulfus.* [*Vid.* Cod. Leg. Antiq. *Edit. per* Fred. Lyndenbrogium. *Præfat. Leg. Ripuar.*]

ſent

fent *France* ; and it may not be amiſs, (after having told you what is moſt re-markable in the Original of each of them) to touch briefly upon the whole, and give a general *Idea* of their Tenour or Contents, and their Style or Method, in order to know of what uſe and ſervice they may be to Us.

WE muſt not let the Word *Law* de-ceive, and perſuade us, that theſe were the Reſult of Learned Mens Conſultations, or the Fruits of a conſummate Prudence, as the Laws of the *Athenians* and *Lacedemonians :* No, they were, properly ſpeaking, no more than Cuſtoms that obtain'd among the People, and were afterwards ap-prov'd and recorded by their wiſeſt and moſt experienc'd Men, in their judicial Deciſions, and followed by the reſt in all their Judgments. This is plain, from the an-tient Copies of the *Salick Law*, which nominate in barbarous Terms, the Pla-ces where ſuch Judgments were given, and ſometimes the Quality or Nature of the Fact.

THESE Laws, notwithſtanding, were afterwards digeſted into Order, by Publick Authority, and had not only the *Fiat* of the Kings, but Approbation of the Peo-ple,

ple, at leaſt of their Repreſentatives : Therefore the *Salick* Law is called the *Covenant*
or † *Treaty of the Salick Law* ; and that
of the *Burgundians*, has the Names of
Thirty ‖ Earls to it, who promiſed for
themſelves and their Deſcendants to keep
and obſerve it.

Their Con-
tents.
THE Matters they chiefly treat of, are
Criminal, and ſuch as are moſt incident
to Barbarous and Savage People, as Rob-
beries, Murders, Injuries, Inſults, and all
manner of Violence : There is little ſaid
of Succeſſions, Inheritances, or Contracts.

---

† *Pactum, Tractatus.*

‖ Sig. *Abgaris*, Com.
Sig. *Aunemundi*, Com.
Sig. *Unnani*, Com.
Sig. *Hildeulfi*, Com.
Sig. *Hildegerni*, Com.
Sig. *Uſgildi*, Com.
Sig. *Waleſti*, Com.
Sig. *Audemundi*, Com.
Sig. *Audahari*, Com.
Sig. *Amgathei*, Com.
Sig. *Auderici*, Com.
Sig. *Aunemundi*, Com.
Sig. *Willimeris*, Com.
Sig. *Conigiſeli*, Com.
Sig. *Comarici*, Com.
Sig. *Wallacrii*, Com.

Sig. *Sigonis*, Com.
Sig. *Fredemundi*, Com.
Sig. *Wanabarii*, Com.
Sig. *Wilfilæ*, Com.
Sig. *Sigiſwldi*, Com.
Sig. *Soniæ*, Com.
Sig. *Godemundi*, Com.
Sig. *Widemeris*, Com.
Sig. *Wadahameris*, Com.
Sig. *Silvani*, Com.
Sig. *Gomæ*, Com.
Sig. *Faſtilæ*, Com.
Sig. *Suldi*, Com.
Sig. *Gundeulfi*, Com.
Sig. *Offini*, Com.
Sig. *Walarimi*, Com.

IN

In the Laws of such of those Nations as had been lately conquer'd, and converted to the Faith, I mean the *Germans, Saxons,* and *Bavarians*, there are particular Punishments assign'd for Rebellion and Sacrilege: From whence we may gather, that neither the Civil, nor Ecclesiastical Magistrates, were secure from the Insults of the *Barbarians*.

SOMETHING there is also to be discovered of the Form of their Judgments; They met together in numerous Assemblies, at which all Persons of Distinction were bound to appear, upon certain Penalties, as the Laws of the *Bavarians* declare. The Proofs made use of, were rather *vivâ voce,* than by written Evidence, because the Art of † Writing, was then unknown; and in default of due Proof, they granted the *Combat,* or a Trial by the *Elements.* The Combat, was a *Duel,* fought either between the Parties themselves, or their

---

† Surely Writing was then known and practis'd. And see hereafter another Reason assigned; and indeed the best Reason seems to be, because the Truth would better appear *vivâ voce,* than by any written Evidence. [*See Sir* Matt. Hale's *History of the Law,* Cap. ult.]
Vid. Cod. Leg. Antiq. *L.B. Baiuvariorum,* Tit. 15. *Ut placita fiant per Kalendas, &c.*

Cham-

Champions, within Lifts appointed by the
Judges. The Trial by the Elements, was
either *Scalding Water*, into which the
accufed put his Arm a certain depth; or
Cold Water, into which he was plung'd,
to fee if he would fink: And fometimes
the Trial was made · by a *Red-hot Iron*,
which he was to carry fo many Yards,
in his bare Hand : Then it was bound and
feal'd up ; and after fome Days, unbound,
to fee what Effect the Fire had produc'd.

THESE Trials lafted many Ages, and
were fo currently received, that they were
call'd *God's* Judgments; and for that Reafon perform'd with Church-Ceremonies ;
the Forms of which, and Prayers ufed on
fuch Occafions, and the Exorcifms of
Fire and *Water*, are ftill to be feen : So
Ignorant were they in thofe Times, as
to believe, that God would work a Mi-
racle in favour of Innocence; and the
many Inftances of Succefs mention'd in
Hiftory, helped to confirm them in that
Belief. However, 'tis certain they were
not able to invent a better, or more convenient Method to determine in Cafes of
Intricacy, and where their own Skill
failed.

THIS

THIS is called in the Canons † *Vulgar Purgation*, and ever condemned by the Church of *Rome*, notwithſtanding the Influence of Common Practice : 'Tis called *Vulgar*, to diſtinguiſh it from *Canonical Purgation*, which was done only by *Oath*.

THE Nature of the Penalties inflicted by theſe Laws is no leſs remarkable than the reſt, moſt of them being Pecuniary ; Or, where the Convict was not able to pay, a Corporal Puniſhment : Scarce any were Capital, but Crimes of State. Thoſe Penalties were called *Compoſitions* ; being only a Tax of Coſts and Damages, made with ſurpriſing Exactneſs. There are an Hundred and ſixty four Articles in that of the *Friſons* only ; which is one of the

---

† Theſe kinds of Vulgar Purgation were in uſe in *England* till the time of *Hen.* III. They were called *Fire and Water Ordeals.* Queen *Emma*, Mother of *Edward the Confeſſor*, was tried by the Firſt, paſſing blindfold over a certain Number of hot glowing Plough-ſhares, with a Succeſs worthy of her Chaſtity. An Example of the Second kind, we have in the Reign of *William* II. who ſuſpecting a Company of Fellows to have ſtollen his Deer, enjoyned them to carry burning Irons ; which they did without Hurt. And the King being told of it, replied, *Quid eſt id ? Deus eſt juſtus Judex ; pereat qui deinceps hoc crediderit.* Eadmerus.

ſhort-

fhorteft : 'Tis properly, a Tariff of all
kinds of Wounds, in which the feveral
Parts of the Body are enumerated, and
even thofe which ought to have been o-
verlook'd, and every' way in which they
may be hurt, fet down, with the feveral
Dimenfions of each Wound. For Example ; the Maiming of a Hand is taxed in
fo many different Articles; as, the Fourth,
Third, Second, or Firft Finger cut off;
and a difference made in the Penalty, if
it be a Thumb, Fore-Finger, Middle-Fin-
ger, and fo of the reft : Nay, the feveral Joints of each Finger have their feveral Fines. They alfo diftinguifh, if the
Part be entirely cut off, or hanging to
the reft of the Body ; and if a Wound
only, then the Length, Breadth and Depth
are fully defcribed. Among the reft, there
is a particular Tax upon Wounds of the
Head, when the Scull is broken, which
feems very extraordinary; but yet is re-
peated in many of their Laws : It is,
* that if a Piece of the Scull be broken
off, big enough to make a Shield found,

---

* Si quis in Capite, vel in quocunque libet membro
plagatus fuerit, & os exinde exierit quod fuper viam
12 pedum in fcuto jaƈum fonaverit 36 fol. faƈum
ejus culp. jud. [See the Ripuarian Laws, Cap. 68. de
Offe, &c.]

being

being caſt into it at the Diſtance of twelve
Paces, the Offender ſhall pay ſuch a
Fine.

Opprobrious Words are tax'd with
the ſame Exactneſs: And hence we may
learn, what Words were accounted infamous in thoſe times.

Some may think it hardly worth while
now a-days to take notice of ſeveral
things that are particulariz'd in thoſe
Laws. There is proviſion made to puniſh
ſuch as ſhall ſtop another in a Road;
ſuch as uncover a † Woman to affront
her; thoſe who dig up a Dead Corpſe
to plunder it; and him who skins another Man's Horſe. In ſhort, there are
particular Articles againſt ſtealing all ſorts
of Beaſts, down to Dogs, the different
Kinds of which are therein ſpecified.
I thought it would not be altogether uſeleſs, to enter into this brief Detail, how

---

† Si qua libera fœmina virgo vadit in itinere ſuo
inter duas Villas, & obviavit eam aliquis, & per rap-
tum denudat caput ejus, cum vi. Sol. componat; ------
----- Et ſi ejus Veſtimenta levaverit, ut uſque ad
genicula denudet, cum vi. Solid. componat; & ſi eam
denudaverit ut genitalia ejus appareant vel poſteriora,
cum xii. Solid. componat. [Lex Alman. Tit. 58. De
eo qui mulierem, &c.

[34]

low foever it feems, in order to give fome
Idea of thofe Laws, as well as a Notion
of the People for whom they were ordained.

Their Style.   THE Style in which they are wrote, is
fo plain and fuccinct, that they would be
eafily underftood, if they were not full
of Barbarous Terms, which have crept in,
either for want of proper *Latin* Words,
or by way of Explanation : And this is
another clear Proof of my Affertion, that
thefe Barbarians † *wrote nothing in their
own Language ;* for certainly, if they had,
thofe Laws might have been much more

---

† The Reafon why the *German* Nations did not
Write their Laws, was (fays *Spelman*) becaufe they
were originally a *Grecian* Colony, coming out of
Lacedemon, and the Territory of *Sparta* ; where
Lycurgus being King, ordained, *That their Laws
fhould not be Written, but Imprinted in every Man's
Memory :* And therefore they were made Short
and Summary. [*Spelm. of the Terms,* Cap. 8.]
   And Monfieur *Pezron,* in his Treatife *of the Antiquities of Nations,* Lib. 1. c. 17. has with great
probability of Truth, endeavour'd to prove, That
the *Spartans* or *Lacedemonians* originally fprung from
the *Celtæ :* From whence alfo, both the *Antient
Gauls,* and our *Britons* were defcended. He, in the
fame Treatife, fhews their Analogy or Conformity
in Manners, Cuftoms and Laws ; and particularly,
of having their Laws unwritten, and preferving them
only by means of their *Druids,* &c.

com-

commodiously wrote in the *German* Language, than in *Latin*, stuffed with *German*
Terms. Yet, it appears there was Writing in the *Teutonick* Tongue, an Age or
two after these Laws were digested : For
not to mention the Ancient *Version* of the
Gospels, of which there are some Fragments in the Inscriptions of *Gruter*, we
have the Laws of the *Anglo-Saxons*, wrote
in their Vulgar Tongue, from the Beginning of the Reign of † King *Ina*, in 712.
to the End of that of *Canutus* the *Dane*,
in the Year 1035. These, by the way,
have a great Affinity to the rest of the
Barbarian Laws ; and were also enacted
in the Assemblies of their Bishops and
Elders.

---

† We have also lately Published, by the Reverend
Mr. *Wilkins*, the Laws of divers *Saxon* Kings, antecedent to those of King *Ina* : *viz*. The Laws of
Æthelbirht; who began to reign, as *Bede* says, *Anno* 613.
or according to the *Saxon* Chronology, 618. Those
of King *Lotharius* ; who, as *Bede* says, began *Anno*
673. or as others, 675. And those of King *Wihtred*,
who began about the Year 691. All which were
Kings of *Kent*, before the Union of the *Heptarchy*,
under King *Egbert*. And no doubt, other *Saxon*
and *British* Princes before these, Published divers
Laws ; as may be Instanced from the Laws of
Howel Dha, which as we hear, will speedily be published by the Reverend Dr. *Wotton*.

THE

THE *Gothick* Laws are in a purer *Latin* Dialect, according to the Learning of thofe Times, than any of the reft; that is, they have fewer Barbarous Expreffions, altho' more Phrafes and fuperfluous Words.

Laws of the Francs *under the Firft Race.* THUS 'tis eafily known, what Laws were in force in *France,* under the Kings of the Firft Race. The *Francs,* who were Mafters, obferv'd the *Salick* ; the *Burgundians,* the *Gombette* ; the *Goths,* who fettled in great Numbers in the Provinces on the other fide of the *Loire,* followed the *Gothick* Laws, and all the reft, the *Roman*; which the Church-Men univerfally follow'd, of what Nation foever they were: 'Tis true, there were few Ecclefiafticks, but what were *Romans* ; but had it been otherwife, their Intereft was to cultivate that Law, for the fake of the great Privileges, and Immunities granted them by the Conftitutions of the Emperors. Befides this, they were obliged to obey the *Canon Law* ; that is, fuch Rules of the Councils, as are compris'd in the Antient Code of the Canons of the *Univerfal Church,* and fome Decifions of the Popes, who were often confulted by the Bifhops.

THE

THE *Barbarians*, and even the *Francs* themfelves, were frequently forced to have recourfe to the *Roman* Law, becaufe their own was deficient in many Cafes. Thus, *Agathias* fays, the *Francs* were directed by the *Roman* Law in their Contracts and Marriages. And *Aimonius* relates, that in the time of *Dagobert*, the Children of *Sadregefille*, Duke of *Acquitain*, were, in purfuance of the *Roman* Law, excluded from his Inheritance, for not revenging their Fathers Death. Befides, it is natural to fuppofe, that thofe who drew up the Publick Inftruments and Writings, being all *Clerks* or *Monks*, as *Marculfus*, whofe Formularies we have, adapted them as much they cou'd to their Law and Style: So that the *Roman* Law was univerfally obferved through all *France*, under the Kings of the Firft Race, and never thrown afide, but when it crofs'd fome *Barbarian* Law in Force.

Now whoever has a mind to fee an Abridgment of thefe Laws in their greateft Luftre, together with the State of *France* under the Firft Race, their manner of adminiftring Juftice, and Government; let him look into the Hiftory wrote by M. *Cordemoi*, at the End of King *Dagobert's* Reign.   D 3   THE

Laws of the
Francs
under the
Second
Race.

THE Emperor *Charlemagne*, having re-united all the Conquests of the *Francs*, *Burgundians*, *Goths* and *Lombards* under his Empire, suffered each Nation to enjoy their own Laws; and had them all reviv'd, through his great Care that every thing should be administred according to Rule and good Order: Perhaps, 'tis to him we are indebted for those Copies that have been transmitted unto us.

IN the Year 788, he order'd the *Theo-dosian* Code to be Copy'd and Publish'd, according to the Edition of *Alarick*, King of the *Visigoths*; and by means of this Edition, we have all the *Theodosian* Code, or rather, an Abridgment of all it contain'd: For, comparing it with that publish'd by *Theodosius* himself, which was much larger, we have but half of it. In the Year 798, *Charlemagne* had the *Salick* Law transcribed, and added several Articles thereto: In 803, *Louis the Debonair* likewise made some Additions. So that the same Law was in use, as well under the Kings of the Second Race, as of the First: The only Addition to them, was the Capitulars, which are General Laws, and deserve carefully to be examined.

IN

In order to which, we muſt underſtand, *The Capi-tulars.*
the Kings of the Firſt Race, for many
Years, held a great Aſſembly on the Firſt
Day of *March*; in which, all Publick Af-*Vide* antè.
fairs were debated, and Mutual Preſents
made between the Prince and People.
This they call'd *the Field of* * Mars : A
Name long before in uſe under the *Roman*
Emperors, to ſignifie a Military Congreſs or
Meeting. The *Francs* held it in the open
Air, for want of Buildings large enough
to hold them ; or rather, becauſe it was
cuſtomary among the *Germans* in their
own Countrey, where they had no other
Dwellings but Caverns and ſcatter'd Huts.
It was, probably, this Cuſtom of Meeting in the Field to hold theſe Aſſemblies,
that fix'd the time of keeping them to
the End of the Winter, which had confin'd them to their Habitations ; and before Summer, that they might employ
it wholly to execute the Reſolutions of
the General Council : For War was the
Principal Subject of their Debates.

This Field of *Mars*, through the Indolence and Inactivity of the ſuceeding Droniſh

---

* From the Roman *Campus Martius.*

Kings,

[40]

Kings, dwindled into a mere Ceremony; and *Pepin* changed the Day to the Firſt of *May*: After his Time, it was uncertain, altho' the Annual Meetings were regularly kept up.

THIS Aſſembly confiſted of the Chiefs in Church and State, as of *Biſhops*, *Abbots* and *Earls*; and I am apt to believe, that all thoſe that were *Francs*, had a Right of coming to it. The Queſtion was propounded by the King; who, after it had been freely debated, pronounced the Definitive Sentence or Reſolution. The Reſult of theſe Meetings was put into Writing, and every Biſhop and Earl obliged to take a Copy from the *Chancellor*, for the Direction of their Inferior Officers, and that no Man might pretend Ignorance. As the Queſtions and Reſolutions were put into a ſhort Form, under ſeveral Heads, they were called *Chapters*; and Collections of many Chapters, *Capitulars* †.

THE Capitulars, I think, ought to be diſtinguiſhed according to their Subjects: Thoſe relating to Church-Affairs, which

† See the Preface of Monſieur *Baluze* upon this Subject.

are

[41]

are very numerous, are really *Canons*; as
being Rules eſtabliſh'd by Biſhops lawfully
aſſembled: Therefore moſt part of thoſe
Aſſemblies, are reckon'd as Councils.
Thoſe Capitulars which treat of Secular,
but General Matters, are truly Laws:
And ſuch as refer to particular Perſons
and Caſes, are to be conſidered only as Private Rules.

WE have ſtill a great many Capitulars
of the Kings of the Two firſt Races; from
Childebert Son of *Clovis*, to *Charles the
Simple:* The greateſt part are of *Charlemagne* and *Louis the Debonair*; which, till
now, were no where to be found, but in
the Collection of Abbot * *Anſgiſe*, and
Benedict || the Deacon. At preſent, we
have the Capitulars entire, in the ſame
Order of Writing and Time, as they were
drawn up in each Aſſembly. They were
thus publiſhed by M. *Baluze*, in 1677.
with an ample Preface, and very Learned
Remarks on the whole. He hath alſo
put in its proper Place, *viz.* at the End
of the Capitulars of *Louis the Debonair*,
Anſgiſe's and *Benedict*'s Compilation. It is

* Afterwards Biſhop of *Sens*.

|| Deacon of the Church of *Mayence*.

divided

divided into Seven Books : The Four firft, were compofed by *Anfgife* in 827. for the better Prefervation (as he fays) of the Capitulars, which were in loofe Sheets. In the Two firft Books, he places thofe of *Charlemagne :* The Firft contains Eccle- fiaftical, and the Second Secular Matters. In the next Two Books, the Capitulars of *Louis the Debonair* and his Son *(viz.) Lothair :* In the Third, the Capitulars relating to Ecclefiaftical, and in the Fourth Book, thofe relating to Secular Matters. The other Three, were compiled by *Bene- dict,* Deacon of the Church of *Ments,* about 845. and contain more Capitulars of the fame Princes, omitted by *Anfgife,* either defignedly or for want of knowing where to find them, and which *Benedict* recover'd in feveral Places ; particularly, the Archives of his own Church †.

THERE are juft Grounds to accufe either *Benedict,* or thofe whofe Memoirs he hath compil'd, of not having been fo exact as they ought, in their Choice of what Ma- terials they have inferted in thofe Capi- tulars : For at the Beginning of the Sixth Book, we find Fifty three Articles taken

† *Mayence.*

from

from the Law of *Moses*, which certainly
did not suit with either *Charlemagne's*
Time or Countrey. After thefe Seven
Books, are fome Capitulars of the Emperor
Louis the Debonair, concerning Ecclefiaftical Regulations, difcover'd fince *Benedict's* Collection, and divided into Four
Addenda; the Firft of which, merely concerns the Monaftick Difcipline.

THE *Authority* of the Capitulars, muft
needs have been very great, being Enacted
by the Advice of the Nobles, and Confent
of the whole Nation; fo that they were
in force throughout the whole *French* Empire, that is, almoft all over *Europe*: Efpecially under *Charlemagne*, *Louis the Debonair* and his Children. Befides the Pains
taken to inculcate them into the Minds of
the People, it was a chief Branch of
the Duty of thofe Minifters called * *Miffi
Dominici*, to fee them duly executed in
the Provinces under their Charge. Nay,
the Capitulars were a long time after
efteemed Laws, as appears by the Letters
of *Ives de Chartres*, the Decretals of *Innocent* III. and the Decree of *Gratian*, where-

* A kind of Surveyors or Commiffaries, fent by
the Prince to infpect the Government of the Provinces.

in

in many of them are inferted. This was
the State of the Law of *France*, under the
Second Race of our Kings ; when the
Capitulars, the *Salick* Law, and the Laws
of each particular People, but efpecially
the *Romans*, were in ufe.

The Ro-
man Law
under the
Second
Race.
THE Care thofe Princes took, to preferve the Ufe of the *Roman* Law, is manifeft, by an Article of the Capitulars of
Charles the Bald; wherein, after the Penalty fix'd upon Falfe Meafures, 'tis provided, *That in all the Provinces fubject to*
the Roman Law, *the Delinquent fhould be*
punifh'd according to that Law ; adding,
That neither He, nor his Predeceffors, had
ever defign'd to Enact any thing repugnant
to it : Which he often repeats in the
fame Edict. Befides, the *Roman* Law was
equally ufeful to thofe who were not *Ro-*
mans, as under the Firft Race of our Kings:
For the Capitulars, which were the only
New Laws, contain very little of the Fun-
damental Maxims and Principles of Law.
The greateft part of them relate only to
Church-Difcipline ; infomuch, that many
Canons of the Antient Councils, are tran-
fcribed among them. Thofe which concern Temporal Matters, often relate only
to Private Cafes, for which they were calculated. Others, are plainly but Inftructions and Minutes, for the Commiffioners

ners fent into the Provinces. The few
remaining General Articles, are very defective Laws: They are rather Exhorta-
tions to Virtue, than Penal Laws. And
as 'tis known, the Authors were Ecclefiafticks, 'tis natural enough to think, they
did not fufficiently diftinguifh between the
Style ufed in Laws, which command and
force Obedience, and that of Charitable Ex-
hortations and Moral Precepts. So that
it was neceffary to have recourfe to the
Roman Law, in Matters of Right; efpecially Contracts and Conditions: For
moft of their Difputes were about Vaffals.

HERE follows a Memorable Inftance of
the Laws ufed in *France*, under the Second Race of our Kings. *Adrivaldus*, a
Monk of the Monaftery of St. *Benedict
upon Loire*, who Flourifh'd in the Time
of *Charles the Bald*, tells us, That there
was a Difpute between the *Patrons* of that
Convent, and that of St. *Dennis*, concerning fome Vaffals: To decide which, a Plea
was held before One *Bifhop*, and One * *Earl*

---

* An Earl, in the Signification of *Comes* or *Comte*,
was not originally a Degree of Dignity, as it is now,
but of Office and Judicature. [Spelman *of Feuds, &c.
Cap. 6.*] Or rather, all *Dignities* imply'd an *Office*
annexed thereto. In the fame Manner, the Bifhops
formerly ufurp'd a Lay-Jurifdiction in this Kingdom;
and were Judges in Trials of Criminal, as well as Civil Matters. [*Vid. Concil. Brit.* 182. *Anno* 693. *vid. etiam
Leges Æthelftani.*] on

on the King's Part, and several Judges and Doctors of Law ; who at the First Meeting could come to no Refolution ; becaufe the Judges of the *Salick* Law, were unacquainted with the Courfe of the Ecclefiaftical Courts, which proceeded according to the *Roman* Law : This oblig'd the King's Minifters to appoint another Meeting at *Orleans* ; where, befides the Judges, feveral Doctors of Law, both of that Province, and the *Gaftinois*, were order'd to attend. And after all, it ended in a *Duel* between the Witneffes.

THIS Piece of Hiftory, fhews, the *Roman* and *Salick* Laws, were at that time both in Force ; that the Church obey'd the *Roman* Law ; that there were Perfons, who made it their Bufinefs to read Publick Law-Lectures ; and that fome of them then lived in *Orleans :* That the Prince's Minifters, were Prefidents of the Court ; and that fometimes, the Witneffes were order'd to end the Difpute by *Combat*.

WHAT I have hitherto treated of, is what I call the *Antient French Law.*

The New Law. IN order to underftand, how the *New Law* was modell'd and introduc'd, we muft firft examine, how the *Old* was reduced

into

into Cuftom; and how the Study of the
Roman Law, came to be revived. The
Origine of all Cuftoms is obfcure; becaufe
they differ from Laws, only in not being
committed to Writing: So that if ever
they are put into Writing, 'tis not till after they have been eftablifh'd by long
Practice. But there is a particular Reafon,
why the Origine of the *French* Cuftoms
is difficult to be traced; *(viz.)* becaufe
they firft grew into Authority, in the Tenth
and Eleventh Centuries; which is the
darkeft Period of Time in all our Hiftory.
But this is what I Conjecture.

ABOUT the End of the Second, and Be-
ginning of the Third Race of our Kings, *Troubles of the Tenth Century.*
both *Italy* and *Gaul* fell into Anarchy, and
a General Confufion. Thofe Troubles
were firft occafion'd, by the unhappy Divifion between the Sons of *Louis the Debonair*; and were greatly increas'd by
the Hoftilities and Ravages of the *Hungarians*, and *Normans*, who gave the final
Blow to the poor Remains of the *Roman*
Spirit and Cuftoms.

BUT this Misfortune, was carry'd to the
utmoft Extremity by Private Wars; not
only betwixt the Dukes and Earls,
but generally, all that had any Caftle
or

or Place of Strength for Retreat: For every Man appear'd in Arms; even the very
Bifhops with their Clergy, and Abbots with
their Monks, to fecure themfelves from
being Plunder'd; when they found their
Prayers and Ecclefiaftical Cenfures inef-
fectual.

THESE Bickerings were agreeable to the
Antient Cuftoms of the *Barbarians*; the
Seeds of which, appear in their very Laws:
For befides the *Duel*, one of their ordinary means of Decifion in doubtful Cafes,
they encourag'd the Law of deadly *Feuds*;
which allow'd the Kindred of the Deceas'd,
to kill the Murtherer where-ever they met
him; except in certain Places, as * the
Church, Royal Palace, Publick Affembly,
the Army, or in his way to any of them :
For upon thofe Occafions, the Perfons
liable to this Revenge were protected.

* *Homo faidofus pacem habeat in Ecclefia in domo
fua, ad Ecclefiam eundo, de Ecclefia redeundo; ad
placitum eundo de placito redeundo, qui hanc pacem
effregerit & hominem occiderit, novies xxx. fol. componat. Si vulneravit, novies xii. fol. componat ad
partem Regis.* [Add. fapientum Leg. Frifonum,
Tit. 1.]

THUS

THUS one Murder, tho' accidental, often produc'd a Train of many Murders: And 'tis likely, that this was the Reason, why the Law did not inflict the Punishment of Death upon Murderers; but only a Pecuniary Mulct, or rather Costs and Damages, which were call'd Compositions: For it was left to the Choice of the Kindred, either to revenge themselves by the Death of the Murderer, or be satisfy'd with a Fine. However it was, 'tis certain Family-Quarrels were universally established in *France*, in the Tenth Century.

As it is difficult to bring to a due Temper, the Minds of a People once exasperated; all that the Zealous Endeavours of the Church-Men, and best of Princes could at first do, was only to obtain a Cessation of Arms for certain Days; that is, every Week from *Wednesday* Evening, to the *Monday* Morning following: During which time, all Acts of Hostility were forbidden. Besides, some sorts of Persons were never to be ill-treated; as Priests, Pilgrims, and Day-Labourers, upon Pain of Excommunication: And this is what they called *God's Truce*, which was since confirm'd and enlarged.

E   ONE

ONE may easily imagine, that during these Troubles, Ignorance and Injustice insensibly abolish'd the Antient Laws; and that being much disregarded, they grew out of Knowledge. Thus the *French* fell again into almost the State of *Barbarians*, who have as yet, neither Laws nor Civil Government: Nay, in this respect, they were more unhappy, in having retained some Remembrance of Arts; which they chiefly employed in Forging Arms, and Building Fortifications: So that they had many more ways of doing one another Mischief, than mere Savages have. They were more ignorant of Good than Evil; and had all the Ferocity of their Anceftors, without their open Simplicity and Innocence.

HENCE came our old Fabulous Stories of *Robbers*, that insulted the Weak and Defencelefs; block'd up the Roads, and interrupted Trade and Commerce; and of *Knights-Errant*, who went up and down in defence of the Innocent, and to succour Diftrefs'd Damfels. But methinks, the Authors of these Romances, were not guilty of any Novel Inventions; since they only copied the real Characters of those Times, embellishing them with Giants, Conjurers and Fairies. BUT

BUT notwithstanding this Confusion, there still remain'd some Forms of Justice; for all Disputes were not determin'd by Force. The *Nobles* and *Roturiers*, or *Plebeians*, were under distinct Jurisdictions. I use those Appellations, tho' of later Date, because the Degrees were then known, tho' not the Names: And I place the Peasants, Artisans, and the rest of the Freemen and Vassals, which compose the Body of the Common-People, under the Denomination of *Roturiers*. These were judged by the Nobles, that is, the Knights, and other Men of Power, who began about this time to erect themselves into Lords, and usurp'd the Publick Authority; of which, they had before, at most, but the executive Part: For as long as the Royal Power was in its full Meridian, particularly in the Line of *Charlemagne*, there was no other Lord but the King; nor any Justice administred but in his Name, or of those put in Authority under him. But in the troublesome Times, every Man took upon him the Prerogative of judging, as well as of making War, and raising Taxes upon the People.

THE Foundation of this Incroachment, was, in all likelihood, owing to the Domestick Power over Vassals: For *France*

was

was ſtill full of that ſort of Vaſſals, who
were accounted Parcel of the Lord's Eſtate
and Inheritance ; and it was no hard Matter, in reſpect of them, to change their
Private into Publick Authority. I am of
Opinion, that many Freemen were confounded with theſe Vaſſals ; either by their
Conſent, in order for Protection in this
time of General Hoſtility, or by down-
right Force : For in the Capitulars, there
is frequent mention made of the Oppreſ-
ſion of Free Poor Men. The Ringleaders
of this Uſurpation, were, probably, the
Earls ; that is, the Governors of Conſiderable Towns, who were before, in right
of their Offices, inveſted with a Power of
Juriſdiction.

THESE Lords, from what Spring ſoever
their Power flow'd, adminiſter'd Juſtice,
either in Perſon, or by Officers choſen
out of their own Domeſticks : Their Stewards were made *Seneſchals* ; their Inten-
dants and Receivers, *Bailiffs* and *Provoſts* ;
and their Footmen, *Serjeants.* Nay, in
looking farther back, we ſhall find, that
the Seneſchal and other Officers, were
not only Domeſticks, but ſometimes Slaves ;
for the *Salick* Law, amongſt thoſe Slaves
valued at a certain Rate, names the *Mayor*,
Cup-bearer and *Mareſchal* ; and the *German*
Law, the *Seneſchal* and *Mareſchal* : But
theſe

thefe Names were not given to Publick
Officers, till the Third Race of our Kings.

THIS Authority was Sovereign; and
Juſtice render'd in a Summary Way. The
Penalties they inflicted, were Cruel : For
it was common to put out * Eyes, and to
cut off a Foot or a Hand : Whence it is,
that the Acts of thoſe Times fo frequently
mention *Mutilation*; and it ſeems too, that
thefe Puniſhments were Arbitrary.

THESE Nobles, who thus fat in Judgment upon the *Roturiers*, were ſubject alſo to the Judgment of their Superiors :
A *Knight* or *Caſtellan*, for Example, was
ſubject to the Juriſdiction of that *Earl* whoſe
Vaſſal he was ; and the Earl, in order to
Judge the Knight, ſummon'd the Peers of
his Court, who were Knights, Vaſſals of
equal Rank among themſelves, and the
Perſon under Proſecution. The Earl himſelf, was one of the Peers of his Lord Pa-
ramount's Court; either an *Earl* of greater Power, a *Duke*, or a *Marquiſs :* And
this Subordination, was obſerved from the

---

* *Interdico etiam ne quis occidatur vel ſuſpendatur pro*
aliqua culpa, ſed eruantur oculi, & abſcindantur teſticuli,
vel pedes vel manus ita quod truncus vivus remancat.
[*Vid. Leg.* Gulielmi Conqueſtoris.]

Pea-

Peafant to the Prince; for the King's own
Court, was made up of the Peers of *France*,
his chief Vaffals.

But this Order was not always obferv'd,
for fome of the Nobles, knowing their
own Strength, refus'd to obey their Chiefs,
who had no other way of doing themfelves Juftice, but by Force of Arms.
The King himfelf, was many times forc'd
to make War, not only againft fome Peers
of *France*, but other inferior Lords. The
Abbat *Suger* tells us, that *Louis the Grofs*
fent an Army againft *Bouchard de Mont-
morency*, in favour of the Abbat of *St. Dennis*; that he Befieg'd *Gournai*, and took it
by Storm; that he Defeated the Lord
Puifet en Beauffe; and at laft fubdued the
Lord of *Montlehery*, who had tir'd out his
Father, *Philip the Firft*, and even ftopp'd
his Communication between *Paris* and
Orleans.

Another way of compofing Differences
between Great Men, was Arbitration, efpecially when the Church was concerned:
And the Writers of that time, as *Fulbert*
and *Ives de Chartres*, frequently mention
thofe Conferences. It feems, that before
the Degrees of Subordination among Great
Men were fettl'd, every one look'd upon
him-

himself as a Sovereign, whose Disputes
were not to be ended but by Victory, or
a Treaty of Peace. This irregular way
of doing Justice, and this Usurpation of
New Jurisdictions, very much contributed
towards those Customs whose Origine we
are looking after : But several other Rights,
introduc'd in these times, had a considerable Share in them. *Fiefs,* * which before
were only Grants for Life, became Perpetual and Hereditary. And to these times
of Disorder, are justly ascribed, the Source
of the greatest Part of those Services, due
from the Tenant to his Lord ; which, 'tis
believed were settled by Private Agreement
or Usurpation.

When Feuds or Fiefs became first Hereditary.

INDEED, there is no likelihood, that the
People should voluntarily invest particular
Great Men with so many Rights, preju-
dicial to their Common Liberty, as are mention'd in most of our Customs ; many of
which are still in Force, as in passing of

---

* When *Hugh Capet* usurp'd the Kingdom of *France,*
to fortifie himself, and draw all the Nobility to his
Faction, he granted their *Feuds* to them and their
Heirs for ever ; this was the Beginning of Hereditary *Fiefs* : And *William the Conqueror* brought the
same into *England.* [Spelman *of Feuds.*]

Rivers ;

Rivers; thofe Rights call'd * *Peage*, † *Travers*, ‖ *Rouage*, ‡ *Barrage*, and many others, as ** *Gifte*, †† *Paft*, ‖‖ *Logemens*,

---

* *Peage.----* A Cuftom or Toll paid for Paffage; which the Lords of Mannors have a Right to demand, within their Jurifdictions.

† *Travers.----* Much the fame as *Peage.* Crofs-Toll, Paffage-Toll, or Thorough-Toll; called with us *Toll-Travers.*

‖ *Rouage.----* Wheelage, a certain Toll or Impofition upon Wine fold in Grofs, and carried away in Carts: Levied before a Wheel thereof be fuffered to ftir.

Droit de ‡ *Barrage.----* A Paffage-Toll, fo call'd from the Bar or Turnpike where 'tis Levied.

** *Gifte.----* Power to lie at the Houfe of a Tenant, Vaffal or Subject, in paffing along by it.

Sir Henry Spelman, *in his Treatife of* Parliaments, *fays, the fame Impofitions were in ufe in* England, *after the* Conqueft,

†† *Paft.----* The fame to require a Meal or Refection of a Tenant or Vaffal.

‖‖ *Logemens.----* An annual Fee due unto fome Lords, for the Lodgings their Vaffals have in their Caftles, in time of War.

and were call'd Cofhering. *In* Ireland *they were termed* Cuttings, *from the old Word* Tallagium.

‡‡ *Fourni-*

[57]

‡‡ *Fourniture*, * *Courvées*, † *Guet*, and ‖ *Garde* ; the sole Right of ‡ *Ovens*, *Mills* and *Wine-presses* ; the Prohibition of selling * *Wine*,

Droit de

‡‡ *Fourniture*.---- A Right of demanding Provision, Implements, or Equipage, from a Tenant or Vassal.

* *Courvées*.---- A Day's Work due from the Vassal to his Lord, to be done in Person, or by his Cattle, Plough or Team.

† *Guet*.---- Castle-Guard or Ward, whereunto the Vassals of Lords that have Castles, are bound in Time or Expectation of War.

‖ *Garde*.---- The Wardship of Lands, due to the Lord of whom they are held.

Bannalitez. { *des fours.* { *des moulins.* { *des pressoirs.*

‡ The Royalty or Sovereign Power of causing all the Bread to be brought to such an Oven to be baked; all the Corn to such a Mill, to be ground; and all the Wine within such a District, to be press'd at the same Press ; for all which the Lord or Owner of such Oven, Mill, or Wine-press, receives a certain Toll.

Ban --- a Vin. * A Privilege some Lords have, of hindring their Vassals to sell their Wine, till they have dispos'd of their own.

and

and many others of the same kind; which relish very much, either of the Slavery of those on whom they were impos'd, or the Violence of the Imposers.

I cannot say, but they are become Lawful, by Prescription and Approbation of those Princes, who have authoriz'd the Customs : Nay, I am willing to believe, many had a Reasonable Foundation ; as, the Re-imbursing a Nobleman the Expence he had been at in building a Bridge or a Causey ; or for retaining some Token of that Servitude, from which he had deliver'd his Subjects. Many of them, are the very Conditions on which Estates are convey'd, as the † *Cens*, || *Rentes foncieres,*

---

† *Cens*--- Rent of Affize, Quit-Rent, Old-Rent, Chief-Rent, the first Pecuniary Charge laid on Conquered Lands, as a Sign and Acknowledgment of the direct Seigniory of him that grants it. This was impos'd by the Captains and Leaders of the *Francs*, when they conquer'd *Gallia*, in imitation of the *Roman Census*, and is still continued as a Mark of Base or Servile Tenure.

|| *Rentes foncieres*.---- These are certain Rents of Accession, or Additions unto the Antient *Cens*, or Chief-Rent ; *viz.* Rent-Service, Rent-Charge, or Fee-Farm Rents.

payable

payable in Money or in Kind; the ‡ *Champarts*, * *Burdelage*, and other like Rights. I only say, that those Services or Rights, are for the greatest part, owing to particular Causes; as is plain from their Names, according to the different Countries where they are in use; and from certain Fantastical Customs, which even want a Name, and could have no other Beginning but the Caprice of a Master.

As *France* grew more Uniform in its Government, Time swept away many of these Irregular Customs; some were entirely abolish'd, others confounded, or mix'd with those, to which they bore the nearest Resemblance; and in short, such as were more universally receiv'd, were taken into our Common Law.

---

‡ *Champarts.---* Field-Rent. Half, Part, or the Twelfth-part of the Crop due by Bargain or Custom, unto the Lord or Owner of the Land.

* *Bordelage.---* Is a Condition by which Lands are held, paying a certain Annual Acknowledgment to the Lord or Owner: It is so call'd from the old *French* Word *Borderie*, which signifies a Quantity of Arable, Meadow, or Pasture-Ground.

THE

Rights of Corpora-tion. THE Rights of Communities and Corporations, alfo introduc'd great Innovati-
ons: For 'twas about this time, that the
Inhabitants of Towns and Cities, began
to unite in Societies, under the Protection
of fome Great Man, able to skreen them
from the Oppreffion of others; and obtain'd the Privilege of being try'd by their
Peers. 'Tis likely, that the firft that began this Cuftom, were the Inhabitants
of Epifcopal Cities, and other Free-Men:
But in time, the Vaffals or Servile Tenants,
belonging to feveral Towns and Villages,
purchas'd their Freedom of their Lords,
at high Rates; in order to have the fame
Liberty of uniting for their Common Defence, and to have feveral fpecial Privileges.

IN the time of the *Romans*, there were
in *Gaul*, as well as every where elfe, abundance of Slaves: But the Gentlenefs of
Chriftianity, and good Ufage of the *Germans*, who were unaccuftom'd to be waited on, by degrees, render'd their Condition much eafier; fo that in the Age our
Cuftoms were formed, they were in no
other ftate of Bondage, than the Obligation of taking care of certain Lands, and
not to difpofe of Themfelves and Goods,
by

by Will, Marriage, or Religious Vow, as
they fhould think proper. By this means,
the Power of the Lords was reduced chiefly to Three kinds of Right; * *Pourfuite*,
† *Formariage*, and ‖ *Mainmorte*, which are
very famous Cuftoms : Hence it is, that
Vaffals are often call'd *Gens de Pourfuite*,

---

* *Pourfuite*.--- A Right of obliging Vaffals to dwell
upon and cultivate fuch Lands, thefe were
call'd *Gens de Pourfuite*; becaufe they were
liable to be purfued, and reclaim'd by their
Lords, where-ever they went, for the Labour and Service due to them.

† *Formariage*.--- The Half or Third, or as the Cuftom is, other part of a Villain's Subftance,
payable to his Lord, if he marry a Woman
that is Free, or a Foreigner : And this, altho' he has leave to do it ; for otherwife,
he lofes Sixty Shillings more.

‖ *Mainmorte*.--- The Right a Lord has to the Eftate
of a Villain dying without Heir of his Body, and no Tenant in common with any
other of his own Condition. There is a
Difference between the *Gens de Pourfuite*
and *Mainmorte* : The firft were born Vaffals, and could not by any means become
Free, without the Confent of their Lord ;
but were like the *Roman* Slaves, *adfcriptos
Glebæ* ; the latter were Vaffals, only rela-
tively, as they held certain Lands by that
Tenure ; but leaving the Land and Goods
upon it to the Lord, might make themfelves
Freemen when they pleas'd.

Main-

Mainmorte, or *Mortaillables*; becaufe they
were fubject to pay Toll or Tallage to
their Lords : They were likewife called,
Hommes and *Femmes de Corps*, or *Gens de
pote*, or *Villains*, from the Villages they
inhabited. But Enfranchifements became
fo common, after the Reign of St. *Louis*,
that there are very few Footfteps remaining, of that Rank of Men.

*Ecclefiafti-
cal Power.* A third Caufe of Alteration in the *French*
Laws, was the Exorbitance of Ecclefiafti-
cal Power : Under the *Roman* Empire, the
Bifhops frequently exercis'd Secular Jurifdiction ; and decided Controverfies between the People ; who, perfuaded of their
Integrity and Prudence, chofe them for
Arbitrators. The Ufefulnefs of thofe Arbitrations was fo apparent, that they were
authorized by a Law in the *Theodofian*
Code, importing, That if one of the Parties, declar'd himfelf contented, to ftand to
the Bifhop's Decifion, the other fhould be
obliged to agree to it, whatever ftate the
Suit might be in.

THIS Law, no doubt, was duly obferv'd
by the *Gauls*, when, during the Time of
Theodofius, there were fo many Bifhops
celebrated for Piety and Learning . And
tho' the Church's Authority was fomething

thing leffen'd, by this frequent Change of Mafters, and under the Kings of the Firft Race; yet, the Bifhops were ever in great Power and Efteem; not only with the *Romans*, but even with their New *Converts*, over whom they had fuch an Influence, as to make them tremble at the very Name of St. *Martin*.

IN the Time of the Second Race, we find the Law of the *Theodofian* Code, folemnly authorized: For the Emperor, after enumerating the feveral Nations under his Dominion, in order to repeal their particular Laws, takes exact notice of the Place from whence that Conftitution is drawn; and orders it fhould be held of equal Virtue with the Capitulars, by Priefts as well as Lay-Men, and then fets down the Words of it at Length. This Law therefore, was obferved, as long as the Regal Power ftood undiminifh'd; and the Acts of thofe Times, make it evident, that Bifhops and Abbats, as well as Earls, were fent into Provinces to fee the Laws executed; and were admitted into the Councils of State.

THE low Condition Monarchy was then in, rather increas'd, than abated the Ecclefiaftical Power: For before thefe New-

coin'd

coin'd Jurifdictions could gather Strength
and whilft the ill Effects of thefe lafted,
'tis natural to fuppofe, the People were
more inclined to fubmit to the Ecclefiaftical Power, than to the Secular ; which
was either unfixed, or fo new, that the
Ufurpation was plainly feen through it :
Befides, the Laity were fo profoundly Ignorant, that they ftood in need of Clerks
in all their Affairs, not only to debate
and refolve Doubts, but even to read and
draw up their Deeds and Inftruments.

In a Word, there being no fix'd Rule
of Juftice left among the Great Men, the
Interpofition of Bifhops and Abbats, became more neceffary than ever : So that
generally fpeaking, they were the only
Peace-makers ; and fummon'd, and made
part of thofe fo frequent Affemblies. 'Tis
certain, that their thus preferving Peace,
and the Injuftice of Lay-Judges ; gavè
grounds to the Bifhops, to ftretch their
Authority fo far, that the Laity at length
complain'd of, and oppos'd it : And this
occafion'd thofe long and cruel * Divifions,
which diftracted *Germany* and *Italy*.

---

* The Faction of the *Guelfs* and *Gibelines*.

BUT

But without dwelling any longer upon the History of Ecclesiastical Jurisdiction, I shall content my self, with having
observ'd the Changes it brought into the
Civil Law; by enlarging the Canonical,
and making it a principal Ingredient in
the Composition of the *French* Law.

This is what occurs to me concerning
the Origine of Customs; and to close my
Conjectures, I am of Opinion, that the
Study of the Antient Law, became then
discontinued, tho' not the Practice; which
was carried on, without Distinction of
Laws, as the People had none left between
them; that it underwent great Alterations
by the New Laws, that were established,
especially in Relation to Publick Power,
and great extent of the Ecclesiastical
Jurisdiction: Those Alterations increa-
sed by degrees, by reason of the little
Correspondence between the Provinces;
and even between all the little neighbouring Districts: For the Division was
so wide, that in the Days of King *Robert*, an Abbat of *Cluny*, being invited
by *Bouchard* Earl of *Paris*, to settle some
Monks at St. *Maur des Fossez*, look'd upon
it as a long and fatiguing Journey; com-
plaining, how great a Hardship it was up-

F

on him, to be oblig'd to go in a ftrange and unknown Countrey.

Thus, the fame Caufes which brought forth the Cuftoms, gave them a different Form in each Countrey. I call that a Countrey, which, by the Acts in the Reign of *Charlemagne* and his Succeffors, is term'd *Pagus*; that is, the Diftrict or Territory of every City, govern'd by an Earl, and was generally a Diocefs. This Variety of Cuftoms, arofe, as *du Moulin* conjectures, from the feveral Means ufed in ufurping the Publick Power; from the Difference in the Treaties and Contracts of the Lords between themfelves, and between them and the Commons; from the peculiar Style of each Jurifdiction, and the various Opinions of Judges.

The ftate of Hoftility thofe Countries liv'd in, did not a little contribute thereto; being ever at Defiance with each other: Infomuch, that great part of their Cuftoms confifted of the Laws of War, which had its proper Rules and Maxims. And for this Reafon, the Diverfity is much greater, in the Provinces fubject to different Princes, as thofe under the Dominion of *England*, and thofe of *France*. Reafons of State too, often interfer'd; every Prince

being

being defirous to keep his Subjects, in all
refpects, at as great a Diftance as poffible, from thofe of his Neighbours; in order to render a Re-union or Agreement
the more difficult. But in thofe Countries
that obey'd the fame Sovereign, the Jealoufie which is natural among Neighbours,
made their Judges and Magiftrates affect
different Rules and Maxims, and trafmit-
ted that Emulation to Pofterity.

THIS was the State of *France*, when *The* Ro-
the Study of the *Roman* Law revived; man *Law*
not of the *Theodofian* Code, which before *reviv'd.*
the Troubles was call'd the *Roman* Law,
both in *Gaul* and *Spain:* But known, at
this Time, only to a few Learned Men;
and afterwards, lay buried in Oblivion,
till the Beginning of the laft Century.
In the Year 1528. it was printed after
Three Manufcripts found in *Germany*; and
this Edition, is that of *Charlemagne*, which,
as I faid before, is the fame with *Alarick's.*
Another Piece of that Code, as it was
modell'd by *Theodofius* himfelf, has been
fince recovered.

THAT Law, which began to be ftudied *The* Jufti-
in the Time I fpeak of, was the fame nian *Law.*
that is read now, I mean *Juftinian's*;
till then, fcarce heard of in the *Weft:*

For

For when *Juſtinian* publiſh'd it, about the
Year ʒ30. there were but *Two Provinces*
in all *Europe*, that paid him willing
Obedience ; *Greece*, and the greateſt Part
of the Countrey under the Governor of
Illyrium. *Gaul* and *Spain*, had both ſhaken
off the *Roman* Yoke, above an Age before ; *Germany* never felt it ; and as for
Italy, the *Goths* held out long againſt *Be-
liſarius*, and were ſucceeded by the *Lombards :* So that the *Juſtinian* Law, was
no where in uſe, but in *Greece*, *Illyrium*,
and a ſmall Part of *Italy*, then ſubject to
the *Romans*.

'TIS foreign to my Purpoſe, to enquire
what became of this Law in *Greece*, and
the *Eaſt* ; 'tis ſufficient to ſay, they had
no other for Three Ages ; and that Three
Hundred and fifty Years after, the Emperor *Leo*, Sirnam'd *the Philoſopher*, order'd
a new Collection of all *Juſtinian*'s Books,
which he mix'd and diſpos'd after a different Method, dividing them into Sixty
Parts ; intituled, *The* Βασίλικα. They were
written in *Greek*, becauſe the *Latin* Tongue
was grown Obſolete, and not underſtood
by thoſe under the Empire of *Conſtantinople* ; altho' they ſtill affected to be call'd
Romans, (as their Poſterity do to this
Day :) So that it was *Juſtinian*'s Law,
in

in Subftance, which was preferved there,
till the Downfal of that Empire.

But its Fortune was quite otherwife
in the *Weft* : In *Italy* it maintain'd its
Ground ; and the *Roman* Law obferved
there from *Juftinian*'s Time, was his own,
and not the *Theodofian*, as in *Gaul* and
Spain : Some Proofs whereof, we have
in the Epiftles of St. *Gregory*, who Flou-
rifhed under *Mauricius* and *Phocas* ; and in
the Second Council of *Troyes*, held by
John VIII. in the Year 878. where *Juftinian*'s Law, is quoted in the Article a-
gainft Sacrilege.

But it was very much chang'd, in the
Four following Ages, by the Mixture of
different Nations, that fucceeded in the
Poffeffion of *Italy*. The *Lombards* expell'd
the *Exarchs* of *Ravenna*, and were again
themfelves fubdued by the *Francs*. After
the Line of *Charlemagne* was extinct, *Italy*
became a Prey to the *Hungarians* and
Saracens ; who feiz'd upon the Kingdoms
of *Naples* and *Sicily*, and maintain'd their
Conquefts, till driven thence by the
Normans. In fhort, the *Saxon* Kings being acknowledg'd Emperors, held the Command of *Lombardy* and *Tufcany*.

After

AFTER so many Transmutations of People, and Changes of Governments, there were, doubtless, very few that stuck to the *Roman* Law; and the rather, because such as did, were obliged to own themselves *Romans*; a Name, at last, in great Contempt, as appears by *Luit-prand*, who lived in the Tenth Century, and says, that in his Time, *the Name of* a Roman, *gave the* Idea *of a Faithless Wretch, without Honour or Courage.*

THE Law of *Justinian*, however, was not so entirely lost in *Italy*, but that they had some Knowledge of it in the Eleventh Century; especially in the Places where the *Greeks* remained longest; I mean, in *Romagnia*, and the Kingdom of *Naples:* This is to be seen, by the Heresie of the *Incestuous*, who in their Marriages, were for following the same Rules as the Law appoints in Successions; and were therefore condemn'd by Pope *Alexander* II. in 1065. But his Constitution quoted in *Gratian's* Decree, mentions only *Justinian's* Law in General, without naming either * *Code* or

---

* In the References made use of by Civilians, *Apud Justinianum*, it denotes the Institutes: But if the Code or Digest be referr'd to, they are either named, or express'd by these Abbreviations, *C. ff.*

Digest,

Digeſt, and cites only a Paſſage of the Inſtitutes.

ABOUT Fifty Years after, a *German*, call'd *Irnier* or *Warnier*, who had ſpent ſome time in Study at *Conſtantinople*, began publickly to teach the Laws of *Juſtinian*, at *Bolognia* in *Lombardy* ; and the Occaſion was this : *Irnier* taught the Liberal Sciences at *Ravenna*, when a Diſpute aroſe between thoſe of the ſame Profeſſion, about the proper Signification of the Word *As :* They ſearch'd the Books of the Civil Law for it ; and liking them, reſolv'd upon a cloſer Application to the Study of them. So that *Irnier*, who came to *Bolognia*, upon the Diſpute concerning the Word *As,* began there to read Lectures upon it, in 1128. according to the Tradition of that School.

HE firſt took in hand the *Code*, then the Firſt Part of the *Digeſt* ; after that, the Laſt, call'd the *New Digeſt* : Then he found out the Second, call'd the *Inforttat* ; and laſt of all, the *Authentiques*. This is what the Cardinal of *Oſtia*, and *Odofredus*, Diſciple to *Azonius*, whoſe Maſter *Bulgarius*, was One of *Irnier*'s Four Chief-Scholars, report of him. So that he began Teaching, of his own Authority, which

F 4   is

is no Argument, but that he might be afterwards Licenfed by the Countefs *Maud*, as the Abbat of *Ufpreg* fays; or the Emperor *Lothair* the Second, as is more generally believed.

SOME little time after, about the Year 1137. *Amalfi*, in *Apulia*, being taken by the Emperor *Lothair*, and Pope *Innocent* II. affifted by the *Pifans*, from *Roger* King of *Sicily*, a Manufcript Copy of the *Digeft* was found among the Plunder, and carried to *Pifa*, and from thence to *Florence*, by *Gino Caponi*, when he made himfelf Mafter of *Pifa*, in the Year 1407, This is what they call, the * *Florentine Pandects*, which awaken'd the Study of the *Juftinian* Law; and has ever fince been reckon'd the moft Authentick Copy.

THEY had many Tokens, which difcover'd them to be written by the Hand of a *Grecian*; befides, the Province where they were found, was that, wherein the *Greeks* maintain'd themfelves longeft in *Italy*.

---

* See *Francis Torellus*, in his Preface to the *Florentine Pandects*.

THE

THE firſt Interpreters, upon the reviving of the *Roman* Law, made only a few Gloſſes, References, and Concordances, as the *Greeks* had done, upon the Βασίλικα : But they had this great Advantage, of having receiv'd the *Roman* Law from their Fathers, by Tradition ; whereas, it had been ſo long difuſed in the *Weſt*, that it was almoſt unintelligible to the *Latins*, from whom it originally came : So that judging it impoſſible, as well as unprofitable, to arrive at the true meaning of the Text, they were ſatisfied with ſuch Conſequences as could be drawn from it ; and Study'd it after a Scholaſtick Method, full of *Sophiſtry* and *Chicane*, as they did the reſt of the Arts and Sciences.

IN theſe early Times, the Study of the *Juſtinian* Law came into *France*, and was publickly Profeſs'd and Taught, at *Montpellier* and *Tholouſe*, before the Foundation of thoſe Univerſities. An Attempt was alſo made, to teach it at *Paris* ; but Pope *Honorius* the Third, forbad it by a Decretal, which deſerves Examination. *Obiit.* 1227.

THE

THE Subſtance of this † Decretal, is, that tho' the Church does not refuſe the Aſſiſtance of ſuch Secular Laws, as tread in the Paths of Equity and Juſtice; neverthelefs, becauſe the Laity, both in *France* and ſome of the Provinces, make no uſe of the *Roman* Law, and that there are very few Ecclefiaſtical Cafes, but are ſufficiently provided for in the Canons; to the End therefore, *that every one might apply himſelf more cloſely to the Study of the Holy Scriptures*, the Pope forbids every Man, to Teach or Learn the Civil Law at *Paris*, or in the Neighbourhood, under Penalty of being render'd incapable to Plead at the Bar, and Excommunicated by the Biſhop of the Dioceſs.

---

† This Decretal was called *Super ſpecula*. Monſieur *Claude Joſeph Ferriere*, in his Hiſtory of the *Roman* Law, ſpends a whole Chapter in ſhewing, that the Study of the Civil Law at *Paris*, was not forbidden, either before, by, or ſince that Decretal; which he proves, had a view only to Eccleſiaſtical Perſons: And that the Edict of *Blois*, made upon the Foundation of that Decretal, was, upon a Repreſentation to *Louis* XIV. of the Inconveniencies that attended, Repeal'd, ſo far as it related to the Study of the Civil Law in *Paris*.

I ſhall

I shall not take upon me to determine, how far this Decretal ought to have been obey'd in *France*; whether it were Obligatory to the Laity, or whether that be the true Reason, that there have been no Professors of the Civil Law to this Day in *Paris*: My Intention, is only to take notice of some Things therein mention'd, conducive to the Design of my History: As, that the Ecclesiasticks gave the Preference to the Canon, before the Secular Law; that they and the Laity, were govern'd by different Laws, in the Thirteenth Century; and from the Words in the Decretal, it may be safely concluded, that all Ecclesiastical Causes, for which the Canons had made no Provision, were decided by the *Roman* Law.

As for the Laity, 'tis said, they made no use of it, being guided by such Customs as I have already mention'd; for altho' the *Roman* Law, was the Foundation and Chief Part of those Customs, yet it was so Interwoven, as not to be distinguish'd.

But what is most worthy Observation in this Decretal, is, the Name of *France*, which is there used in a very confin'd Sence;

Sence; and, if I am not miftaken, for
the Ifle of *France* only; fo that by the
other Provinces, we are to underftand
Normandy, *Burgundy*, and the moft Northern Parts of the Kingdom: From whence
it may be inferr'd, that fince that Time,
the Countries govern'd by Cuftom, have
been diftinguifh'd from thofe that follow'd
the Written Law.

THUS the Law of *Juftinian* was reftor'd
to the World; became more Famous in
Italy than ever; and fpread over the reft
of *Europe*, where it had never before
been heard of: And indeed, 'tis very
furprizing, that Books compiled at *Conftantinople*, Six hundred Years before, and
funk into Difufe there, being partly abolifh'd by the Βασιλικα, fhould meet with
fo much Regard and Countenance, in
Countries that were no part of *Juftinian*'s
Dominon, as *Spain*, *France*, *Germany* and
England; without the Sanction of Ecclefiaftical or Secular Powers: And that it
fhould be Cuftomary to call them, the
Written, *Common*, *Civil*, and by way of
Excellence, *the Law*; as if there had
been none other Confiderable. However,
this is what I am apt to believe, might
be the Caufe of fo ftrange an Event:

IN

In the utmoft heighth of *Barbarifm*, fome fmattering of the *Latin* Tongue, and Footfteps of the *Roman* Cuftoms, were ftill preferv'd. *Glaber* the Monk, who flourifh'd in the *Eleventh* Century, calls the Chriftian Countries, at that time, the † *Roman World*, and the reft *Barbarians*. 'Tis true, the *Francs* and other Conquerors, had a great Averfion and Contempt for all that then called themfelves *Romans*; that is, the Subjects of the Empire of *Conftantinople:* But ftill, they had a confufed Notion of the Excellence of the *Roman* Manners and Actions, efpecially of the Wifdom of their Laws ; notwithftanding, its Books were very little known, and hard to be procured. The Law of *Juftinian*, therefore, met with good Reception, as being that of the Antient *Romans* ; for the Wifeft in thofe Days, had not Skill enough to diftinguifh it from the true *Roman* Law, *i.e.* the *Theodofian* Code ; nor to know when *Juftinian* liv'd, and of what Authority his Laws were : The Name of the *Roman* Emperor was all they regarded.

---

† *Orbis Romanus,*

MOREOVER, thefe Laws were of general Ufe and Advantage: for therein, the
Principles of the Civil Law were well
eftablifhed; not only in Relation to the
Romans, but all other Nations: For there
is fcarce any Maxim, in either Law of
Nature or Nations, but may be found in
the *Digeft*; befides an infinite Number of
accurate Decifions, in particular Cafes.
But it was chiefly of fervice to Princes,
whofe *Prerogative*, is therein extended in
its full Dimenfions, free from thofe fatal
Blemifhes it had fuffer'd in the foregoing
Ages; nay, it furnifh'd them with Matter to build very high Pretenfions. The
Emperor of *Germany*, as fome Doctors
explain'd this Law to him, had a Right
to Univerfal Monarchy; and others faid,
that Kings were Abfolute Emperors, within their own Dominions.

IN fhort, the whole Defign of thefe
Laws, was to render Mankind more Can-
did and Humane, more fit for Society,
and obedient to the Supream Lawful Powers; and to extinguifh all † Unjuft and

---

† Yet *Grotius*, in his Book *de Bello Gothico*, proves
the Laws of the *Goths* and *Vandals*, to be more
Equitable and Juft than thofe of the *Romans*, in
Juftinian's Time.

Tyran-

Tyrannical Cuſtoms, introduced by the Barbarous Nations. 'Tis not therefore ſo much to be wonder'd, that this Law, firſt brought to Light by the Curioſity of Learned Men, ſhould, through the Intereſt of Princes, and Approbation of the People, infenſibly eſtabliſh it ſelf.

It met, however, with a different Reception, according to the Diſpoſition of the People : The *Italians* eagerly embrac'd it as ſoon as it appeared, they were but juſt delivered from the burthenſome Impoſitions of the *Germans*, whom they look'd upon as *Barbarians*, (tho' no better themſelves ;) and labouring to reſtore the *Roman* Name, and the Memory of their Anceſtors, or rather of the Antient *Italians* ; they were, beſides, no longer apprehenſive, by becoming *Romans*, of being ſubject to the Emperor of *Conſtantinople* ; for about that time it was taken by the *French :* And as the *Eaſtern* and *Weſtern* Empires, were in the Hands of thoſe call'd *Francs* or *Latins*, to diſtinguiſh them from the *Levantines* and *Grecians* ; this contributed very much to the Propagation of the *Roman* Laws throughout their Dominions.

Conſequences of the Study of the Roman Law.

But

But, notwithſtanding this, 'tis certain, the Study of it in † *Germany*, was never heard of till towards the Fifteenth Century ; but its Authority quickly ſpread over all that Countrey, being *then* call'd the Empire.

But to confine my ſelf within *France :* It has ever had the Force of Law, where the *Roman* Power took deepeſt Root ; as, in *Languedoc, Provence, Dauphiné* and the *Lyonois ;* thoſe Places having been the firſt conquer'd by the *Romans*, and the laſt by the *Francs ;* and the greateſt Part, acknowleging at that time, the Emperor of *Germany* as their immediate Sovereign. Beſides, their bordering upon *Italy*, gave them better Opportunity than they could otherwiſe have had, to ſtudy the *Roman* Law : For this Reaſon, altho' ſeveral Cuſtoms ſtill remain in thoſe Provinces, different from this Law, yet they are not directly contrary, nor of any great Extent.

On the other hand, the Cuſtoms prevail in the reſt of *France*, and the *Ro-*

† Herman. Coringus, *de Orig. Juris German.*

man

man Law is not there obferved, in all
thofe Cafes where Cuftom has made other
Provifion, which are very numerous.

THIS is the Difference between the *Cuftumary* Countries, and thofe which obferve the Written Law. Whether the *Roman* is the Common Law, in the Countries governed by Cuftom, in Cafes omitted by the Cuftoms, has been a famous
Queftion, argued *Pro* and *Con* by the
Two Prefidents, *Lizet* and *de Thou*; and
I have not heard it is yet decided.

THE Study of the *Juftinian* Law, introduced great Alterations in the *French*,
confifting only at that time of certain
Cuftoms : For the *Roman* Law, as little
as it was underftood, was thought fo neceffary, that no Body who had not ftudy'd
it, was employ'd, either in Judging, Pleading, or drawing up Contracts : Infomuch,
that all the Officers belonging to the
Courts of Juftice, even the Attorneys, and
Notaries, were in thofe early Times, *Graduates*, and confequently *Clerks*; for as
yet, the Laity had no Tafte of Learning :
Thefe, thinking to make themfelves more
neceffary, or perhaps more correct than
their Predeceffors, changed all the Forms
of the Publick Acts, which till then were

G   in

in a plain eafie Style, except fome forry
Preambles ufed in all Inftruments of the
fame kind ; but from the Year 1250. or
thereabouts, they are clogg'd with an In-
finity of Claufes, Conditions, Reftrictions,
Renunciations and Proteftations, in order
to exclude the moft General Rules; and
often fuch, as could in no wife affect the
Parties : In fhort, they frequently inferted, what would have been clearer and better underftood, if left out.

THE Spirit of Diftruft, at that time
very prevalent, and doubtlefs the Effect
of the late Diffentions, made every one
fond of thefe *Cauteles*, as they are call'd ;
and he that ufed moft, and the longeft,
was accounted the ableft Lawyer. The
fame Humour infected the Proceedings
of the Courts of Juftice : Formerly, Judgments were pafs'd fummarily, and with
little Ceremony, by the Lords and others
moft knowing in the Cuftoms ; but fince,
have been loaded with fo many Forms
and Delays, as not to be ended without
the Affiftance of Clerks and Doctors :
Hence are fprung Deputies, Bailiffs,
Stewards, and other Judges of the Long-
Robe.

YET

Yet, the Study of the *Roman* Law, had its Advantages as well as Inconveniencies; It greatly foften'd the Rigour of the Cuſtoms, and eſtabliſh'd ſure Maxims, by arguing from one thing to another; which is certainly the Reaſon, why we have left off quoting, and even reading the Antient Laws of the *Barbarians*, that were ſtill in Practice, when the Study of the *Roman* Law firſt began, according to *Otho de Friſingue*; who reports, that in his Time, the Nobility of *France* follow'd the *Salick* Law : And the Author of the Second Book of the *Fiefs*, ſays, that in *Italy* Cauſes were determin'd either by the Laws of the *Romans* or of the *Lombards*, or by the Cuſtoms of the Kingdom ; that is, as 'tis underſtood, the *German* Empire.

Since that time, the Antient Laws have been laid aſide, and in the Reign of *Philip* of *Valois*, when it was pretended the *Salick* Law was of ſuch Service, for the Succeſſion of the Crown ; the Text was not cited, as of a Written Law, but the Force of it was urg'd, as of an Inviolable Cuſtom : Nay, the very Name of *Salick Law*, was not made uſe of ; and, I think, *Claudius de Seiſſel*, Biſhop

G 2   of

of *Marfeilles*, in the Reign of *Louis* XII.
was the firft that mention'd it. So that
the Cuftoms received a notable Alteration, as well by the new Forms of Practice
in Bufinefs and in Judgments, as by the
new Maxims and Rules which were about
that time firft admitted, or at leaft explained. And this Mixture of the *Roman*
Law, with the Cuftoms, makes up the
Body of the Laws ufed in *France*.

Cuftoms
firft re-
duc'd into
Writing.

IT remains now, that I explain how
this Law has been tranfmitted to the
prefent Age ; *viz*. how the Cuftoms were
reduced into Writing.

THE Diverfity of Cuftoms proved very
troublefome, after the Provinces were
united under the King, and Appeals to
the Parliament became frequent : For as
'twas almoft impoffible the Judges of
Appeal fhould be acquainted with all
particular Cuftoms, when they were not
committed to Writing, by any proper
Authority ; there was a Neceffity for
the Parties agreeing what thofe Cuftoms
were, or making proof thereof by Witneffes.

By

By this means, all Queftions in Law, were reduced to Facts; upon which, Inquiry was to be made * *Par turbes*, a very expenfive and tedious Method, and yet not a fure one, to come at the Truth; fince it depended greatly upon the Influence and Induftry of the Parties, and Experience and Integrity of the Evidence: Thus, fometimes, equal Proof was made of two Cuftoms directly oppofite, in the fame Place, and upon the fame Fact.

It is eafie to conceive, how far this Convenience, of fhaping the Law to one's own Purpofe encourag'd Perjury; and how difagreeable the Study of the Law was, fince, after a Man with great Pains and Application, had made himfelf Mafter of the Written Law, or by Reflection, drawn good Confequences from its eftablifhed Rules, all his Arguments and Authorities might be defeated, by pleading a Contradictory and often a Falfe Cuftom.

---

* When the Cuftom, or Explanation of a Cuftom was in doubt, the Parties concern'd, were oblig'd to make it good by Twenty Witneffes, at leaft: This Enquiry was called, *Enquête par turbes*; from *Turba*, a Troop or Company.

And

AND indeed, the Cuftoms themfelves were render'd very precarious, by the Corruption of Bailiffs and other Officers, who to ferve their own Ends, often laid them afide; and the Prefumption of others, who inclin'd more to their own headftrong Opinions, than to the Tradition of their Forefathers. Thus *Peter de Fontaines* complains, that in the Time of St. *Louis*, his Countrey was in a manner deftitute of all Cuftoms, and fcarce any one could be afcertain'd by the Knowledge of Three or Four Perfons.

THE Study of the *Roman* Law, I believe, very much contributed to this Uncertainty; for it was in univerfal Credit; and tho' little underftood, nor lawfully authoriz'd, yet every one followed what he beft approved, or was moft able to underftand. Befides, thofe who had the greateft Infight in the Law, had not always the moft compleat Knowledge of the Cuftoms, which was not to be attained without long Practice; yet their Opinions were very much regarded and followed, in the Decifions of Caufes, and many of them were received as Cuftoms, and fo remain.

WRI-

WRITING was the only means of fixing the Cuſtoms, notwithſtanding their Variety, to ſome Certainty : This Work was therefore undertaken, ſo ſoon as the Troubles which had cauſed it were over, and Time had ſomewhat fix'd them ; which was about the End of the Eleventh Century : And tho' we have very few Remains of thoſe old Law-Books, yet, I preſume, that whatever appears to have been done in one Place, was practiſed in others ; and that Time and ſubſequent Works of the ſame Nature, have ſwallowed up thoſe that were more antient : The oldeſt I know of, are the Uſages of *Barcelona*, authorized by Earl *Raimond Berenger* the Elder, in 1060. and the *Fors* or Cuſtoms of *Bearn* ; which are, at leaſt, of equal Antiquity, being ratified by Viſcount *Gaſton* IV. in 1088.

ABOUT the ſame time, that is, in 1080, *William the Baſtard*, having conquered *England*, aſſembled the Nobleſt and Wiſeſt Men of each County, and upon their Teſtimony, commanded the Cuſtoms of the *Anglo-Saxons*, and of the *Danes* that were mixed with them, to be digeſted into Order, which was

G 4 ac-

accordingly done, by the * Archbishop of
Tork and Bishop of *London*, in their own
Hand-writing.

UNDER this Head of Digested or Written Customs, I rank the Books of the
Fiefs of the *Lombards*, compiled about
the Year 1150. by Two Consuls of *Milan*, and intituled, *Customs*; but are in
reality only Antient Usages, collected by
experienced Judges : Of this kind also is
Speculum Juris Saxonici, the oldest Original of the *German* Laws, tho' the Learned
say, it was not wrote till about 1220.

NEAR the same Time, they began to
write their Customs in *France*. These
Writings were of Three Sorts ; the particular Charters of Towns, the Custuma-
ries of Provinces, and Treatises of Practitioners : Let us examine each separately.

Charters and Customs of Cities, &c. TOWARDS the close of the Twelfth,
and during the Thirteenth Century, they
wrote the Rights of several Corporations,

---

* *Alfredus autem Eboracensis Archiepiscopus, qui Re-
gem Willielmum coronaverat, & Hugo Londiniensis
Episcopus, per praeceptum Regis scripserunt propriis ma-
nibus omnia quae praedicti jurati dixerunt.* [Chron.
Ecclesiae Lichfield.]

whose

whofe Charters, I am perfwaded, were
the Originals of their Cuftoms. I fhall
fpeak only of thofe I have feen, either
intire, or recited in part by our Hiftorians ; becaufe they will fuffice to form a
Judgment of the reft.

THE oldeft is the Charter of the Corporation of *Beauvais*, granted by *Louis
the* † *Young*, in 1144. containing an exprefs Account of feveral Cuftoms relating
to the Jurifdiction of the Mayor and Com-
mon-Council: It is nothing elfe but a
Confirmation of thofe Rights before given
by *Louis le Gros* ; but there is no mention of the Letters Patent, and therefore
probably, the firft Grant was only verbal.
After the fame manner, they pretend
William Talvas, || Earl of *Ponthieu*, made
Abbeville a Corporation, about 1130. altho' the Charter of *John* II. which they
fhew, bears Date only in 1184.

I find alfo, in 1173. * *Henry* I. of *England*, gave Licenfe to the Inhabitants of

---

† Or *The Devout*.

|| Hiftory of the Earls of *Ponthieu*.

* Chron. *Bourdeg.*

Bour-

Bourdeaux, to choose a Mayor. In 1187.
Hugh Duke of *Burgundy*, granted the same
Rights to * *Dijon*, that were enjoy'd by
the Corporation of *Soiffons* ; which of
Confequence are more ancient, tho' their
Charter have no Date. That of the
County of *Beaune*, is dated in 1203.
That of *Bar fur-Seine*, in 1234. and that of
Semur, in 1276.

I could mention the Charters of feveral other Places of Note. Of this nature
I take the Eftablifhment to be, made at
† *Rouen* in 1205. between the Clergy and
Barons of *Normandy* ; containing feveral
Cuftoms relating to the Ecclefiaftical Jurifdictions, certified by Men of Experience. The Charter of *Rouen*, given by
Philip the Auguft, in 1207. confirming the
Antient Rights and Privileges of that City,
which relate to the Corporation and Traf-
fick. Laftly, The Inftitution of the Corporations of *Rouen* and *Falaife*, and that
of *Pontheau de Mer*, which is without
Date, (but feems to be the more Antient,)

* Collection of Pieces relating to the Hiftory of
Burgundy, by *Peyrat*.

† *Du Chefne's* Hiftory of *Normandy*.

and

and regulates the Election and Power of the Mayor and *Efchevins* or Sheriffs.

BESIDES these Charter-Deeds belonging to particular Cities, the Customs of whole Provinces began about the same time to be put into Writing ; which, is the * *Second fort* I took notice of : Such were the Antient Customs of *Champagne,* publifh'd by *Pithou* ; thofe of *Burgundy,* which are in *Du Peyrat's* Collection ; the Notorious Customs of the † *Chatelet,* publifhed by *Brodeau* ; confifting of the Refolutions of the Inquiries *Par turbes,* from the Year 1300. to 1387. the Antient Customs of *Normandy,* and of *Anjou* ; the the Antient Ufages of *Amiens,* and many others ftill to be feen in Manufcript.

Cuftoms of Provinces.

BUT the moft Confiderable, are thofe of St. *Louis,* given us by Monfieur *du Cange* ; containing the Customs of *Paris, Orleans,* and *Anjou,* as they prevailed at that Time : Wherein, 'tis to be obferv'd, the Word *Eftablifhment,* is Synonymous with *Edict* or *Ordonnance.* This appears

* The *Cuftumaries.*

† The Town-Houfe or *Guild-Hall* at *Paris.*

by

by *Peter de Fontaines*, who lived at that
Time, and in his Tranflation of a Law
taken out of the *Digeft*, calls the *Prætor's*
Edict a *Ban ou Etabliffement*. I rank
them, however, among the Cuftoms, becaufe the Preface exprefsly mentions their
being made to confirm Good Ufages and
Antient Cuftoms, with fome Improvements extracted from the Laws and Canons : They were made by St. *Louis* in the
Year 1270. before his Expedition into *Africa*.

*The Wri-
tings of
Antient
Lawyers.*
THE Third fort of Writings, which
contain much the fame Things, and may
very well pafs for the Originals of our
Cuftoms, are the Works of able Men,
compofed about that Time, for the Benefit and Inftruction of others : As, The
Advice of *Peter de Fontaine*, put out by
Monfieur *du Cange*; The Book infcribed
to Queen *Blanche*, fuppofed to be by the
fame Hand; The Cuftoms of *Beauvoifis*,
written by *Philip de Beaumanoir*, in 1285.
The *Rural Summary*, by *Boutelier*; the
Great *Cuftumary* made in the Reign of
Charles VI. and the Decifions of *John
de Mares*, publifhed by *Brodeau*, together
with the Notorious Cuftoms.

As

As I am of Opinion thefe Records were the Plan, upon which our Cuftoms were afterwards more folemnly reduced ; it may not be improper to give fome Account of their Contents.

THE Words, *Ufage* and *Cuftoms, Immunities* and *Cuftoms, Franchifes* and *Privileges,* are not Synonymous, as fome have thought. The Word *Cuftoms* fometimes fignifies *Ufages,* and in that Sence is directly contrary to *Immunities,* which denote the Privileges of Corporations, or whatever relates to Publick Right : Sometimes *Cuftoms* are oppofed to *Ufages,* and then they fignifie the particular *Rights* or Laws of a Place, but more efpecially, the *Services* due from the Tenant to his Lord ; whereas, *Ufages* fignifie General Rules applicable to all alike. *Franchifes,* are chiefly Exemptions from referv'd Services, (as *Mainmorte, Formariage,* &c.) whereby Vaffals enjoy'd the Benefit of the Common Law ; and *Privileges* are Rights granted to Freemen, beyond what the Common Law entitled them to ; as *Common* or *Town-Field, Running in the Foreft,* and *reftraining of Caufes to a certain Court or Jurifdiction.* 'Tis very probable, however, the Words *Ufages, Cuftoms,* &c.

may

may have been differently taken in different Countries, and I don't pretend to infist, that they are oblig'd to receive them in the fame Conftruction I have given them.

The Contents of thefe antient Originals of our Cuftoms, relate chiefly to the New Rights or Rules eftablifh'd during the troublefome Times: Firft, the *Rights* of the *Prince*, *Earls*, and the reft of the *Nobles*, with the Jurifdiction of the *Lords*, and that of the *Commons*. In the next place, the Right of *Fiefs*, Tenures in *Capite*, *Bannalities*, and other Signioral Rights, (as *Gifte*, *Fourniture*, *Courveés*,) due from the Vaffals to their Lords. The Diftinction of *Gentlemen* and *Gentlewomen*, from *Copyholders* and *Villains*, *Free* or *Bondmen*. The Right of *War*, *Duel*, and *Champions*, &c.

But what they treat of moft at Large, is, the Form of Juftice, and Method of Procedure in the Lay-Court : For they never fail to make that Diftinction, becaufe of the Ecclefiaftical Power, at that time in the Height of its Pride. So that one may perceive, the Compilers of thefe Cuftoms, always fuppos'd another Law to govern in Matters of Contracts and Succeffions,

ceffions, and did not offer to take notice of any thing but what derogated from the Common Law.

Now I am at a Lofs to know what this Common Law fhould be, unlefs it were the *Roman*. Indeed they often quote it by the Name of the *Law*, and the *Written Law*. And tho' in thofe Days, every thing almoft was wrote in *Latin*, yet thefe Cuftoms were in *French*, as treating of Matters which could not be well explained, but in the Vulgar Tongue, and neceffary to be underftood by every one.

In thefe Writings, one may obferve the Changes our Law has fuffer'd : The oldeft retain much of the *Barbarian* Severity, frequently mentioning, *Wounds* that draw Blood, *Mutilations*, *Fines* upon *Forfeitures*, *Security* or *Safe-Conduct*, and *Breach* of the *Peace* : But what has been written within thefe Three hundred Years laft paft, comes nearer to the *Roman* Law, and that which is now in Ufe ; and treats of *Succeffions*, *Wills*, *Marriages*, and other *Contracts*, and much about the *Forms* of *Proceedings*.

I have

I have been the more large upon the
Subject of thefe antient Originals, as being, in the Opinion of the Learned, the
beft Comments upon the Cuftoms, becaufe
they difcover their Spirit, and Succeffion
of their Changes.

Cuftoms re-   BUT all thefe Writings could not pre-
duced with vent the Uncertainty of the Cuftomary
greater Ex-
actnefs.   Law, being either, without Authority, too
Old, or too Succinct ; wherefore, 'twas
thought advifable to make a more Exact
and Formal Digeftion of the Cuftoms.

THE Project was laid in the Reign of
Charles VII. who, after he had driven the
Englifh out of *France*, undertook a general
Reformation of every Branch of the Conftitution ; and among the reft, iffu'd a
long Edict, dated at *Montil-les Tours*, in
1453. the Hundred and twenty third Article of which, declares, That thenceforward all the Cuftoms of the Kingdom
fhould be put into Writing, and agreed to
by the Practitioners of each Place, then
examin'd and confirmed by the great Council and Parliament ; and that the Cuftoms
fo written and approved, fhould be obferved as Law, and no others quoted.

Du

Du Moulin fays, the Defign was, to jumble all the Cuftoms together, in order to extract one General Law, and that the Writing of each particular Cuftom, was only Provifional, that the People might have fomething certain to depend upon, whilft the general Work was upon the Stocks.

It was, in truth, the beft way that could be taken to give *France* a Sett of Good Laws : 'Tis what the firft Legiflators follow'd: And *Plato* fays, as in the Beginning, States were form'd out of many Families affembled together for Convenience ; fo the Laws were form'd out of the Cuftoms of thofe Families, of which the Beft and moft Reafonable were chofen, and by fome Wife Man made a Rule for the whole Body ; abolifhing fome Things of fmall Moment, peculiar to each Family.

And the fame Method might be practifed in *France*, confidering each petty Province as a Family, in refpect of the whole Kingdom. This is what *du Moulin*, who lived near that time, fays was intended ; and it feems to be fupported by *Philip de Comines*, who reprefents *Louis* XI. as very defirous of having only one Cuftom,

H

ſtom, one ſort of Weight and Meaſure ;
and that all the Cuſtoms ſhould be regi-
ſtred in *French*, in a Book fairly written.
Hitherto, the firſt Part only of this great
Deſign has been put in Execution, that
is, digeſting of the Cuſtoms ; and it was
ſo long a doing, that it was not finiſh'd
in above a Hundred Years after *Charles*
the Seventh died.

THE firſt digeſted, were the Cuſtoms
of *Ponthieu*, under *Charles* VIII. and confirmed by him in 1495. There were
ſeveral finiſh'd under *Louis* XII. After the
Year 1507, the Work was carried on
by Fits, under *Francis* I. and *Henry* II.
and there were ſtill ſome left undone in
the time of *Charles* IX.

THE Number of theſe Cuſtoms, including the *Local*, and Cuſtoms of neighbouring Provinces, as the Low-Countries, who
copied after *France*, are 285. but reckoning only the Principal Cuſtoms of the
Kingdom, amount to no more than 60.
moſt of them differing from one another.
In the mean time, it was obſerved, about
a Hundred Years ago, many Alterations
had crept in, ſince they were firſt reduced in the Beginning of the laſt Century,
and that there had been conſiderable Omiſ-
ſions

fions ; fo that many Cuftoms were amend-
ed, as thofe of *Paris*, *Orleans*, and *Amiens*,
which was done with the fame Solemnity
as at firft.

In order to make thefe Cuftoms better
underftood, 'tis neceffary to be acquainted
with the Ceremonies ufed on the Occafion of their being new-modell'd. In the
firft Place the King iffued his Commiffion,
by Virtue of which, the Three Eftates of
the Provinces affembled : The Refult of
the firft Meeting, was to order all the
King's Judges, Regifters, and fuch as had
born that Office, and the Mayors and
Town-Clerks, to fend in a Lift or Catalogue of the Cuftoms, Ufages and Styles,
which they knew were conftantly in Practice. The States appointed a Committee
to put thofe Lifts into Order, and reduce
them into One Volume ; which being
read in full Affembly, they agreed to, or
alter'd what was proper, and then fent
them to the Parliament to be Regifter'd.

This Method is fully explained in the
Verbal Procefs of the Cuftoms of *Ponthieu*,
which, as I faid, were the firft digefted,
and done by the Magiftrates of feveral
Places ; the greateft Part of the reft have
been reduced by Commiffioners from the

Par-

Parliament, *viz.* such as had presided at
the Assemblies of the States, where those
Lists of the Customs were read ; but 'tis not
to be suppos'd they were the Authors, nor
that they had time to correct them ; That
was left to the Practitioners of each Place,
who, no doubt, transcribed them from
those antient Originals before mention'd :
We are not to expect any great Elegance
or Method from these Gentlemen, and
'twas impossible to think of Order or Style
when they came to be read in the Af-
sembly ; 'tis enough things are regulated
in Substance; for on those Occasions, every thing is done in haste : No wonder
therefore, the Customs are ranged in so
ill Order, and so uncorrect a Style, notwithstanding the Commissioners, whose
Names are prefix'd, were Persons of great
Character and Abilities.

Laws first called Or-donnances. I come now to the *Ordonnances* : We
call none so, but those under the Third
Race; the rest are better known by the
Title of *Capitulars*, which make part of
what I call the Antient *French* Law.

However, the Word *Ordonnance* seems
to have had its Origine, from the Regulation made every Year by *Charlemagne*,
for the Management of his own Estate
and

and Houfhold; for this Word has been long in ufe: And in the Time of St. *Louis, That* was call'd an *Ordonnance*, which now is the *Eftablifhment* of the King's Houfhold: Since that, it has been given to all forts of Letters Patent, by which the King propofes any thing to be generally obferv'd.

But I fee nothing like this, before the Reign of St. *Louis*; what they give us of his Predeceffors, are only Charters of Privileges, and Private Regulations, in favour of Churches, Corporations, Towns or Univerfities. But it looks as if they did not pafs thofe Acts as Kings, fince every Nobleman did the fame in his own Mannour; and the greateft part of their Regulations, having grown into Cuftom, are inferted in the written Law-Books: For when any new Law was to be eftablifh'd, or important Queftion decided, the King did it in the Affembly of his Barons; and the Lords in Proportion, ufed the fame Method with their Vaffals: So it was like an Agreement between them all, or a Judgment given by their Advice.

The Affize of Earl *Geofrey*, is an Example of thofe kinds of Agreements, being a Regulation made in *Britany*, in 1287.

H 3   for

for the Succeſſion of Noble Dignities.
Another Inſtance is, the antient Regula-
tion of *Philip the Auguſt*, touching the
Deſcent of partable *Fiefs*, by and with
the Conſent of ſeveral Lords, whoſe
Names, as well as the King's, are in the
Front of it.

As to Judgments, we have the Antient
Arrêts, reported by *du Moulin*, at the End
of his Book call'd *Style du Parlement* ;
they are indifferently term'd *Edicts* or *Arrêts* ; ſo that the Word *Arrêt* ſignified
only the Reſult of a Debate.

I fanſie, by the way, 'tis from hence
the Practitioners derive the great Authority, they now aſcribe to the *Arrêts of
Parliament*, conſidering them as Laws :
Beſides, before the Cuſtoms were reform'd,
there was no ſtronger Proof of any Uſage,
than the Conformity of ſeveral *Arrêts*,
which is the Reaſon, that at the End of
the antient Manuſcript Cuſtoms, we generally find the *Arrêts* of the County or
Provincial Court.

To return to the *Ordonnances :* Thoſe
of St. * *Louis* were in ſo high Eſteem, that

---

* See *du Cange*'s Notes on the Life of St. *Louis.*

the

the Authors of the Hiftory of his Life,
have been at the Pains to recite them :
They are upon feveral Subjects ; as, For
the Encouragement of Religion, againft
Jews, Blafphemy, and the Ambition of
Church-Men ; For Juftice, Of the Duty
of Bailiffs and other Officers ; For the
Government of the City, againft Gaming
and Bawdy-Houfes, &c. One might alfo
recapitulate the Heads of the *Ordonnances*
of the reft of our Kings ; but that would
be writing a Hiftory of *France*, by the
Laws, which is not confiftent with my
Purpofe ; they are to be feen in the
Chronological Tables, made of them, at
the Beginning of the Conference of *Gue-
nois :* I fhall only fay, They, in general,
treat of Publick Right , and fettle the
King's Prerogative, and the Power of the
Magiftrate. From whence it proceeds,
there has been a far greater Number of
Edicts, fince the Acceffion of *Francis* I.
than in all the preceding Reigns ; becaufe,
'tis fince that time moft of the Subfidies
have been levied, and Titular Offices created, in order to make them Venal.

THERE are likewife abundance of *Ordonnances* for regulating the Proceedings
and Forms of Juftice, but very few of
fervice in the Conduct of Private Life,

or

or that contain any Maxims or Rules of Law : So that the *Roman* Law is of the fame ufe now, as when the Study of it was firft reviv'd ; notwithftanding, there were neither Cuftoms nor *Ordonnances* at that time.

FOR if on the one Hand, it has loft Ground by our rejecting the * *Senatus Confultum Velleianum* ; yet, on the other, it has gain'd, by Admiffion of the Edict of † *Second Marriages :* And all the *Ordonnances* have ever been drawn up by Men learned in the *Roman* Law. The moft celebrated, are fuch as have been made

---

* The *Senatus Confultum Velleianum*, was a Law to hinder Women being bound for others, *ne pro ullo fœminæ intercederent :* It is fo call'd from *Velleius Tutor*, in whofe Confulfhip it was made. The ufe of this Law in *France*, was abrogated by an Edict of *Henry* IV. but fome Indulgence of this kind is fhewn to the Women of the *Lionnois Forêts*, *Beaujollois* and *Mafconnois*, for the Encouragement of Trade.

† The Edict concerning Second Marriages, was made to prevent the Wrong that might thereby be done to the Child by the firft Hufband ; and therefore, the Law is very fevere upon fuch Women, as marry again within the Term of a Year. This is ftrictly obferved in all the Provinces of *France*, where the Written Law takes place, except *Bourdeaux*.

in

in the Affemblies of the States, as thofe of *Moulins* and *Blois*.

THE Parliaments, and other Courts, whofe Jurifdiction is Sovereign, because the Prince is fuppofed to be prefent, had a Right to examine the Edicts directed to them, and to remonftrate against them, if they thought proper, before they were publifh'd; but this is now quite out of ufe, and they are oblig'd to Regifter and Publifh whatever the King fends them, faving the ufelefs Privilege of Remonftrating afterwards.

THIS is the Beft and moft Exact Hiftory I am able to give of the *French Law*. If any one is inclined to look into thefe Matters, no doubt, he may find many things that have efcaped me; but I fhall be highly fatisfied, if fuch whofe Profeffion obliges them to be skill'd in our Laws are encouraged by this Difcourfe to fearch more exactly after their Originals.

I N-

INDEX.

I N D E X.

Com-

INDEX.

F. *Field*

INDEX.

F.

INDEX.

INDEX.

INDEX.

FINIS.

www.ingramcontent.com/pod-product-compliance
Lightning Source LLC
Chambersburg PA
CBHW031943090426
42739CB00006B/71